Acknowledgements

After many years of encouragements from Christian friends, I have finally written this book. Without such promptings, especially from Tony May, I am sure that this would not have happened. My deepest gratitude is blessed upon Rev. Judy Turner, spiritual director extraordinaire, who took on the daunting task of reviewing the structure and flow of the content with gently and gracefully offered suggestions and changes. She and her husband John founded and serve Christview Retreat Center in Arkansas (judy@christviewmin.org). Because of my proclivity to not recognize mistakes in details, I greatly appreciate my editors, Judy Parker, Rich Haynes and Susann Brinkley, who also doubled as my publicity consultant. In addition, I deeply appreciate Brad Rickey's (Rickeybrad@gmail.com) crafting of the book cover which came from the description of the spiritual journey included in the book. And I am thankful for my wife, Patricia, not only for providing endless uninterrupted hours for writing but also for her undying love and support. The Spiritual Road: Helping Others Grow spiritually would not have been written without all of you.

I am further indebted to all of the people who have allowed me to accompany them along parts of their spiritual journeys. Many thanks for the use of those stories, with some changes to conceal identities, which have been included within this work. Their vignettes have not only informed the validity of the process of spiritual growth but they have also added depth and reality to it.

Finally, I am humbled by how God placed people and opportunities in my way so to sculpt my personality to be able to intuit, organize and summarize the process of Christian spiritual growth and development. Mostly, I am pleasurably mystified by the personal faith relationship God engendered in me that has totally transformed how I live and look at life. And I pray that this book will somehow encourage and enable the same in each reader.

Richard A. Haynes
Spring 2012
Beautiful Little Fox Lake
Brown County, Indiana

The Spiritual Road

Helping Others Grow Spiritually

By

Richard A. Haynes

The Spiritual Road
Helping Others Grow Spiritually
by Richard A. Haynes

Printed in the United States of America

ISBN 9781622301799

www.xulonpress.com

As a pastor and spiritual director, I've read many books on spiritual formation, pastoral counseling and spiritual direction. This is the book I've been waiting for! The Spiritual Road: Helping Others Grow Spiritually is a comprehensive manual for those wanting to encourage spiritual growth in others. The book provides understanding of the spiritual growth process and practical tools for conversations with people who want to move forward in life with God. The book is based on scripture, includes the wisdom of classic Christian writers through the centuries, and the insights of modern psychology - all brought home in a very practical way. Dick Haynes has done a marvelous job of making a wealth of information very accessible to anyone interested in serving as a spiritual helper. Although clergy, professional counselors, and spiritual directors will find this a good resource, it is also written for any Christian who wants to be a better listener, friend, or small group leader. I may be one of the first spiritual helpers to thank Dick Haynes for this book, but I think there will be many others!

Judy Turner, co-founder of Christivew Ministries, retreat leader, and spiritual director. She was formerly the Church Growth Consultant, Homeland Ministries of the Christian Church (Disciples of Christ).

Dedication

In memory of my father, Elmer R. Haynes, who to the best of my recollection said, "Son, remember that every good story tells truth. Never tell a lie; but don't ever let the truth stand in the way of a good story."

Table of Contents

Tools for the Journey—200

Praxis for Spiritual Helpers—318

Introduction

One day after a retreat with his staff, I noticed a pastor of a large congregation staying after everyone else had left. He was pacing in and out the door and then up and down the deck while he talked on his cell phone. His friendly tone disguised his agitated movements, furrowed brow, intense listening and pithily interjected comments as he talked with a series of parishioners – defusing potential disagreements, clarifying possible points of contention and doing conflict resolution. Obviously, he was very skilled. I know because I had so often had to practice that same proficiency of "putting out fires" and "taking care of business." The subject was financial in nature and the need of filling the vacancy for some constitutionally-designated church officer. I felt for him.

After the armada of phone calls had seemed to maintain the cold war among the different personalities with some kind of cease fire, the pastor started to pack up all of the scattered papers, calendars and program planning ideas in order to head back to the church office, check on emergency needs that required immediate pastoral care and hopefully go home to begin packing for a much needed vacation trip that started the next day.

As he littered stuff into his brief case, I engaged him in some light conversation in regard to the beauty of the day and the time of retreat with his staff. Then, I interjected a comment, "I hope you might let me help you with your ministry." He politely responded that he had already set up a conflict management seminar, as well as a how to be a good chairperson of a committee and long range planning retreat; and that he didn't think that he needed any help at this time. In reply I noted, "Most of my retreats are more spiritual in nature; focusing on prayer, personal evangelism and biblical application." I guess I should not have been surprised by his near anger and his voice's sudden rise in volume as he retorted, "Oh, the kind of things we are supposed to do!"

Whether this stressed senior minister really didn't spend much time providing relational spiritual help or was simply frustrated that his work load kept him from doing that, the result was the same. An overemphasis on church work overwhelmed the spiritual purpose for which it was created.

Now, please understand that I have GREAT SYMPATHY for leaders of local congregations, where I spent my entire professional religious career. I know the pressures and the expectations. I know the exhaustion and the stretched to the limit feelings. After the sub-committees, boards and meetings are held with the associated managerial phone calls made, then come the church programs and activities as well as the taking care of the needs of people. Of course, people die, get married and have problems which need to be addressed; thus, funerals, marriages and consoling become the tasks of the minister. Oh yes, don't forget to throw in sermon preparation to the list of church work that has to be done on a regular basis. Unfortunately after all of the administrative tasks and the showing concern for the variety of life problems of all the people is done, little time or energy is left. As a result, spiritual growth is left half done or abandoned.

Indeed, the ministry that God unfolded through the person of Jesus is not about church work! It is about assisting people to grow in their personal spiritual relationship with God so as to transform the world into the Community of God. Nevertheless, the Church, the structured group of Christians, is absolutely essential! The first part of God's purpose for The Church is that it be the model of the Holy Community that God desires. The second part of God's purpose for The Church is to be the agent to implement God's form of mercy and justice into the world. **Christians-in-relationship as The Church, as the representative of God, is the only way to accomplish these external purposes.** However, when maintaining The Church becomes the higher priority, its God-designed purposes are diminished or eliminated. In addition, when Christians stop growing in their personal spiritual faith (belief), being the Holy Community and metering mercy/justice into the world (application) also comes to a halt, or at least becomes severely limited (inconsistent and non-concentric)!!!

The aim of this book is encourage all spiritually mature Christians to emphasize spiritual growth and development for the benefit of others as well as the Church. Just like it takes all of the mature adults in a village to rear a child, it takes all of the spiritually mature Christians in a congregation to assure spiritual growth and development. Spiritual helpers include all who provide leadership in whatever ways in the church from nursery attendants to the pastor's emeriti/emeritae, from teachers and program directors to religious, counselors, ministers and spiritual directors. To each, I say, **"There is a process to spiritual growth. Do you know what it is? Can you assist others through it?"** This book will guide you to understand and help you be a better spiritual helper.

As an INTJ on the Myers-Briggs Type Indicator, I have always been interested in overall patterns, especially of spiritual growth; and my ability to help people see what has been and project what will potentially happen in their lives has benefited many people. Perhaps, I can do that in these chapters. That is my hope. The structure of the book includes a theory of spiritual growth and development (chapters one through four), a comprehensive description of its pattern (chapters five through eleven), the integration of spiritual growth with psycho-social models (chapters twelve through fifteen), some practical tools for overcoming issues that deter spiritual growth (chapters sixteen through twenty-one) and a summary of the practice of being a spiritual helper (chapters twenty-two and twenty-three).

Biblical references are included throughout each section; Christian lyrics are scattered supportively; and a multitude of real life stories illustrate from beginning to end.

My intent is that <u>The Spiritual Road: Helping Others Grow Spiritually</u> is an accurate description of the process of spiritual growth that includes simple, practical ways to view it and encourage it. In addition, I hope that this material will help average church members/leaders and those who they may influence to grow spiritually in the Christian faith. Thankfully, God is part and parcel to spiritual growth so sometimes even blind travelers reach their destination. However, Christians can do much to cooperate with what God is doing for and with them. That is the purpose of this book – to help Christians to be able to work together with God toward the level of spiritual intimacy that Jesus calls "oneness" and for the strengthening for the church.

Overview of Spiritual Growth

There is a process to Christian spiritual growth just like there is a process to growing through life. In life, people call it maturing; in spirituality, St. Paul talked about Christians who needed spiritual milk in order to grow into those who required spiritual meat. No one formally taught me the Christian growth process although they assisted me through it – most assuredly not understanding exactly what they were doing. Growing up I experienced God though Jesus the Christ; and I received teaching, love and support from many Christian adults in church families. College and seminary enabled me to do academic and critical thinking in regard to spiritual matters, but left the process uninformed. Family and friends, especially my wife, opened my emotions and guided me into matters of the heart. The people who I served as a Christian pastor, especially my spiritual directees, provided revision to the application of my spiritual understandings. God was guiding each experience; but also each milestone along the way was responsible for bringing me closer to God. A seemingly inexplicable intersecting of God and life events occurred on this journey. But it did not seem to be random, just unknown – this process of Christian spiritual growth.

I believe that knowing the way helps people to get where they are going, but at the very least allows them to know that they are heading in the right direction and perhaps even confirms when they have arrived. Cartographers are unusual people: part adventurers and part helpers who don't want others to have cut the path through the landscape like they had to do. They are practical, overview kind of people. Reflecting on my spiritual journey and those I have guided, I have both drawn and collected maps so that people might envision The Spiritual Road ahead of them. In order to communicate this information, I have begun with a theory of spiritual growth, detailed the process of Christian spiritual growth, overlaid other maps for the purpose of supplementing that process, provided tools to deal with the difficulties that happen along the way and finally encouraged people to be spiritual helpers who employ the process for the good of others.

CHAPTER 1

Defining Spiritual Growth

O ne day a middle aged man in a sharply tailored pin-striped suit walked up to me with a handshake extended and boldly announced, "Hi. My name is Jim and I'm in the car business!" Not to be outdone, I returned the remark with equally eager tones saying, "Hi. I'm Dick and I'm in the spiritual growth business!" That may have been the only time in the last half century that this used car salesperson had ever been speechless. But he was.

What is it about spiritual growth that makes one speechless? First of all, it is hard to define or at least the variety of ways that people explain and approach faith is often confusing. In fact, a diversity of approaches actually does work; and I don't intend to explain all of them nor discount any particular means of spiritual growth. Instead, I will concentrate on ways that Christians have used, which I have found typical in my personal life and in the lives of hundreds of people from both Christian seekers and believers, whom I have guided spiritually.

What is spiritual faith and spiritual growth? Truly, all growth always involves change from one thing to another. **Growth is spiritual when it involves movement from one way of recognizing God to another as well as any transition in applying that understanding.** The purpose of our Christian spiritual faith (about which Jesus was quite clear) is to become closer to God.[1] Jesus described this as becoming "one" with God – a goal for which people need God's help to obtain and is approximated in a variety of ways as people seek to think as God would think, feel as God would feel and act as God would act. Growing in spiritual faith is necessary for this to happen. In addition, Christians understand that Jesus models this oneness with God and that "personally knowing" Jesus is also the best way of reaching this oneness. **So, an over-simplified definition of spiritual growth is that it is the purpose of spiritual faith because growing brings people closer in oneness with God.**

What are the components of spiritual faith and how does it grow?

Let us begin by understanding that spiritual faith is two dimensional; <u>it is about gaining belief in God and applying that understanding in real life practical ways. Belief together with application is what I call faith in God</u>. Both belief and application need to happen although the process is not necessarily linear. In other words, people can practice faith long before they know precisely what they believe; and they can also understand before they put that belief into action. However, both are necessary for what I call "spiritual faith." In addition, Christian spiritual faith always includes a centered focus on Jesus of Nazareth as God's chosen way to bring people and God together. I am using this phrase "faith in God" in a very general sense. Paul Tillich discussed faith with the depth and nuances which that complex term deserves.[2] However, I simply want to use the term "faith" as a way to describe the spiritual connection that is established between people and God – whether that happens when the beauty of a sunset first overwhelms a young child or when a seasoned elder is caught up in an ecstatic contemplative vision of the resurrected Christ.

As a male, I learned about the difference between boys and girls at an early age; it was so long ago that I'm not exactly sure when that happened. However, with two sisters in my household of origin, I increasingly realized more and more differences. While in my adolescence, my siblings and I played baseball together in the backyard and wrestled playfully in the basement romp room – I knew my sisters and I were not the same but it didn't much matter. One day, I looked across the room and saw a <u>girl</u> – and I couldn't stop thinking about her or stop looking at her. I was so attracted and fascinated and uncertain – all at the same time. It was puppy love. I started spending more time with that girl in order to get to know her, enjoy her, learn from her and share my life with her. It was a great experience and hopefully it has happened to others, too. Eventually, this association with "the other" grew into something more serious until I made a commitment to be engaged and eventually married. And as every person in a long-term relationship knows – that was only the beginning to the depth and height and the width of love. If nurtured, the love relationship grows into an intimacy in which couples finish each other's words as well as support and defend each other; and this connection develops into a deep union that cannot be fully explained with words.

Analogously, faith in God is like a connection with another person that begins with the simple acknowledgement that someone "other" exists. However, "faith" as I am using it is not limited to, and is much more than, just mere belief that the other is alive. This recognition extends to simple interaction until the association becomes a friendship that grows into a relationship – a love that eventually makes the two inseparably bonded. Likewise, <u>faith in God is relational and takes time</u>; it begins and grows not unlike a connection with another person. In order to discover whether this kind of faith connection has occurred, my Christian evangelical brothers and sisters sometimes ask, "Do you have a personal relationship with Jesus Christ?" While this query sufficiently identifies a certain type of faith relationship, it does not include the kind of connection with the divine which happens toward the beginning of coming to "faith in God" and prior to a "Christ relationship."

The Christian religion teaches that this spiritual faith is initiated by God wanting to connect (actually re-connect) with us – a love to which people are invited to respond. Scripture passages such as "God was reconciling the world to himself in Christ" [II Corinthians 5:19] or "For God so loved the world that he gave his only son that whoever believes in him shall not perish but have eternal life"[3] [John 3:16] illustrate this. When people even entertain the notion of God, they have "responded" and a fledgling "personal relationship" has begun. Although it is not a fully developed personal relationship, it is the beginning of "faith in God" and needs to be honored and nurtured as the spiritual faith that it is.

In summary, spiritual faith/growth at its most basic level can be viewed as gaining belief in God and applying that belief in real life practical ways. In addition, spiritual faith is about having a connection with the divine that is experienced in ways similar to the manner in which we relate with other people. Thus, this "faith in God" is experienced differently at various times and according to the multiplicity of circumstances in people's lives. When people move from one expression of faith to another, they have experienced spiritual growth.

CHAPTER 2

Making It Real

I am fond of asking a riddle question: **"There are five frogs sitting on a log. One decides to jump. How many are left?"** By the twinkle in my eye and the all-knowing smile on my face, people infer that this is probably a trick question. Many people answer, "There are four frogs left on the log." Occasionally, someone will say, "When one frog jumped; they all jumped. So there are no frogs left on the log." After their responses, I simply note, "There are still five frogs sitting on that log because 'deciding to jump' and 'jumping' are two different things."

There is a big difference between thinking and acting. I may think that I am a Christian or believe that I should love my enemy; but until I do something about it I am just thinking about it … sitting on the log, not jumping.

Thinking + acting = decision

Any counselor knows that speaking an unspoken truth is better than just thinking it; and saying it out loud causes a reality that can often be visibly noticed in a client. People who have had this experience understand and even remember that particular moment when their insight or admission became real and made an impact. That occurred when their thinking took on form – it emerged from an internal thought to an external spoken word. Then, when it was spoken to another person, that truth became even more real because it became relational.

As a minister, whenever I would be visiting with a person at home, hospital, restaurant, after committee meetings or in a private counseling/spiritual direction setting, I would be particularly aware of times when people would uncharacteristically pause and be absorbed in an unspoken thought or idea. So, I would give them a bit of silence to process what the "busyness" of their world would not let them. Often I would see them look up as to visualize the story of what was happening within; and then suddenly look down when they connected with its emotional content. At that particular moment, I would ask, "What were you thinking?" and then typically follow that question with the encouragement, "It's ok. You can say that." The next words spoken were usually important; but in numerous instances people would begin by saying, "Pastor, I have never said this to anyone before." Helping people speak what they have been thinking, especially if it had never been said before, is helping them birth their thoughts into reality. It is also helping them grow spiritually if what they say can be related to God or if some healing can be gained that allows for a deeper God connection.

Thus, the first step in making faith real is to let it move from the inner world to the outer world. Now, faith-thinking is very important. It is the incubator of the Spirit that God has conceived within us. Within this safe, protected place, people are able to consider different options and grow in understanding before they have to let others know what is happening. However, as all parents know, they cannot remain pregnant forever – in order to become real people's faith-thinking must be born into the world. People have nurtured and loved it the best they could in the spiritual womb, but this new faith-thought must be born. When this new birth is pushed into the world, it comes with joy and danger, excitement and anxiety. But it is real.

For example, as a child I had a sense that I was taken care of and provided for. At some point, I began to think that along with my parents, it was God who was taking care and providing for me. At home my parents taught me to pray before our meals. As my faith-thinking grew, I considered bowing my head in prayer before eating my food from the cafeteria at school to say "Thank you." (School lunches absolutely need prayer!) When I finally let my inclination to pray embody external action, my faith-thought was brought to life as faith-action. There was joy in what I had just completed as God's pleasure was instilled within me. On the other hand, now I had to address the question of my school mate, "What are you doing?" And I had to face the criticism, "He thinks he's some kind of holy-roller." However, I also found an unexpected friend who said to me while playing at recess, "I think about saying grace, too. Maybe we could do that together?" When my faith-thoughts were born and became real, they could then begin to grow in strength and stature. This action together with my thought equaled a decision I had made. My faith-thought that had become action elicited joy as well as criticism; but I also developed a living faith.

In summation, the connection people have with the divine needs to take form in order for spiritual growth to occur. This is a continuous life-time process of conceiving and giving birth, of bringing forth what is internal into the light of the external world. <u>It is making internal reality into external reality.</u> **Helping people "make it real" is the beginning of the process of naming, claiming and proclaiming God in life. Spiritual growth has begun.**

CHAPTER 3

Uniting Belief and Deeds

A s people go through life they are always making decisions that have the effect of uniting their beliefs and actions, or disconnecting them. One of the primary goals of spiritual helpers is to assist others in uniting belief and action. New Testament passages certainly provide much instruction regarding faith-belief and faith-action. In one section, the writer of the book of James provides commentary about belief and action which the biblical writer calls "faith" and "deeds."

[14]What good is it, my brothers, if a man claims to have faith but has no deeds? Can such faith save him? [15]Suppose a brother or sister is without clothes and daily food. [16]If one of you says to him, "Go, I wish you well; keep warm and well fed," but does nothing about his physical needs, what good is it? [17]In the same way, faith by itself, if it is not accompanied by action, is dead.

[18]But someone will say, "You have faith; I have deeds."

Show me your faith without deeds, and I will show you my faith by what I do. [19]You believe that there is one God. Good! Even the demons believe that — and shudder.

[20]You foolish man, do you want evidence that faith without deeds is useless? [21]Was not our ancestor Abraham considered righteous for what he did when he offered his son Isaac on the altar? [22]You see that his faith and his actions were working together, and his faith was made complete by what he did. [23]And the scripture was fulfilled that says, "Abraham believed God, and it was credited to him as righteousness," and he was called God's friend. [24]You see that a person is justified by what he does and not by faith alone.

[25]In the same way, was not even Rahab the prostitute considered righteous for what she did when she gave lodging to the spies and sent them off in a different direc-

tion? [26]As the body without the spirit is dead, so faith without deeds is dead.[1] [James 2:14-26]

A careful reading of this passage indicates that the writer makes the contrast between keeping something to one's self and putting it into action. The biblical writer calls these two concepts "faith" and "deeds" and teaches that these two spiritual dimensions both need to be employed.

James claims that faith without deeds is "useless" (verse twenty) and infers that it has no power to save (verse fourteen). In one example, he indicates his affirmation that people believe in God. However, he notes even the devil also "believes" in God, but does not act in accord with God (verse nineteen). In other words, just believing is neither adequate nor sufficient, but following through on what people believe is necessary – faith and deeds need to go together.

Given the context and the message of this biblical passage, it is best understood that James is contrasting what people think or believe with how they act. His instruction is that just thinking without real life application of that thought is useless.

My question to the text is: "What do you call it when "faith" and "deeds" are actually put together?" The writer of James does not say. It would be useful, even essential, to have a name for this interfacing of "faith" and "deeds." I suggest that instead of the word "faith" it would have been better if James would have used the word "belief" to describe the truth he was attempting to teach. Belief is something that people do in their heads. I prefer to reserve the word "faith" for when people put the internal and external together. In addition, faith, as I am using the word, is relational – bringing a thought into relationship via action in the world or in the lives of other people.

Following my definition, "faith in God" is belief in God together with practical real life application of that understanding. Truly, "belief" without "deeds" is dead or at least stuck in one's head. "Deeds" without "belief" is empty. Putting these two spiritual dimensions together fashions spiritual faith and often brings spiritual growth as people reconcile the inconsistencies that emerge between what they believe and how they live.

FACILITATING SIMPLE SPIRITUAL GROWTH

I want to focus on some practical, everyday kinds of examples of uniting belief and deed. Hopefully, people will identify with at least some of these situations; and spiritual helpers will realize these as opportunities to assist in spiritual growth.

Helping people grow spiritually does not have to be difficult. In fact, it can be as easy as getting people to say what they are thinking. This task becomes less complicated when the helper is aware of what he or she is hoping to assist. The hardest part is to really listen to others so that they believe it is safe to say what they are thinking. In my experience, this happens when listeners are truly interested in others. After a trusting conversation has been elicited, spiritual helpers need to succinctly interject a question or comment that will allow people to take the next step, followed by silence that is designed for them to choose and act. The process is simple, but takes practice and great skill – listening, trusting, questioning and silence.

One scenario has happened quite often in my life. People would say, "I need to make an appointment to see you sometime" or "I need to talk with you." These statements, of course, indicate that people have something on their minds – a belief or a thought. Typically, these folks have been thinking about making this comment for some time, but have not acted on it. At that moment, I would typically take out my appointment book, which I carried in my shirt pocket, and ask, "When would you like to do that?" This is rudimentary spiritual growth, but growth none the least – making a decision to meet is action. Indeed, the act of inviting people for an appointment gives them the opportunity to make their belief real – at the very least it has helped them to consider that possibility, which they may decline. If people make the appointment, their personal will has been engaged and a decision has been made which potentially allows them to say out loud what they have been thinking at three o'clock in the morning when they couldn't sleep.

How is this spiritual growth? Allowing people to speak what is inside helps them to make their thinking external and especially makes it relational. God can work inside people's heads; but is more likely to be effective in relationship with others in the external world. This is part of the impact of Jesus' statement "For where two or three come together in my name, there am I with them."[2] [Matthew 18:20]

Faith in God cannot be relational if it remains in people's minds. It has to be expressed in real life practical ways. "Now preacher" says the objector. "You mean that I can't just talk to God in my head?" Of course, people pray to God in silence. However, ask yourself, "When did you feel the closest to God or when did God seem the most real to you?" When people's prayers were answered in external ways especially at the beginning of their lives as Christians, then they knew that God was real. God certainly talks with people though their minds in silence. However, God never stays in people's heads but is always manifesting in real life practical ways.

I believe that God is often trying to break through into people's busy lives. Agreeing to sit down and talk on any subject that seems personally important can allow God to do just that and effect spiritual growth in the process. When people help others establish a time for such reflection, they are enabling a connection with God and potentially spiritual growth. Attending a Bible study/prayer group also holds the same possibilities. Whether more spiritual growth actually happens in the conversation depends on if what is said is related to God so that healing or change occurs.

A similar circumstance reveals itself when people say, "We should do that." or "I would like to do that." At that time I began using the phrase that helped me to overcome my procrastination and resultant lack of spiritual growth, saying, "There is no time like the present." Then suggest, "Let's do it now." In committee meetings, people wonder if a particular person is willing to do a task or someone may suggest that the group should set a time to serve at the soup kitchen. I respond, "Let's call them now." At noon, someone might suggest the need to have lunch sometime. I would say, "Let's do it now."

Another example occurs when people have asked me to pray for someone, or even for them; I have learned to make it real by again pulling out my appointment book, asking when to pray and how to spell that name – then wrote it down. This action made their request more real and it actually helped me to remember to pray for that person. On the other hand, I actually recommend that praying in that particular moment is the best way to respond – unless the situation says "no."

Furthermore, praying aloud with someone often helps people verbalize what they have not been able to do – perhaps being emotionally honest with God. It can be a very cathartic and freeing moment. It certainly takes beliefs, makes them into deeds and presents them to God. In this way, spiritual helpers assist others by using their own spiritual energy to connect others with God (via the helpers' faith and action on behalf of others). In addition, this faith-action also models for people how they may do the same for others.

Praying in public is often discouraged in today's society as if it is something to be ashamed of. However, <u>Christians have one true privilege which is coming into contact with God together</u>. Make that belief real and affirm your Christian faith by praying together, boldly. The scripture proclaims, "I am not ashamed of the gospel, because it is the power of God for the salvation of everyone who believes."[3] [Romans 1:16a] Truly, whenever Christians come together, they should affirm the most important part of their lives – their faith. Praying together is an excellent way to do that. "Let's do it now."

> Gracious and ever-loving God, you have brought me to this particular moment in my life and I am grateful for the guidance and blessings. But I also confess that I have not trusted you but have worried and wondered what was happening. What I believe right now about you is _____. Help me to act the way I believe. Help me to change what I believe if that is better. Enable me to move toward a more mature faith. Inspire me to say what I believe and mean what I say that I may grow in spirit and in truth and be so partnered with you that we are as one. I pray in the name and for the sake of my Savior who prays that we will be united. Amen.

DIFFERENT STROKES FOR DIFFERENT FOLKS

For spiritual growth to occur, some people need to verbalize while others need to stop talking. People sometimes put mouth in motion before they put mind in gear. In other words, they speak out of habit or are motivated by their emotions. So, another way to help people grow spiritually is to assist them to think about what they are babbling. Numerous people, particularly those who need to talk in order to think, become overwhelmed, confused and even disoriented when they talk. They are trying to process too much information, options and possibilities; and they become like a pinball bouncing wildly, and sometimes erratically. Enabling people to sort and organize the multiplicity of information can be very helpful.

One of the most unique and exquisitely simple techniques for inducing spiritual growth is to call for silence. I regularly met with Julia who often became overwhelmed by all of life's issues including her spiritual beliefs which were also swirling around inside of her. As a result, she exhibited some inconsistent, sometimes marginally irresponsible, behavior; and she appeared to some people to not be very smart. However, this mother of two adult children had never learned to stop long enough to process the confusion within. (This tendency was compounded by her obsession to serve others and her fear of what others might say about what she really thought – a typical mode of operation for many Christians in the culture.) However, Julia was far from unintelligent and had a survivor's ability that she had gained via all the challenges and abuse she had overcome in her life. What she needed was silence.

While talking one day, I discovered quite by accident that what Julia needed was silence. I suggested, "Why don't you take a moment to think about what you just said?" I also recommended that she take a couple of deep breaths which she did. Her body began to relax as she let her head settle back onto the chair. She gently closed her eyes and began to reflect. I anticipated that this silence would last about a minute or perhaps two. So, I watched for signs that she was becoming uncomfortable or done with her time of processing. However, Julia was fully engaged in this exercise for at least twenty minutes. When she opened her eyes and smiled, I asked, "Would you summarize what you have been thinking?" What materialized was no more than a three sentence synopsis of all that had attacked her sensibilities. This scenario was no accident. From that day forward whenever Julia came for spiritual direction I would let her regurgitate what was overwhelming her; and then call for silence which was often for an extended amount of time – time that was always purposeful and meaningful. Silence truly is golden.

Talkative people (about sixty percent of the population) need to stop talking for spiritual growth to solidify. When people are overwhelmed as was Julia, silence may be the best response. However, other conversationally-oriented people might benefit more by stopping them with a succinct, reflective question. What is helpful spiritually is to ask them what kind of thinking is motivating their speaking. "Is what you believe consistent with what you are saying?" "What does your faith advise you to do with that anger?" Or "What you are saying about all those people sounds a lot like gossip to me. Is that what you want to do or would talking with them be better?" Or "Where do you see God in what you just said?"

Make sure to ask questions instead of making statements. For example: announcing, "You are gossiping" will elicit a far different response than "That sounds like gossip; what do you think?" The first assertion will bring a defensive attitude; the second comment invites people to be aware and then choose. Remember, the job of spiritual helpers is not to fix anyone; the role is to invite, encourage and create the opportunity for others to allow God to do that.

Now, colleagues remind me that some people just want to talk, inferring that I might offend someone by trying to get them to think about what they are saying. I certainly understand that people are like this; and I don't intend to upset folks. I simply want to do my job of helping others grow spiritually. In order to do that, I need to invite them to act or reflect depending on who they are. If they don't want to follow through on what they say, it is really ok because either their will is not set or they really don't want to change; so they are not actually ready to act anyway. If they don't use the silence or the reflective question for their own benefit, the same is true. However, unless someone invites them to unite their deeds to beliefs, they will most likely not grow spiritually. Think of it as extending people a helping hand, not giving them a push. If they don't reach out and take the hand, they are not ready. But unless spiritual helpers offer assistance, people will not be lifted out of the place where they are stuck.

All through the Gospels, Jesus asked questions that had the import of encouraging people to grow spiritually. Such is the case of the blind man who was sitting alongside the road to Jericho.[4] [Luke 18:35-42] The blind man hears that Jesus is coming and must "believe" that healing is possible or else he would not have called out, "Jesus, Son of David, have mercy on me." What does Jesus do? He asks what is much more than a rhetorical question, "What do you want me to do for you?" He invites this man to verbalize what he has been thinking. The blind man says, "Lord, I want to see." Jesus replies, "Receive your sight. Your faith has healed you." (Verse forty-two) Truly, there is something about putting belief and action together that allows "faith" to heal, to save or to make people whole! It allows the blind to see.

CHAPTER 4

Concentric Faith

As people live their faith decisions (thoughts + actions), the next part of the faith journey (which happens repeatedly) is to be consistent with what they think and do. This step of their spiritual lives is what I call "concentric faith" which is being consistent and authentic. While people do not live that way most of the time, concentric faith needs to happen at every level of faith – whenever they gain new understandings or behaviors. On the other hand, being inconsistent or unauthentic is not bad except if people plan to remain in that condition and live that way. In fact, unless people are perfectly lucky or someone is Jesus Christ, their faith is never concentric neither from the beginning nor all the time.

People are interior and exterior beings. In other words, all human beings think and act. What people think and how they behave do not always match. What people say they believe and how they live are often inconsistent. Although the internal and external don't match or are incompatible, it is best that they do. For example, I can believe that I am an American patriot and talk passionately about the democratic process, but I never go to the polls and vote on Election Day. So, what I think and how I act are inconsistent. How do people typically feel about others who think they are patriots but never vote? At best, people might think they are shallow; on the other hand, people might consider them liars. The opposite situation is equally unsettling. People who drink a quart of vodka a day and do not function well in society are alcoholics. However, if they do not believe that they have that problem, what do people think about them? Some people might just regard them as in denial; or at worst, others might crusade against them because they are a serious danger to others.

Does God want people's faith to be concentric? I believe so; at least God does not want them to consistently be shallow or in denial, to be a danger to society or a liar. In these two scenarios, what people believe is not consistent with how they act – and neither do they intend to change. I am reminded of what my ol' pappy used to advise: "Say what you mean and mean what you say." In this regard when it comes to spiritual faith, the saying would be, "Do what you mean and mean what you do." **At best people's beliefs and actions coincide. When this occurs, they have concentric faith.**

The last time I had my eyes examined at the optometrist, an apparatus was placed in front of my eyes. As I looked through the goggle-like lenses two circles were visible – one on the right and one on the left. The doctor said, "I am going to move these circles of light toward each other. Please tell me when they come together." When these objects became superimposed, I said, "That's it. They are together." These two objects were the same size so when they intersected, they were actually one thing. They were "perfectly" overlaid. However, they could have been different size circles. When they would have united, their centers would have been superimposed although one circle would have appeared larger than the other. They would not be "perfect" but they would be concentric.

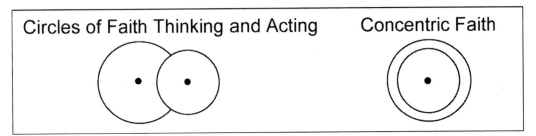

Graphic 1: Concentric faith occurs when the circle of faith-thinking (belief) and the circle of faith-action come together.

Concentric faith occurs when the circle of faith-thinking (belief) and the circle of faith-action come together. Most of the time the size of the circles are not the same (our thinking and our behaviors are rarely the same). They do not have to be superimposed, or perfectly as one, to be consistent and authentic as long as they coincide at the heart. Whenever the circles are centered, the focus becomes clear just like two lenses – even though they are different in size. When this happens, people gain a glimpse of truth as part of their thinking and part of their behavior have come into agreement. Clara H. Scott's 1895 hymn "Open My Eyes, That I May See" affirms this process as we get keys to seeing God's Will and being content or free in God's Spirit.[1]

Developing concentric faith is a process. It takes time for the circles' centers to align. In other words, it takes time for the thinking and behavior of people to become consistent and authentic. In practical terms, it means people will seem to be inconsistent (because they are) but they are actually in the process of growing toward concentric faith (assuming that is their intention). However, as the circles begin to merge together, people do see more clearly. An interesting example may clarify this concept. When I was at the eye doctor's office, before the examination began I looked up at the eye chart and thought to myself I can read that bottom line. Then, the doc covered one of my eyes and asked, "What is the lowest line you can read?" Much to my surprise, I not only could not see the lowest line, but could only read the fourth line from bottom. I had to ask why and was told that when both eyes work together, human vision is more accurate. The same is true when it comes to using belief and action in tandem together. When I focus my belief and action in the same direction on the same subject, my vision is unambiguous. The more closely aligned my thinking and behaving become, the more concentric my faith is and the clearer spiritual focus I have.

Indeed, when people's beliefs and actions are concentric, so are their lives. Even in the midst of chaos, life is easier. Part of the benefit of concentric faith is the greater certainty and contentment that accompanies it. In Paul's letter to the Philippians he affirms, "I have learned the secret of being content in any and every situation, whether well fed or hungry, whether living in plenty or in want. I can do everything through him who gives me strength."[2] [Philippians 4:12-13] **This strength that brings contentment is not the ability to do what I want to do. Instead, this strength is living consistent with what people believe and how they act.** The apostle Paul referred to this as having the mind and heart of Christ or being "in Christ." The phrase "in Christ" is used ninety times in the New Testament letters mostly to refer to people who were committed to following Jesus as Savior and Lord. However, a somewhat mystical or supernatural element is implied in this phrase because the divine and the believer are put together. Some people can actually experience this truth in a physical way.[3]

Being concentric with Christ at any level of faith is mature thinking and behavior combined. This is the ideal of the spiritual life – to live with such an interconnected belief and conduct. In those fleeting transitory moments, people are truly content because they are in God's Will albeit only partially. Cherish the moments of perfect clarity or beautiful contentment! And praise God! They will last for only as long as God allows – until God pulls people farther along the spiritual path.

For example, Eldon believed that God wanted him to "love his neighbor." Accordingly, he attempted to be nice to everyone he met and dealt respectfully with them. He participated in providing food for church funeral dinners, even when he had little time to do that, because he want to "make real" what he "believed." Also, the man across the street was typically negative and critical of Eldon's children, but Eldon had even started talking with him. Eldon was practicing love for his neighbor.

One day, an elder from the church asked if he could talk with Eldon about "prison ministry" which the elder described as regularly visiting men in jail and sharing Christianity with them. He wanted Eldon to do that. Eldon weaseled his way out with various excuses and the elder responded, "I thought you meant it when you said that you were putting into practice Jesus' command to love your neighbor!" (First of all, this elder does not understand spiritual growth and needed to be schooled – or removed from his position. Inflicting such guilt and shame often retards people from further spiritual growth.) In truth, Eldon's faith was very concentric because he had a faith-belief that he had made real by practicing it. His Christian faith was absolutely ok. On the other hand, his faith was not perfect because he didn't love everyone. Later, in his faith growth he may integrate "prison ministry" into his neighbor-loving activities. However, his faith would not be perfect then either.

ON BEING PERFECT

The Sermon on the Mount records Jesus as concluding, "Be perfect, therefore, as your heavenly Father is perfect."[4] [Matthew 5:48] Now, I confess that reading this Bible verse almost destroyed my plan to become a Christian. You see, I knew that I could not be perfect; I couldn't even follow all the rules that my parents laid down for me; and there was always improvement that needed to be done. Because I had internalized that whatever I did would never be good enough, I knew that I could never measure up to Jesus' command to "be perfect." Obviously, I could never be a good Christian.

Fortunately, I learned that sometimes what the Bible says in English is not what was meant by the original language in which it was written. The Greek word used for "perfect" in Matthew 5:48 is "τέλειός" (teleios) which according to the Greek lexicon means "to carry through completely, to accomplish or bring to an end." When this word is applied to human beings, it means "full grown, adult, of full age, mature."[5] Teleios is translated "make perfect." Our typical definition of "perfect" is "without flaws." However, when an apple, for example, is "made perfect," it has completed its journey from seed to blossom to full-grown fruit – it is at the end of the process and is ready to harvest. It has accomplished the goal for which it has been made even though it is flat and discolored on one side and that there is a worm hole at the top. However, it has been made perfect, in the biblical sense. When the end result of an apple is done, it will not be without flaws. Likewise, in the spiritual life, people are to grow to the end, to mature ... which in all the cases I know contain imperfections. Jesus communicates the goal of the spiritual life by claiming that we need to become "τέλειός" like God is. **So, l invite people to grow into the maturity that God has – making lots of unintentional errors along the way. As they do, they will be "made perfect." When people experience concentric faith with that sense of contentment, they know that they are traveling the right road**.

Do not be discouraged by what seems to be unreachable demands of some Christian teachings. While the goal of the spiritual life is to mature into the character of Jesus in order to experience oneness with the divine, the spiritual path is not about "getting it right" or "being flawless" along the way. In fact, people cannot be perfect in that sense. However, people can work toward making their faith concentric – with their thinking and acting consistent and authentic.[6] In this sense, spiritual faith is more about having a smooth, productive journey than reaching the destination.

If people have a connection with God that brings them to faith-belief which they then make real by their actions, they are in the spiritual growth process. Moving these two parts of spiritual faith together so that people mean what they do and do what they mean is having concentric faith. **As long as people intend and work toward being consistent and authentic, their faith is being "made perfect."** When people stop growing and integrating whatever is new in their lives, their spiritual life becomes stagnant and begins to die. Concentric faith comes when people's faith in God is consistent and authentic. It is then that more of God's power is released into their lives. Be intentional and always move toward concentric faith.

Traveling the Spiritual Road

Spiritual growth has a progression which can be identified. The process, like all developmental maturing, is not exact and has numerous exceptions caused by life circumstances. However, it is valuable to understand that an infant will have mouth pain and whine or cry for seemingly no reason. Teeth are starting to form and push through the tender gums. Also, knowing ahead of time that puberty will happen can help ease the stress of a first menstrual cycle or changing voice tones. While such life events do happen, their precise timing cannot be anticipated. **Accordingly, certain key happenings in the spiritual life can also be anticipated and identified. Those who help others grow spiritually and those seeking God can benefit from understanding the spiritual growth process and make it smoother by doing so.**

As described in the opening section, spiritual faith includes belief, application and consistency. However, it is essentially relational – people's relationship with God but also with each other and the world. Spiritual growth is always about people's ability to respond to the initiative of God; and people's ability to respond is the direct result of the capability that they have to do so emotionally, ethically, intellectually, experientially and so forth. Indeed, one type of relating affects the others. For example, when people believe that God desires that they love others, then they begin to think differently and act accordingly. On the other hand, a crisis in the world or near fatal automobile accident can reorient people into a closer and more obedient relationship with God. Indeed, events and experiences can also have adverse effects on either people's spiritual faith or the way they function in the world. Spirituality and worldliness directly influence each other. While understanding the process of spiritual growth is the primary focus of this book, at least a working appreciation of the ways people develop in the world is essential to best help people grow spiritually.

In the next seven chapters, I will describe the most basic and classical roadways on the Christian spiritual journey. Whether using or not using a map, spiritual growth is developmental and intimately intertwined with people's ability to function in society. In subsequent chapters, I will present additional growth models that can be superimposed onto the spiritual growth-process map in order to provide detailed information that can clarify the various ways people travel as well as the understanding of detours and delays they may encounter on their road trip.

There are different maps that are valuable for the roads Christians travel – all are helpful, none are perfect. Remember that the map is not the territory. All of these maps are intended as a general overview and do not consider the academic scrutiny or the harsh criticism to which each view has been subjected. If, as helpers of spiritual growth, they are useful, please employ them as a way to guide thinking and counsel. However, do not use them as the ultimate truth. If spiritual helpers see no value in them, of course do not utilize them. I prefer a map; and so invite Christians to pick which map and which legend to use as they or those they assist travel to their not yet arrived-at destination.

CHAPTER 5

The Roadways

I grew up in the days without automatic Geographical Positioning Systems and computer mapping programs. It was a day and time when people actually needed to read and figure out what a map was telling them in order to get where they wanted to go. Every map had a different legend and scale to follow. Some maps were pretty simple; while others included so much information that they were challenging to read but of course more informative.

When I was a young teen, our family was traveling in a white Chevy station wagon on a family vacation. My father was driving and following the instructions of my mother who was looking at the map. Dad was frustrated probably because he was lost and didn't want to admit it. Impatiently, he was awaiting instruction from Mom on what to do next. When he glanced over and saw her reading the map upside down, he was none too happy, took the map, and gave it to me. "Here," he said. "See if you can figure out where we are!" That's how I became the family navigator. In the process, I learned that the blue squiggly lines were rivers and that black lines with marks on them were railroad tracks – we didn't want to follow them but they could actually be good information about where we were and where we wanted to go. I learned the differences between county, state and national roads; and the speed that a car was likely to travel on each. I discovered the little numbers on the left and right on every road that indicated the distance between intersections. Dad taught me my first mathematical formula, D=rt or Distance equals the rate of travel multiplied by the time of travel. So, if I added and multiplied correctly, I could actually estimate a time of arrival pretty closely. That was quite important for lunch and bathroom stops – not to mention calming the "anxious mob" of two girls and a dog in the back. Consequently, at an early age I learned the advantage of anticipating and projecting the events. Sometimes, however, the map was not accurate or road construction altered what was expected. So, while I discovered the advantage of anticipating what came next, I also learned that the map is not the territory.

I am telling you this fascinating story from my childhood to illustrate that having a map and learning to read it can be helpful in getting to one's destination. Actually, it is invaluable, even comforting, especially for the person in charge of getting to road's end. Likewise, having and using maps for the spiritual journey can be equally helpful. In fact since the likelihood of having a computer program to automatically guide people to the final destination is not very likely, learning to read and discern the spiritual journey maps is essential – unless you don't care where you are going.

THE THREE WAYS OF CHRISTIAN SPIRITUAL GROWTH

As early as Origen of Alexandria (185-254 A. D.) in Christian history, leaders of the Way[1] [Acts 9:1-2] had been writing about the experience of growing closer to God. Among his six thousand writings, Origen described three stages of personal spiritual growth that he discerned, respectively, from the Old Testament books of Proverbs, Ecclesiastes and the Song of Solomon. Around 500 A. D., **the Christian writer with the pen name of Pseudo-Dionysius first labelled these stages – purification, illumination and union**; and those in those stages were called beginners, proficients and perfects, respectively. In the thirteenth century, these stages were more formalized into what has been christened the "Three Ways."[2]

This long-established system refers to Christian spiritual growth that occurs after a person has confessed faith in Jesus Christ as Lord and Savior. However, since belief in and movement toward God actually begins prior to the classical descriptions of the Three Ways, I will start by supplementing this system with that preceding stage of growth. I will also convert the archaic language and concepts contained in earlier writings and will be as precise as possible about the "tasks" that need to be completed for each part of the journey. In addition, I will provide questions and examples to assist those helping others grow spiritually to progress along the spiritual road. Particular types of prayer forms typically coincide with each stage; these will be described later in chapter sixteen.

Please, keep in mind that the following outline of the spiritual growth process does not always take place in the exact order; also each concept does not have to be "completed" before moving onto the next and each is often repeated and/or adapted in later stages. For example, an annual budget accurately approximates income and expenses but never precisely reflects the final data; but the budget does allow people to count the cost. Estimating the process of spiritual growth has similar value.

The following disclaimer applies to the whole of spiritual growth: First and foremost, God desires to be in a mutual love relationship with each believer and consequently works incessantly to make that possible. Yet, our human nature, unredeemed and unsanctified, makes that impossible. Accordingly, God's Holy Spirit attempts to make such necessary transition occur. **As people grow in spiritual faith, it may seem that they are doing the work but actually God makes it possible and draws them into relationship via the Holy Spirit working in them.** However, God, whose essential nature is perfect love, will not do so without people's consent and cooperation. God does the work *if people cooperate* in the growth; this happens throughout the spiritual growth process.

What is traditionally called the Three Ways actually only has one destination, a perfect loving relationship with God. **On this road trip, travelers navigate three types of pathways.**

✝ <u>The first road surface</u> is analogous to a gravel or country road. It has sharp curves and hills, is uneven and often full of pot holes. This road surface ends in road construction that tests the resolve of everyone to continue the journey.

✝ If travelers stay the course, <u>the second road surface</u> is amazingly smooth, wide and easy; and it takes travelers to all kinds of places fast. Near the end of this second super highway road surface, travelers enter into a forever-long tunnel that has no light so as to blind the trekkers and makes them feel despairingly lost.

✝ If hope is not lost, travelers emerge from the tunnel onto an exquisitely, very familiar pathway which, in time, reveals itself as the "road to grandma's house." At this point, <u>the third road surface</u> and all external circumstances are inconsequential because the travelers are raptured in delightful and loving memories and at the same time in joyful anticipation of all that awaits them at that numinous location.

It is worthy of note that each part of the journey ends with a crisis or "dark night."

THE SPIRITUAL ROAD

The Pre-Christian Way ➡		The Purgative Way ➡		The Illuminative Way ➡		The Unitive Way	
✝ Awareness and Naming of God ✝ Awakening to the Need for God ✝ Identification of Sin ✝ Acceptance of Grace ✝ Moment of Decision	C O N F E S S I O N A L T E M P T A T I O N	✝ Purging of Sins ✝ Adopting Ethical and Moral Standards ✝ Establishing Spiritual Habits ✝ Coming to Basic Trust in God	D A R K N I G H T O F T H E S E N S E S	✝ Learning ✝ Clarification ✝ Devotion ✝ Mission and Generativity	D A R K N I G H T O F T H E S P I R I T	✝ The Experience ✝ The Secret of Contentment ✝ Watching and Waiting ✝ The Temptation ✝ Living in Love	H E A V E N

Graphic 2: The Christian Spiritual Road has four pathways:
The Pre-Christian Way, the Purgative Way, the Illuminative Way and the Unitive Way.

The Three Ways of Christian spiritual growth begins at confession-baptism (or via baptism-confirmation in some traditions).[3] Regardless of the order of the belief and application, it begins when people have been "born from above" or confessed their belief in Jesus as Lord and Savior. At this point, new Christians enter onto the first road surface called the Purgative Way, which is primarily about purification from sinful tendencies. The second roadway is called the Illuminative Way where Christians discover, interpret and apply deeper godly truths. The Unitive Way, about union with God, is where God's Spirit is infused into travelers in small but pure amounts so they think, feel and act as God would while sensing the sin of the world as God does. The Three Ways describe stages, or different roads surfaces, along which Christians travel. However, prior to these road ways, people spend time in spiritual preparation deciding if they want to go on the official journey that leads to a mutual loving relationship with God. I call this the "Pre-Christian Way."

CHAPTER 6

The Pre-Christian Way

The "Pre-Christian Way" is primarily about increasing people's awareness of the reality of God until that makes a personal difference. It includes all that prepares and leads to God's justification by grace – when God declares people accepted. Various sign posts, which often occur as a natural progression in children, will be passed; however, adults also need to go through a similar chain of events. These include:

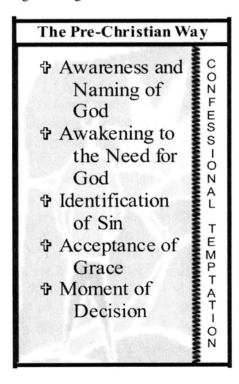

Graphic 3: The Pre-Christian Way includes the necessary steps for coming to a decision to accept Jesus as Lord and Savior.

AWARENESS OF GOD

If infants know God (as some people claim), they certainly need to learn how to name God in life. Ernest Cassirer in the <u>Philosophy of Symbolic Forms</u>[1] illustrates that life is fundamentally about pictures and making meaning. Infants experience and observe life before they can say anything about it. One day, a mother or father will hold up a ball and speak the name "ball" directly to the infant. An object has been given a name and language has begun. Images are the permanent building blocks of all that people understand. Eventually, to the object-words people add actions that get names like "throw" which people connect with "ball." They now have "throw the ball." Later, children learn words for concepts like numbers or love; however, even these concepts still have their roots in pictures like in two pieces of candy or a mother's kiss. <u>Words are always images before they are words</u>.

What does baby talk have to do with spiritual growth? Someone has to name the object or action. **Someone has to name God.** Infants may actually know God, but making God incarnate (into real life) happens in the act of naming. Praying hands sculptures, a cross on the wall, little boy/girl praying artwork, a picture of Jesus welcoming children, saying grace as a family, going to church and so forth, all provide "names" for God. **Naming God and teaching where God can be identified becomes an important way to assist in the awareness of God.** In Christian families, the naming of God is often part of the natural process of spiritual growth.

Children ask questions, sometimes really deep questions. Someone has said, "All 'why' questions lead to God." If that is true and it seems so, then children, teens, young adults and all question-asking people are seeking information about God. It seems to be imbedded in people's very being. In the groundbreaking work, Ana- Marie Rizzuto discovered that children revealed what they believed through drawings of pictures about God.[2] Long before they could verbalize what they thought, they depicted their understanding of God which sometimes reflected the views of their parents but included a collage other cultural influences as well.

Children think about God, ask about God, and picture God. Even when people don't tell children about God, in their search to understand and make meaning of the world children will discern the Presence of God. The apostle Paul claims that such information is readily available, "Since the creation of the world God's invisible qualities – his eternal power and divine nature – have been clearly seen."[3] [Romans 1:20] <u>To help people on "The Pre-Christian Way" clarify their awareness of God, ask them "How do you see God?" or "If you needed to draw a picture that expresses God what would it look like?" Or give them paper and crayons and have them draw</u>.

An engaging contemporary television commercial begins with an eight-year-old boy holding a spotlight for his father who is working on a vehicle's engine. The boy asks one question after another often before the previous question has been adequately answered.

His first simple comments/questions quickly turn into excruciatingly difficult ones. For example, he asks whether his mother or father is the oldest. When his father claims to be the oldest, his son immediately wants to know: "Does that mean that you will die first."... We didn't see that coming! The life insurance company that sponsored the commercial wants people to "protect" their loved ones by purchasing their product. At the root of this vignette is every child's unspoken concern: "Where is my protection and strength when you are gone?" Thus, this boy's probing question provides a much greater opportunity: to say "Only God knows who will die first. Have we talked about who God is?"

Children and others on the "Pre-Christian Way" ask serious life-questions which always lead to God. Helping them to name God is essential to the spiritual growth process. However, this God-seeking and meaning-making cannot remain an intellectual exercise, but needs to include personal application. **When God is connected personally to what matters most, people move toward claiming that they need God. This makes the relationship with God spiritual – the engaging of spirits.**

An essential part of my picture of God came from times of worship that I experienced at James W. Riley's Children's Hospital in Indianapolis, Indiana while recovering from polio at age four. My picture is still clear and communicates a mix of hope and healing which is what God wants for everyone. This spiritual faith was initiated by the courage and strength given in what Jesus did on the cross, which I needed for my life and recovery. Accordingly, my God-understanding began with power beyond myself to do the impossible [Philippians 4:13];[4] it became an in spite of "being hard pressed we are not crushed" theology [II Corinthians 4:8-9];[5] and finally it transformed into because of weakness "God's power is made perfect" life-meaning. [II Corinthians 12:9][6] My awareness of God has increased, been reframed, deepened and transformed; although awareness needs to occur at the beginning of faith, it is continued throughout the spiritual life.

Indeed, awareness is the first step in all spiritual growth. That is especially true during the "Pre-Christian Way." **Helping others grow spiritually at this stage is in part about naming God and how God's relates to people.** At the beginning of this part of the journey, a clear, decisive teaching manner is needed. This is why classes or Sunday school that includes instruction, catechisms or disciplining is so important. Those who want to help people grow spiritually need to remember that such lessons must be more than imparting information; the spiritual journey is relational so what is learned must make a personal difference. This type of teaching is most effective for children who are eager to absorb. However, also on the "Pre-Christian Way" are many adults, who in my experience desire a "Christian Basics 101" course, but these grown-ups bring lots of life-learned objections. Nevertheless, the need is the same – to help them become aware of the presence of God. They often have the pictures and the experiences within them. So, ask them, "When was the first time you remember that God was more than just a name to you?" They will become aware of and/or affirm their faith in the process.

41

For example, adults will experience a "divine" life moment and continue living without any awareness unless someone helps them name God. A glorious sunset will be etched on the brain as a beautiful picture or it can be a sign that points to the creator. A powerful and even life-changing insight that could not have "come from me because I don't think like that" could just be from nowhere – unless someone notes, "That's how God communicates." I often respond to people who have just spoken a passionate hope, "If you put 'Dear God' before your statement and 'Amen' afterward, that would be an awesome prayer. Sometimes writing down what is prayed for as well as the corresponding answers can be an effective way to identify God. Any way that adults can identify God in their lives enables them to become aware of the Divine.

People themselves can also be the pictures that lead children or adults to God. A saintly grandmother, a loving father, an ethical friend, a sports figure who gives God credit, a beloved Sunday school teacher or camp counselor can easily have a dramatic effect. Early in their lives, children come to recognize that all adults are bigger, smarter and more powerful than they are. This corresponds to a beginning definition of God: as eternal, omniscient and almighty. The relationship children have with adults directly determines how and what they think about God. I was proud and totally embarrassed when my son at age five publicly announced during a children's time, "My daddy is better than Jesus." **The examples we set for children help determine how they see the divine. This is also very true for adults on the "Pre-Christian Way."** They need mentors, elders who are responsible for their spiritual learning and small groups where they can grow in the awareness of God as they see God working in the lives of more mature Christians.

In order for faith to begin, God initiates contact with people in ways that provide glimpses of goodness and grace – something positive that is "other than" human. People's spiritual "task" is to identify and name this experience as "God." Accordingly, individuals need other people to help them grow spiritually in this way, which may be the summit of spirituality. Whether that recognition of God comes in the sweetness of mother's milk or in a moment when all seems right with the world, people have a beginning sense of trust. In the most inaugural way, this is God, who needs to be named. <u>Awareness is the first step in all spiritual growth</u>.

THE NEED FOR GOD

After becoming aware of the existence of God and having it matter personally, individuals can only grow closer in their relationship with God if they need and desire God. This "need for God" dynamic happens quite naturally in children and with age becomes progressively more difficult. In fact, adults, who come to the "Need for God," often have a complete attitudinal change which has been called an "awakening."[7]

42

Not long into life, children realize that the world is not as secure and safe as they would like; they feel really vulnerable and in need of protection. Responsible parents try to keep their children safe from harm and even teach them to protect themselves, but ultimately they will fail because something is always, bigger, stronger, faster or smarter. This desire to be safe can lead to the need for God, who is defined as bigger than the biggest, stronger than the strongest and so forth. **Most certainly there is an element of fear associated within this "Need for God" transition.** The Old Testament asserts this stage with the teaching, "The fear of the Lord is the beginning of wisdom"[8] [Proverbs 1:7] and Jesus also instructs, "Fear the one who can destroy both the body and soul in Hell."[9] [Matthew 10:28] Children especially can become totally afraid of God and adults can become defensive unless their "fear of God" is closely connected with a God who is also benevolent. Personally, I would prefer that no one have such a fear of God, whose ultimate goal is for all to abide harmoniously together forever. Nevertheless, this larger than life view of God understands that God is in control and in charge – a principle that needs to be affirmed for those on the "Pre-Christian Way" even if people might like to make some modifications or distinctions. Thus, to ask probing questions designed to deepen one's faith, such as, "Does God actually control everything?" or "Can God lift a rock bigger than God can make?" are not helpful or appropriate for people at this stage of development. Leave these kinds of questions for later as they are best asked of those beginning the "Illuminative Way."

One way of helping those on the "Pre-Christian Way" to claim their need for God can be done simply by suggesting that they address God in prayer as "Almighty God" or "Heavenly Father" or "Lord of all creation" or "Master of the Universe." Even the youngest child can learn the route bedtime prayer: "Now I lay me down to sleep. I pray the Lord my soul to keep. If I should die, before I wake, I pray the Lord my soul to take." Such application of belief helps to cement the ability of God to protect; and it increases the need for God.

A second way that is natural for children to accept their "Need for God" comes in the interplay of good versus bad. Children don't innately know right from wrong; and parents and others provide this distinction. From birth, they associate warmth, mother's smile and milk as good things which are perpetuated and increased if children act in a certain way. However in the process, children make mistakes. They are told "No!" Such corrections are followed by displeasure and the withdrawal of what they desire. Consequently, children want to please those who are bigger, stronger, faster and smarter than they are – if for no other reason than to get what they want. This normal developmental process can also be translated into the "Need for God," saying, "If you do what God wants, you will get good things, approval and blessings from God. God has rules to be kept and laws to be followed. Follow them and you get God." **At this point in the spiritual faith process, the view of God as one who takes charge of life and gives the desired security and approval, is fundamental.** Affirming for others that God is in charge and wants to give good things is enabling spiritual growth especially for those who are on the "Pre-Christian Way."

There is a corollary to the interplay of good versus bad. When children do not follow the rules or make mistakes, especially those actions that hurt others, they are taught to say, "I am sorry and won't do it again." Such apologies apply to God in the form of seeking God's forgiveness. Accordingly, if I violate God's rule by hurting my younger sister, then God is not happy with me. I may not really care if my younger sister is mad at me or not, but I do want good things from God so I need God's approval. Because I need God, I ask for God's forgiveness.

For teenagers and young adults who are on the "Pre-Christian Way," coming to the "Need for God" can be much more difficult. Teenagers, of course, feel like they need to 'break free' of parents to become their own person and don't "need" anyone. And certainly, young adults have life skills and abilities that allow them to take care of themselves and consequently not feel the insecurity and dangerousness of the world. So unless previously attained, the "Need for God" is not a priority for either teens or young adults. **Since the appropriation of spiritual faith at this time of life is most readily done through community, the influence of other people and society is a key.** In his stages of faith, James Fowler phrases it, "I believe what the group believes."[10] Church youth groups focused on a single theme can highlight the "Need for God" so that teens accept that truth because "we" believe it. Thus, even for young adults, focusing of God when part of a group is particularly important. Our contemporary society is not particularly supportive of overt spiritual faith expression. However, this can happen when grandma asks that her whole family, including the teens and young adults, attend church together as her birthday present. It can happen when a family at Christmas time gathers to go to Christmas Eve service or the patriarch decides to take five minutes to read the biblical Christmas or Easter story. Congregations with homogeneous views and proclamations can be very helpful to adults who need the group to affirm their need for God.

Another key way for the "Need for God" to emerge is through the influence of individual people. I remember Forest 'Murph' Friend, an elder in my first congregation, who always said, "I need to go to church." Mr. Friend was one of the highest quality people I had ever known. I couldn't imagine why he would say this was his "need." Forty years later I understand and have never forgotten the influence that his simple insistence had on me. In addition, when accepted groups of people like celebrities or sports stars credit God with their success, teens and adults who still "need God" listen. If those people who "have it made" think God is important and necessary to their success, then maybe they might need God as well. The most successful groups who have engendered the "Need for the Higher Power" are Twelve Step recovery programs like Alcoholics Anonymous. In this setting, the "Need for God" comes not via teaching or preaching but though the consensus of the group – people all need God who can restore their lives to sanity.

Adults in the middle ages of their life can accept their "Need for God" through the emptiness brought on by the human condition called "existential anxiety."[11] While this may be casually dismissed as a mid-life crisis, more typically the depressing angst is rooted in unanswerable concerns about anticipatory dying, guilt and uncertainty. These concerns only have resolution in God who mid-lifers need. In addition, those adults in later years or in the midst of a health predicament as they face their own demise and coming death can come to affirm their need for God – often someone needs to suggest that they take this spiritual step of faith.

If adults have not moved through the spiritual progression of the "Pre-Christian Way" and found their "Need for God," spiritual helpers can be of assistance. However, direct conversation about that issue is most likely the best way for that to happen.

IDENTIFICATION OF SIN

The "Need for God" is often intimately linked to "Identification of Sin." The most basic and simplest definition of "sin" is that it is separation from God. An old adage states this in a different way: "I have learned two inconvertible truths in life. First, that there is a God; and second, that I am not God. God is 'other than' I am." The same is echoed when the Bible quotes God: "'My thoughts are not your thoughts, neither are your ways my ways,' declares the Lord.' As the heavens are higher than the earth, so are my ways higher than your ways and my thoughts than your thoughts.'"[12] [Isaiah 55:8-9] This separation from God is innate and ontological... it is a given. God is "other than" a human being. <u>The human condition is separation from God... this is sin</u>. People may need God because they can't do something or need to feel secure, because they have hurt others and need forgiveness or because they want to have a relationship with God (now and in Heaven) and cannot do that by themselves. <u>What is most important is that people are not where God is and cannot get there by themselves.</u>

One of the most profound influences in my life occurred when I read a sermon by Paul Tillich called "You Are Accepted."[13] In the message, Tillich taught about the ambiguous use of the words "sin" and "sins" in the New Testament. <u>"Sin" is about human separation from God. "Sins" refers to the wrong actions and bad attitudes that people have</u> (which have the result of separating people from each other and from God). All bad-behavior "sins" cause people to be separated from God – they intensify the fact that human ways are not God's ways. Nevertheless, even if people never committed any bad-behavior sins, they still would be separated from God.

For those who did not grow up in the church or who have made poor choices that have resulted in wrong actions and bad behavior, especially those that have caused injury to others, "Identification of Sin" is straightforward. Some people on the "Pre-Christian Way" have clearly committed sins. Murderers on death row, for example, can understand their bad behavior and clearly realize how they have sinned and have need for God. People in Twelve Step Programs have no trouble identifying their sin and often feel it very deeply. Accordingly, they often "grieve" their sinful behaviors which can intensify their need and desire for God.

On the other hand, people who have grown up in the church and have spent their life being the best they can be, following the rules and doing good for others, can have a more difficult time identifying that they are sinners even though the Bible clearly teaches "All sin and fall short of the glory of God."[14] While "good church people" may have more difficulty sensing their separation from God and feeling it, "Identification of Sin" is essential for spiritual growth. Thus, asking long-term, upstanding Christians, "What is your signature sin?" or "How do you know that you were once separated from God?" can be helpful.

I was teaching a Bible study in which I focused on personal application of the biblical content. The group, consisting of long-term church members, was working its way through the letter to the Romans and was in chapter three. As the discussion proceeded into the application section, one of the most respected elders of the congregation commented about Romans 3:23, "Then that means I am no different than those people across the hall." What the elder was referencing was the room where one of the seven Twelve Step Groups, that rented the church space, met. At that point in the life of the congregation, no people "in recovery" were officially part of the church. That changed in the months that followed.

Regular church participants may actually identify sin after a number of years of life experience. As a pastor, occasionally I would have someone who wanted to be re-baptized because "When I was first baptized, it didn't mean anything." Instead of saying, "You don't need to be re-baptized," I always took this as an opportunity for spiritual growth and theological conversation. First, I recognized that this person was obviously identifying sin in their life so we would talk about what that was. Second, I would clearly teach that taking this action and being re-baptized in no way changed what God had already done at the time of their original baptism. However, I would affirm that now the baptismal candidate would realize, even feel, what God had done for them. Thus, it was important for spiritual growth.

Spiritual helpers need to be ready and able to assist people in identifying sin which is not the easiest topic to broach. Nevertheless, formally recognizing sin, whenever it happens, is needed for spiritual growth and makes the acceptance of God's Grace powerful. While "Identification of Sin" is absolutely essential for spiritual growing, it can also be precarious. Those children who have been told over and over that they are "bad," or adults who have committed and/or repeated horrific crimes as well as those who are abused or trapped in the battering of the legal system, can take on a destructive level of guilt – a feeling of guilt that is so internalized that seemingly no one can dissolve it. Thus, the balance needed at this precipice is to identify sin but not to the point of de-habilitating guilt.

ACCEPTANCE OF GRACE

"The gift of God is eternal life" may be the absolute best phrase in the Bible! This sentence, however, begins with "The wages of sin is death" and ends with "in Christ Jesus our Lord."[15] [Romans 6:23] **Two important points need to be made: first, God's free gift needs to come "as soon as possible" on the heels of identification of sin; and second, grace must elicit appreciation and responsibility.**

The best definition of grace that I know of is: "Grace is the unearned and undeserved gift of God." Thus, feeling unworthy to receive such an extremely generous endowment without the ability to have ever earned the right to have it is necessary at this point for spiritual growth. Eternal life is the final payment but it comes in installments, according to individual need, and may be received as new life, forgiveness, second chances, as well as feeling loved and accepted.

I had a family member who was diagnosed with terminal cancer who I will call Alice. Alice asked me to be her personal pastor because she knew she needed God. Although Alice had a tender heart, she had not lived an exemplary life and certainly stayed as far away from religion and God as her conscience would allow. In addition, Alice had suffered abuse and had a hard life. On the other hand, Alice had some early religious training and for her lack of regular church contact had a pretty good knowledge of the Bible. Alice clearly knew how sinful she had been and felt unworthy. On one of my visits to the hospital, Alice wanted to talk about God. I presented the plan of salvation in a very informal but biblically accurate manner. Alice comprehended what I had said and knew her opportunity to believe that Jesus was God's gift to her for the forgiveness of her many sins. However, Alice baulked when I asked if she was ready to do that. After an uneasy moment, she blurted out with great angst, "But I have lived so badly and I don't deserve it!" I calmly affirmed, "That is exactly the point! This is how much God loves you and wants you." The result was a flood of tears, a strong assertion of belief and an emotionally free and floating demeanor out of this life and into the next.

Alice had come face to face with God's grace and her response was incredulity and astonishment. No wonder people love John Newton's hymn, "Amazing Grace;" it resonates in their souls.[16] The hymn begins, "Amazing Grace how sweet the sound that saved a wretch like me." Even if people are not as wretched as Newton, who practiced human trafficking – slavery, they do take grace personally because they still don't deserve it.

This same experience could have happened for Alice decades before it did. However, it did not, because she had come to feel so unworthy and had not received God's Grace in a timely manner. **Spiritual helpers need to be ready to offer God's Grace precisely at the moment of the feeling of greatest unworthiness. The Bible puts sin and grace together in one sentence and so should spiritual helpers.**

The above story that illustrates "Acceptance of Grace" is a classic example of the forgiven adult sinner who receives the promise of eternal life. However, <u>grace can also be gathered in the form of love, second chances, exoneration or absolution – all that are unearned and undeserved</u>. For example, a child who has broken a rule deserves the appropriate consequences. If such discipline was intentionally not enforced, then grace would have been given, which is the perfect moment to teach what God's Grace is like. Personally, while I intellectually understood grace from a theological perspective, I first appropriated the feeling of grace and thus the intent of God through my wife. This happened years after becoming a Christian, which is an example of how spiritual development is not always linear. However, when I appropriated "Acceptance of Grace" my spiritual life and helpfulness was catapulted forward. It happened in this way: being physically deformed, I came to believe that I was not good enough to be loved in a heterosexual interpersonal relationship. Not long after we had been dating, Pat would spontaneously say, "I love you;" but I have not done anything or said anything to deserve such affirmation. In fact, it would not be inaccurate to say that during our early years she would tell me that she loved me a couple of hundred times a day – until I finally came to believe and feel the love-given grace. After thirty-five years of marriage, Pat has come back to reality. She now graces me with "I love you" only about fifty times each day. Everyone should be so divinely blessed!

The point is that grace not only needs to be understood biblically and theologically but also needs to be felt as it is applied to real life. This best occurs immediately after sin and/or sins have been personally identified. When people grasp what God has given and have felt that grace via life experience, they are truly grateful for the gift. Grace cannot be earned; but it sure can be appreciated. I could not earn my wife's love but in response I certainly can live faithfully with her. God desires the same. "Your new life is God's gift to you; but what you do with it is your gift back to God."

Dietrich Bonhoeffer's contrast between "cheap grace" and "costly grace" provides the perfect explanation.[17] Grace is cheap when people receive God without personally identifying sin(s) that needs to be forgiven. In addition, **people make grace cheap when they behave without gratitude for the gift**. God's gift of grace (forgiveness, love, and new life) comes at the moment a person accepts Jesus as Savior and Lord. **Following, learning, trusting and becoming like Jesus are what make God's Grace costly**. Indeed, when people develop in the natural spiritual progression, they know God, need God, feel their sin, accept God's free gift – and consequently they respond gratefully with their life.

MOMENT OF DECISION

Every important period of time warrants summary. Years of education completed should be celebrated with a graduation ceremony. Courtship and love definitely need affirmation at the wedding event. Pregnancy is best culminated with a beautiful birth. Indeed, the transition toward a life lived in God at its center also needs a "Moment of Decision." Some people say, "I didn't have a dramatic conversion like St. Paul so I don't know when I started believing in Jesus." While this can be true, everyone still benefits from a moment of putting their growth toward God all together. Typically, these are reviewed with any good evangelistic "Plan of Salvation" Christian tract. Be sure to have one available, write your own as I have, or be able to use the scriptures to facilitate a "Moment of Decision."

Billy Graham's Christian crusades have become famous for the summarizing the Christian faith and calling people to a moment of decision. Graham would invite people to accept Jesus as savior with the same hymn of his conversion experience, "Just as I Am."[18] The hymn reflects God's request to simply come with Jesus' promise of John 6:37, "whoever comes to me I will never drive away." God will be in the moment of surrender; trust it.

Just as I am - without one plea,
But that Thy blood was shed for me,
And that Thou bidst me come to Thee,
-O Lamb of God, I come!
Just as I am - Thou wilt receive,
Wilt welcome, pardon, cleanse, relieve;
Because Thy promise I believe,
-O Lamb of God, I come!

Spiritual helpers need to be ready to assist people through the "Moment of Decision" which best begins by summarizing the "Pre-Christian Way" period of time (included in the bullets at the beginning this chapter.) However, the most important parts of the "Moment of Decision" are asking for the decision and speaking it out loud in prayer. The way I have typically phrased the decision question is, "Do you believe with all of your heart and the best of your ability that Jesus is your Lord and Savior and that you want to follow him with your life?"

Then, I would ask that person to repeat aloud the words that I would pray. This prayer sometimes called "The Sinner's Prayer" can be personalized to reflect the individual's spiritual journey and experience. The particular words of the prayer are not as important as the themes that need to be included.

✞ Address to God
✞ Understanding their sin and/or separation from God
✞ Asking for forgiveness
✞ Accepting Jesus as Savior and Lord
✞ Promise to follow with the rest of their life (beginning with baptism/confirmation)

A Sample Sinner's Prayer: Gracious God, I confess that I am a sinner and separated from you. Please forgive me. I now believe in my heart that you sent Jesus to save me – to reconcile us. I believe he is my personal Lord and Savior. So, I promise to do my best to follow you and your ways; and I will begin by showing that I mean what I say with my baptism. In Jesus' name. Amen.

Do not underestimate the value of having a person pray that prayer – it is a moment of summary, an emotional release and a choice to be responsibly honored. **Do not underestimate what God does whenever such a prayer is prayed.** Theologically, this is called "Justification." "Therefore, since we have been justified through faith... God has poured out his love into our hearts by the Holy Spirit, whom he has given us."[19] [Romans 5:1,5] **In the act of decision, God has made something definite happen. It is when God's power is infused into a person. It is when God forgives and accepts; it is when a person is "born from above." It is when the inheritance of eternal life is bestowed. It is when God substantively abides if even for a brief time; and pure joy is released.**

CONFESSIONAL TEMPTATION[20]

"I didn't see that coming!" is what people might say after a total surprise event has occurred. What I call "Confessional Temptation" fits into this description. **"Confessional Temptation" is the strong enticement to return to the way people used to be before they accepted Jesus as Savior and decided to follow the spiritual path.** It happens soon after (or sometimes just before) believer's baptism or confirmation. As a result of their new life (or anticipated new life) in Christ, many new Christians are euphoric and joyfully enthusiastic for God. When all is well; and they have a new lease on life, that's when it happens – temptation. Seemingly, the opposite would be expected, but I have observed confessional temptation over and over again.

The New Testament account of the baptism of Jesus by John the Baptist concludes with God's words, "This is my Son, whom I love; with him I am well pleased."[21] [Matthew 3:17] It doesn't get any better for children when they hear such affirmation from their parent. With such an emotional and spiritual summit, we would anticipate only greater experiences to come. Nevertheless, the very next biblical verse records what happened, "Then (at once) Jesus was led by the Spirit into the desert to be tempted by the devil."[22] [Matthew 4:1] This picture of Jesus' personal spiritual life is a paradigm for the spiritual life of believers. In some way, it is the first occurrence of a new believer; but it is best viewed as the last struggle in the "Pre-Christian Way." **It is God asking the question a second time, just to make sure the first answer was the real one. "Do you really want to follow me?"** For Jesus the test was about whether he would inappropriately employ God's power (to turn stones into bread); whether he would accept what God gives in the midst of insecurity (to call angels to protect him); and whether he would focus on what he could get for himself (to seek the fame and glitter of the world) instead of worshipping God. Jesus accepted the mission to transparently model the love of God and bring reconciliation to humanity. Succumbing to the devil's offers would not allow this mission to be accomplished – thus the test. In order to affirm their new found belief, those at the end of the "Pre-Christian Way" go through a similar test.

Three things are noteworthy about "Confessional Temptation." <u>First</u>, the timing makes it directly related to the experience of saying "Yes" to God (through the acceptance of Jesus). Implicitly the question is asked, "Do you really believe what you say you believe?" As such, "Confessional Temptation" is a test. Tests are neither good nor bad; they are simply a mechanism to evaluate learning. However, they often feel a whole lot worse than that. <u>Second</u>, God's Spirit initiates this spiritual test. Since God's power is given with forgiveness and salvation, God tests how responsible the believer will be with the gift? <u>Third</u>, it's a real test because the devil is in charge of its intensity. The demonic always brings to the minds of new believers what they might have to give up in order to follow God. Whether an attitude or an action, whatever a person had to surrender or change will be tested. They will be tempted to return to their former life (ill chosen friends) or compromise what they need to do (stay out late on Saturday nights and miss Sunday worship). **During this time of "Confessional Temptation" (unlike the intensity and duration of later spiritual trials), God is very close at hand.** Words of instruction that counter the temptation are available if asked for. Comfort and "ministering to their needs" is close by. God does not want newly confirmed children to fail; just to make sure this is what they really want because the tasks ahead are difficult indeed without such clarity and commitment.

CHAPTER 7

The Purgative Way

People on the Purgative Way have started to be a follower of Christ. They want to know what is right and what is wrong – they need to know the difference and insert this discerned correctness into their lives. <u>Accordingly, they are very dependent on structure and spiritually clear-cut guidance which is best received through connection with a spiritual community and/or mentor.</u> Using the question, "What would Jesus do?" in order to discern the Christian right way from the worldly wrong way is a simple and effective although unsophisticated way to focus the Purgative Way's tasks, which include:

Graphic 4: The Purgative Way
commences the official Christian journey
and includes purging sins
and adopting Christian practices.

PURGING OF SINS

As a Christian, I believe that Jesus died to save me from my sins. However, at the moment that I accepted Jesus as my Lord and Savior, my personal sinful behaviors were not automatically all gone. I assume that neither did the sins of others suddenly halt. **What does happen at the moment of confession/baptism is that God releases people from the consequences of their Sin – from eternal separation from God**. Truly, when people receive Jesus as Savior, first and foremost, their "Sin" or separation from God is forgiven, removed and/or becomes no more – accordingly God establishes a relationship with the believer. The fact of this divine decree allows the possibility for all sinful attitudes and behaviors to be removed. In other words, believers' sins are "in principle" forgiven; but "in fact" sinful actions and behaviors still remain until these new Christians, and sometimes long-term Christians, want their sins to be gone – and work toward that goal.

"Purgative" refers to the purging of the negative from people's life. It is about removing perpetual or habitual sins; and that takes time. Certainly, God "could" do that for people; but that would defeat God's purpose – that people will voluntarily choose to return God's love with a life lived that is appropriate to being part of God's Holy Community.[1] In other words, people need to eliminate perpetual sins from their life and replace them with godly behaviors and attitudes. And this, like any change or new habit, takes time. The Spirit of God, placed within believers at their confession of faith, gives new Christians the necessary power to root out the sins from their lives. Actually, <u>God does the work if and only if people cooperate</u>. **So even after the Holy Spirit gives birth to new Christians, they still have sin-removal to accomplish, ethical/moral standards to adopt and spiritual basics to establish – moving toward a lifestyle that can be described as "basic trust" of God and God's ways. These primary tasks of the Purgative Way often take many years to complete.** The Purgative Way begins the process of Christian "Sanctification"[2] or being set apart for the purpose of becoming Christ-like which is also called "discipleship" or "holiness" in some traditions. The New Testament says it this way, "Work out your salvation with fear and trembling, for it is God who works in you to will and to act according to his good purpose."[3] [Philippians 2:12b-13]

The Purgative Way is a struggle. It takes strong consistent effort to effectively remove sin. Truly, God does this work but requires new Christians to will and to work for sin-removal to occur. Accordingly, Purgative Way Christians need to focus on God so that God will think on them. A very ancient hymn of the faith, "Lord Jesus Think on Me" is a favorite of mine for this part of the spiritual journey. The spiritual master, Synesius of Cyrene, around 430 AD, penned the words that were later put to music, which is simple and methodical – a song that could be sung all day because it would be hard to get out of one's head. The structure is so basic that a contemporary musical sound could easily be composed. For the purging of sins and the remembering to do so:

Lord Jesus, think on me
And purge away my sin;
From earthborn passions set me free
And make me pure within.[4]

The Purgative Way is like being on probationary status. The offenders' sentences have been deferred and they are given a period of time to see if they can "stay out of trouble." In other words, the Purgative Way is about whether people can move into a life as responsible "citizens of Heaven" and adopt a life style that reflects that way of living. Noteworthy is that God as the Righteous Judge is more patient and tolerant than those in the earthly legal system, who often assume that once a person has been "bad" they are doomed to get "worse." **The basic tools to use for this "sin-removal" process are confession, penance and repentance**.[5] God closely works with people to keep them moving along the Purgative Way; and when they get off the path, God provides "motivation" to keep people moving along.[6] In fact, for confessed believers in Jesus Christ, sincere and serious work toward sin-removal guarantees that their sins will be totally removed – even if God has to do that for them after they have taken their last breath on earth.

In order for new Christians to choose "sin removal" they need to know what is right and what is wrong; what is good and what is bad; what is black and what is white. Subtleties, complexities and options are not only unhelpful, but they are typically destructive to the process of spiritual growth for those on the Purgative Way. Working with these people means: being clear, precise, basic, fundamental and as black and white as possible. Listing all the sins that might be purged and how to do that is not within the scope of this book. However, the New Testament and other writers spend much time teaching that the "sins of the flesh" are bad and "life in the Spirit" is good.[7]

So I say, live by the Spirit, and you will not gratify the desires of the sinful nature. For the sinful nature desires what is contrary to the Spirit, and the Spirit what is contrary to the sinful nature. They are in conflict with each other, so that you do not do what you want. But if you are led by the Spirit, you are not under law…Those who belong to Christ Jesus have crucified the sinful nature with its passions and desires. Since we live by the Spirit, let us keep in step with the Spirit. Let us not become conceited, provoking and envying each other.[8] [Galatians 5:16-18, 24-26]

This explicit dualism is helpful for those on the Purgative Way because it aids in stopping sins and adopting ethical/moral standards. Such rigid strictness will not be as helpful for those on the Illuminative Way; and those on the Unitive Way will not want to even be bothered debating which approach is best.

When I was pastor of a congregation, I would occasionally be told, "Preacher, I haven't heard you preach on 'salvation' lately." Now, the sermon I just finished may have been about having the truth set a person free which is certainly about not lying and becoming redeemed by God's truth, which includes the activity of God's saving grace in a person's life. However, what my congregant was really saying was, "I need repetition and reinforcement; I am on the Purgative Way and it is hard. I need the basic message of the Church regarding Jesus dying on the cross for the saving of my sins.... If I don't get that, Preacher, I am going to waver off the side of the road." So, I would soon deliver a more traditional gospel sermon because those on the Purgative Way need it for their spiritual health and wholeness.

In addition, for those on the Purgative Way it does matter "who is in" and "who is out." Jesus was clear that everyone would be judged and a division would be made between the sheep and goats,[9] [Matthew 25:31-46] between those in the Holy Community (Kingdom) of God and those who were outside of it "wailing and gnashing of (their) teeth."[10] [Matthew 13:41-42, 49-50] Those who are making progress in the "tasks" of the Purgative Way are actually encouraged by references to where they could have been – separated from God. They were once in that condition and could return to it if they choose to. Accordingly, in order to continue in the right direction, they need to continue to adopt positive spiritual attitudes and actions. Those mature spiritual helpers who have moved farther down the faith pathway can affirm this black and white teaching and at the same time guard against making God a vindictive and judgmental tyrant.

The first task for Purgative Way Christians is to purge their sinful attitudes, behaviors and concerns – the ABCs of faith. Clearly identifying what is good and what is bad is necessary to accomplish this undertaking. As a result, a new system of values will be initiated.

ADOPTING ETHICAL AND MORAL STANDARDS

After "sin removal" has begun, the next step is to replace the old life with new ethical and moral standards. Typically the "Purging of Sins" and the "Adopting of Ethical and Moral Standards" occur simultaneously or at least alternatively. The process is inherently intuitive: whenever people remove something then they put something in its place. Eliminating an old behavior like lying when it is convenient for one's own personal benefit can be replaced with a positive God-authorized value of telling the truth, which will set people free.[11] [John 8:32] Repeating this process, the "rejection of one's sinful values and the substitution of godly values," leads to the adoption of an ethical and moral system which can be called Christian.

Here are some examples of how the "Purging of Sins" and the taking on new ethics and morals intersect. The Ten Commandments are important Hebraic basic principles that have been morphed into the Christian ethical and moral system. These principles, which include lying, cheating, honoring, stealing, faithfulness, not to covet and to have a primary focus on God, are guidelines for a Christian who is on the Purgative Way. The Golden Rule to "do unto others as you would have them do unto you"[12] [Matthew 7:12] is a generic but a guiding standard. Absolutely, the Great Commandment, to "love God" completely and other people "as you love yourself,"[13] [Matthew 22:38-39] is foundational to the spiritual life as Jesus affirms. These Christian rules can lead to discussion about what is love and who I am to love. Furthermore, some of Jesus' other teachings, especially in the Sermon on the Mount,[14] provide fundamental lessons to be put into new Christians' lives. Overcoming the Seven Deadly Sins,[15] which have corresponding replacement virtues, also give black and white instruction. Implementing such ethical and moral values occur over a period of time often with lots of trial and error.

The Bible records and churches teach much about the need for "sin-removal" but very little is described about how to actually accomplish that task. **Awareness, willingness, CPR, persistence, spiritual disciplines including focused prayer as well as review and encouragement are the tools.** Those who help others grow spiritually through the Purgative Way must be willing to "live with" these Christians because it takes so much time to move along this part of the spiritual road, which has lots of ups and down, U-turns, slippery slopes and deep pot holes to navigate. Especially helpful for these Christians is review and encouragement. They desperately need to see how far they have come and how much progress they have made; putting this in writing for them is even more supportive. After talking/counseling with Purgative Way Christians, I often write an immediate summary of our conversation and send or email it to those people; almost always this correspondence will be used for further reiteration. Encouragement, it goes without saying, is necessary – the apostle Paul was doing this for the Philippians in New Testament letter to them. Reading that book with its theme, "I am sure that God who began this good work in you will bring it to completion,"[16] [Philippians 1:6] can also help. While review and encouragement are always excellent spiritually helpful tools, they are especially needed for those on the Purgative Way.

Now some "sin-removal" and values-adoption may have already been established prior to a person making a Confession of Faith and officially enters onto the Purgative Way. This can happen with children and youth if their spiritual growth takes place in a chronologically developmental manner – growing up they learn right from wrong. In this case, the Purgative Way task of "Adopting Ethical and Moral Standards" can become much easier because some of the work of aligning with God's principles and practices has already been done. Accordingly, as children become new Christians, they do not need to change these already-adopted godly practices, only intentionally affirm that they choose to live this way for God.

On the other hand, while some children travel a relatively smooth ethical and moral road, some rebel when they become teenagers. They seek independence from authority and the rules they have been taught; they go out on their own and make their own mistakes. While they may actually know right from wrong, they now have the task of seeking to reform their manner of living. The psalmist recalls what this was like, "Remember not the sins of my youth and my rebellious ways; according to your love remember me, for you are good, O Lord."[17] [Psalm 25:7]

In another scenario, **the Purgative Way is often experienced differently for adults who become Christians later in life**. While people are somewhat tolerant of the mistakes that children and youth make, they become increasingly intolerant as sinfulness is carried on into adulthood. Indeed, those adults moving onto the Purgative Way often have more difficulty because of the complexity of their lives, the disdain of other adults and the potential increased quantity of "bad" habits to overcome. People critique that adults should know better and are more judgmental of those adults. Perhaps they "should." But the Purgative Way process still needs to be gone through and harsh criticism deters that from happening. Nevertheless, the "tasks" are the same: to remove sin, adopt ethical/moral standards and establish new spiritual habits; and **all Purgative Way Christians need the same things: patience, persistence and clear teaching**. In the past, those who have helped people grow spiritually have afforded these attitudes with children and youth; but have often been severely lacking when it came to adults.

However, Alcoholics Anonymous and other twelve step programs have had amazing success in helping adults stop detrimental habits and also adopt new ethics and morals. This is accomplished without one individual telling another what to do – although the group consciousness is clearly a strong instructional voice which comes from the similar and repetitive stories of its participants. While these adults may have rejected the teaching of Christians, God has found a way to use these secular programs.

I used to think that Alcoholics Anonymous was just a group that helped people get sober until I attended a seminar on small groups led by Lyman Coleman.[18] He informed us that the principles behind the present-day twelve steps programs began when Father Sam Shoemaker of St. Stephens Episcopal Church in New York helped Bill Wilson, co-founder of AA, with his alcoholism. Together they outlined twelve tasks that needed to be done in order to recover from this unhelpful habit. Each of these steps was based on and originally included references to biblical passages. The scriptures were later omitted and the step's references to God changed to the "Higher Power" so as not to be a deterrent to those who had been rejected by religiosity adherents. Indeed, the recovering alcoholics I met had already named and claimed the Higher Power; they were firmly in the process of purging sins and adopting ethical and moral standards. I was able to easily "translate" the Twelve Steps using biblical passages and affirm how the AA principles, which God desired, came from within Christianity. Helping these people to make a "Confession of Faith" was then relatively simple. Those in recovery did not need to change, only confirm, their ethical and moral standards. However, God always honored their statements of faith and those in recovery often felt genuine relief and joy. As one man told me, "AA saved my ass; but the church saved my soul."

One of the most important qualities for those who help others on the Purgative Way is not to get discouraged or disappointed with them. If intolerance or impatience as part of one's growing edge, consider referring them to someone else. Purgative Way Christians need consistent, patient help with lots of prayers on their behalf because they will typically start and stop numerous times as well as take side trips that spiritual helpers know are dead ends. Telling others what to do or explaining rarely helps and often does harm. <u>Experience is the Purgative traveler's best teacher; someone just has to be there to catch them when they fall or else they may not get up very quickly</u>. It is a thankless job daily "leading a horse to water." Someone has to do it; but please don't drown them just because they won't drink.

I ask Purgative Way Christians who are struggling to overcome sins, "How long did it take you to get into this condition?" The answer typically comes back in terms of many years. I follow up with the question, "So, how long do you think it will take you to get out of this condition?" To which most people become very uncomfortable thinking that it will take as long to get out as it took to get into this state of being. Having people feel the immensity and the seeming hopelessness of this change is part of my purpose. I then affirm for them, "No. It will not take that long. You got into this situation accidently, unconsciously. You are going to get to a better place intentionally, consciously and with the power of God." This simple Socratic conversation is designed to be encouraging and also has the potential to overcome the "fear" or "resistance" that often keeps Purgative Christians from constructive choices.

Moving forward as consistently as possible, however, is very important. Consider the scripture passage about cleaning the house of an evil one and quickly filling it before seven more come and fill it.[19] [Luke 11:24-26] As new Christians are changing their old negative habits there is a void in them, which needs to be filled with positive Christian ethics and morals. The vacuum will be filled! Sometimes the new system of values may be filled with an entire scheme like a cult, a good project or an organization to give one's life to. On the other hand, a particular philosophy like humanism or new age thinking may take the place of the old sinful life. Other people may reorient their lives around social activities, consumerism or building a better life for their families. While most likely people's new lives are better than their old lives, they are not focused on adopting the ethical and moral standards that God wants. Consequently, many Purgative Way ministers fervently preach a black and white message designed to counter such new "better" ways of living, but which are not strictly God's standards. This clarity can be helpful to Purgative Way Christians, while others may see it as rigid and judgmental. Nevertheless, getting off-road is to be expected; and someone needs to help get them back on track or clean out the mess they have allowed to occur in their own house. This is often the spiritual helpers' tasks when working with those on the Purgative Way.

While Purgative Way Christians best learn through instruction and limited choices, they also can become exceptionally good at repeating the answers and precepts they have been taught. In the beginning, parents don't really care if children understand why they need to look both ways before they cross a street or the need for them to eat their spinach... just DO IT. But eventually, parents want children to know why they are doing what they are doing so they will continue to do so when their parents are not around and so that the children will pass those lessons onto their own children. In the finally analysis, Purgative Way Christians need to own what they believe; they need to do this because they believe it, not simply because they have been indoctrinated with it. They need to accept and implement because they choose to do so.

Thus, for people who help others grow spiritually, even those on the Purgative Way, asking questions is the best policy. Consider for example this sample conversation: "John, what do you think you should do?" If John provides a clear, godly answer (even if he does not consider all the options), affirm that response by saying, "Yes. You can do that (or think that) if you choose." This reply is designed to evoke John's personal will. The follow-up question is, "Do you really want to do that?" When John espouses a particular godly value and chooses to do it, then "sin-removal" begins to take place. (If John wants to follow through with this choice, then spiritual helpers need to pray with John specifically to ask the Holy Spirit that is within him to provide the necessary assistance.) Or if John has previously known what is right and even practiced it, this spiritual conversation has the effect of reinforcing what is good for his continuation of the spiritual journey. On the other hand, given the opportunity that questions instead of instructions afford, John may want to ask about what he has been taught, which is good because it can lead to deeper commitment of what he already believes or to a newly revised understanding, which may be God's luring him into the Illuminative Way. Nevertheless, patience and gentle questioning can help Christians to grow spiritually in whatever direction they need and to continue on the Christian journey.

In summary, "Purging of Sins" and "Adopting of Ethical and Moral Standards" best go hand in hand. A clear understanding of right from wrong is necessary. And supporting this new system development for Purgative Way Christians takes patience, repetition and clarity. While this process is primarily about increasing their knowledge and willingness, new Christians certainly need to affirm that their ethical and moral attitudes and behaviors are in accord with God's Will.

ESTABLISHING SPIRITUAL HABITS

Having good spiritual habits are the means to confirm, solidify and expand what has already happened along the Spiritual Road. However, spiritual habits are not the end of the journey! Jesus warned the religious people of his day about this caveat when he said, "Woe to you, teachers of the law and Pharisees, you hypocrites! You clean the outside of the cup and dish, but inside they are full of greed and self-indulgence. Blind Pharisee! First clean the inside of the cup and dish, and then the outside also will be clean."[20] [Matthew 23:25-26] People incessantly ask, "Tell me. What am I supposed to do?" They want to change. They want to get better. They want to do what is right. They want the right spiritual habit. They need to practice what they have come to believe. They need to do something positive in place of what they used to do. They need to practice what has been preached to them.

However, be warned.

This society is primarily focused on "What do I need to do?" By this people mean, "Give me a task to accomplish." So, spiritual helpers tell Christians to go to church twice a week, sing in the choir, become a deacon or serve on a committee or in a soup kitchen. **However, spiritual habits cannot substitute for the hard work of purging sins and living with different morals/ethics which have as their goals becoming more like Christ and having an interactive "personal" relationship with God.** <u>When performing the tasks become the highest priorities, the spiritual growth process is halted abruptly.</u> People can practice spiritual habits without purging of sins; and Christians can observe spiritual habits but still maintain dual or inconsistent ethics and morals. This scenario happens all the time, which is not necessarily to be considered "bad" and often just means that people have tried to move too fast spiritually. Bruce Wilkinson writes about a good Christian woman named "Catherine" who was disturbed because she was not growing spiritually.[21] Dr. Wilkinson diagnosed that it was because of unforgiveness in her life; unforgiveness is an inside the cup dirtiness that listening to/agreeing with a good sermon in worship cannot clean. This story is not atypical as I have encountered it in literally dozens and dozens of such practicing Christians; and it is very painful to them because they have been doing so many good things for so long. But they missed a step or need to repeat a step in the spiritual growth process.

Richard Foster in <u>Celebration of Discipline</u> provides a representative summary of spiritual habits that every Christian needs to establish.[22] Foster includes four internal, four external and four corporate disciplines or habits which corresponds to the three unique ways of appropriating the Christian faith via pathos (heart), logos (mind) and ethos (group) expressions of faith. All three ways are necessary; and one approach is typically intrinsic to each individual. Included are: meditation, prayer, fasting, study (internal disciplines); simplicity, solitude, submission, service (external disciplines); confession, worship, guidance and celebration (corporate disciplines). This list is not an exhaustive summary of good spiritual habits. Numerous variations of these and other spiritual habits exit and are useful. **In order to help Purgative Way Christians grow spiritually ascertain whether these are being practiced or not. At least, one in each category is desirable**, while progressing toward including all of them. In addition, Christians on Illuminative and Unitive paths of the spiritual road also need to embrace and continue these disciplines; retarded spiritual growth in these "further down the road" Christians can sometimes be attributed to neglecting previously learned spiritual habits.

New Christians need to establish regular spiritual habits and there are very simply ways to help them. If they don't have a Bible, give them one. If they have a Bible but don't know where to start reading, assign them something to read or give them a reading program to use. If they don't pray, write out a prayer for them to read, including the Lord's Prayer. If they don't go to church, take them to worship. If they need to learn, get them into a study or Bible group. If they need a new set of friends, go to church dinners and fellowship gatherings. Introduce them to Christian leaders so they will have mentors to contact. If they don't focus on others, enable them to provide some help at a local food pantry or at least make a donation.

In addition to these traditional spiritual habits, I suggest awareness, willingness, CPR, persistence, intentional prayer as well as review and encouragement.

<u>Awareness</u>: **New Christians need to get into the habit of becoming more deeply aware of themselves, others and God**. They have already become aware of God, sinfulness, their need for God and grace. In order to continue growing spiritually, this awareness must continue. When did they think about God during their day? What part of their Bible reading seemed most important or applied to them? Did they think about the needs of others and what did they do or not do about that thought? Awareness is the first step in all spiritual growth. An important part of Christian spiritual growth is developing a natural sensitivity to the spiritual world that God has created – it is everywhere.

<u>Willingness</u>: New Christians have chosen God. It is an act of their personal will. The ultimate goal of growing into the maturity of Christ is that people will think, feel and act in a godly manner. This means that our human will is in accord with God's will. The entire spiritual goal has been summarized as "having God's will to be our will." However, I do not want to trivialize "spiritual willingness" because it is not easy, ever.

At an elementary level, deciding to overcome any sinful habit begins this process. Yet, when Purgative Way Christians first think about doing what God desires, they may not be able to do that and rarely are able to do so consistently. Nevertheless, because they are a Christian, God is on their side and wants to help them to align their will with God's will. **Willingness is the key to unlock the door to God's help**. All they have to do is pray to begin what they have chosen to do. They may choose to stop lying, which they have practiced to make themselves look better – laudable sin-removal. However, establishing the corresponding spiritual habit of "truth telling" as a godly behavior takes a further willingness – especially since such honesty can allow people to see more unflattering parts of themselves. Being willing to grow spiritually via sin-removal and spiritual habits is ONLY effective when people believe that God is in the process with them to help them. Otherwise, they may believe that God is displeased with their inability to change, which is hard. "God does not blame the lame – only the unwilling."

On the other hand, some new Christians may not be quite ready to change. Getting ready is part of the spiritual process. Thus, the alternative prayer is, "God, make me willing to... (to change, to forgive or go to church, and so forth)." Very often people do not consider this optional prayer and it takes spiritual helpers to make the suggestion. In addition, another unconventional prayer may be necessary to suggest: "God, make me willing to be willing to..." Honesty is especially important when it comes to spiritual willingness. Accordingly, people need to pray the prayer that is in conjunction with where their willingness factor is. This prayer God will honor; and God honors the prayer.

CPR: **Since unforgiveness and holding onto resentments are primary blocks to spiritual growth, CPR needs to become a mainstay tool. Confession, penance and repentance are biblically-based principles that are absolutely necessary for new spiritual life.** These crucial concepts are real and powerful – and neglected. In recent decades, psychological research has actually been done on the process of forgiveness, which totally confirms the necessity of the biblical emphasis on forgiveness. Because it is so important I have included an entire chapter called "CPR for New Life" that outlines what is needed. Suffice it to say that CPR must be a regular spiritual discipline. Christianity has neglected or reduced the prominence of confession. Roman Catholic Christians have minimized the opportunity for official confession. Protestant Christians have moved it to the pastoral counselor's office. All Christians have relegated confession to something that can happen between God and themselves which absolutely does not work. Thousands seek professionally trained therapists, who are needed for serious mental disorders. However, so much could be accomplished with simple confession with appropriate follow-up and accountability.

Intentional Prayer: All and a variety of spiritual disciplines are helpful for spiritual growth. **However, from start to finish, prayer is most important. My definition of prayer is communication with God.** However, prayer comes in so many different forms and actually has its own spiritual progression, which ends in God giving Christians exactly what they need WITHOUT any effort on their part. Nevertheless, Christians begin a lifetime of prayer with a great deal of effort and they need to intentionally do so. The various forms of prayer, corresponding to different stages of spiritual growth, will be outlined in chapter sixteen "Prayer Forms." For a temporary conclusion, **the practice of prayer, in whatever form, is essential and needs to be part of Christians' spiritual habits.**

Review and Encouragement: The word "remember" occurs in the Bible countless times and for good reason. **Human beings need to remember what happened in the past in order to appreciate the present moment and in order to wisely move into the future**. Remembering what God had done anchors the Old Testament exodus of the Israelites from slavery in Egypt; remembering the crucifixion and resurrection of Jesus has a similar impact for Christians. The review of what God has been doing in Christians' individual lives is just as essential to keeping the faith. One of my mentors recommends that the spiritual discipline of review occur an hour each week, a day each month and a week each year. Too much? Start with half of that. In addition, review is best done with a trusted and spiritually wise person; at least the summary of one's review. People are really good at fooling themselves, even when they want to be completely honest. **Working with another person who wants the best for them but who will not let them be less than honest is the pinnacle of the spiritual practice of review**. Also, such a person must always be an encourager for them and desire whatever will assist them to travel their Spiritual Road. Find that person for you and cherish the counsel he or she has to offer.

COMING TO BASIC TRUST IN GOD

The Christian life is most essentially about a relationship with the Divine. In order to have a good relationship with anyone, people must come to believe the other person will be good to them and wants the best for them. Christians who have moved across the Purgative Way have come to this conclusion and have changed their lives accordingly; they have come to the life stance that following God via the example of Jesus Christ is the only way they ever want to live. Coming to this "Basic Trust in God" and God's ways is the final destination of those traveling the Purgative Way; but the process of traveling the Purgative Way road is not easy to which this following true-life story will testify. Nevertheless, making consistent progress moves Christians toward a life stance that can be called "Basic Trust in God."

James was firmly on the Purgative Road. A mid-forties divorced father of two adult children, James had successfully made his way through life events of career and child-rearing to a place where he was seeking a little happiness for himself. James' background is important for understanding his current spiritual struggles on the Purgative Way.

James was raised in a good family with strongly-espoused religious standards with parents who clearly delineated right from wrong valuing the austere truth. Over the objections of many people, he married young vowing to prove all the naysayers wrong that the marriage was doomed to fail. His wife turned out to be irresponsible and repeatedly unfaithful. For various reasons which included the religious stigma that accompanies a theologically conservative denomination, James put up with this inappropriate behavior for a dozen years before divorcing. During this time, he became a strong and powerful man who possessed superior abilities to argue, persuade and forcefully state his opinions. I call him General James because he demands accuracy and high standards; and he has no trouble telling everyone, including himself, exactly what is right and needs to be done.

While life had never been very easy for him, in recent years it had become increasingly more stressful and painful,[23] especially in relationships that he really wanted to work. Upon the recommendation of a competent friend, he sought the counsel of a spiritual director. While these sessions at first centered around relationship skills, after a few months James would lament with statements like, "I really need to get closer with God." and "I need to get back to church." and "I'm not a real Christian." The forthcoming conversations revealed that while he had been baptized as a child, James did not feel like a Christian. He also affirmed that he could not be a Christian and continue to sin willfully. He knew right from wrong; he knew and proclaimed his own sinful behaviors; he knew that Jesus had died for his sins – but because he could not maintain a morally and ethically perfect life, James could not/would not receive the gift of justification. He desperately wanted to live up to the accurate, godly standards his parents asserted and make them proud, but he could not. James confused being good for God with being accepted by God. At his emotional center, James, even though he knew he could never be, wanted to be good enough in order to be accepted as a Christian.

Reviewing the positive growth that occurred in him including the releasing of anger and unforgiveness that he held as well as his demanding and controlling nature, James moved toward receiving the grace that God wanted to give him. He made plans to attend the Great Banquet, a multi-day event for adults to be immersed and inundated with the Christian message. However, right on "cue" James had a "spiritual meltdown." It was his (pre) "Confessional Temptation." His backsliding began with acting out sexually and was confirmed by the guilt he felt just days before the event. Accordingly, he planned not to attend the Great Banquet. Thankfully, God was close and encouraged him to seek counsel. After the divinely inspired Great Banquet touched him deeply and following a second retreat on spiritual growth, James got down on his knees, confessed his sins and Jesus as his savior, but more importantly he RECEIVED the grace that God accepted him "warts and all." James nowadays begins some of his sentences, "Now that I am a Christian..."

James still struggles. Of course, he is still on the Purgative Road which is extremely uneven and full of pot holes. But now he has received the power of God that has been poured into his heart to strengthen and enable him. Jim continues with some of his same problems, but now he has God's help to overcome them. He prays to be "softer" and not drive people away with his strongly, asserted (albeit accurate/truthful) statements. He is beginning to substitute impartially-spoken questions for his typically stated harsh opinions. He is not quite as hard on himself as he used to be. James is also building good spiritual habits that assist his spiritual progress. He bought a modern English Bible he could understand and has started reading it. He is seeking a church that satisfies his current spiritual need and attends weekly, sometimes twice a week. He receives and circulates Christian-based emails for encouragement and inspiration. He has new friends from the Great Banquet community and keeps in contact with them. James is purging, with God's help, the sins that plagued him and is substituting new godly disciplines. I pray for Jim because the Purgative Way is hard; and I thank God that I had a strong theology of grace because without it, James would not have made the progress he has made.

Purgative Way spiritual growth is hard. The author of the book of Hebrews writes about the spiritual growth transition that Christians make through the Purgative Way with these words:

> We have much to say about this, but it is hard to explain because you are slow to learn. In fact, though by this time you ought to be teachers, you need someone to teach you the elementary truths of God's word all over again. You need milk, not solid food! Anyone who lives on milk, being still an infant, is not acquainted with the teaching about righteousness. But solid food is for the mature, who by constant use have trained themselves to distinguish good from evil.[24] [Hebrews 5:11-14]

Indeed, Purgative Way Christians are slow learners and often need to re-learn the lessons "all over again." This is certainly true in the life of James. Part of the laborious nature of this path is because it takes a long time to un-learn bad habits and put new ones in their place. There seems to be a fight between an "old self" and the New Creation that is trying to emerge. While it is easy to conclude that this transition happens in a single moment, it really is developmental, occurring over time and sometimes with a great deal of effort. Constant training is required to distinguish between good from evil, especially to do so naturally and effortlessly. Those who are learning to choose between good and evil have most certainly had to face that dualism within themselves. They have increasingly rejected sinfulness and accepted godliness. They are getting ready for solid food as they travel the Purgative Way.

Certainly, even consistently-faithful Purgative Way Christians still have sinful behaviors. Nevertheless, they are better now than they used to be. While comparison can be a defensive justification to the reality of actually accomplishing, Purgative Way Christians increasingly do have less world and more God, less sin and more Spirit in their lives. **Signs of progress** occur in the removing of negative behaviors and increased ethical and moral behavior. Furthermore, Purgative Way Christians actually start doing really good things with their lives that honor and glorify God as they move into a closer relationship with God. They also have developed positive spiritual habits, sought the company of other Christians, prayed regularly, learned some parts of the Bible and have found them helpful. They have come to consider Jesus in a friendly manner and have appreciated him as their savior; and have reverenced God as well. The byproduct of this spiritual struggle has been that lots of time has been spent with God. **All of these "tasks" have led them to a basic and genuine attitude of love and trust in God.** The Basic Trust in God may have begun with fear or a need for protection but has developed into a deepening sense of affection and fondness. However, before this "Basic Trust" can grow into the "Mature Faith" of Illuminative Christians, it must again be tested.

DARK NIGHT OF THE SENSES[25]

The story and teaching in the tenth chapter of Mark is a paradigm for the Purgative Way.[26] [Mark 10:17-30] The rich man says he desires eternal life. First, Jesus tells him that he first needs to keep the law which he had done. Secondly, Jesus instructs this man that he must surrender all his wordily possessions. This he was unwilling to do; he wanted to do it his own way. Now some may want to conclude that selling all worldly possessions is necessary to follow Jesus or have eternal life; but the issue is about this man's willingness, not about doing certain things. (For example, Jesus promised the theft on the cross eternal life without any requirements; and because of their faith prostitutes would enter the kingdom of heaven before the Pharisees.)[27] [Luke 23:39-43; Matthew 21:31] In the teaching to the apostles that follows this encounter, Jesus indicates that entering God's Kingdom for a rich man is difficult, but that all things are possible with God. In verse twenty-eight, Peter said to Jesus, "We have left everything to follow you!" Then Jesus affirms that doing so will produce great reward including eternal life.

The Purgative Way tasks are not about surrendering all worldly possessions but it most certainly is about being <u>willing</u> to do so! **The Purgative Way is about training the personal will to have its primary focus on God and God's ways.** Thus, Purgative Way Christians may need to detach from the desire for things of the world; and they certainly must make a habit of not practicing sinful behaviors. They are to leave every impediment behind and follow Jesus. Now Jesus ate food, kept a treasury of money, had many friends, and even accepted expensive gifts. While Jesus did not reject such worldly things, they were never his primary focus – the Community of God was. This is the transition which Purgative Christians need to make. **Just before they are about to come to the end of this first road of the Christian spiritual journey, they will encounter a major "under construction" road block – the "Dark Night of the Senses."**

Christians have been progressing along the Spiritual Road by stopping detrimental physical habits and replacing them with godly actions – reading the Bible, going to church, serving others in tangible ways and so forth. Christians have rightly and necessarily used their physical abilities to accomplish their personal spiritual growth. They are doing so well and that is why the "Dark Night of the Senses" is about to begin! **Naturally, what happens while Christians are traveling the Purgative Way is that they come to believe that what <u>they</u> are doing will lead them up the Spiritual Road to their final destina-**

tion. They have been doing so by means of their "senses" which includes everything that a person can do **with their five physical senses** – yes, these are carnal or worldly things, but they accrue spiritual growth. <u>The "Darkness" refers to the fact that this no longer works</u>.

Benedict J. Groeschel comments on how Purgative Christians try to manage their faith journey. Based on Friedrich von Hugel's stellar work in religious development,[28] Groeschel, using the labels of child faith and adolescent faith, describes two different ways this is attempted. "The child attempts by cultic faith to manage the fear of life by attempting to control God with good works; the adolescent uses curiosity and rational analysis to control the divine by deciding what God can and must do.... The child's cultic works become the good deeds of charity; the adolescent's questioning becomes a reverent philosophy and theology."[29]

Because of all the positive things Christians have learned to do for God as well as all they have come to know about God, the scripture and what is right and true, **they have a kind of "spiritual pride" that makes them think that they have been accomplishing their own faith.** <u>God needs to correct this faith attitude, unconscious though it may be, and will do so through a crisis of faith that has been called the "Dark Night of the Senses.</u>" It must be felt deeply so the lesson is best learned experientially. As a result, the quality of the relationship these Christians have with God will fundamentally change. **In order to move further along the Spiritual Road, Purgative Way Christians need to conclude that their egoistic self is not in charge, God is – which requires a deep moment of surrender not unlike their Confession of Faith**. The prayer, "Not my will; but yours be done" applied to whatever is their crisis of faith needs to happen in the heart of their hearts.

The Apostle Peter thought he knew what the spiritually correct action to take was when he told Jesus in no uncertain terms that he and the apostles should not go to Jerusalem, which was the prudent and understandable way to manage growing the faith and staying out of danger. Of course, Jesus thought differently and completely rejected Peter's comments by saying: "Get behind me, Satan! You are a stumbling block to me; you do not have in mind the things of God, but the things of men."[30] [Matthew 16:23] In a separate incident, again Peter, one of those Purgative Way Christian slow learners, refused to let Jesus wash his feet. (Peter thinks: A spiritual novice never should allow his feet to be washed by a spiritual master – especially because this action indicated submission of the one doing the washing.) Peter's "Dark Night" is Jesus' comment: "Unless I wash you, you have no part with me."[31] [John 13:8] This action would have caused a total break in their relationship. However, Peter surrenders by saying that Jesus should then wash all of him. These biblical examples are to emphasize that even the commonplace, religious way of doing things that have been learned must be yielded so that the Divine is in charge. Indeed, following and trusting Jesus, even though it does not make sense, emerges as a basic tenant.

"The Dark Night of the Senses" can be triggered by any negative external event which causes a conflict between what is experienced (sadness, tragedy, pain, loss)

and the faith which the Purgative Way Christian has come to espouse and live. This spiritual event can be indicated by any of the following: "I prayed and didn't get what I wanted." Sometimes people will ask, "How can a good and loving God allow such awful evil?" Other types of comments might be voiced but <u>everyone juxtaposes what I have done with what God "should" do</u>. For example: "I thought if I prayed God would do it (my way)." "I thought if I was good, I would not have to feel this pain." "I thought if I became a Christian, I would know exactly what to do and it would all make sense." Because Christians cannot understand or change their problem by their own tangible efforts, they experience a "Dark Night."

St. John of the Cross[32] describes this condition of faith in terms of light.[33] Throughout the Purgative Way, Christians are moving toward the Light of God which they do through the tasks they have accomplished. This process provides them with the light of faith that can be gained via natural human means – by means of people's senses, intellect, emotions and so forth. St. John notes what happens when people bring their little light of faith into the perfect, holy Presence of the Light of God. People are so outshined that everything seems dark and they become temporarily blind; it is just like being indoors and then walking outside into the full brilliance of a sunny day. Christians wanted God. They move toward God. And thus "darkness" has surrounded them. They are in the "Dark Night of the Senses." This experience is not to be confused (but often is) with the "Dark Night of the Spirit," which occurs years later at the end of the Illuminative Way and with far different circumstances, although the "darkness" itself feels much the same.

For most people, I greatly simplify what is happening by saying, "You have come to an extended "under construction zone" on the spiritual road. You do not know what is going on. You cannot hurry the work that needs to be done or figure it out. You certainly can't do anything to fix it. You are stuck here. It is where you wanted to be... really. You just don't know it. The only option you have is to choose whether you will stay the course or turn around and go back. At an "under construction" zone with a flagger holding a stop sign, travelers are halted. "For how long?" people impatiently wonder; and the unwanted rhetorical answer is "Until God invites you to move forward." People know what is back there; but not what is ahead. Will they or won't they completely trust that God has them exactly where they need to be (even though they can't see it)? And will they trust that God loves them, wants the best for them (just the way they are), and will find a way for them where there seems to be no way?"

<u>A Word of Warning</u>: Faith crises can occur because of people's sins. Unfortunately, the "Dark Night of the Senses" can be repeated as travelers double-back and re-experience the same under-construction and decision-making process of faith all over again. Indeed, such "backsliding" can and does happen at any time and at any stage of a Christian's life, and is especially prevalent at this juncture.

In order to discern if a person is in a "Dark Night of the Senses" first ask, "Do you have serious, persistent sin currently in your life?" If the answer is yes, then what is happening is not this dark night. Because of the presence of persistent sin, the process of confession, penance and repentance is needed. If the answer is no, then those who help others grow spiritually need to explore further. What do Christians believe about their crisis and how God relates to it? Equally important is the role of guilt. Some Christians who earnestly strive to be good enough or who just genuinely desire to be good Christians may feel tremendous guilt when the "Dark Night of the Senses" happens. Their own pseudo-guilt, or guilt imposed upon them from religious authorities, will cause them to try to be better, pray harder, and do more by their own efforts. This is exactly what is counterproductive. Spiritual helpers need to relieve this sense of guilt, especially since these Christians have not done anything wrong! Sometimes the contemporary phrase, "Let go and let God" can help assuming that this "letting go" does not mean to stop all the positive Christian things and spiritual habits that followers are doing. Instead, the "letting go" is to release the conviction that these quality Christians can affect the outcome of this situation by the good that they do. "Let God be God and stop trying to fix it." Not unlike the "Confessional Temptation," the "Dark Night of the Senses" is a test that seeks to confirm, "Are you really ready to follow even if everything seems out of control? Will you let God lead?" The words of the contemporary song, "Blessed Be Your Name,"[34] reflect the attitude of non-control and acceptance that is required while in the "Dark Night of the Senses."

Blessed be Your name
On the road marked with suffering
Though there's pain in the offering
Blessed be Your name

If and when Christians consent, God moves them forward with a combination of intuition given from beyond themselves and a kind of divine revelation that provides them with a "Mature Faith" that is expressed in a genuine trust and love of God and God's Ways. **In God's own time and in God's own way, God will move Christians through this crucible of the "Dark Night of the Senses."** Initially, people may not recognize the new maturity of their faith but they often identify how much smoother their life has become. Afterward, most people cannot explain what happened except that they made it through to the other side and they have a deep sense of gratitude. They just trusted God. Like the blind man asked to explain what happened, he simply could respond, "One thing I know. I was blind, but now I see!"[35] [John 9:25] Likewise, people can be heard to say, "I don't think I could have made it through without God." But often times they cannot explain what they mean or exactly how that happened.

I sometimes use the analogy of how ozone is created to paraphrase what God has done. I say that Christians have, by means of the power of God, become ozone. The normal oxygen molecule that people breathe in the atmosphere is always made up of two unpaired electrons going around in an endless orbit until lightning strikes. Then it becomes triple ionized oxygen or that sweet-smelling, "spring-like fresh air" that happens after a thunderstorm. Likewise, sometime after a Purgative Way Christian comes to their "under construction" zone and decides to continue on the Spiritual Road, God, in God's own time and way, zaps or graces them. Accordingly, they become new souls who have been lifted above the road construction they were stuck in and placed on an awesomely smooth, beautiful superhighway. It is an amazing, "miraculous-like" experience. People never know when lightning will strike. This begins the Illuminative Way, the second leg of the Christian spiritual journey.

Consider the following two vignettes that describe the various ways Christians move through the "Dark Night of the Senses." One reflects a real-time life event and the other is a composite of various folks' narratives. Both are true to the experience of moving through the "Dark Night of the Senses."

Jennifer is a dedicated Christian in her early forties who has grown up in a Protestant tradition since birth. She has committed her life to Jesus as Lord and Savior in a developmentally traditional manner. She has adopted good ethical and moral standards, especially when it came to considering the needs of others and providing service for them. She has consistently practiced spiritual habits like regular worship, studying the scripture, intercessory prayer and service to others. Unfortunately during her twenties and thirties, Jen experienced life difficulties in both an abusive marriage as well as a demanding and demeaning job. While she navigated her way through this uneven surface, Jen became increasingly anxious and fearful which resulted in a persona of distrust that limited her ability to move forward in daily life and well as her spiritual life. In addition, her good Christian attitude of putting others first kept her stuck in this darkness as somehow she thought that doing what everyone (including God) wanted would make her life better.

Just prior to starting spiritual direction and part of the reason for doing so, Jennifer's emotional discomfort was so great that she needed to resign from the job that was causing her so much angst. After discerning her situation and recognizing that Jennifer did not need therapy, her spiritual director initiated conversation about the underlying anxiety which was keeping her from moving forward both in her daily and spiritual life. As Jennifer found another job where her skills and dedication were both valued and rewarded, she came to experientially "believe" that God really wanted good things for her. Because there were no persistent sinful behaviors in her life, her spiritual director suggested that she boldly ask to be blessed and pray that she would follow where God would lead. Within an amazingly short period of time, she stopped feeling so anxious, was able to constructively deal with criticism at work that would have previously filled her with fear. In addition, she was able to participate in ministry projects that required some risk into new territory. The final confirmation was given when Jennifer stated, "I have prayed all my life. But lately it has been different. Before it seemed like I did all the talking, but now it feels more like conversation and I hear God communicating with me." Jennifer had been transported through the "Dark Night of the Senses" and her fearfulness that she had previously attempted to manage via appeasement. Her life was now smoothly moving into the Light of God's Presence where newness and free-flowing communication had started because she had boldly chosen to follow whenever God would lead in spite of her anxiety-orientation.

Timothy also made it through the "Dark Night of the Senses" but with a totally different set of circumstances.

Timothy was a very mature, young twenties Christian who had "done everything right" throughout his few years. He had been a model student, dutiful son and active Christian who was polite, gentle and considerate of others. He had strong values and sought to follow biblical teachings. Tim had graduated from college and was looking forward to a career as an educator. He met a young woman, fell in love and they married. In less than two years, his wife announced that she did not love him anymore and wanted a divorce. Marriage counseling was begun in order to repair the relationship. However, the wife did not want the marriage to continue; so they divorced. Tim had always wanted to be in a long-term marriage relationship, be a faithful husband and rear a family. Being a biblically informed Christian, Tim was thrown into despair because he realized that the scripture taught that remarriage after divorce would make him an adulterer (especially when no unfaithfulness occurred). He struggled emotionally and spiritually. Did God want him to be single the rest of his life even though he had done everything right and the divorce was not his fault? He wondered whether or not God wanted him to be happy or whether God even cared. If he remarried would God condemn him as a sinner, who would be living in a perpetual state of living in opposition to God's law?

Quite by accident, Timothy, seeking some emotional relief from his internal conflict and being a Christian, found a spiritual director who was willing to "see what she could do." While Timothy wanted to follow what the scriptures taught, he hoped that God did not want him to live a life of celibacy. He sought to do what was right and follow what God wanted him to do. He noted that he was a young man in his twenties who had already been a sexually active married man; and he felt this sexual passion acutely. Furthermore, he recognized that the scripture taught that those who were unmarried or widowed should marry if they could not control themselves and move into fornication.[36] [I Corinthians 7:9] He hoped that this "rule" might apply to him. Tim also knew that one sin would be as condemning as another. What should he do?

Since Timothy found value in the scripture, his spiritual director suggested that along with prayer that they might study the biblical passages on marriage, divorce, remarriage and adultery. First of all, while they recognized some inconsistency among the sections, they had to conclude that God wanted faithful marriage relationships and noted that marriage was to be for life regardless of who was unfaithful and who was not.[37] These were God's rules so that people would establish a moral and ethical style of life that would be worthy of the Holy Community which God desires. Secondly, the director and Timothy studied the parable of Jesus in which an owner of a vineyard hired workers; the parable was taught to especially describe the Kingdom of Heaven and its owner.[38] [Matthew 20:1-16] The hired employees were to work a certain prescribed number of hours and receive an agreed upon wage in return. In the parable, throughout the day the master hired other workers who were not able to work the entire length of the day; some could actually work for only one hour. When it was time to pay all of the workers, the owner gave the full day's wage to all who worked the entire day and the exact same amount to those who worked only part of the day, including the one who had labored only one hour. The workers who toiled the entire day were angry over what they thought was unfair treatment. To this, the owner replied, "'Friend, I am not being unfair to you. Didn't you agree to work for a denarius? Take your pay and go. I want to give the man who was hired last the same as I gave you. Don't I have the right to do what I want with my own money? Or are you envious because I am generous?"[39] [Matthew 20:13-15]

In reflection on the parable, the spiritual director asked Timothy, "Who was the owner of the vineyard/ the Kingdom of Heaven; and who the workers were?" Tim replied, "God is the owner; and the workers are those who do what God instructs them to do for which they receive payment." The spiritual director affirmed his answer and then she asked, "Does God have the right to do with whatever God has to give?" "Yes. I would think so as long as God didn't treat people unfairly," was Tim's cautious response. Now I have a much harder question for you to think about, "Do you think that God can treat people differently and still be fair?" Tim grimaced with his retort, "That is hard. I guess it would say that "fairness" does not mean everything has to be exactly the same. It is like in the story. The vineyard owner paid all the workers a fair wage; he just gave more to some than what was required. He wasn't unfair, just generous. So, yes I guess God can act differently and still be fair." The director smiled and replied, "Ok. What does God have to give that no one else has to give?" "A trip to Heaven," Timothy blurted out. "And what does God do for people to allow them to take that trip?" "God forgives our sins," was Tim's rhetorical response.

Finally, the spiritual director wondered, "In what way might this teaching of Jesus apply to your marriage situation?" Tim reflected, "I tried to stay married and wanted to. I would have worked the whole day. It was not my fault that I couldn't stay married. Do you think that God would be so gracious to me to give me a second chance?" Wisely, the spiritual director responded, "I don't know what God will do; but it does seem clear that God will choose what God will choose. As we have studied, the scripture decrees allow, even encourage, remarriage if a spouse has died [I Timothy 5:14];[40] but scripture does not allow remarriage in the case of a divorce because "adultery" would be the result (except in the case of unfaithfulness). In other words, it would seem that while divorce *legally* ends a marriage, it is not terminated *spiritually* or in God's eyes. However, it also seems that God makes an exception to spiritually end the marriage and allow remarriage for those who have experienced an unfaithful spouse.[41] [Matthew 19:9] Forgiveness is God's prerogative. Forgiveness is given and available to those who accept Jesus as savior; also forgiveness is given to those who confess their sins. However, forgiveness belongs to God and God can do with it as God chooses while still not being unfair to those who have kept the agreement. Truly, I don't know what God will do. But, I recommend that you spend some intense time praying your heart out to God, including how much you want to work for God as well as your own personal heart's desire for a marriage companion. And we will reflect on what happens in your prayer time."

Tim later reported that following this conversation, he felt almost immediately relief emotionally; he started obsessing less about his former wife and about his future. Although he felt better, he could not confirm from his prayers any particular ways that God might be gracing him. It took nine weeks, which seemed like an incredibly long time to a twentyish-year-old. God answered with an unprompted and unplanned grocery store meeting of Angela, a woman who had almost the same experience as Tim. Standing in line they exchanged comments about being on their own again; and outside in the sunshine, they talked for a long time. While Angela was not as active a Christian as Timothy, she had been abandoned by her husband and felt like damaged goods. Angela wondered if God was punishing her although she could not figure out what she had done that was so awful. Timothy interjected that he wondered the same thing but had come to reaffirm that God was not doing that. When he noted that a spiritual director had helped him, Angela was intrigued and asked if she could meet this woman.

Making a long story shorter, Angela and Timothy reconfirmed their desire to seek what God wanted for their life; and they also started dating. While Timothy believed that Angela was God's answer to his prayers, he agreed to keep praying and "take it slow" to make sure it was God and not his own self-interest speaking. In the process, Tim's life became genuinely energized and focused. Angela came to a deeper commitment of faith. At a particular joint spiritual direction session, the director led Timothy and Angela to a prayerful conclusion. Their mutual happiness seemed to be genuine and divinely enriching experience for both of them. However, their being together could only be because God had decided to "pay them for the whole day." Thus, recognition of and living in the midst of God's radical grace would necessarily be the best way for them to live and honor God in the process. A year later, the spiritual director attended their joyous wedding celebration.[42]

In summary, the Purgative Way begins with a major conversion or confirmation to Jesus as Savior. While many people believe that this is the whole of the Christian life, it is just the beginning. Indeed, the Purgative Way **often reflects an intense struggle and radical shift in the manner of living**. People become different. Their transition is reflected in moral/ethical standards, healthy spiritual practices and also a basic trusting relationship with God. However, via the "Dark Night of the Senses" at the end of the Purgative Way, this "under construction" zone prepares Christians with an even deeper level of trust that transcends rules and being good. Speaking about the psychology of spiritual development, Benedict Groeschel instructs that the major overall trend describing the Christian spiritual journey is about the decrease of anxiety and the increase of peace-freedom.[43] Nowhere is this sweeping transition noticed more than as Christians move through the "Dark Night of the Senses" and onto the Illuminative Way.

CHAPTER 8

The Illuminative Way
An Introduction

The Illuminative (or Enlightenment) Way is the "superhighway" of the Spiritual Road. The surface is smoother, wider and without obvious pot holes. The speed and ease of travel is much faster and more enjoyable. Getting to one's desired destination is much less of a chore and affords greater variety with lots of things to do and see and learn about. Accordingly, **Christians in this stage of spiritual growth learn quicker, are eager to do so, absorb the reasons for faith more rapidly and also begin to serve others whole-heartedly in God's name. In addition, they enthusiastically want to put into practice and perpetuate what they believe.** An orthodox description for this attitude is "zeal" for the Lord (not to be confused with the short-lived, manic fervor that often occurs immediately after conversion). The traditional Spiritual Road name given to these Christians is the "Proficient" largely because they are becoming skilled at what they believe and do.

On the other hand, the characteristics that describe Illuminative Way Christians are very diverse. Part of the reason for this range of qualities is generated by, can be discerned from and attributed to the stages of personal and social development that this large age group goes through. The Illuminative Way can begin when Christians are in their twenties and extend into their sixties or seventies.

A LONG AND VARIED JOURNEY

First, the Illuminative Way can be lengthy simply because so much is required in order to complete the tasks of these years and simultaneously build healthy relationships in the process. During these decades, people typically focus on the question of "Who am I?" and skill development. They also will move toward a career, marriage and rearing a family. As a result, they will likely develop concern for taking care of others and eventually for passing on what they have learned and built. Indeed, the life-tasks that people go through directly affect their spirituality which is primarily about one's personal relationship with God. For example: As young people are discovering who they are, they also consider "Who they are" in relationship to who God is, which necessarily includes learning more about the characteristics and qualities of the divine. Also, building a life can correspond to building a church. While people may simply think they are just living life, they can simultaneously grow in relationship with God. **Helping people grow spiritually during the Illuminative Way often occurs by helping them link their life activities within the aura of God.** Representative questions to help this process are: "What is God doing in your life?" or "Where have you sensed the presence of God?" (Using God-focused questions rather than person-oriented ones such as "What are you doing for God?" are best because they put the emphasis on God's work instead of the person's efforts.)

Secondly, the Illuminative Way can be lengthy because people often have to relearn or repeat previous lessons. There is plenty to learn and consequently a lot to be integrated into what has already been gained. Learning these life lessons is important because certain personality qualities are needed for spiritual progression. For example, trust is an essential part of faith in God; without trust, reliance upon God, God's Word and God's people is convoluted at best. Those who have suffered abuse, especially at a young age, may have a particularly difficult time trusting others or matters of faith. In addition, trust is an important part of daily living and in order to become a strong quality its practice may need to be repeated during progressive life events. Such lessons often need to be reaffirmed through life situations that are increasingly complex and have more at risk. Thus, spiritual growth and one's relationship with God frequently, but not always, depend on completing this kind of "unfinished business." In the past century and into this one, numerous people have turned to psychotherapy in order to work through certain life issues that cause them problems and make them unhappy. While those who help others grow spiritually may not be therapists, nor try to do therapy, the manner in which life issues limit or strengthen Christians' relationships with God needs to be paramount for those on the Illuminative Way. The classic volume Atonement and Psychotherapy by Don Browning illustrates where therapy and Christian theology parallel in this regard.[1]

The real life vignette of Ned may be instructive. Ned has been on the Spiritual Road for decades but is stuck in a roundabout, which is a two-lane circle designed to increase the speed and ease of traffic flow. Nevertheless, people can loop the roundabout continuously instead of heading off toward their destination. The necessary background of Ned's life includes three sisters who got all the attention from their father. Regardless of what Ned did, he never ever received the affirmation that he needed and deserved from the kind of exemplary childhood he lived – smart, skilled, moral and faithful. Ned was a good boy and tried to be first-rate at everything; and his father was not all that commendable. In fact, when their father died, none of the three daughters came to the funeral which Ned arranged and attended – almost no other people visited.

Ned has been a Christian for most of his life. Currently, he is an active member and a spiritual leader in a local congregation; he attends meetings, visits shut-ins, goes on retreats, consistently helps others, and assists in outreach programs and work day projects. His relationship with God is prayerful and committed as well. He has extremely high expectations of himself... and yes, of others as well. He believes that whatever kind of good he does for others, they will (are supposed to) return to him. And when they don't voluntarily return the favors he gets angry, secretly because he would be bad if he showed it. Unconsciously, Ned is probably mad at God but most certainly would not allow himself to feel that.

Today in his early sixties, Ned has a long-term marriage and is a doting grandfather. Unfortunately, Ned's wife has suffered numerous de-habilitating medical conditions; Ned has been a caregiver for twenty some years and a good one as might be assumed. He also is a self-employed construction worker who supports the family at the same time he takes care of his wife, who like many with long-lasting illnesses has given up hope of ever getting better. Ned has been a strong advocate, emergency room nurse, nutritionist and encourager for two decades – he is totally exhausted and frustrated especially when his wife refuses to take his well-conceived, designed-to-get-her-better good advice. While other people admired him and shake their collective heads in disbelief of all that he does, Ned can never do enough.

One of Ned's close friends was a pressure relief valve for Ned. The friend listened intently for years. While still willing to be there for Ned, he discovered that his support was of little help and suggested that Ned go talk with someone. Ned did not understand why his life was so difficult, but accepted that God must have wanted it to be that way. He figured that it was something he just had to live with and talking about it wouldn't do any good. Finally, the friend convinced Ned to see a counselor who was also a spiritual director. During this process, Ned found a safe place to verbalize all those things he would think about during the middle of the night after his wife would wake up.

At one of his sessions, Ned reflected on how hard and exhausting care giving had been. When asked, "Why do you do so much?" Ned responded, "If I don't succeed, I must have done something wrong." And with this frustration gestalted to the foreground Ned blurted out, "I would be OK if she would just do what I said!" To which the counselor replied, "Did you hear what you just said that <u>you</u> would be ok if <u>she</u> responded positively to you?" Ned immediately made the connection: he was repeating his long-practiced pattern of working hard to get affirmation in order to feel OK about himself.

"How is that working for you?" was the rhetorical question as the counselor seamlessly morphed into spiritual direction. Gently grasping this opening in order to connect some of Ned's life patterns, the director spoke, "While working hard in your life may never give you the positive that you probably deserve, God sees you and loves you just the way you are. God has all the Fatherly affirmation to give you that you could ever need and you can't do anything to deserve it; it's just waiting for you! If you get that then you might want to soak it up. What do you think?" Ned, much calmer now, said he was ready for something good for himself. So, the director asked, "Well then. How would you want to pray about this in the days ahead?" Ned replied, "I want to ask God to help me stop worrying about everybody and everything." It was a good start toward releasing his obsessive-compulsive working for affirmation attitude that was affecting his relationship with God. Ned had a long way to go but he left that day more hopeful.

The spiritual problem was that Ned kept trying to get affirmation by doing good things. And Ned was absolutely doing well but would not accept that he had ever done enough to be considered OK. Because of Ned's interpersonal need for affirmation, he obsessively tried and tried hard to do good expecting that he could "earn" what he needed. So, he was "unable" to believe that he was good enough; and he was also "unable" to just trust that God would give him exactly what he needed (which may not be what he thinks he wants.) Ned was stuck in a spiritual roundabout.

While Ned's life as well as his spiritual relationship would improve if he had adequate self-esteem and limited his "serving others to satisfy self" attitude, spiritual growth is not dependent on such emotional healing. Spiritual direction, as practiced by those before the advent of psychological understanding, would have directed Ned to pray about his frustration seeking God's relief and insight. He might also be advised to consider the relationship with his father and the possible unforgiveness (which is the ultimate spiritual dilemma) he has. This form of prayer instruction is still effective – in other words God persists in answering the deepest desires of peoples' prayers. Nevertheless, understanding (plus appropriate action) of the psycho-social roundabout in which Christians circle can rid them of "stinking thinking" mantras and open their lives to a deeper relationship with God. God will always continue to work in people; I just believe that psychological understanding/healing helps people to cooperate with what God wants to do.

Third, the Illuminative Way is often lengthy because Christians need to go through an ever deepening process, designed to prepare them for a life of eternity. The process, which will become clearer by the end of chapter nine, goes like this. Christians learn about themselves (the person God is creating them to be). As this occurs, they receive spiritual insights, making clarifications to their faith, which they apply to life especially in terms of service to others. During this time of servicing, Christians in relationship to their new environment learn even more about themselves because they have given of themselves. As a result, Christians gain deeper self-understanding, fuller appreciation of God and God's ways as well as clearer commitment to their personal relationship with God.

As a synchronized theme for traveling the Illuminative Way, **there is some indication that following one's life plan, which is indicated by the patterns in one's life, can increase the speed and purposeful direction along the Spiritual Road.** For example, did Saul of Tarsus know that he would become the greatest evangelist and missionary for the churches of Jesus Christ? Certainly not, but he did discover that truth along the way. Indeed, his life was uniquely prepared for that spiritual task and to be in a united relationship with the divine. He was both a Roman citizen and like Jesus a devout Jew. He was extroverted and a great public speaker. He was exceptionally intelligent, fluent in both the Old Testament Hebrew and the New Testament Greek languages, making him suited to interpret and translate the unique faith that Jesus brought. He was a respected and high-level official, a Pharisee, in Judaism. He was deeply insightful, spiritually devoted, a problem-solver and a negotiator. Saul was perfectly suited to become the Apostle Paul. Understanding how he had been equipped and then cooperating with that preparation allowed St. Paul to rapidly move along the Spiritual Road, become effectively used by God to spread Christianity and write much of the New Testament. God did the work; and as Paul recognized what God had in mind, he cooperated. Likewise, Illuminative Way Christians also can benefit as they read the road signs especially as they travel this part of the Spiritual Road.

In the way of an introductory summary, the goal of the Illuminative Way is for Christians to come into a much deeper relationship with God through increased knowledge and activity as part of the Community (Kingdom) of God. These Christians are also living through and relating life's activities with the divine. Concurrently, they may need to be taking care of "unfinished business" regarding their personality and life issues which restrict their spiritual relationship. Failure to do so may keep Illuminative Way Christians on a perpetual roundabout instead of moving forward on the Spiritual Road.

Describing the tasks to accomplish, or the steps to take, on the Illuminative Way are best done in generic terms because there are so many variations. Movement along the Illuminative Way is dependent on and is related to whatever life circumstances are prominent in Christians' lives. However, **what Christians learn, clarify, love, apply, share and spawn are the means to this part of the journey's end.** Yet, the particular actions that are permeated are not as important as the development of one's relationship with God.

Throughout the long journey of the Illuminative Way, God must guide and light the path. God must be sought out to be the vision, the wisdom, the strength, the encouragement and the victory so that Christians neither get lost along the way nor believe that their skill-driven and task-based development has been accomplished on their own. "Be Thou My Vision" has always reminded me of where to keep the focus.

> Be Thou my Vision, O Lord of my heart;
> Naught be all else to me, save that Thou art.
> Thou my best Thought, by day or by night,
> Waking or sleeping, Thy presence my light.[2]

In fact, developing a quality personal relationship with God is supremely important in order to be able to face the extreme trial that comes at the end of the Illuminative Way, the "Dark Night of the Spirit." The traits of the Illuminative Way may be summarized to include the following:

✟ Learnings

✝ Clarifications
✝ Devotion
✝ Mission and Generativity
✝ Dark Night of the Spirit

Because the "Illuminative Way" covers so much information, I have divided it into three chapters – this one as an introduction, chapter nine to summarize the process and chapter ten to consider the "Dark Night of the Spirit" which typically comes near the end of the "Illuminative Way."

CHAPTER 9

The Illuminative Way The Process

The process of going through the Illuminative Way includes following very fluid stages and "tasks" that need to be completed. They include:

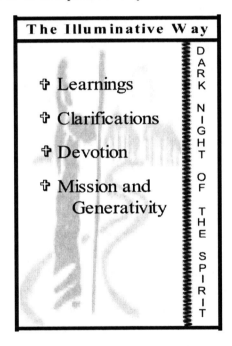

The Illuminative Way

✞ Learnings

✞ Clarifications

✞ Devotion

✞ Mission and Generativity

DARK NIGHT OF THE SPIRIT

Graphic 5: The Illuminative Way rapidly builds and expands upon the new Christian lifestyle with mature learning, devotion and practices.

LEARNINGS

Truly, learning is important all along the Spiritual Road. However, the "Learnings" that takes place on the Illuminative Way must be distinguished from other gains in knowledge.

The story-example that goes with making this distinction occurred early in my ministry when a seven-year-old wanted to make her confession of faith. Shelly was able to voluntarily speak basic information about her faith and answer questions to determine that she was not just parroting someone else's words. Now did Shelly know everything about Jesus or have a developed, sophisticated faith? Of course not, she was only seven years old! But "Does she know enough?" was always the question asked by those who were on the Illuminative Way and were learning a great deal daily. This "adultish" question was code for "I can't believe I didn't know all that I am learning now. How can a seven-year-old make an informed decision?" But it was actually the wrong question.

As I know now, but only intuited then, my only concern needed to be, "Does Shelly have a genuine seven-year-old expression of faith?" If so, then I needed to honor the faith she had and keep her growing. Henceforth, my profession of faith/confirmation question for everyone became, "Do you believe with all of your heart and the *best of your ability* that Jesus Christ is your Lord and Savior; and that you want to follow him with your life?" This question works equally well for seven-year-olds as for seventy-year-olds or even those who were mildly mentally challenged. By the way, I visited with Shelly, not her real name, just last year. She is still a member in the same congregation where she made her confession of faith, still actively learning along the Illuminative Way and also passing on the faith to her children and others.

The commentary that goes with this story is: Illuminative Way Christians need to grow spiritually into a well-versed, knowledgeable, informed faith. On the other hand, those who are about to start on the Purgative Way, whose mode of transportation is jump-started by the spark of the Holy Spirit, need to express only a rudimentary faith and a willingness to begin.[1] Requiring a refined faith of a seven-year-old is tantamount to "squelching the Spirit." Shelly, ready to become a Purgative Way Christian, had already learned the basis of Christianity and her faith needed to be honored, not held to the standard of the learning which Illuminative Way Christians experience.

Truly, the learning that takes place on the Illuminative Way is a different kind of knowing than either the learning that it takes to become a Christian on the Pre-Christian Way or the learning that happens on the Purgative Way. On the Purgative Way, people's relationship with God is expanded via learning right from wrong, spiritual habits and coming to rely on God. As a result, Christians' lives change according to the rules and instruction. Their learning comes as they do what is right. On the Illuminative Way, Christians' relationships with God become more give and take – yet with God (and spiritual others) still being the teacher and Christians still being the students. Via an analogy, Pre-Christian Way people have not enrolled in school. Purgative Way Christians are in early elementary school. Illuminative Way Christians are in higher grade levels where they are encouraged to take initiative, explore, ask probing questions and generally discern the reasons for what they believe. In fact, they are genuinely excited to learn more using this approach.

Accordingly, the Illuminative Way "Learning" is not just learning facts or details but learning how to use this information rightly, according to the way God intends. Also, it is about understanding the reasons that underlie what was learned during the Purgative Way.

GROWING IN TRUTH

The Apostle Paul counsels Timothy, who is a minister and not just a Christian beginner, to be as one "who correctly handles the word of truth."[2] [II Timothy 2:15] The Greek word, ὀρθοτομοῦντα, which is translated "correctly handles" literally means "to cut straight or divide correctly." Since this phrase is not used elsewhere in the New Testament, some discussion as to its precise meaning has taken place over the years. Given that this section of scripture is about learning, how are people to understand its application to Christians on the Spiritual Road? First of all, the "word of truth" cannot mean all New Testament scripture passages because they were not even compiled when II Timothy was penned. On the other hand, what the Apostle Paul wanted Timothy to handle correctly was the spiritual faith, based on the life, death and resurrection of Jesus, which God had given to individuals. While Paul absolutely wanted this "Christian" spirituality to be used as God intended it to be used, what was infinitely more important was helping Christians grow stronger in their faith. And that always depends on who you are talking to![3]

Those who help Purgative Way Christians need to keep the "words of truth" clear, straight and simple. As Paul discusses in a separate passage, they need "spiritual milk."[4] [I Corinthians 3:1-2] Hence, the II Timothy passage advises that quarreling over words, moving away from the basic truths of the faith like the belief in the resurrection of Jesus or participating in godless chatter are never helpful, especially for Purgative Way Christians. On the other hand, those who are farther along the Spiritual Road, i.e., Illuminative Way Christians, need "spiritual meat" – they need something more nourishing to chew on so that they can grow. For example, Jesus was rightly handling the message of God when he taught (Illuminative Way people) with sentences that began: "You have heard that it was said... but I tell you..."[5] [Matthew 5:21, 27, 33, 43] As Jesus was correcting scripture, he was also teaching people to expand and deepen their understandings. As a clarifying example, one might ask, "How do you accurately teach the meaning of family?" When you are a child your family is mom and dad; later the people of the church or other relatives will be family; and to Unitive Way Christians it is all of creation. The word "family" is re-taught, re-formatted, depending on people's life circumstances. In a like manner, the "word of truth" must be taught and re-taught accordingly in order to be correctly applied. Absolutely, there is a time to stick to what is simply written. There is also a time to espouse the deeper insightful meanings that come from within the message of God. Knowing when and where and how to do this is necessary for everyone who "correctly handles" the meaning of God.

Helping make the transition between the Purgative and Illuminative Ways deserves special consideration. Spiritual helpers know that Christians are ready for or moving onto the Illuminative Way when they say, "I know that we are not supposed to question, but..."[6] and they are honestly seeking more. Purgative Way Christians with their right versus wrong perspective, believe (and might have been taught) that they are never to question authority, the rules or to think for themselves – indeed, previously that would have been counterproductive since the rules give spiritual strength to their lives. Thus, they have not allowed themselves to doubt because "it is bad" to do so. However, when Christians verbalize a form of the above question, I know it is time to have my "doubt is belief's twin brother" discussion, which I do in order to give them permission from a spiritual authority figure, which Purgative Way Christians need, to proceed.

I would begin, "You know that there are two very different kinds of doubt, don't you?" Because they don't, I continue. "There is genuine doubt and double-minded doubt. Genuine doubt is when a person really wants to learn but does not know the answer; and they are honest seekers. On the other hand, the purpose of "double-minded" doubt, described in the book of James, is to discount and destroy faith.[7] [James 1:6-8] Double-minded doubt is unhelpful and counterproductive to growing in faith. Conversely, in order to grow in faith, people need to learn and in order to learn people need to ask questions. Therefore, asking honest questions is not only good but also absolutely necessary. <u>The basis of every authentic question is uncertainty or doubt. In order to find a new or deeper truth a person must begin with doubt in the form of an honest, seeking question</u>. That's why I say that doubt is belief's twin brother. So, ask questions, even those that might seem not allowed, in order that you might better believe."

At other times, Purgative Way Christians who are ready to move through the "Dark Night of the Senses" may actually get the courage to describe how their current relationship with God no longer seems adequate; it may be inauthentic, seem immature or simply feel oppressive. A divine relationship can be inauthentic when what people espouse to believe is not the way they actually experience life. Or it may feel oppressive when a loving God who controls everything must be punishing people via cancer. These are all openings to discuss alternative ways to describe their presently-held characteristics of God in relationship to their personal faith. Hopefully such discussion leads to a deeper, more mature and fully loving portrayal of the divine as well as their relationship with God.

The apostle Paul had a similar desire for Christians to expand their understanding of God when he offered this prayer for the Ephesians,

For this reason I kneel before the Father, from whom every family in heaven and on earth derives its name. I pray that out of his glorious riches he may strengthen you with power through his Spirit in your inner being, so that Christ may dwell in your hearts through faith. And I pray that you, being rooted and established in love, may have power, together with all the Lord's holy people, to grasp how wide and long and high and deep is the love of Christ, and to know this love that surpasses knowledge — that you may be filled to the measure of all the fullness of God.[8] [Ephesians 3:14-19]

Paul not only desired that people have Jesus in their hearts but also that they would subsequently experience the deepest spiritual growth possible. This means learning and asking questions. Certainly, divine love goes beyond human knowledge but learning is the only way for people to grasp this truth. In other words, God's Spirit enters people to help them receive the love of God given in Jesus; and when this faith is solid, God provides additional power to grasp a more completed understanding of that divine love – which solely cannot be acquired through learning but requires it.

This kind of Illuminative Way learning has been the subject of theologians, philosophers, poets and musicians. Anselm of Aosta (1033-1109 A.D.), the Archbishop of Canterbury, England, coined the phrase "faith seeking understanding." This phrase captures the truth that Christians at first come to faith without full understanding, but the Illuminative Way process of spiritual growth actually moves Christians toward deeper knowledge and even wisdom that fortifies faith. Therefore, **Illuminative Way Christians seek understanding, through genuine questions and honest exploration, in order to gain more of the "fullness of God."** In so doing, they come to know God with more certainty and assurance than ever before. **They not only know what they believe, but also why they accept it as true.** Thus, while the Purgative Way is largely about loving Jesus with the "heart," the Illuminative Way focuses on knowing the divine with the "mind." Perhaps the motto for the Illuminative Way was best captured by the prayer phrase ascribed to the thirteenth century English bishop Saint Richard of Chichester.[9] It was also popularized in the 1971 Stephen Schwartz and John-Michael Tebelak's musical <u>Godspell</u> with the song "Day by Day."[10] In order to follow God on the Illuminative Way, Christians need to "See thee more clearly, love thee more dearly, follow thee more nearly day by day" and understand what they are doing in the process.

LEARN ABOUT WHAT?

What should these Christians learn? Just about anything that enriches their faith. People learn best if they are interested and by doing. Thus, Illuminative Way Christians might best learn what they do and gravitate toward what they desire most. <u>However, the learning must not be solely for the purpose of acquiring trivia but for growing spiritually in relationship with God.</u> A very simple but effective way to engage Illuminative Way Christians is to ask, "Where are you putting most of your energy?" After listening intuitively to whatever they have been doing, spiritual helpers could easily respond with some form of

"Where is God in all of that?" and "What do you think God is trying to teach you through it?"

Examples of what to learn are copious; here are a few ideas from what people do at church and in life.

What do Illuminative Way Christians do in the church? Certainly, they go to worship, sing hymns, read the Bible, pray, give offerings, share faith and serve others. Do people understand the parts and purpose of worship? Can they express that? Do folks understand the words of songs they sing in church and why the composer wrote those words? Can Christians know where to find or even recite particularly significant biblical passages? Have they read the entire Bible or learned how to do a contextual Bible study? What are the different types and parts of prayer? Can people recite the Lord's Prayer? What, why and how much should people give? Do people have a personal faith story they can express? Can they lead other people to accept Jesus as Savior? Christians serve others but can they articulate how that is important and how it is part of their faith; and do they have opportunities for outreach activities and mission trips? Indeed, every fellowship dinner and every committee meeting could easily (and briefly) highlight one of the above – and actually help people in their personal spiritual growth and relationship with God. (And it does not take clergy to make that happen!) Part of the success of Rick Warren's books <u>The Purpose Driven Church</u> and <u>The Purpose Driven Life</u>[11] is that they provided a forum for Illuminative Way Christians to consider, discuss and understand faith in deeper ways, even when folks did not agree with what was written.

What do Illuminative Way Christians do in their lives? Are these folks beginning to learn about their own skills, gifts, abilities and the opposite of their strengths? Then, they could enjoy focusing on the personal values and characteristics that God desires for people to have as well as how to value and appreciate others who do not have the same qualities. Are they in or wanting to be in a relationship? Learning what the Bible or Christian-based writers teach about love and relationships would be of great interest to them. Christian-based child rearing principles would be an authentic concern for families. In addition, a "sharing Christian faith with children" workshop would be an excellent way to develop evangelistic skills and hone Christians' own faith narratives as well. Work, money and business dealings would capture the attention of those with careers. Do they know how to implement "spirituality in the workplace"[12] or have meaningful social and political conversations? Discussion groups about current events or films can be an excellent way to seek new understanding that can augment Christian faith. <u>The possibilities are endless to learn and enrich faith as it is applied to daily living</u>.

So that the above suggestions do not become just another church program, certain questions must become the most significant focus for Illuminative Way Christians. Near the end of each of the above ideas ask questions such as: "What does this subject say about God?" "What does God desire or require of you?" "How does this knowledge strengthen your understanding of God and your faith?" "How are you living or not living in a manner that is pleasing to God?"

THREEFOLD LEARNING

The "Learnings" along the three plus decades of the Illuminative Way includes at least three major foci – **learning to understand the reasons for faith, learning the intricacies of Christian loving (God and others) and beginning to enter into a broader perspective that not only sees value in others and their thoughts but also sees those things as absolutely necessary to God's plan.** Each "Learning" guides Christians into a closer relationship with God by helping them internalize the quality and character of God. In the history of Christianity, this long process has been called the "Training of the Will." In other words, Christians are learning to think God's thoughts, feel God's emotions and align with God's will – or to do so as well as finite human beings can. Consider each of these tasks.

First, Illuminative Way Christians attend to "Learnings" to gain the reasons for their faith. Even in non-doctrinal churches, an incredible number of teachings and doctrines are impressed on Purgative Way Christians. This type of training is not only necessary but also most effective for beginners. Illuminative Way Christians have already learned most of the basic Christian principles. However, **they need to understand what the rationale is for those doctrines, teachings and catechisms they have been taught**. As mentioned above, these Christians are motivated and eager to learn – and there is a lot to discover.

In the process of learning to understand what they already believe, Illuminative Way Christians have a tendency toward apologetics, which is the discipline of defending or proving Christianity; also evangelistic enthusiasm to share their faith may accompany this learning. More than occasionally, Christian folks will justify what they believe as if their lives depended on it. This proclivity often happens at the same time that young adults are coming to claim "who they are." So, such passion in a sense reflects whether their lives have value and meaning or not; and it can take on a larger than life intensity. Christians, especially at this stage of claiming the truths that determine everyone's personhood, may feel like defending the faith, even fighting to uphold its principles. Yet the passion to preserve the faith may be the flames that set fire to the world that God wants to save. The Medieval crusades, the abrasive barrage from street corner evangelists, arrogant condemnation of other Christians from liberal-minded theologians or the bombing of abortion clinics can all be evidence of this mind-set. While the faith principles behind such actions may be laudable, the practices do not reflect the character of God. Accordingly, spiritual helpers need to evaluate these types of behaviors as sin not spiritual growth along the Illuminative Way.

Second, Illuminative Way Christians attend to "Learnings" to love as God loves. During the Purgative Way, Christians learned the Great Commandment to love God and others. In the Illuminative Way, they deepen the understanding of that doctrine by bonding it with life experiences.

Long-term loving relationships are the best God-designed way for people to understand God's love, sacrifice and grace. This understanding of God's love is deepened with increased life experiences. The Illuminative Way is particularly good for making the connection between the love in life and the love of God. Assuming a positive relationship, when children move out of their nuclear family, they often realize all that their parents have done for them including the sacrifices of selves that their parents have made over the years. When this occurs, a simple parental statement (or a similar one made about them) can be spiritually instructive: "If you think that I love you, have sacrificed for you and given graciously to you, then you have a better understanding of God's love, sacrifice and grace." Correspondingly Jesus teaches, "Which of you, if his son asks for bread, will give him a stone? Or if he asks for a fish, will give him a snake? If you, then, though you are evil, know how to give good gifts to your children, how much more will your Father in heaven give good gifts to those who ask him?"[13] [Matthew 7:9-11] Furthermore, the love of spouses can also increase this God-understanding because spouses' loves are freely given, unearned and underserved – parents are "supposed" to love their children. The above important, but simple naming is an essential task for those who help others grow spiritually.

Finally, after young adults acknowledge parental love and young spouses experience deep love, they eventually move to teaching, modelling and sacrificing that "divine" love for others. Christians can acquire the deeper understanding that taking care of others is in essence doing what God wants, building the Holy Community (Kingdom) of God and serving Jesus at the same time. Jesus' parable that highlights this teaching concludes, "The King will reply, 'I tell you the truth, whatever you did for one of the least of these brothers (or sisters) of mine, you did for me.'"[14] [Matthew 25:40] Hopefully, as Christians serve other people, their actions develop into a godly manner of living. These "Learnings" occur especially when adults, trending toward middle age, have children who need taken care of. As a result of this life development, Christian parents begin to identify and appreciate the effort and importance of the love and care that their parents put into rearing them. As they are able to make this connection with the love of parents or other guardians, these adults comprehend how the Heavenly Parent has taken care of them. Certainly, having this life experience allows this learning to be most effective. Appreciation and praise for God becomes even more profound in this transition if the correlation between life and God is made. If this learning takes root, these Illuminative Way Christians value and increase their efforts to take care of and love others because they internalize how much God wants this to happen.

The corresponding danger for Illuminative Way Christians is that they can have the tendency to love only those other people whom they consider worthy. They may also focus on limiting their love by "taking care" of their own which can be as limited as individuals' immediate families. Clarifying what God intended by the word "neighbor"[15] – that love was to be extended to even enemies as agape love (unconditional positive regard, not necessarily warm-fuzzy feelings) – is designed to expand the understanding and the practice of divine love.

Third, Illuminative Way Christians attend to "Learnings" to see how God envisions value, importance and necessity in all of creation. As Christians learn the reasons for their faith and practice loving others, they gain decades of life experience. Accordingly, they have encountered an array of diverse situations, types of people and different viewpoints. If the love of God has guided their interactions, they have honestly seen value in these opposite positions. What have they done with them? How would God deal with the diversity? Illuminative Way Christians are invited to integrate and attain the broader perspective that God has in order to value the good and affirm the design for the creation. This third learning often occurs as adults move toward the empty nest syndrome when children leave home or employment seems to lose meaning. The limited activity or lessening of responsibility can enable them to see beyond their own lives.

These more mature Christians will typically show greater evidence of the personality characteristics that are identified as divine. The spiritual writers in the first fifteen hundred years of the Christian church summarized these emerging qualities both as the theological virtues of charity (love), hope and faith but also the moral virtues of prudence [careful intellectual discernment], justice [respecting the rights of others which needs perspective], fortitude [courage to do right in the midst of difficulty/danger] and temperance [restraint of the desire for sensual pleasures].

These virtues are seen in persons who exhibit measured discernment, who consider a variety of opinions in order to gain a larger perspective and who have the ability to speak and act on the truth even when to do so would be unpopular or dangerous. For example, people who formerly displayed prejudices will begin to see the good in those same people or situations previously distained. Alcoholics who seemed to be unable to quit drinking suddenly are able to successfully resist the temptation. Dyed in the wool politicians begin to work with those of differing viewpoints and for a common good. Significantly, these "divine" attitudes are not temporary, but have become part and parcel of these Christians' modes of operation.

While people may have these qualities as a "natural disposition," in order for these virtues to be steadfastly part of peoples' characters these new outlooks must be "engrafted" into them by God's Holy Spirit.[16] In addition, the list provided by the Apostle Paul which has been label the "Fruits of the Spirit" can also be used to discern the presence of divine qualities within Christians. I have often heard the teaching that people should work to acquire "love, joy, peace, patience, kindness, goodness, faithfulness, gentleness and self-control."[17] [Galatians 5:22-23] However, while these qualities may tend to be innate, they are truly "God-given gifts" typically bestowed during the Illuminative Way that cannot be earned. As Janet Ruffing explains, Christians grow "deeper and deeper into the life of God. New facets of the mystery [qualities] of God open for us. God indwells us, gifts us with the Spirit, and manifests love to the world, in and through us."[18]

FOCUS ON PHILIPPIANS

Some additional insights about the "Learnings" along the Illuminative Way can be gleaned from scripture. For centuries recommendations have been made or Illuminative Way Christians have discovered for themselves the value of the letter to the Philippians. The letter to the church at Philippi is written to Christians who had made much progress along the Spiritual Road. The references to joy, celebration and affirmation would signify Christians on the Illuminative Way. Paul's opening prayer for them includes:

"That your love may abound more and more in knowledge and depth of insight, so that you may be able to discern what is best and may be pure and blameless until the day of Christ, filled with the fruit of righteousness that comes through Jesus Christ – to the glory and praise of God."[19] [Philippians 1:10-11]

His hope for their increase in knowledge and spiritual insights points to learning that needs to take place on this second leg of Christians' faith-trek. In addition, Paul refers to them as "mature" people who need not just to believe but also to "suffer" for Jesus as well as to adopt his manner of living and thinking.[20] [Philippians 1:27-29] **This identification of and participation in divine intent also happens as knowledge leads to a deepened understanding**.

In chapter two, St. Paul encourages the Philippian Christians to literally "let this be thought in you."[21] [Philippians 2:5] Then in verses six through eleven, he goes on to describe the character of Jesus by quoting a poem that many scholars claim to be a hymn of the early church. The suggestion is that these Christians need to let this thinking be in them so as to "imitate" the attitude of Jesus in their daily lives. To have this "Mind of Christ" includes but is not limited to humility, servanthood and obedience – definite personality qualities that occur to Illuminative Way Christians. This classic section is worthy of careful studying, especially for Illuminative Way Christians, so as to gain from the deeply insightful teachings that are contained in it. Paul further emphasizes having a thought-based faith when he encourages the Philippians to focus on anything that is true, noble, right, pure, lovely, admirable, excellent or praiseworthy. He counsels that they put this mind-set into practice. When this is done, he claims, the God of peace will be with them.[22] [Philippians 4:8-9]

Learning in the form of thought development is encouraged in the letter to the Philippians. Part of this includes "What was Jesus thinking?" when he did whatever he was doing. Of course, people cannot completely merge with another's mind; but the process of digging deeper into the motivation and intention of Jesus allows spiritual growth for those who are ready. When, for example, Christians begin to understand how much Jesus gave up when he took human form, they begin to make a deeper personal connection with him. This is the purpose of the learning that is to take place along the Illuminative Way.

LEARNING FROM THE "LEARNINGS"

All of the above Illuminative Way "Learnings" potentially lead to great changes in Christians' knowledge, personality and how they handle life – not to mention a significant change in their personal spiritual relationship with God. In fact, so much is realized that people begin to believe that they have learned everything all by themselves – when in truth only God can infuse them so that they are able to think, feel and will as God. In addition, what is learned does not automatically enhance their personal spiritual relationship with God. All Illuminative Way "Learnings" moments need to be consciously lifted in prayer in order to strengthen, affirm and build the relationship with God. This is so simple; yet so profound. These prayers are best fashioned in the form of genuine thankfulness and appreciation for what has been learned and how God has changed Christians from within. They are called "prayers of the heart" which are generally more affective and spontaneous.

What happens in a marriage when partners don't say "Thank you" and offer appreciation when it is honestly due? The partners start taking each other for granted which begins a time of "creeping separateness." If not changed, the relationship stops growing, is ignored, becomes dull or non-existent and even leads to divorce. What happens in a marriage when partners do say "Thank you?" The people feel valued and more of the same is given and received. The relationship becomes special, enjoyable and enduring. Likewise, expressing a genuine "thank you" to God when people do not really have to (because it will not cause hard feelings if they don't) enhances the relationship. Prayer conversation with God raises the relationship to a higher or deeper level.

In summation, Illuminative Way Christians spend decades learning which corresponds to **loving God with their minds.** This typically includes, but is to not limited to, understanding what they believe, increasing the ability and depth of loving God/others as well as gaining a larger outlook on life that mimics how God sees, loves and integrates the multiplicity that makes up the creation. As this spiritual learning grows, a major transition normally takes place. **Indeed, two primary characteristics of Illuminative Way Christians are the decreasing of anxiety-driven behavior and the increasing display of positive divine qualities.**

Finally, as Christians move along the Illuminative Way, their "Learnings" curve bifurcates via a hopscotch movement into "Clarifications" and "Devotion." While learning, Christians also are involved in clarifying. While learning, Christians also become devoted.

Sometimes these next steps occur simultaneously. While I have elected to list "Clarifications" next in the steps along the Illuminative Way, "Devotion" may actually occur prior.

CLARIFICATIONS

I have listed "Clarifications" as a separate step in the Illuminative Way process, yet "Clarifications" often go hand in hand with the Illuminative Way "Learnings" that are taking place. **"Clarifications" is essentially about deepening the information and dogma that was gained during the Purgative Way.** The Purgative Way learning leaned heavily upon getting the facts and determining right from wrong. As Christians move onto the Illuminative Way, they begin the "Learnings" stage by asking honest questions designed to enhance and increase faith. Often times, some of the information they receive may seem at odds with what they already have learned. Now, they have more questions about the prior clear and definite "answers" which can often result in "shades of gray" kind of conclusions. This is not to say that people's Christianity is destroyed, actually it is most often enriched. Consistently this stream of questions leads to an extremely deep and unshakeable faith, which is God's purpose for the process of "Clarifications."

Making these statements may already put some Christians on guard, ready to defend anything that would potentially be changed from what they originally learned. Absolutely the most important concern, at least for helping people grow spiritually, is whether or not Christians' relationships with God are strengthened and deepened toward the intimacy and oneness that Jesus desired for all followers. If change makes the relationship better, then the change is good. If the change hinders or limits the relationship, it is not good. Thus, if "Clarifications" does not reinforce a people's faith, then do not go there. This also is a note of warning for spiritual helpers: **Assist in "Clarifications" only when it helps the personal spiritual relationship with God**.

The process of "Clarifications" is rarely easy and quite often demands great struggle in order to come to a place of relative peace and harmony. Much deep and sincere prayer over a period of time was absolutely needed for most all the "Clarifications" I have received and witnessed in others. I am fond of using a little comic relief for Christians in the midst of "Clarifications" by saying, "You know that it is absolutely true what Jesus said, 'The truth will set you free.'[23]... [John 8:32b] However, it is likely to make you miserable in the mean time!" This is my way to ease the tension of the topic and encourage people to continue the search for the truth of God, which is worth the effort.

THE MIND OF CHRIST

In essence, "Clarifications" relies on moving toward acquiring the "Mind of Christ." So I have reflected on what the apostle Paul has to say on this subject, which is so intricate I have included the scripture passage below.[24] [I Corinthians 2:6-11] Paul begins chapter two noting that he did not originally speak to the Corinthians relying on persuasive worldly thinking (superior wisdom). However in verse six, he is now ready to speak to mature Christians using his critical thinking skills, empowered by the Spirit of God.

We do, however, speak a message of wisdom among the mature,[25] but not the wisdom of this age or of the rulers of this age, who are coming to nothing. No, we speak of God's secret wisdom, a wisdom that has been hidden and that God destined for our glory before time began. None of the rulers of this age understood it, for if they had, they would not have crucified the Lord of glory. However, as it is written:

"No eye has seen,
no ear has heard,
no mind has conceived
what God has prepared for those who love him"[26] —
but God has revealed it to us by his Spirit.

The Spirit searches[27] all things, even the deep things of God. For who among men knows the thoughts of a man except the man's spirit within him? In the same way no one knows the thoughts of God except the Spirit of God. We have not received the spirit of the world but the Spirit who is from God, that we may understand what God has freely given us. This is what we speak, not in words taught us by human wisdom but in words taught by the Spirit, *interpreting spiritual truths to spiritual men*.[28] The man without the Spirit does not accept the things that come from the Spirit of God, for they are foolishness to him, and he cannot understand them, because they are spiritually discerned.[29] The spiritual man makes judgments about all things, but he himself is not subject to any man's judgment:

"For who has known the mind of the Lord
that he may instruct him?"[30]
But we have the mind of Christ.

In the above passage, the Apostle Paul is contrasting natural human wisdom with the kind of wisdom that God has. Especially noted is the "mysterious or secret" wisdom, which refers to God's plan to incarnate Jesus for the purpose of salvation. This wisdom was available only to God (or the Spirit) in that it was hidden for centuries, until God was ready to release the information. Even though it has been made known, some people do not understand it – only those who are "spiritually" minded have received it.

Many commentators make the point that the Spirit is revealing the meaning of Old Testament passages in order to refer to God's salvation in Jesus. The Spirit, who comprehends the "thoughts of God," can also teach them to whoever has access to the Spirit. This is how contemporary Christians grow spiritually toward intimacy and oneness with the Divine – they have received the Holy Spirit. Accordingly, the Apostle Paul claims that "We have the mind of Christ."[31] [I Corinthians 2:16] Nevertheless, St. Paul's assertion may be a little hyperbolic and presumptuous! It may be more accurate to say that Christians are growing into the mind of Christ.

The apostle argues in this passage that only an individual can know his or her own mind. I certainly can know myself, in part, especially as I seek to better know my own motives and mental abilities. However, I am dramatically assisted in knowing myself through the reflection from others; and actually I must have the knowledge that comes from others in order to totally know myself. In fact, often others see in me what I have not recognized in myself; and they can also assist me in deeper understanding of myself. The same is true in regard to the mind of Christ.

Who can know the mind of Christ? Yes certainly Christ can know his own mind. "In the same way no one knows the thoughts of God except the Spirit of God."[32] [I Corinthians 2:11b] If I have this mind infused into me, then I might potentially have access to this information. Belonging to Jesus by means of being "born from above" infers that the Spirit of God is placed within people or at the very least available to them.[33] [Romans 8:9] New Christians have this Holy Spirit placed within them although they still "groan" to be able to use it. And this Spirit has the ability to "search all things, even the deep things of God."[34] [I Corinthians 2:10] Thus, through what God has given, people have the ability to obtain the mind of Christ.

So, if Christians need to grow into this mind of Christ, how do they get there?

Certainly reading the Bible is a primary source for procuring information about Jesus and certainly for coming to understand some of his thinking. **On the other hand, having information or knowing what Jesus did and said is not having the mind of Christ.** Consider having the responsibility of judging an adulterous woman (as Jesus did in John 8:1-11) and the Law (of God) required that she be condemned to die. Jesus had this information that was included in the Law of God firmly fixed in his mind, but he did not make up his mind to put it into practice. Thus, having knowledge about how Jesus acted does not guarantee Jesus will do so exactly the same every time. In other words, having biblical knowledge and strictly applying (a Purgative Way approach) it is not the same as responding with the mind of Christ (Clarification that comes during the Illuminative Way). Although understanding what Jesus did can help and is the first place to start, it is not having the mind of Christ – only information about him.

What did God think would be the best way for people to obtain godly thinking? Laws and lessons helped for awhile, but proved not to be inadequate. Thus, God became incarnate, born in human flesh, in Jesus. In order to get to know the mind of God, people need to live with it; or as Jesus affirmed near the end of his earthly life, "Anyone who has seen me has seen the Father."[35] [John 14:9] While Jesus no longer lives on the earth, "the Counselor, the Holy Spirit, whom the Father will send in my name, will teach you all things and will remind you of everything I have said to you."[36] [John 14:26] The Spirit of God is given to all who believe so that they will be able to live toward obtaining the mind of Christ. But how do Christians get to that state of mind? Just like the Apostles did – by living with Jesus and learning daily. As they did, Christians increasingly approximate the mind of Christ. **Christians are a work in progress and so is having the mind of Christ.** In addition, Jesus' mind becomes available as two or more people are connected in his name and for his purposes. Having the mind of Christ is a progressive discernment process; accordingly, the spiritual step of "Clarifications" which requires deep discernment especially needs assistance from Christian helpers.

The Illuminative Way is the path on which Christians form the mind of Christ within them. During this passage, they are transformed by the renewal of their minds, moving toward consistently practicing the will of God in their living. **Via "Clarifications," Christians gain insight after insight; and God corrects their wrong concepts and "stinking thinking." As such, Christians gather deeper meanings from the scriptures, deeper insights into their own beings and greater ability to love God, self and others**.

About this time in the process, Christians realized that they are not really so smart as to be able to have made such tremendous transitions and know so much. And it dawns on them that God must have had something to do with this. In fact, maybe God has been doing all of their spiritual growth all along. But they reason, "I have done some of this, haven't I?" Then they begin to understand a deeper meaning to what they have been saying, "God does the work, if I cooperate." Yes, Christians have been trying; but God has been so much more in charge and working so much harder than they ever recognized. Consequently they are so thankful and deeply humbled at the same time. Their commitment is increased as they realize anew, on a much deeper level, that God has everything that they need. Finally, Christians affirm that those wonderful moments of prayer which they have experienced in the past have been God inviting them into a closer relationship where God desired to do even more for them. And they are moved to pray...

Something about this process of obtaining the mind of Christ via "Clarifications" is uniquely interesting and divinely profound. Christians receive a thinking-confidence that actually makes them stand straight and tall and then upon self-reflection drops them humbly down to their knees in prayer. But there is no shame in this dramatic turnabout because God knows that Christians need to exercise their minds in human thinking and spiritual discernment in order to arrive at this relational place. Actually, the reader may anticipate that this process of loving God with the human mind can lead to "Devotion" as well as to the "Mystery" of God.

THREE "CLARIFICATIONS" EXAMPLES

In order to explain this complex topic, I will provide three different ways that "Clarifications" can be manifested.

- ✝ Clarifications can be about modifying some of the originally learned Christian teachings.
- ✝ Clarifications can be about finding a larger common denominator by which to understand and validate seemingly conflicted issues.
- ✝ Clarifications can be about revising how Christians understand how to live.

Often "Clarifications" occur in regard to expanding the understanding of a teaching that was first learned. While these nuances rarely change the truth of the original instruction, they certainly can reorient Christians' belief structure as well as their life actions. These modifications certainly can have implications for other areas of Christians' daily life and spirituality.

Purgative Way Christians are typically younger and often necessarily centered on themselves (if not selfish). So, when it comes to the Christian teaching on love, they may have been taught the helpful rule: **J**esus first; **O**thers second and **Y**ourself last. Or as the acronym goes Christian J-O-Y comes as a result of living in this manner. Purgative Way Christians require structure in order to internalize the teachings and qualities of God. However, after living by this standard for a long time, Illuminative Way Christians, although they know that it is right to love others, start feeling burned out, depleted and sometimes even resentful that others are getting all the attention.[37]

For Illuminative Way Christians who know what is right and have been practicing love for others consistently, a "Clarifications" of Christian love is a promising next step. They might benefit from understanding what I call "teeter totter love." After reviewing the J-O-Y rule, I revisit the scripture from where this rule originated, "love your neighbor as you love yourself."[38] [Matthew 22:39] Then, I would teach: "We are to love others AS we love ourselves. This instruction indicates that we love others to the degree that we love ourselves or at the same time as we love others; assuming that is possible. There seems to be an inherent balance that is needed. Think about it as being on a teeter totter with yourself on one end and others at the opposite end. We need to have Jesus in the center of the relationship at the fulcrum so that the teeter totter goes up and down, giving both yourself and others a joyous ride, alternatively. There is a lot more J-O-Y and positive relational energy in a teeter totter ride than in always pushing someone else on a swing set. Since we already know and practice God's teaching to love others, it is more than ok to love ourselves also. In fact, that may actually be necessary in order to practice Jesus' teaching accurately – to love others AS we love ourselves."

This "Clarifications" does not actually change the teaching of Jesus but it does change its understanding and application. In my experience, women who need and receive this "Clarifications" experience it as freedom. Because they are "allowed" to take care of their own needs, they are especially freed to deal with stages of arrested emotional development which may have occurred between the ages of three to twelve. Because of such, many women feel guilty when trying to take the initiative or feel inferior when attempting to learn and make things (Erikson's stages three and four). These tendencies often keep them from "owning" their own spiritual faith or moving onto stage four, synthetic-conventional faith, of James Fowler's stages of faith. By being given biblical permission and spiritual encouragement not to have to love others before taking care of themselves often allows them to move forward in their personal relationship with God.[39]

For a second example, some forms of "Clarifications" that involve two very different ways of believing can be resolved through understanding them from a larger perspective that embraces both of the former ways of thinking. For example attempting to add the fractions one-quarter and two-thirds is not possible while maintaining each of their current forms. However, if one-quarter is translated into three-twelfths and two-thirds is converted into eight-twelfths, then they can be put together with the answer being eleven-twelfths.

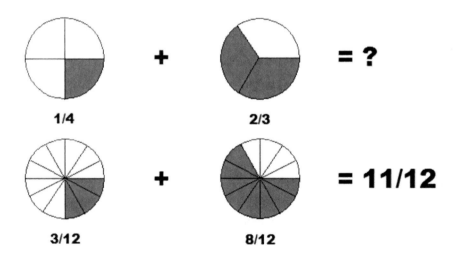

Graphic 6: Reconciling some information requires a new but common way of understanding similar to the way that different fractions need a common denominator in order to be added together for the answer. This is a form of "Clarifications."

Spiritual "Clarifications" can occur by similarly finding a larger common denominator by which to understand and validate seemingly conflicted issues. This action takes new thinking or a broader perception which typically must come from beyond the person. <u>Spiritual helpers are actually assisting Christians who are ready for "Clarifications" by gently introducing alternative ways of harmonizing paradoxical thoughts</u> or suggesting a book that might do the same. Nevertheless, some Christians are unwilling (and sometimes unable) to let their concepts of one-quarter or two-thirds go. Change is too difficult for them. If they are "forced" to do so, they will often rigidly hold to their former understanding. Spiritual helpers often wonder whether it is best to keep silent or offer suggestions to Christian travellers. The answer in this case is that spiritual helpers need to discern whether Christians are ready for "Clarifications" and to stop assisting with it when resistance to change or new insights are experienced.

With this in mind, Illuminative Way Christians may start asking questions, for example, about the creation of the world as recorded in the book of Genesis and compare that to the conclusions of scientists regarding the origins of the world. The results of the "debate" contrasts God's truth expressed in a literal inerrant reading of the Bible with following a strict evolutionary theory of natural selection. If "Clarifications" progresses on this subject, both positions can discover better ways of understanding that typically involve adopting new perspectives. For example, people can come to understand that statistical analysis indicates the extreme improbability of evolutionary theory, which is a statement of belief, actually occurring as described; on the other hand, people also discover how early biblical authors used stories to express spiritual truth but not necessarily facts. Thus, re-assessment is needed from both perspectives. People have offered various conclusions on both sides of this "debate." While objections continue, the important point is that both sides have and need to continue to find a common denominator in order to "solve the problem."

One reframing of this issue was offered by Pierre Teilhard de Chardin who was a paleontologist as well as a dedicated Roman Catholic priest.[40] His "creative thinking" concerning the creation-evolution question forged common ground between the two disciplines of religion and science at least to his satisfaction.[41] He affirmed a divinely created origin to the world and evidenced how God was still using the evolutional process to transform humanity into what God desired – a common ground that valued both religion and science.[42] Nevertheless, on the one hand, many scientists argued with some of his conclusions and on the other hand he was censored and shunned for many years by the church which has since re-evaluated its position.[43] The depth of Chardin's personal, albeit, mystical relationship with God and the extreme centrality of Christ in his faith are supremely evident in his writings, poetry and prayers. Simultaneously, Pierre Teilhard de Chardin was engaged in authentic scientific pursuits while holding an intellectually honest and unwavering Christian faith. He affirmed, not pitted, his Christian faith and his scientific endeavours. In fact, he saw a God, who was part and parcel, fully working in and through, the science he embraced. He found common ground in two seemingly conflicting vocations. While his conclusions are not the only ones, they are examples of how a larger perspective can incorporate different approaches to faith so as to allow for spiritual growth.

A simpler everyday example begins with the assertion that men and women are different. Some have gone so far as to promote the analogy men are from Mars and women from Venus. Following their natural inclinations men and women might never live harmoniously together. Because of the common denominator of love for each other and the purpose of maintaining that expanded form of understanding and living, men and women joyously and even divinely interconnect. Obtaining this common denominator from two different viewpoints is not easily accomplished. God's work of "Clarifications" is definitely needed in the "battle of the sexes" so "they are no longer two, but one."[44] [Mark 10:7-9]

The third example of "Clarifications" is about revising Christians' approach to life and faith which is rarely easy and almost always complex. I am including two vignettes to illustrate how "Clarifications" happen and also how to assist in the process of <u>reorienting the practice of faith</u>. The story about DeShawn is a fairly straight forward approach to a revised faith perspective. Natalie's narrative is more complex because it contains and clarifies not just a single insight but modifies a long-practiced life pattern with a new faith perspective. The better spiritual helpers know the people they accompany, the easier they can enable "Clarifications."

DeShawn is nearing fifty years old, married with two adult children and has faithfully practiced the Christian faith all of his adult life. He is currently an elder in a Protestant congregation, active in the Emmaus Walk movement and in regular spiritual direction for himself. During one of his sessions, he talked about a typical event which became a moment of insight. DeShawn began, "Pastor Robin had two funerals to officiate during Holy Week and on Wednesday before Easter asked if I would be willing to help with the Maundy Thursday worship service with a speaking part. I found out that it would be a reading; and since I would not have to prepare something original, I consented. The reading turned out to be a dramatic portrayal of Judas Iscariot's perspective on how he decided to hand Jesus over to the authorities. Afterward, so many people told me how much they appreciated my presentation and how much they got out of it. But," DeShawn squeamishly said, "I'm not sure that I liked that."

His spiritual director interjected, "That experience seemed to have had an impact on you. Could you say more about what happened to you?" DeShawn continued, "I guess I did a really good job conveying what Judas was thinking and how he felt so I must have really gotten into him or he got into me." "What do you mean," inquired his director? "I think we must all have a little of Judas inside of us," exclaimed DeShawn! "Can you tell me what you are thinking?" was the director's response. "Well, Judas had some mixed feelings about what he was about to do. But ultimately he decided to do what he wanted – what he thought was best. He was self-motivated – selfish. Then after he concluded that he knew what was best to do, he started rationalizing how hurting and disappointing his friends and others was ok. He convinced himself that he was right. That's when I started to feel a little uncomfortable, especially since I was able to communicate so effectively."

"I sense that was a little painful for you," said his director. "So are you saying that there is a little of Judas inside of you and that you are uneasy with that realization?" "Yes. That's it. I think a lot about what I will do and can easily conclude that what I want is what is best; then I convince myself that it is also the best for others who might be hurt," DeShawn replied. "I see," affirmed his director. "DeShawn, is there anything good about feeling uncomfortable like this?" DeShawn thought for a moment and then answered, "It causes me to realize what I am actually thinking and I feel really bad about such self-centeredness." "And what good might come out of this kind of self-examination," probed the director? "Hopefully, it will cause us to think about living the way God wants and to strength our relationship with God" was his synopsis. "Yes," agreed his director. "I hope that you might do that for yourself. Examine how you might have the tendency to act like Judas with self-interest and then justifying your conclusions. After all these years of being as good a Christian as you can be, it is hard to realized that Judas' tendencies are still inside of you. Perhaps God is trying to show you more about yourself than you have previously known. Please consider how this might be true and include those insights in your prayers."

At various times, as Christians participate in typical church programs, they will gain new insights which actually can change their faith understandings and their way of living as Christians. The "Clarifications" that DeShawn experienced helped to clarify his Christian faith. He, like Judas, had lived following Jesus for a long time; and he had a little of Judas' tendencies toward self-conviction and justification inside of him. <u>This experience of "Clarifications" humbled DeShawn and enabled him to live more cautiously and aware of whether he was attuned to God's Will or his own.</u> (This spiritual direction session ended with a discussion of the importance of prayer which is included in chapter sixteen, "Prayer Forms.")

The second "Clarifications" story is about Natalie. Natalie is a very intelligent, single woman in her forties who is solidly on the Illuminative Way. Natalie had been a Christian for a long time and had practiced her faith in numerous ways especially when it came to those most marginalized by society for whom she held deep compassion and concern. As a second career, she entered seminary, at first to find new ways to help the disadvantaged, but had expanded her focus toward other "caring-for" ministries. Natalie had a solidly resolved Christian faith to which she was definitely committed. However, she also saw herself as open and flexible. This personality characteristic was discovered at her second spiritual direction session following a discussion of how she used qualifying words and phrases like "it could also be," "perhaps," and "but also" to offer alternative explanations. Natalie could always find good in every situation and each person in her life – it was one of her personality strengths as well as a result of her Christian approach to life. As a thinking person, she would attempt to weigh every option until she had balanced different perspectives that included finding God in the current circumstances. Natalie was a person who God was using to strengthen God's Holy Community.

Natalie was not about to change her faith, but to clarify it.

At a later session, Natalie and her spiritual director were talking about her genuine openness to opportunities that presented themselves in her life. Her director rejoined, "Yes. I certainly see how you go with the flow." Natalie reacted negatively to the phrase "go with the flow" which she explained meant to her that she would be a person who would not follow through. She continued by asserting that she was a person who was committed to what she would do and would complete whatever she started. Her director affirmed he had no intention of inferring that she would be inconsistent or irresponsible with his comment of "going with the flow." He only saw his comment as a re-phrasing of her reference to "openness."

After coming to the agreement about the meaning of their words, the director asked, "Natalie, how do you decide between ministry opportunities when you have a choice?" She noted that besides how she would feel about any particular form of helping, she would also evaluate practical information like type of job, salary and location. Then, she would just choose. She noted that subsequently she would always be open to and able to find how God was working in whatever situation she found herself. Then Natalie gave an example. Previously, in a peer supervision group, Natalie had talked about a ministry experience where she was feeling unfulfilled which she expressed; "I was not getting what I needed." After saying what was going on, Natalie came back to the group a week later to commentate that the situation was not as bad as she had previously noted and that there were a lot of good people and things happening there. Her director rephrased, "So you used your thinking to find some good in that place even though at first you were experiencing un-fulfilment?"

Natalie paused and looked away. Then she continued, "Sometimes I have a tendency to be committed for too long." When asked to say more about that, Natalie described a previous job in which she was increasingly unhappy, but could still see some good being accomplished. She stayed and stayed... until the job ended when funding ran out. This "forced" unemployment led to her decision to enter seminary.

Her director queried, "If you had been clear and definite about how you were feeling at this job, what would have happened?" "I probably would have quit; but I am not a quitter and people were still being helped," she objected. With gentle patience, the director wondered, "Natalie, do you think that if you are unambiguous about feeling negative in a particular situation that you don't have options?" "I don't know; maybe," was her hesitant response. In this crucible moment, the director asked if he might summarize what he had heard to see if Natalie agreed.

"What I have heard you express is that when you start feeling negative about a particular situation, you will typically work to find God in that place. By citing moments when God is found and how good is being done, you tend to push aside any negative feelings you have and sometimes will stay committed for too long, especially since you don't want to be considered a quitter. Did I summarize that about right?" "Yes. That is pretty much it," Natalie concurred. Her director continued, "Since you can find God and good, you don't seem to have any option but to stay. But I want to suggest that there is another way to look at this without denying your negative evaluation and without being a quitter. Is it possible that God may be using your un-comfortableness to push you in another direction? If so, you would be free to follow God's prompting; you would have the option to embrace a greater openness."

"Yes I think that is right" she responded. Then she began to think out loud, putting into her own words, what was being suggested. Reflecting helped her process this new way of thinking and also affirmed the revised approach to Christian faith that was being revealed for her. Further conversation suggested that Natalie could have a negative evaluation of her situation and still choose to stay the course – just like Jesus clearly did not like going to the cross with the phrase "Let this cup pass from me"[45] [Matthew 26:39] but chose to go forward anyway. The eighth chapter of Luke was referenced as an example of Jesus being clear about what he was going to do, yet remaining open in the midst of that action. He was headed to heal the little daughter of Jairus when he stopped to affirm the woman who touched the hem of his garment (time during which the little girl died).[46] [Luke 8:40-56] Near the end of this clarifying process, Natalie stated, "I see that there is a difference between finding God wherever I am and following where God wants me to go."

At that point, Natalie's director concluded, "You have worked really hard today. I feel sure that pondering all of this would not only be appropriate but also helpful. So in your prayers and in your writing, you might reflect on how your great ability to find God in everything can limit you from following where God wants you to go. You might consider how using your qualifying words and explanations sometimes keeps you from being authentically clear about how you are feeling and even keeps you committed for too long. Remember, being clear about whom you are and how you are feeling does not have to limit your openness. It actually can allow you to be more open to following God."

THE VALUE OF "CLARIFICATIONS"

How does "Clarifications" contribute to the overall process of personal spiritual growth and development? Or in other words why go through such really hard work?

First, "Clarifications" paradoxically re-focuses Christians toward trusting God more completely. This happens because Christians realize that they don't know as much as they thought they knew. When Christians begin travelling along the Illuminative Way, they have changed their lives, have come through hard times, and have established a "Basic Trust" in God. They pretty much feel like they "have it all together." As Illuminative Way Christians eagerly seek to learn and grow, they naturally ask questions that move them into

"Clarifications" which becomes a humbling experience designed by God to increase their trust, reliance and love for God. Their questions provide greater clarity, but at the same time give rise to more and more questions until they are respectfully surprised that Christianity, God and faith are bigger than they ever fully comprehend. Their continuous questioning may lead them into the experience of Christian Mystery, discussed below – which is also humbling. Accordingly, "Clarifications" is also a great corrective to the strong tendency toward spiritual pride that exists at this juncture of faith.

Secondly, as Christians' eyes are open to more of what they did not know, they may say: "I need to trust God more; I need to listen to God more; I need to be open to the greater 'God possibilities' in my life." **As a result, they voluntarily surrender more of themselves, begin to listen more carefully in prayerfulness, and come to believe and look for the meaning and purpose that God must have for their lives.** This response is analogous to Peter's yielding exclamation, "Lord, to whom shall we go? You have the words of eternal life. We believe and know that you are the Holy One of God."[47] [John 6:68-69] Indeed, "Clarifications" brings the fuller knowledge and appreciation for the height, depth, width and length of God's love, which in turn increases allegiance and fidelity. Accordingly, Illuminative Way Christians increasingly commit more and more of their lives and their selves to God. They consecrate their hands, feet, voice, money, intellect, will and heart all to God. This is the theme of "Take My Life and Let It Be"[48] which reflects deepening faith that Illuminative Way "Learnings" and "Clarifications" engender, moving toward "Devotion."

Third, as Christians increasingly trust and rely on God, they typically come to believe that God has plans and purpose for them because God deeply cares about them. They desire to discover these plans yet they feel like they only have pieces to the puzzle. While they search, sometimes Christians lovingly cling to a verse of scripture that affirms their conviction: "For I know the plans I have for you," declares the Lord, 'plans to prosper you and not to harm you, plans to give you hope and a future.'"[49] [Jeremiah 29:11] The process of "Clarifications" can be instrumental in putting together part of this picture. "Clarifications" such as Natalie went through are often contained in the patterns of thought and behavior. Because of the complexity and number of topics to be discussed and integrated, uncovering these patterns may take a number of sessions, or a long session. However, helping people to significantly understand how they can live their faithfulness in new ways frequently assists them toward discovering their life's meaning and purpose. This intensifies God's greatness, sovereignty and deep concern for them.

Fourth, "Clarifications" broadens and enlarges not only Christian understanding but also the ability to draw closer together into the "Family of God" with other Christians as God intends that they all may be one.[50] [John 17:20-21] In addition, "Clarifications" makes it possible for Christians to want to move out beyond themselves in discovery, appreciation and assistance of other people. Their love for God's people and God's creation grows deeper. Assisting with concentric faith development, connecting belief and action, is an especially important goal for those who help others at this point in their Christian growth.

In summary, the process of "Clarifications" is rarely easy and often very complex; it takes time and thought-provoking work. Scores of Christians never ever attempt to clarify their faith and hence slow their travel along the Spiritual Road. On the other hand, making new, clarifying faith discoveries can bring Christians to greater openness and depth in their experience of God. It can be very rewarding and also greatly amplify their love for God.

A WORD ABOUT "MYSTERY"

The term "mystery," at least in the religious arena, does not indicate something that has a solution like a mystery novel or a mathematical problem, but refers to concepts that are irreconcilable. This kind of mystery exists even in science. For example, when physicists study the properties of light, they consistently arrive at conflicting conclusions – light appears as a continuous wave but also as intermittent particles. Logically, light must either be a wave or a particle – but in the human experience it is both. This is a "mystery" to be received and lived with.

On the other hand, there are problems, which seem like "mysteries" that can be clarified, even within faith. For instance, a book or e-reader definitely seems solid but scientists unequivocally inform people that objects are not solid but actually molecularly particles in constant motion – people only experience the firmness. As a second illustration, anyone who has lived long enough comes to realize that many random events occur in life that make life seem chaotic; the same is true for the actions of the molecules and their components that make up the universe. However, chaos theory claims that such randomness, if seen from a long-term, broad perspective, actually constructs patterns. The suggestion is that the larger the perspective the more clearly paradoxical thoughts can be understood.

What does this interplay between "Clarifications" and Christian Mystery have to do with spiritual growth and relationship with God?

At first glance, mystery and "Clarifications" seem to be at odds with each other – but they are not. "Clarifications" is the process of increasing understanding by learning new information which often happens through using a different or broader perspective. **Mystery occurs when the process of "Clarifications" brings the same or similar conflicting results** – then the ideas cannot be solved, dissolved or resolved. Accepting the unanswerable-ness is the answer. In religious terms, it is mystery. Christianity has some of these mysteries. For example, the orthodox pronouncement of the faith is that God is both three persons and one God. Similarly, Jesus is also proclaimed to be both God and human. Other Christian mysteries include the precise nature of God, the relationship between predestination and free will, as well as the interconnection between love, power and justice. "Clarifications" of such subjects consistently lead to the same irreconcilable results.

While complete comprehension of the mysteries of the Christian faith is not possible, learning and clarifying what can be understood about "mysteries," especially while on the Illuminative Way, is extremely important. Thousands of Christians have written on these complex subjects. And using the process of "Clarifications" can significantly increase understanding on these and other topics. **Doing so actually furthers the appreciation for the wisdom and greatness of God, which enhances the personal spiritual appreciation and faith in God**. Such attempt at "Clarifications" is very good. In fact, the scripture even affirms the process. After encouraging a strong and persistent personal effort to strengthen believers' faith, it concludes: "If any of you lacks wisdom, he should ask God, who gives generously to all without finding fault, and it will be given to him."[51] [James 1:5] There are even vignettes of saints, fully immersed in deep Unitive Prayer, who emerge from a vision with understandings that they cannot explain and sometimes are instructed not to attempt explanation. The assumption is that God has revealed to them something that cannot be communicated – a mystery. On the other hand, St. Paul, talking about the process of growing spiritually, affirms the existence of faith mysteries that will become clear later, "Now we see but a poor reflection as in a mirror; then we shall see face to face. Now I know in part; then I shall know fully, even as I am fully known."[52] [I Corinthians 13:12]

Truly, mystery can occur at anytime throughout the process of spiritual development. For example, at the beginning of faith, Pre-Christian Way people may simply not be able to comprehend how such a great God would want to love weak and fallible human beings. That experience is a Christian mystery because people will never understand how that is true. Perhaps, the best explanation is that loving is the essence of who God is. However, while pondering this mystery can help Christians to expand the definition of perfect love, they can only approximate understanding God's love or desire to love people. It is mystery. In the final analysis, mystery will always exist purely and simply because humans are not divine – yet. Some things people simply cannot know because of the limits of the human condition. **While "Learnings" and "Clarifications" can draw people closer to God, the appreciation of divine mystery at appropriate moments along the Spiritual Road also does the same**.

From a spiritually developmental perspective, "Learnings" and Clarifications" are part of the process that enables Christians to understand, within their limitations, the greatness of God with their minds. This process ushers a deep commitment and trust that prepares them for an even deeper relationship with God. The next chapter about the Dark Night of the Spirit describes how Christians, as part of spiritual developmental growth, need to voluntarily yield the use of their personal abilities and will, which includes their formerly God-ordained striving to understand. They have been prepared and are invited to abide in the Mystery. **Indeed, the farther along the Spiritual Road that Christians travel, the more likely they will embrace mystery – and need to do so**.

Spiritual helpers have the opportunity to encourage Illuminative Way Christians to learn and clarify their faith understandings. This can be done through Bible studies, suggested materials or in conversations. Whether to do so depends, in part, on whether the learning and clarifying is strengthening the depth of people's relationship with God? Spiritual helpers also have the opportunity to affirm contact with true mysteries of the faith. Are the people they help ready to surrender intellectual searching and striving? Is coming to accept mystery an important part of "falling" into the embrace of God, of more deeply trusting?

DEVOTION

As expressed above, Illuminative Way Christians are often highly motivated to grow spiritually and learn anything and everything. These "Learnings" spawn both insightful "Clarifications" and lavish "Devotion" which are not necessarily linear and may be simultaneously, as well as alternatively, experienced.

As Christians learn more in depth about Jesus' heart, mind and will, they more completely grasp the character of God. As Jesus noted, "Anyone who has seen me has seen the Father."[53] [John 14:9] As "Clarifications" cause Christians to gain deeper understanding, they not only love God but also know why they love. Accordingly, **Christians become more committed with each successive transformation and with each confirmation**. As a result, the Purgative Way's "Basic Trust" grows into a mature and satisfying faithfulness. It becomes "Devotion."

"Devotion" is about profound love given and received. Devotion is seen as deep commitment; it is evidenced in the earnest desire to live a godly life; and it is expressed as having Jesus as a true friend. This "Devotion" is expressed in many forms and in different ways although certain characteristics definitely accompany it across the long decades of the Illuminative Way.

First, Christians love God sincerely – not that they didn't love God before, but this form has a qualitative difference. Part of this increase in love comes from deeper appreciation of God via the "Clarifications" of faith. Part of this increase in love can come when Christians' actions of loving neighbors enriches the Presence of God. However, <u>most of this increase in love comes because God has infused love into Christians who respond with acts of devotion</u>. This augmented faith occurs when Christians, who become humbled via greater knowledge and life experience, have surrendered "all that they have and all that they are." From this point on, God increasingly becomes the initiator and director of the spiritual life. Indeed, the farther along the Spiritual Road that Christians travel God does more of their spiritual growth and Christians do less – assuming that they don't stop believing and doing.

No longer do Christians go to Mass because that is required; they go because they want to. No longer do Christians read the Bible because they are supposed to; they study because of how much closer to God they feel when they do. No longer to Christians begrudgingly give their twenty dollar contribution during worship; they instead generously give because God is creating a New Earth with what is not really theirs in the first place. Christians no longer do the "right thing" of helping others; instead they have totally invested themselves with godly service in the form of direct participation. Devotion propels itself into pure praise and selfless service.

Second, Christians' sincere love for God morphs into an earnest desire to participate in spiritual things. In fact, Christians begin to see God, to have "God sightings" or "recollections," in the entire world around them. They are sensitive to and aware of how thoroughly God permeates the creation. In addition, the love for God is so natural and certain that Christians are not concerned whether other people approve or not. Their goal is to live life totally devoted to God and the things of God, which now becomes increasingly seen as all of life. Arthur Devine states it this way: "The fundamental virtue of this state is recollection, that is, a constant attention of the mind and of the affections of the heart to thoughts and sentiments which elevate the soul to God... as well as attention to God in all our actions."[54]

Such deep, devoted commitment to God and God's ways comes from the conviction that not only is God in charge but also has people's best interest at heart. As a result, Christians will equally accept the blessings or consolations of life as well as the corrections, difficulties or desolations. Why? Because "we know that in all things God works for the good of those who love him, who have been called according to his purpose."[55] [Romans 8:28] A cute, but still meaningful story from my life can illustrate this unwavering devotion of seeing God work even in the more disconcerting moments of life.

In 1985, I attended a two week spiritual direction intensive retreat with twenty-three other people. Three years earlier, I had discovered and acknowledged that my life purpose, from God's perspective, could be summarized as "to love the strong-willed women in my life." It was a form of penance for attitudes and actions confessed. On the first day of the retreat, the leader announced, "I was going to divide you up into groups of four for the rest of the retreat, but I think that I will just let the Holy Spirit do the selecting. So, take a moment, breathe a couple of calming breathes and allow God to guide you when I ask you to select yourselves into a small group."

When the process began, I watched, almost like an out of body experience, as one woman from the left side of the large circle pointed to a woman directly across from her on the opposite side of the circle. Together, without getting out of their seats, they looked to a woman who was directly opposite of me. Then, simultaneously as if divinely scripted, all three women looked directly at me and smiled. All I could do, and literally did, was look up at Heaven, shook my finger at God and smiled as I said, "It's not fair that I know these things." I was acknowledging, in my most typical humorous-sarcastic way, that I knew God was going to strongly challenge me; and I was ok with that. It did not matter what difficulty I would go through; because I had surrendered to God and was convicted of God's perfect love, I was devotedly certain that God would work to make good things happen. In case the reader was were wondering, oh yes, those three were among the most strong-willed women at the retreat. The women certainly did not disappoint me; and neither did God. Both the gut-wrenching challenges and the divine healing that took place at that retreat formatted the rest of my life, which would not have happened without having a devoted trust in God that allowed me to go through those experiences certain of God's love.

Third, friendship with Jesus is offered and develops to a heightened degree. Christians travelling along the Purgative Way sometimes refer to Jesus as a personal friend. They have been accepted and graced into the Community of God which was likely to have been the most invigorating feeling and the greatest relationship they had experienced to date. Indeed, God's grace is freely given to usher people into Christianity, and people may feel that they have been befriended, when actually they have only been "saved." This expression of "friendship" is not the same as that which is endowed via the Illuminative Way step of "Devotion." In fact, the Christian-Jesus relationship along the Purgative Way is necessarily more like a student to a teacher or a servant to a master although a benevolent one.

At the point of "Devotion" along the Illuminative Way, Jesus, because it is the right time, declares, "I no longer call you servants, because a servant does not know his master's business. Instead, I have called you friends, for everything that I learned from my Father I have made known to you."[56] [John 15:15] The "master's business" includes intimate knowledge (deep "Learnings") coupled with clarity of the master's intentions ("Clarifications"). Jesus and Christians are now partners in this business venture and a devoted friendship is offered. Indeed, **Christians come to have Jesus as their friend not because they resolve him to be so, but because Jesus declares that into being** as a voluntary act of love which actually increases Christians' attachment.

This "friendship" that Jesus gives to the Apostles near the end of his earthly life is bestowed absolutely as a result of lives lived with intention and obedience. The same is true about the friendship that God gives to Christians at this point along the Illuminative Way. Indeed, this devoted friendship does not supersede but is foundational to all that has gone before. In other words, this friendship does not give license to do anything that Christians desire; instead it is actually contingent on obedience.

In addition, Jesus was very clear, "You are my friends if you do what I command."[57] [John 15:14] Purgative Way Christians will tend to say, "I don't want to have to obey someone for them to be my friend."[58] On the other hand, for mature Illuminative Way Christians, obedience is not a problem for they have been doing that for a long time and deeply understand why they will continue to do so. They also realize that it is not about their wanting Jesus for a friend; but it is totally about Jesus offering to be their friend, offering his "sacred heart" to them. These Christians are humbled and exhilarated at the same time by the magnitude of this proposal... they experience "Devotion."

Think of the dynamics of this Jesus friendship-devotion in this way. Teenagers, like Christians, have been graced into their family of origin. They may desire to have keys to the family car. But just because they want this gesture of "friendship" does not mean that it will (or should) be given. When they become sixteen years old, teens may believe that they have the right to the gift of those keys. However, the vehicle is the property of the parents who bought and maintain it; who treat it with respect; who honor the privilege it is; and who abide by the laws and intention that go along with driving. The keys to the family car are appropriately *gifted* at the right time – when the teens are ready to be junior partners in the family business. When is the right time? When teenagers are humbled and exhilarated at the same time by the gift; when they honor and respect the gift; and when they are totally devoted to the commands of the ones who have given the gift. This is not a gift that teens can expect just because they reach a particular age. However, their readiness can be demonstrated by the consistent practice of obedience; then parents can bestow the gift, like God did with the gift of Jesus, at the right time. "You see, at just the right time, when we were still powerless, Christ died for the ungodly."[59] [Romans 5:6] Likewise, the friendship of Jesus is granted at the καιρος time.

Accompanying this time of "Devotion" and friendship given is a kind of communication that may be best described as "mystical" in nature. While Christians have prayed to God for many years; now they definitely "hear" the voice of God being returned to them. If they do not "hear" the voice of God, they sense the Presence of God clearly guiding them. This may be also understood as the "prompting" of the Holy Spirit.

Accordingly a fourth characteristic of "Devotion" is that conversational and "affective" prayers become more typical and a sense of the Holy Spirit is received. Christians' predominate type of prayer begins to change in part because the Christian-Jesus relationship has begun to deepen. "Contemplative Prayer" is often used to name this style of praying. Greater trust has increased the intimacy; also comfortableness in the relationship brings a freedom of expression that is evidenced both as speaking "from the heart" as well as a dedicated, intense listening for God's words. Prayer becomes more spontaneous and full of feeling, even if the praying is not spoken with passionate emotion. In addition, without getting into an entire explanation of the theology of the workings of the Holy Spirit, God allows divine words to be heard – in part because of the closer Christian-Jesus relationship and because the communication will now be understood more in the context and with the intention with which it is given.

Many younger Christians, especially those who grow up in a church atmosphere, often develop excellent praying skills that seem very natural and just like talking to God. This is not contemplative prayer. (In fact, some people can speak publicly in ways that sound very much like the give and take of "Contemplative Prayer" but without having received the friendship God bestows that allows for an interactive, contemplative prayer life. This is not necessarily hypocritical except in case where the pray-er claims to hear the voice of God.) Now, I do not want to say that God cannot "talk" loud enough for anyone to hear because God can and does do that from time to time. However, in my experience, most of these Christians have not experienced enough life to freely surrender in a way that merits God's "gifting the keys to the family car." These Christians are communicating very freely and friendly to God, which is a good thing; and they certainly are being well prepared for contemplative prayer from the human communicating side of it. However, God realizes when Christians are not at the level of intimacy contained in "Devotion" and so God is not ready to initiate a marriage proposal. Truly, God will determine when Holy Spirit communication is appropriate to be given – even the most mature Christians cannot manufacture it.

DEVOTION AND THE HOLY SPIRIT

Earlier in this chapter, I alluded to another gifting that God gives, which often happens during the step of "Devotion" – the receiving of the Gifts of the Holy Spirit or the Fruits of the Spirit. As with the gift of spiritual friendship, these are given when God knows that Christians are ready. Christians should indeed yearn for the higher gifts and train themselves with skills and abilities that parallel these Spirit qualities. However, they are gifts which God gives via the activity of the Holy Spirit and cannot be humanly manufactured even though some basic inclination may exist. In other words, the Spirit's gift of "peace" can be approximated by certain nonchalant attitudes and de-stressing techniques, but only God can change Christians so that they naturally and without effort are intrinsically peaceful.

The fruits of the Spirit are bestowed during the Illuminative Way not only because Christians have been living with their hearts in the right place but also because they understand why and what they are living. People often think that they can make themselves loving like God or joyful like God, but they can't. While Christians should yearn for the Fruits of the Spirit, they cannot make them happen. However, because they are moving through the Illuminative Way and are experiencing a transformative life, God's Holy Spirit may provide one or more spiritual gifts – given as confirmation of the budding divine-human conjunctive relationship. Christians have come to this overall spiritual life attitude, not because life is so easy or they have learned to do so, but because God has graced them. As a result of their deeper relationship with God, Christians have been prepared for and immersed into a spiritual quality that is like God's character.

Now I particularly have made these distinctions for the benefit of spiritual helpers regarding interactive prayer and the Holy Spirit's gifts. Accordingly, some Christians may wonder why they do not hear God answer their prayers or why they don't have the gift of patience they have been trying to obtain. It may be important to help them understand that hearing God or getting a spiritual gift is not about what Christians can do to "cause" God to respond; it happens ONLY when God determines they are ready (and assumes that they continue to practice good spirituality). Thus, for Purgative Way Christians who want to "hear" God, they can be encouraged to focus on the written Word of God as a way to "hear" what God has spoken and also grow closer toward the mind, heart and will of God which is the necessary human preparation for God's real-time messaging. However, it is not the same kind of "hearing" that takes place for Illuminative Way Christians through Spirit communication via contemplative prayer. In addition, those who assist Illuminative Way Christians certainly will want to help them understand that what is heard during prayer can have one of three sources – from God, from the person praying or from the demonic. Chapter twenty-three, "Spiritual Helper Mode of Operation," has more about this discernment.

To recap, Illuminative Way Christians taking "Devotion" steps are typically transported into a new level of spiritual faith, especially in regard to the communication of God in their prayers but also through the receiving of the gift of God's Spirit in different forms.

EXPRESSION OF "DEVOTION"

Finally, Christian "Devotion" is definitely not cookie-cutter in form. **"Devotion" manifests itself in a variety of expressions often as a direct result of the prominent activities and personal emphases in Christians' lives.** In historical descriptions of spiritual growth, "Devotion" often meant spending extended time in deep prayer. Images of priests and religious lying prostrate on the floor of Cathedral naves come to mind. Indeed, the Illuminative Way naturally leads Christians to pray more and seek to spend copious amounts of time with God. However, this predisposition toward internal spiritual expression is not the only way to "Devotion" which can also include outward and tangible displays. Upon occasion, Illuminative Way Christians can use encouragement to explore ways other than prayer that are available to express the "Devotion" they have. In such cases, I may ask, "Where is your energy or passion?" After they describe some person, activity or cause, I will ask the follow up question, "Does God have anything to do with this?" Then, consider if they are (or could) use this passion as a way for expressing enduring love for and with God. Does this action enable the mutual spiritual "Devotion" between God and them? If so, its conscious pursuit as a form of "Devotion" will enhance their personal spiritual relationship with the divine.

As such, "Devotion" can emerge via Christians' preferred path. If they enjoy serving others, then they may choose to increase their extent and intensity of service. If they enjoy learning and teaching, they may decide to put emphasis on deeper understanding. If they have a passion to have others experience the redemption and "saving grace" of Jesus, then they may want to hone their skills as an evangelist. Rearing a family for the good of God can be "Devotion" especially if it is focused on changing generational destructive patterns.

Persons who are always found helping in the church kitchen or loving God as a consistent fixture in worship can also be participating in spiritual "Devotion." All are ways to love God; all are ways to increase one's faith; and all are ways to connect with God in a closer relationship. In terms of application of spiritual gifts, the apostle Paul affirms the use of one's preferred path: "If it is serving, let him serve; if it is teaching, let him teach; if it is encouraging, let him encourage; if it is contributing to the needs of others, let him give generously; if it is leadership, let him govern diligently; if it is showing mercy, let him do it cheerfully."[60] [Romans 12:7-8] Clearly, these external activities must have a conscious and primary component in order to be true "Devotion" – they must be about giving and receiving profound love between God and the individual.

A warning: Spiritual pride is a great danger on this particular part of the Spiritual Road. Illuminative Ways Christians are so convicted and so zealous because of all that God has done for them that they proudly show off their beloved to the world. However, in the process, they may elevate themselves and forget God. They forget that they are not getting better by themselves, they are not getting more knowledgeable on their own and they are not serving because they have become so righteous. In other words, their "Devotion" becomes about what they do instead about thanksgiving for how God brought them to this place. Accordingly, **the actions of pure praise and selfless service become the indicators of true "Devotion."** Spiritual pride may be the most insidious sin of all because it can hide so easily and be so untouchable in all types of "good" actions. If genuine humility does not accompany acts of "devotion" either externally or internally, then spiritual pride may be dangerously close. May clergy and other spiritual helpers without their own personal spiritual helper beware!

In review, "Learnings," "Clarifications" and "Devotion" are not automatically or linearly experienced. However, they are interconnected and contingent on each other. In fact, over the sometimes three to four decades of the Illuminative Way, Christians will cycle through these qualities as "Learnings" may lead to "Devotion" or "Clarifications" may provide additional questions for new "Learnings" and so forth. In addition, there is a developmental inclination to apply whatever has been learned, clarified or is deeply loved. Indeed, spiritual growth cannot progress without some form of application.

MISSION AND GENERATIVITY

While the classic authors who write about the Spiritual Road typically list only three steps during the Illuminative Way, I believe an additional phase, which I label "Mission and Generativity," is necessary and actually takes place. I suspect this difference is primarily due to the original writers' emphasis on prayer and the internal dynamic of the spiritual path – which is about the change that occurs between the "soul" and God. Indeed, God changes souls internally through "Learnings," "Clarifications" and "Devotion;" and individuals respond with knowledge, clarity and deep love for God. While this change should be affirmed via prayer **unless that personal character transformation is extended into the world in people's "vocation," spiritual growth becomes arrested.** Thus, encouraging Christians to apply their matured faith not only enriches their spirituality but also makes a significant impact of Christianity upon the world. Moving into "Mission and Generativity" naturally allows this application of faith to happen and is precisely the result of the changed internal relationship between God and individuals.

"Mission and Generativity" is a spiritual growth category that includes and may best be understood in terms of its developmental life dimension. **"Mission" involves reaching out to care for others; "Generativity" is naturally motivated by the perpetuation of self**.

Consider the natural development toward the service of others. Because teens and young adults need to gain skills and abilities, it is relatively impossible for them to be altruistic. When people are consumed with the responsibilities of family and career, service beyond this focus is severely limited by time and energy. However, when these responsibilities have ended, the ability to more intentionally help others can emerge. As adults live longer and with better health, middle aged adults have greater opportunity to provide service to others before and even including the need to take care of ailing parents. **In fact, honoring the spiritual value of serving others in terms of "Mission" becomes exceptionally important.** Carl Jung says: "Among all my patients in the second half of life— that is to say over thirty-five—there has not been one whose problem in the last resort was not that of finding a religious outlook on life."[61] Indeed, by the second half of life, service and mission become easier and more vital. Part of the reason for this is that people begin to understand their finitude – they anticipate dying and think about what they leave after they are gone. **Thus, "Generativity" or passing on what people have learned and loved becomes of paramount importance.**[62] Thus, there is a natural inclination to forward onto the next generation whatever has been learned, accomplished or accumulated. But why? It can be simply because people need to affirm that their lives have had some purpose. It can be because they want to be remembered. It could be to make a humanitarian difference in society or the world. On the other hand, the efforts of "Mission and Generativity" are not about individuals but about God.

Spiritually speaking, "Mission and Generativity" go hand in hand. "Mission" is about sharing God and helping others in word and deed. "Generativity" is about re-creating or passing on what has been experienced about God in word and deed. Analogously, "Mission" is like running a business to be of service; "Generativity" is building that business to extend it into the next generation. However, an important distinction separates "Mission and Generativity" from other types of service and outreach activity that can and do happen throughout Christians' lives.

Spiritual helpers are often asked to assist others to discern, "What does God want me to do with my life?" The word "vocation," which comes from the root word that means "calling," originally referred to what God was calling people to be and do. Discovering vocational path is important and God has an interest and an informed opinion as to what would be best, which most certainly includes the gifts and skills that God has provided. Understanding and following the God-present abilities and passions within people will bring them closer to God and likely make their life path easier. Doing so can also be preparatory for what God has in mind for them later in life. A helpful way to approach this discernment of vocation is to reflectively ask, "Does that career include the use of the gifts and skills that God has given you?" and "Would God like to be doing that line of work with you?" However, discerning vocation or calling, which typically happens earlier in life, is not the same as the Illuminative Way's "Mission and Generativity."

From the beginning of their spiritual life, Christians are taught to love others. Of course, this service is basic and essential to the growth and development of Christians at every phase of their journey. At first, Christians do this because it is the right thing to do. They likely come to hope that such loving action will be returned to them in time. Hopefully, they continue their loving ways because they see the good that is created and how other people benefit from their service. Eventually, they receive Spiritual Gifts like compassion and kindness so that their love of others is actually initiated via these God-instilled qualities; in other words, God does the loving as Christians cooperate in what God wants to do.

Included in all of the service and mission activity done prior to "Mission and Generativity" is a degree of self-interest, which increasingly diminishes as Christians progress along the Spiritual Road. People love, serve and help others for a variety of reasons. Christians may help others because it is the right thing to do and they want to be accounted good. They may love because they have positive feelings about it. They may involve themselves in mission action – in prison ministries, youth groups or soup kitchens – because of the "personal power" or importance that is generated. (These actions are not selfish when done developmentally to obtain the necessary strong sense of self.) People may participate in a Christian business as a way of serving but also to receive money as a valued benefit. The self-interest contained in such service and mission is unavoidably developmental and not necessarily inappropriate or unchristian.

While "Mission and Generativity" includes caring for and extending the life of Christianity, this phase of the Illuminative Way is not so much about the tasks that are accomplished as it is about the spirit in which they are done. Also, the work of "Mission and Generativity" is distinctively not about quantity or doing more for God which is more thoroughly explored in chapter eighteen, "Dealing with Pain." Instead, its greatest import is perpetuating the Spirit of God and facilitating Christians into greater intimacy with God.

However, as Christians move near the end of the Illuminative Way into "Mission and Generativity," a subtle but major transition takes place. Loving others is done for God. What Christians do and say is almost totally for the sake of loving God alone. The solitary "satisfaction" they have is that God is honored and glorified; and it truly does not matter if anyone knows what has happened – God knows and that is all that matters. <u>In order for this attitudinal transition to have taken place; Christians must have been adopted into God's "family business" which requires clarity about God's purposes coupled with a devoted loving relationship with the Divine</u>. So, while Christian activity or vocation can happen at any time in believers' lives, the "Mission and Generativity" of the Illuminative Way can only occur after some "Learnings," "Clarifications" and "Devotion" have transpired.

Mission may look the same as former life activities; what has changed is the relationship with God and the intention that underlies the service. The Apostle Paul attempted to make as clear as possible this distinction when he said, "I have been crucified with Christ and *I no longer live, but Christ lives in me. The life I live in the body, I live by faith in the Son of God, who loved me and gave himself for me.*"[63] [Galatians 2:20] <u>Paul has become so identified with the divine that all that he does becomes a "direct" extension of God into the world</u>. Jesus taught about the need for and the process of getting to this spiritual place in life. "Then he called the crowd to him along with his disciples and said: "If anyone would come after me, he must deny himself and take up his cross and follow me. For whoever wants to save his life will lose it, but whoever loses his life for me and for the gospel will save it."[64] [Mark 8:34-35] The concept of Christians' "negation of self" can be extremely problematic if literally applied too early in Christians' lives. Jesus never counsels young believers to deny their loving self or their compassionate self which are needed in order to practice Christian principles during the Purgative and Illuminative Ways. However, **near the end of the Illuminative Way, typically later in people's life span, the "negation of self" is appropriate and necessary**. <u>This voluntary surrender or denial manifests as an act of true love; and it allows for God's Spirit to be lived through human beings in the purest way possible</u>. Similarly, the covenant that God established with Abram frames the intension of God for humanity and also overviews the spiritual process of individualization. "I will bless you ... [so] you will be a blessing. ... and all peoples on earth will be blessed through you."[65] [Genesis 12:1-3] This spiritual course of action is about receiving God so as to increase in personal strength and abilities in order to pass faith on to others, which, if done to the maximum, requires the denial of self.

Jesus counseled both mission and generativity. The classic "Mission" statement is "to go into all the world and make disciples."[66] [Matthew 28:19-20] When Jesus was comparing himself and his followers to a grapevine and its branches, he commanded them to "bear fruit."[67] [John 15:8] In other words, they were to reproduce themselves – that is "Generativity." Early in the spiritual procession of his followers, Jesus had consistently taught them the importance of loving others – the standard by which this was to be done was by loving others as people loved themselves. However, at this point in the spiritual growth of his apostles, Jesus' teaching took on a deeper dimension when he re-framed it – "A new command I give you: Love one another. As I have loved you, so you must love one another."[68] [John 13:34] This new form of love that Jesus now required was based on perfect love – divine agape sacrificial love – which takes understanding of Jesus' intentions in order to love this way.

The "Mission and Generativity" focus of caring for others and passing faith to the next generation has changed as revealed in light of Jesus' High Priestly Prayer for all his followers.[69] [John 17:1-26] Although he verifies his "assigned" work done to glorify God, his prayer is totally about the intimate relationship, the oneness, which exists between God and himself. This intimacy is the overall focus for the end of his spiritual life on earth and the goal for all of his followers on The Spiritual Road. It is about knowing God... which is eternal life. It is about honoring God who Jesus asks to protect all followers from the evil one so that they may be one, not so that they would be safe from worldly issues. It is about passing on the love-oneness to the world that exists between God and Jesus – and which is to become manifested in Christian believers. The Christian-God relationship is the ultimate factor, especially at this juncture in the spiritual life. "Mission and Generativity" are increasingly practiced primarily based on Christians' oneness-love with God. Accordingly, the concept of the selfless, suffering servant – a condition into which Christians cannot will themselves – begins to form since Christians are not concerned about worldly consequences but only about pleasing God.

"Mission and Generativity" is about being part and parcel of God's plan for a New Heaven and a New Earth.[70] [Revelation 21:1] It is the materialization of the Lord's Prayer that "your will be done on earth as it is in Heaven."[71] [Matthew 6:10] It requires Christians to become "living sacrifices, holy and pleasing to God – this is your spiritual act of worship."[72] [Romans 12:1] Consequently, Christians quickly come to realize that communicating this Divine Spirit is way above their pay grade. While they are committed to doing this, they need help – realized more than ever before. Prayer deepens because of this need. Prayer becomes a lifestyle; and since all of life is about God and the things of God, prayer becomes "continuous." Indeed, Christians moving through "Mission and Generativity" profoundly understand that nothing of this caliber is possible without the presence and power of the Holy Spirit.

The increased intimacy between God and souls, the loving others with the same love that was in Jesus and the perpetuating the Spirit of the Divine are all essential to the spiritual step of "Mission and Generativity." They are also perfect preparation for the Unitive Way. However, before an opening into this last part of the spiritual journey is granted, a great test awaits Christians – the Dark Night of the Spirit, the second aspect of the Dark Night of the Soul.

CHAPTER 10

The Illuminative Way
The Dark Night of the Spirit

THE DARK NIGHT OF THE SOUL

The phrase "The Dark Night" comes from St. John of the Cross,[1] who used it to signify a particular part of Christians' spiritual journey on which he provides the most significant treatises. Understanding "The Dark Night" is especially important for guiding Christians along The Spiritual Road. Unfortunately, none of the original Spanish works of St. John – only hand-written copies, which include numerous albeit unintentional errors – have survived. His writings from the 1500s are, of course, couched in archaic and diffuse language. His frame of reference is the Scholastic Theology (or Mystical Theology) as well as the Scholastic "psychology," embodied within it.[2] In order to best understand the intent and nuances contained in St. John's literally profound thought, a thorough study is needed. Fortunately, some contemporary authors have made such examinations.[3] I am certain that this kind of precision is needed especially in theological circles. However, because of its complexity and often technical jargon (much like legalese), it is unhelpful for the average person who helps others grow spiritually – but without such understanding there is great danger in misguiding Christians. Thus, with quite a bit of fear and trembling, I have attempted to summarize "The Dark Night(s)" in everyday language, provide real-life examples of them and suggest ways to help Christians grow spiritually that distinguishes between the different "The Dark Night(s)."

Part of the problem is that the phrase "The Dark Night of the Soul," has been popularized and even trivialized in recent literature. It absolutely does not, nor should it refer to, any awful, tragic event that occurs in life. In fact, **the "Dark Night" is best understood as the positive, loving action of God even though it rarely feels that way.** As described by John Michael Talbot, it is a "Holy Darkness"[4] in which God lovingly prepares Christians for new life.

I have tried you in the fires of affliction

I have taught your soul to grieve
In the barren soil of your loneliness
There I will plant my seed.
Holy darkness, blessed night
Heaven's answer hidden from our sight,
As we await you, O God of silence,
We embrace your Holy Light.

What is the "Dark Night?" It is the internal experience, which can have corresponding outer life connections, of the absolute absence of the Presence of God. This state is most often felt as emptiness, dryness and loneliness – what spiritual literature calls "desolations." While abuse, tragic accidents, death and natural disasters are unquestionably dreadfully life-shaking, they are not necessarily spiritual "Dark Nights." On the other hand, depression is often common to both life difficulties and "Dark Nights." Spiritual helpers need to understand when depression becomes clinical and therefore requiring referral for therapeutic assistance.[5]

"The Dark Night" described by St. John of the Cross is a purification process that can pervade much of Christians' lives in which people, or "The Souls," are being prepared to be united with God. John describes two major aspects of this progression – "The Dark Night of the Senses" and "The Dark Night of the Spirit" – each which has its own particular purpose. Since "Souls," or individual Christians, experience these "Dark Nights," the phrase "The Dark Night of the **Soul**" has been coined and popularized. While both of John's "Dark Nights" are part of a "single" process, they do occur separately, generally at different times in Christians' lives and definitely for purifying different parts of the "Soul."[6] Thus, I have elected to identify them at different times in the process of spiritual growth and development. (This can technically be incorrect, but practically more helpful.) Increasing the complexity, the entire "Dark Nights" process includes an "active purification," which includes what people can do and a "passive purification," which is totally done by God alone. Furthermore, I have previously described an additional "Dark Night" experience, in chapter six, because it has been so typical in my experience (and in scripture) and has a different purpose than the two listed by John of the Cross. This "Dark Night" I have called the "Confessional Temptation."

In considering the process of spiritual growth, I have included the "Confessional Temptation" at the end of the "Pre-Christian Way" and the "Dark Night of the Senses" that occurs near the end of the "Purgative Way." While both of these experiences of darkness feel very real, they are to be distinguished from the "Dark Night of the Spirit" if for no other reason than they happen at different times. However, the primary reason is that they happen for different reasons and require different responses to the test that is presented. Nonetheless, **whether Christians trust God more fully is always the basic issue.** Spiritual helpers, upon first discerning that Christians are in the midst of a "Dark Night," would be advised to ask, "Are you willing to trust God with (fill in the blank)?" followed by "What will it take for God to know you are serious about this?" Those questions essentially discern Christians' willingness and ability to move forward.

A brief comparison of these three dark times can help the understanding of the "Dark Night of the Soul." **The absence of God is felt during the "Confessional Temptation" because new Christians are "re-asked" via this darkness whether they really want to follow God with their lives.** These Christians feel lured to return to their former life; and their temptation is appropriately intense to test the person and in their particular situation. On the other hand, God is very close and eager to help so a "sure I want to follow" is all it takes to move through this temptation; but giving that confirmation may actually be very difficult for those ready for the "Purgative Way." A mentor, guide or spiritual helper is very useful at this transitional moment.

The absence of God is likewise felt during the "Dark Night of the Senses." During the "Purgative Way" Christians have purged their lives of persistent sins and started doing all kinds of good things that helped them "feel" the Presence of God. However, near the end of the "Purgative Way" none of these tangible (sensate) things seem to help bring the awareness and positive affirmations of God into their lives. This Darkness is caused by God as a test. In order to proceed along the spiritual road and deepen their personal spiritual relationship, God cannot allow these Christians to believe that what they "do" can in any way control how God does or does not respond. Accordingly, the spiritual habits and good deeds that formerly brought good feelings and internal consolations from God no longer do so. This "Dark Night of the Senses" occurs as long as Christians believe that their actions will bring God's presence and affirmations. Christians must let God lead and stop attempting to expect and anticipate God by what they do. They must "let go and let God." This darkness often persists for an extended time – at least until God is sure these Christians have become truly "willing" to follow and have completely surrendered to wherever God leads, without knowing the details. When they are letting go, Christians may have a sense that God's Holy Spirit is running their lives. Alternatively, when they re-start controlling, the darkness returns until trusting becomes a way of life. A mentor, guide or spiritual helper is highly recommended during this transitional period.

The absence of God during the "Dark Night of the Spirit" is greatly protracted! The "Dark Night of the Spirit" occurs at the end of the Illuminative Way as an entrance into the Unitive Way. Christians have experienced spiritual darkness before, but not like this. In this crisis, Christians need to again surrender. However, they are not required to give up just the things of the Purgative Way but also the Illuminative Way's comfort and assurances of faith as no divine consolation is derived from prayer, worship, study or even service. The activities that once brought the Presence of God no longer do so. The feelings of God's closeness and loving attention cannot be sensed. Mental clarity is so clouded as not to provide assurance. The past was full of memories and evidence of God; but in the present moment Christians only have a profound and extended absence of God.

THE DARK NIGHT OF THE SPIRIT

St. John of the Cross used the Scholastic Theology and its understanding of the psychological makeup of human beings. Accordingly, the individual person, called the Soul, is divided into two parts – the sensory and the spiritual. The sensory portion includes the five senses as well as the "imagination" (which contains an element of intuition). The spiritual part consists of three "faculties" – the intellect, the memory (which includes past recall as well as future projections) and the will. <u>Just as the "Dark Night of the Senses" does not allow physical sensations to bring forth the Presence of God, the "Dark Night of the Spirit" disallows the intellect, memory and the will from doing the same</u>. **The ultimate purpose of the "Dark Nights" is to remove or purify all that is not God from Souls so that "all the fullness of God" <u>that is humanly possible</u> can dwell within people.** Thus, Scholastic Theology's concepts of the sensory and the spiritual aspects of people must become "Dark."[7]

THE COMING OF THE NIGHT

Remember, Christians approaching the "Dark Night of the Spirit" have grown into a mature trust in God and don't need lots of "feeling" proof of God's love and work; and have already come to realize that these former ways of sensing God have mostly stopped working. Instead, they have come to rely on their intellect, memory and will in order to connect with God. These Illuminative Way Christians have no doubt about the existence of God. They consistently continue in spiritual habits; they continue to pray in faith but without feeling God's responsiveness; they have so much more knowledge and insight into the Holy Community that God is creating. They have moved more deeply in love with God – but it is now a love that has less passion and more contentment. Having this level of Christian maturity is absolutely needed to be able to endure the trial that is coming. Throughout the Illuminative Way, God has initiated and sustained the growing intimacy these Christians have enjoyed for so long and they have anticipated a culmination to this wonderful relationship. Unexpectedly, it is gone as if it never ever happened! It is as if on the day of the marriage the bridegroom (or bride) is nowhere to be found. Spiritual helpers need to discern that the above characteristics exist before determining that "The Dark Night of the Spirit" has begun.[8]

One benefit, if it can be called that, is that sometimes Christians can anticipate the coming of the "Dark Night" because of the waxing and waning of the Presence of God they experience over a considerably long period of time. Prayer that had been so rich and rewarding for most of the Illuminative Way becomes dry and empty – and nothing helps for long.[9] Seemingly, God does not want Christians to go "cold turkey." So, the "consolations" or affirmations from God continue to come periodically with feelings of love and assurances. However, even these consolations fade over time into darkness.

For example, while mature Christians who say they are "not being fed" are objecting to the fact that spiritual leaders or a particular congregation are not "making" them feel God, they may actually be headed into a "Dark Night." If they are concerned about not getting new understandings/clarifications or are just spiritually tired from serving without support, the same may be true. Assuming that the cause of their "emptiness" is not sin or unforgiveness (or the ineptitude of church leaders), these long-term Christians actually cannot "be fed" nor is it helpful to try to do that – for God is causing this "dryness." In this situation, I have too often heard spiritual helpers be totally unhelpful by rhetorically asking: "Well, if you feel far away from God, who do you think moved, and it wasn't God?" Such judgmental guilt is so unfair!!! Christians are, of course, taught that the divine is the same "yesterday, today and forever."[10] [Hebrews 13:8] So to them it seems inconceivable that God would have actually moved. But truly, God is the same; **the God of Light always moves away from Christians at the ends of the Purgative and Illuminative Ways so as to allow darkness to emerge in order to draw Christians into a deeper loving relationship**. Indeed, spiritual helpers would be to advised to counsel such mature Christians about what God is doing and how to cooperate with such divine grace. Additionally, understanding how God purifies the soul's intellect, memory and will during "The Dark Night of the Spirit" can be useful.

LOSING YOUR MIND

Through the intellect people gain greater knowledge of God and the things of God. However, the intellect can only approximate God; people's intellect can never fully "know" God and in fact it becomes an obstacle that disallows God from directly connecting with the Soul. In addition to this admonition, St. John of the Cross includes moments given by God via "visions, revelation, locution and spiritual feelings" as received by the intellect which must be refused even those "from beyond us" forms of knowledge. However, as Susan Muto says, "The intellect is not the problem; arrogance is."[11] People need to surrender the "pride of their mind" – that by studying the scripture or theology or life enough, they can know God.

Truly, people cannot comprehend God and attempting to do so limits the ability of their souls to receive the Love-Reality which is God. This principle is echoed by the Apostle Paul who wants Christians, who are well-founded in their love for God, to receive a deeper love, that knowledge cannot obtain or imagination can envision. How is this accepted?

Through God's power in the "inner being." Christians at this stage of spiritual development need other Christians to pray for them as Paul does:

> "I pray that out of his [God's] glorious riches he may strengthen you with power through his Spirit in your inner being, so that Christ may dwell in your hearts through faith. And I pray that you, being rooted and established in love, may have power, together with all the saints, to grasp how wide and long and high and deep is the love of Christ, and to know this love that surpasses knowledge – that you may be filled to the measure of all the fullness of God. Now to him who is able to do immeasurably more than all we ask or imagine, according to his power that is at work within us, to him be glory in the church and in Christ Jesus throughout all generations, forever and ever! Amen."[12] [Ephesians 3:16-21]

Christians are advised to "release and relinquish" what they believe to be true and especially their attempt to acquire this knowledge so that God can fill them more than they can do for themselves through their intellect.

Two brief examples, one classic and the other contemporary, can indicate how God moves Christians toward complete surrender intellectually.

A classic example in the history of Christianity surrounds the events of St. Thomas Aquinas at the end of his life. For the majority of his adult life, Thomas wrote the Summa Theologiae, an absolutely superb systematic theology that has guided Christianity for centuries and Roman Catholic doctrine still today.[13] Before he died Thomas emerged from an ecstatic vision, after which he proclaimed that his entire life's work was "mere straw" in comparison to what God had revealed to him.[14] As a result, he refused to finish his great theological work. God will strip Christians from reliance upon what they know so that The Truth alone remains.

Rev. Lorenzo Dade revealed to me that he was moving in a similar direction. Lorenzo was a well-schooled and extremely academic Protestant pastor who had served some of the most intellectual congregations in his denomination. Now retired, he was engaged in self-reflection and working through some of the concepts that plagued him. After a presentation at a conference, Lorenzo visit with me about his current spiritual condition. He revealed, "The older and more retired I get the more I struggle with free will and predestination. I am thinking that mystery is the way to go." Rev. Dade also noted that he had been dealing with some former decisions he had made and some forgiveness he needed to offer. In his time of reflection, he questioned his decision-making ability. He was an extremely smart man experiencing "self-doubt." All his life, he was a self-determined individual making free choices and living with the consequences; mature in his faith and his understanding of God. However, at this time in his life he was inundated with questions that God typically brings to people's minds, like: "Does God determine our destiny?" and "Do we really have free will?" There is strong evidence for each position. But are people really to know? Can they know even if God reveals truth to them? Rev. Dade, moving toward the Unitive Way, had the conviction, "I am thinking that mystery is the way to go." Accepting "Mystery" is akin to surrendering one's intellect; it is a surrendering so that God can be "in charge." Lorenzo was becoming ok with being in the darkness of not-knowing, the opposite of what he had built his life on, in order to simply be and allow the Presence of God.

How do people help others who are in the midst of the "Dark Night of the Spirit's" darkening of the intellect? First, make sure that people are at this stage in spiritual process. Purgative Way Christians <u>must</u> come to the knowledge of right and wrong – and intellectual sloth is extremely destructive at this point. Furthermore, Christians, only beginning the Illuminative Way, benefit greatly from broadening their intellectual understanding of God and God's ways because it increases their devotion, service and commitment. However, if people are in or coming to this "Dark Night," then helpers could affirm this uncertainty as "good" because God is opening them. Authenticate with them that knowing God completely is not within human ability. Suggest that in essence people can only know "about" God. Ask how important is the intellectual effort to imperfectly know (about) God especially if another way is available? Suggest that not-knowing God (via surrendering our intellectual ability) may actually allow the true God access to them. Say: "It is ok not to grasp at God; but instead open your hands so that God can take hold of them." St. John of the Cross suggested that what was needed was the supplanting the Christian virtue of <u>unwavering faith</u> in the place of knowledge.

THE POWER OF THE PAST

The purification of memory is also part of the "Dark Night of the Spirit." Memory is typically the storage place of past experiences. However in the Scholastic Theology which St. John used, it also includes imagining or projecting the future.

During the Illuminative Way, Christians have been encouraged to learn, clarify, serve and become totally devoted to God. Accordingly, Christians have experienced the divine via confirmations, answered prayers, blessings and affirmations, which they have come to enjoy and anticipate. Indeed, believers have come to expect that this is how God "works" and they also believe that the same will continue. In this process, **Christians have accumulated a storehouse of impressed memories to which they have become strongly attached; and in their actions, prayers and imaginations they desire to recall or even recreate them.** "Paradoxically, there is a stage of forgetfulness we must go through if we are to grow more mindful of God as a mystery of love and not an object of our own mastery."[15]

<u>In a sense, the Illuminative Way experiences have been immortalized in memory; as such, Christians are able to "recall God" on demand.</u> Thus, **these memories determine**

what is to be hoped for. But only God can be the hope of Christians – not the remembered transcendent moments of God nor the experiences, teachings or service done for God. In other words, the memories that have served Christians so well for so long have become a hindrance for God's coming to them in purer ways. As St. John says, "None of the supernatural forms and ideas[16] that can be had by the memory is God, and the soul must empty itself of all that is not God in order to go to God."[17]

Memory can be powerful. Through it and the hope it aroused, Victor Frankl and others were able to survive Nazi concentration camps. On the other hand, memory has the ability to capture and torture without any outside assistance. One of my early spiritual mentors would often cliché a freeing truth, "The past is forgiven; and the future is open." Or as a spiritual director, I now know, "The past needs to be forgiven; and the future needs to be seen as open." Unfortunately for many people what keeps them spiritually enslaved is the unforgiveness in their past and the demanded-expectations of their future! Consider this example.

Nariko, the Japanese name for "gentle child," surprised me one day by announcing that she wanted to begin spiritual direction as she said, "I have thought about this for quite a while and have decided that I have a spiritual problem." Nariko is a very intellect, compassionate and talented ordained minister. She had always been part of the Christian community, but she was having trouble sensing any close connection with God. At her request, we worked together about every other week for more than two years. A trusting and appropriate friendship fostered that enabled much spiritual growth, which mostly included connecting her life experiences with what she already faithfully affirmed, but did not "feel." Nariko had participated in psychotherapy for a number of years because of the serious mental and sexual abuse she suffered from age four. She had made much progress in therapy but residuals surrounding the issues of anger, unforgiveness and lack of self-confidence remained. Many therapy topics were discussed but with the spiritual intent of discerning, "What does God have to do with this topic?" and "What is the spiritual lesson you need to learn?"

After a while, Nariko revealed a pattern that she had been experiencing for a number of months. On her day for spiritual direction, she would increasingly become deathly afraid. She remembered former criticisms, abuse and being "looked at;" and she would anticipate that the same was going to happen in her spiritual direction session. Her created word that described this experience was that she "catastrophized" her life, almost to the point of a "panic attack." She also noted that she did not experience criticism or abuse from being "examined" in spiritual direction and after an hour that included much affirmation and encouragement, she always felt better. I was intentionally using the therapeutic tool of "building a bridge" – but not simply for the interpersonal relationship but to enable Nariko's connection with God.

The revelation of her "catastrophizing" led to discovering how she would keep God at a safe distance, like she had done with most everyone in her life. This was indeed a spiritual issue. Much of Nariko's past had been forgiven and her future was opening to goodness. However, Nariko, in order to protect herself from the genuine danger that intimacy always affords, would bring the feelings of her horrendous past and dump them into her present (as well as her emotional God-moments) whether they deserved to be there or not. Her daily life was not any more unpleasant than anyone else, but her "catastrophizing" would make it so. Accordingly, future sessions were spent together affirming: that the present was not the past; that God had a new future that had nothing to do with her awful former experiences; and that taking the past and dumping it into her present was not only harmful to Nariko but also unfair and counter to what God desired for her. We were building new memories to replace the destructive ones; memories that were always sealed with prayer.

Nariko was far from her "Dark Night of the Spirit" and was not likely to enter it with her obsession about past negativities. On the other hand, her experience was instructive regarding what it takes to empty the memories so that God's perfect love can transform people – to make them ready to be loved by Love itself. ... But all who are on their way to the "Dark Night of the Spirit," should "forget" that I even mentioned that.

MAKING SPACE FOR GRACE

By the time that most Christians come to the "Dark Night of the Spirit," they will have matured enough so as not to have serious unforgiveness nor have excessively programmed their minds with what God will or will not do. But if they have such tendencies, then they have significant work that needs to be done before God will allow them to move closer via the "Dark Night." **The "Dark Night of the Spirit's" purging of memories is not about helping Christians remove serious unforgiveness or projected imaginations, but about "forgetting the memory" of ever having those issues**.

Memory/imagination has a lot to do with the emotional attachment to past events as well as the projection of what will occur in the future. These can keep Christians drowning in negative experiences and unforgiveness that keep God at bay. Or these memories, even "godly" ones, can simply take up space and consequently leave no room for God.

Indeed, spiritual and/or emotional pain can occur in the lives of Christians who need to forgive.[18] However, spiritual and/or emotional pain can also occur in the lives of Christians who are experiencing the "Dark Night of the Spirit." How do spiritual helpers determine what is needed? Forgiveness is needed when the memory of the event and/or person in it "causes" Christians to be triggered or trapped into feelings or actions, especially those which are more intense than the current situation elicits. On the other hand, forgiveness has been completed when "the power" goes out of the memory – not when the memory has been forgotten.

The "Dark Night of the Spirit" seeks to purge the remembering of "already forgiven" memories. The purpose is not because the memory deserves to be forgotten, but simply to make room for God. **Whatever attention Christians place on their memories limits their ability to remain in the present moment where God is.** All memories as well as anticipated happenings regarding one's life, heaven or the rapture need to be gently released.

To some bystanders, this advised "forgetfulness" seems like being uninterested in God or God's ways. However, the opposite is actually true: **Christians are making space for grace.** <u>All that is not God – including that which is just about God – is being released and relinquished so that God can fill the Soul</u>. A revised colloquial expression might be of assistance for those in this part of the "Dark Night of the Spirit." "There are two rules to follow. First, don't remember the small memories. Second, all memories are small ones (in comparison to God)." Centering Prayer, which gently releases all unwanted thoughts except the one on which a pray-er is focused, is good training for letting go of memories.

Memories determine what is to be hoped for. People use their past to pre-determine the future – what God will give. In other words, Christians preempt God with memory. If they want what God wants for them, if they desire to be at one with God, then they must release all memories. These memorialized-expectations and anticipations, on which Christians have come to depend, must fade. After all are purged, then God can deliver the real future that comes only via the Christian virtue of pure hope for those "who have been called according to his purposes."[19] [Romans 8:28]

IDENTIFYING WITH JESUS

The final component of the "Dark Night of the Spirit" is the purification of the human will, which needs to be surrendered to God's Will. As St. John proclaims, Christians have to withdraw their "affection from all in order to center it wholly on God."[20]

When St. John of the Cross comes to the purification of the will at this point in the "Dark Night of the Spirit," I believe that the Scholastic Theology and its psychological overlay of how human beings are to be understood have reached their limits. In accord with the thinking of his day, St. John described the human will as having emotions.[21] If the Scholastic model is replaced, at least in regard to the human psyche, with a clearer replica, then a viable solution might be approached.

Modern psychology defines the personal will, which Gerald May correctly notes, as "the capacity to make choices, form intentions and direct actions."[22] Thus, the will does not contain emotions and is to be distinguished from the intellect as well. Think of the human will as the Director of Actors, like in a motion picture film production. The human will directs the other psychological functions of the brain – coordinating them and making the final decisions that launch them into "action." Psychosynthesis characterizes the human will in this manner and also lists the functions that the "will" controls which includes thought, intuition, imagination, feelings, sensations and impulse-desire.[23]

Following this model, the human will can be visualized in the center with the functions around it. **In the center of the human will, is the Conscious-I or what is also called the Soul-Self.** According to Psychosynthesis, this Soul can be in direct contact with the Higher Self which is beyond the individual and has also been identified as the Holy Spirit. When the human will, via our individual active choices, has done its work of "purifying" the six functions around it, then what is left "to do" is to will one thing – God.

This surrender of the will is based on intention – actually the freely giving of all personal willingness for the good of the Other which is the only way that pure love can be transmitted. In other words, during the "Dark Night of the Spirit" Christians lovingly give away the only thing they have left – themselves, their Soul-Self. In the words of Jesus, "Father, into your hands, I commit my spirit."[24] [Luke 24:36] God responds with "passive purification," transporting people into moments of Union with God – the Unitive Way.

I believe that the God-given, human free will is centric to Christians' ability to love – including the ability to love as God loves. Even though God must supplant agape love within people for them to be able to love divinely, people must be willing for that to happen. In other words, if love is not freely given, it is not love at all; and if Christians do not willingly love, they cannot unite with God. **Love freely given is the only way to unite with God; and this requires the act of the individual human will in order to do so.** (Note: people cannot make union with God happen, but God honors their surrender and accomplishes the union when "permission" is given.) Accordingly, since God wants people to respond freely in love, God will not take their human will from them. With this supposition, I will explore the "purification of the will" which occurs during the "Dark Night of the Spirit."

Everything, and I mean everything, in life can at best only be an approximation of God. Thus, everything that people's thinking, feeling or action does is at best an idol – because it cannot conceive, praise or worship who God *really* is. This is why, in the final analysis, the "Dark Nights" of Sense and Spirit must occur – to remove our senses, imagination, intelligence and memory from attempting to come to the idolatrous-God of human creation. People's human will directs these functions. When the will lays itself down, after it has freely surrendered all of the functions it directs, unity with God can occur – BUT NOT BECAUSE OF WHAT PEOPLE HAVE DONE BUT BECAUSE GOD THEN COMES AND MAKES IT HAPPEN. God as Pure Love responds to the purest act of love within Christians' ability to give.

SURRENDERING THE HUMAN WILL

While it is difficult to conceive and put into words, there are some "active" ways to surrender the will at this point on The Spiritual Road. Remember, that the previously described forms of "Dark Night" purifications must be happening or what I describe below is not part of the "Dark Night" process.

The basic tenant for "purifying the will" is *simply* **that Christians willingly relinquish any desire for anything except God**. Thus, Christians approach everything through God and experience life in a totally different way. Besides being extremely difficult to do, having vested interests – like rearing a family, running a business, being passionate for a cause, or having a strong commitment to support a spouse (or anyone else) – makes total surrender very difficult, but not impossible. No wonder that the "Dark Night of the Spirit" typically takes place after much life has been lived.

People who help others grow spiritually can discern if Christians are moving toward this "surrender of the will" part of the "Dark Night of the Spirit" and assist in the following ways:

First, consider the motivation for which Christians love God. All Christians at this point in their lives are loving individuals and concerned about loving others as well as God. However, their love cannot be formed from fear, or offered because of duty or even because it is the right thing to do. Their love cannot be for the purpose of countering sinfulness. Although Christians normally have already "purified" these motives long ago, making sure they have done so is appropriate and necessary discernment. **The way Christians are to love is for God alone – not for others, the world or even themselves. Their effort is to be much more closely aligned to loving God "for whom God is."** A clue about whether this is being done can be noticed in their use of words. If people consistently think, feel or speak "me" "mine" or "I," they are not close to, ready for or part of the "Dark Night of the Spirit." Likewise, if their conversation is consumed with excessive concern for children, the church or any other human entity, the result is similar.

In the Sermon on the Mount, Jesus has a simple yet profound teaching that seems to directly apply to this time in Christians' lives, even more than at other times. The passage can use some "Clarifications." It reads: "The eye is the lamp of the body. If your eyes are good, your whole body will be full of light. But if your eyes are bad, your whole body will be full of darkness. If then the light within you is darkness, how great is that darkness!"[25] [Matthew 6:22-23]

Biblical commentators have struggled to interpret this text, largely because the correct physiological function of the eye is not accurately represented in the passage. For example, the human eye does not shine light, like a lamp, but actually needs external light in order to see. So the eye is not like a lamp and does not radiate light, which makes the analogy of the scripture problematic. However, it is commonly spoken that people see with their eyes; and the goal of the passage is to get the "body" to be full of light. Light can be understood as God – especially since these verses are written as an analogy. Now the translation is typically interpreted that if people's eyes are healthy, they will be able to see well because they have light inside of them. Conversely, if the eye is "bad" or diseased, then they will not receive light, and consequently have darkness inside.

A "Clarifications" emerges when the phrase "If your eyes are good (clear)" is alternately understood. The Greek for the word that is translated as "clear" or "good" is ἁπλοῦς (aplous), which means "single, pure or uncomplicated." Now to translate "if your eyes are single" is not to advocate being a Cyclops, but to be focused like a laser beam on one and only one thing. When this happens, people become full of light – that is, full of God. Conversely, the Greek word, πονηρὸς (ponēros), which is translated "bad" really means "evil" or "hurtful" because it is being compared to the opposite of God. Jesus is teaching that for people to be full of Light – to have all of God that is possible for them to contain, they must be totally focused with a single center of attention on God. This understanding is confirmed by the following verses that instruct that people cannot serve two masters.

This single focus on God alone is not easy and it takes a spiritual lifetime of being prepared and purified in order to just get to the place where being "full of Light" is even possible. Considering where people spend their time is often an excellent way to discern whether they are serving two masters or not, especially if they are unaware of their egotism. Discerning the singularity of people's will is important for determining if they are ready for or already in the "Dark Night of the Spirit." Indeed, **Christians, in the process of surrendering the human will, will be attempting to focus only on God.**

Second, surrender of the human will is evidenced and perpetuated via free and willing choices that are correct and right regardless of the consequences. While discussing how to work with directees who have moved far along the spiritual path, Janet Ruffing references Karl Rahner in order to describe difficult circumstances and responses. I see these as very reflective of people in the midst of the "Dark Night of the Spirit" especially because of the selfless-willing that initiates their actions. While the following "situations" could occur at various times in Christians' lives, the nearly automatic "responses" point to those in the midst of the "Dark Night of the Spirit." Consider my paraphrasing of Rahner's examples in the following situations and the responses.[26]

Situation – a man, although he could defend himself, chooses to keep silent and be unjustly treated; The Response – is not just the self-sacrifice, but a deep conviction that the noble action will result in some unnamable good.

Situation – a man does his duty in the midst of a feeling that he is denying himself and doing something nonsensical; The Response – he experiences a sense of freedom that no earthly compulsion can take away from him.

Situation – a woman struggles to come to a place where she can forgive a horrific past event; The Response – she receives "silent forgiveness" from the other side that is taken as self-evident that God is taking care of it and her.

Situation – a woman who prays and attempts to love God, but receives no confirmation for the years she has put into the effort; The Response – she knows that she knows that she knows God is always there in the nothingness.

Each of these examples can occur at various times within people's lives. However, **the consistency of such free, non-compulsive actions, which are not rooted in automatic reactions or habits, is the key to whether the will is being surrendered.** These responses are certainly not for self-interest; but neither are they made to prove a point. Furthermore, such free, non-compulsive, faithful responses are not "in spite of" sin, evil or wrong – **they are motivated by pure and simple choices for God.** These faithful notions are also free of what has been previously determined as good and right and true – there is no compulsion in the choices that these "Dark Night" folks make. Their initiative is from pure trust; and throughout they are fixed with loving attention on God. The human will is freed from "habitual, compulsive ways of loving and behaving righteously."[27]

When working with people who have seemed to release all automatic, compulsive activity in their life, spiritual helpers may find that they may be extremely reluctant to talk about their own experience. However, after spiritual helpers have taken the opportunity to ask about the situation, they would be advised to clearly echo back to these Christians the "unconditional loving, godly choice" that was made by these people. Helpers may also choose to comment on what they see as the benefit of this non-compulsive, loving action. For example: "Thank you for sharing your life. What I hear is that God was honored with such little concern for your needs. My faith is encouraged." Then follow up with the question, **"How do you get the power to act like that?"** The answer will come as some form of: the Spirit of God gives the power to act in godly ways in spite of the present life situation. **Indeed, God's Spirit provides the ability to act as God would act.** This is evidence that because of the "surrender of the human will," God is incarnate and working through the lives of these Christians.

Mother Teresa of Calcutta lived a non-compulsive, faithful life choosing to sacrificially serve the poorest of the poor in India. For years her prayer life was without positive feelings, even emptiness, from God – yet she continued to affirm her belief in God. "Rising above the pain of feeling 'unloved and unwanted' by Jesus, she did her utmost to show her love for him … She sought him in each person she met … holding fast to His words, 'As you did it to one of the least of these my brethren, you did it to me.'"[28] She consistently asserted such goodness in her life and instructed others to always see Jesus in the people they served … to be His Light. At some point, Mother Teresa was not serving because she wanted to help others but did so purely because she was receiving God in the persona of other people.

Third, moving into the "surrender of the human will" as part of the "Dark Night of the Spirit" can be indicated by beginning to identify with God. This can occur with deep feelings of unworthiness. This attitude is not to be confused with the self-condemnation that happens as Purgative Way Christians realize their sinful nature and feel appropriately guilty about that. Neither is this attitude about the "ashes and sack cloth" self-denying behavior as Christians are attempting to purify themselves. Also, it is to be distinguished from the Illuminative Way Christians' depreciative mind-set of releasing the things of the world because the things of God are more important.

At this stage, Christians' feelings of unworthiness are seeded from a different source. They will actually be identifying with how God is touched by the sins of the world. Jesus took the weight of the sins of the world into himself when he hung on the cross – which was extremely painful and full of sorrow. When Christians surrender their human will, they open themselves up to the nature of God. Accordingly, they can begin to feel, but only in a small portion, the overwhelming grief that God feels about sin. Nonetheless, the realization causes incredible shame and a deep sense of not deserving any of what God has given to them.

In addition, Christians at this stage may also have a sudden revelation, as if God just infused this truth, about how God has "felt about" their own personal sins. They may talk about "my sins" but the focus is not about them as it is regarding how God could actually forgive their unworthiness. Key to this issue is the fact that these Christians absolutely know that God has forgiven them and has a place in Heaven for them BUT now they have a profoundly deeper regret – which God has placed within them. If they are to experience union with God, they must also begin to experience how God feels about sin!

On the other end of the spectrum, Christians may also begin to experience, in part, the fullness of God's Love for all things. **As a result of their surrender of will, they may also be brought into a fledgling experience of the perfect love of God**. When Jesus left the upper room on the Thursday before his death, he took time to instruct his Apostles on their way to the Garden of Gethsemane. Using the analogy of the grape vine, he repeatedly told them to "abide in me." The Greek word, "μείνατε" (meinate) is translated as stay, abide or remain and indicates "dwelling within." Jesus' teaching clearly states that his words must abide; his love must abide; his commandments must abide; and his will must abide in them. Accordingly, Jesus commands his followers to "Abide in my love.[29] [John 15:9] This is the ultimate goal for Christians. "Abiding in Jesus' Love" is very different than thinking loving thoughts, feeling love or even doing genuine acts of love. It is living within the "soul of Jesus" – within his very nature – which is not possible to humanly accomplish. **Christians and Jesus are to abide in each other as Jesus and God had done – this is a union of spirits. While Christians cannot make this happen; they can be solely focused on "God alone" in order to be prepared for the moments when God will fill Christians with this sense of Divine Love.**

As a result, not only do these Christians begin to see glimpses of good in the worst of evil; also they believe way beyond proof that through the Power of God ALL are redeemable. This attitude can reside ONLY in the Love that is contained in the basic nature of Jesus, who freely gave himself up for all of creation. When agape love flows in and through and around, Christians begin to appreciate why God loves and they also act the way God does. Such agape love may be experienced in mystical, non-rational ways. It may be noticed in altruistic actions that seem to have "no common sense." The classic Christian hymn, published in 1747, "Love Divine, All Loves Excelling" by Charles Wesley comes to mind. It reflects that God's Love has to come to earth and to be "fixed" within people, God's humble dwelling; God finishes forming the New Creation, as Christians are changed from glory into glory until Christians are "lost in wonder, love and praise."[30]

Fourth, the surrender of the human will can be evidenced as Christians identify with what Jesus went through at the end of his earthly life. During the last week of Jesus' earthly life, he summarized and reaffirmed his purpose; he yielded his own life into God's hands; and he surrendered his human will as especially evidenced in his Garden of Gethsemane prayer, "Not my will, but yours be done."[31] [Luke 22:42] The darkness that Jesus went through at the end of his life was no accident. He modeled for Christians what is necessary in order to experience the greatest possible relationship with God – or as Jesus says, "That they may be one as we are one."[32] [John 17:22]

The following real life story of assisting Billy Joe through the latter part of his life includes spiritual darkness as well as some identification with Jesus. I hope it will be an effective example for assisting mature Christians during the surrender of the human will part of the "Dark Night of the Spirit."

Billy Joe was in the later stages of his life on earth if his deteriorating physical condition was any indication of that fact. He and his wife of many years had gone through the ups and downs of rearing five children on minimal income. He had been legally blind for a number of years and now could no longer walk. All the while, Billy Joe had done the best he could as he would go to church and be involved in his children and grandchildren's lives. He had been a Christian for as long as he could remember and continued to practice the faith as his body would allow. He read only with the help of very large print and a powerful magnifying glass. Mostly, he listened to books on tape, especially the audio Bible he had. He had always been a reflective person and genuinely open and honest. He actually wrote his own history, his own funeral as well as letters encouraging others. He certainly attempted to live by Christian principles and by his perseverance enabled others to do so; that is when he was not telling them that they should do so. Billy Joe was a faithful Christian.

Within the last year, Billy Joe had suffered a debilitating stroke, a heart attack and had needed a half a dozen blood transfusions because of a small hole in his colon. In addition, he had been in the hospital three more times for what was determined to be panic attacks. After doing all of the spiritual things he knew to do which had always helped in the past, Billy Joe was still feeling suffocated and had trouble breathing. The doctors provided some calming medication to ease his anxiety; however, the symptoms of fear persisted.

Billy Joe telephoned John, a former pastor, who he knew to be a trustworthy and spiritually insightful person. He set an appointment to talk about how Pastor John could help improve his spirituality and be able to handle his current situation; and because of distance and physical limitation they decided to visit on the telephone. At the meeting, Billy Joe described his problem and concluded, "I know what the solution is. I have to totally trust in God and have more faith which I can get through prayer and scripture reading and so forth." The spiritual pastor affirmed that was of course true but then asked Billy Joe to "tell me about the fears you have been talking about." Billy Joe talked about often being in the hospital and knowing that his physical body was getting worse, saying, "You know what happens when you anticipate that you are not going to get better but only worse. I am anticipating the pain and discomfort and wonder if I will be able to handle it. I am not peaceful at all like I am supposed to be about the end of my life here on earth. I know I will go to heaven; but I'm afraid that I won't act like a Christian should. I need more faith. I need your help, please."

Pastor John attempted to comfort Billy Joe with a brief summary of the Christian man that he knew him to be. Then he interrupted himself to say, "I would like to change the subject a little bit if that is ok. Especially since we are in the season of Lent, I want to remind us about the events when Jesus was preparing to go to the cross. As you know, he anticipated his death and taught his apostles in the upper room on the Thursday before Easter. Then they went out to the Garden of Gethsemane to pray. While there, he prayed, "let this cup pass from me." What do you think that meant and what was Jesus feeling at the time?" Billy Joe responded, "Pastor, as I remember I believe that Jesus was asking not to have to go to the cross." "Do you mean that he did not want to die – just like you?" queried John. Billy Joe hesitatingly answered, "Yes, it seems like that is the case."

Then John continued, "The scripture also tells us that his sweat was like great drops of blood and that his three most trusted apostles could not stay awake to be with him although he specifically requested their support. So what do you surmise that Jesus was feeling as he approached the end of his life on earth?" Billy Joe paused and then said, "Well when you put it like that. Jesus wasn't happy and probably felt alone and abandoned by his friends. He was addressing the most intimate and personal subject so I expect that he was definitely anxious to get an answer." John interjected, "That is a good description; but what are the feelings that go with that?" "If I have to be honest," Billy Joe said cautiously. "I would guess that, even though he knew what was going to happen, Jesus must have felt uneasy, a little afraid maybe. But some of the other things he said when on the cross lets me know that he was deeply trusting in God."

Pastor John noted, "You are right Jesus had human feelings of anxiety in spite of his perfect relationship with God. And I am glad that you brought up his words on the cross. Do you remember when he said 'My God, My God, why have you forsaken me?' What was he feeling then?" Billy Joe responded, "I have always wondered about that time when he cried out. It seems that he felt forsaken – totally lost as if abandoned by God." Pastor John then taught, "Do you know that many scholars believe that Jesus may have been quoting Psalm 22; that line is the first verse. The psalm begins by expressing the human feelings of abandonment, fear and anxiety which Jesus as a man was certainly feeling. However, as the psalm continues to its conclusion, remembering all that God had done in the past, it ends up affirming faith and glorifying God."

John paused and then waited until Billy Joe finally broke the silence, "If the Son of God felt this way and was even a little panicky, then I am not so bad!" "Did you think that you were," sympathized Pastor John? "Yes! We are taught about how peaceful and content we are supposed to be and I haven't been. I thought it was all my fault!" At this point Pastor John smiled although Billy Joe could only feel it over the phone line, "Well, I am here to tell you, Billy Joe, that you are doing what you need to be doing and it is not your fault! What you are experiencing is a normal and natural part of the spiritual process which Jesus modeled for us. He showed us how to go through these times. Saints down through the centuries have called what you are going through the "Dark Night of the Spirit." Now, there are some end of life items that I would like to make sure you have done like any forgiveness you need to offer and affirmations that you would like to make to family and friends. I would also like to remind you of some scripture passages that are appropriate especially at this part of your life; you can use them as part of your normal devotions. But mostly you just need to express how you feel, remember how God has bless you in the past, and seek a spiritual companion to be with you as you go through this darkness time. But please remember it is not your fault." They closed with prayer and agreed to get back together in about a week to talk again.

*****

A week later, Billy Joe and Pastor John again visited via telephone. Billy Joe reported that his anxiety level was definitely lower and he was able to reflect on the many former times when he had felt the real closeness of God's Presence. Then, he intensely spoke, "But I am in a real spiritual crisis. I have been listening to a tape that someone gave me about anxiety and what to do about it. Pastor, I have always trusted God whenever I asked for forgiveness, but I have not repented like others. They cry and have such an emotional upheaval. I feel sure that I have not taken my sins seriously. I need to repent more and pray harder."

With a bit of concern in his voice, John responded, "Billy Joe, do you have serious persistent sin in your life?" To which he immediately replied, "I have become aware of things about myself that are worse than I first realized, like words I said that hurt people and my attempt to control when it was not my place to do so." "But are those things for which you have sought God's forgiveness and some reconciliation when possible," re-asked Pastor

John? To which Billy Joe honestly responded, "Yes. I have always done that; but I feel so awful about how sinful I have been."

John pointedly inquired, "Billy Joe, do you think that by taking your sins more seriously as you say that you will get God to forgive you?" And Billy Joe objected, "Oh, no; I know that God has forgiven me. It is not that at all. I feel the weight of my sins more than ever. It feels like I am before the 'Judgment Seat.' So I think that if I would repent more, God would make me feel less anxious and smile on me." Pastor John politely interrupted, "I am glad to hear you say all of this except for your last sentence. You cannot get God to make you feel better by repenting more. Your spiritual crisis is not that you need to repent more; your spiritual crisis is that you think by doing the right things even better, you can somehow persuade God to give you peace. But it does not work like that. The peace that passes understanding is beyond our comprehension and therefore outside our ability to figure out or make happen. Remember, Jesus felt anxious and abandoned even though he had done everything right. All he could do was feel the sins of the world weighing on him; and finally say, "Into your hands I commit my Spirit."

"I think I am starting to get this. It seems to be something that I just have to go through; I can't change it or fix it; and my only recourse is to trust God as I have always done. But why do I feel so awful about my sins? All of a sudden, I have these things and people I have offended that just pop into my mind. I have wondered if it was the Devil bringing these to me; but really it feels just like when the Holy Spirit comes to me."

"Billy Joe, I have a suggestion. When the Holy Spirit brings these memories, you might think about them as a gift handed to you. God is giving you a birthday present ready for you to unwrap. This present is an opportunity to prepare you for eternity. Very truly you have been forgiven, but God is inviting you to feel the depths of your sins in ways that you have not felt before. And when you do, just say, 'God, I feel how awfully sinful I have been; and I'm so sorry.' Then God, with arms wrapped around you, simply says, 'I know, Billy Joe, and it is ok. I know how you feel. I have felt the same way about your sins.' Do this for every gift that God brings to your mind. Each time you do this, it is like dross being burned away from your soul, so that you can shine like silver."

After a moment, Billy Joe said, "Thank you, Pastor. I can do this and I feel so much clearer about what is going on." John concluded, "You are most welcome. I'm glad it has been helpful. Let's end our time today with prayer."

An insightful reader might have recognized that Billy Joe's story seemed to have elements of the "Dark Night of the Senses" in it, especially in regard to his wanting to "repent more and pray harder" to get God to make him "less anxious and smile on him." However, other factors help to determine his experience as the "Dark Night of the Spirit." First, Billy Joe is not at the end of the "Purgative Way" since he has been learning, growing and loving God deeply more many years. Second, the depth of his spiritual pain described as the "weight of the world" is another strong indicator. Finally, while continuing the practice of correct spiritual habits, his identification with Jesus, his sincere trust in God as well as his passionate desire to follow God also point to the "Dark Night of the Spirit." <u>Billy Joe was being moved to the place where he would have to experience, not just understand, what Jesus went through</u>.

The apostle Paul also expressed arriving at a similar time in his life when he wrote: "I want to know Christ and the power of his resurrection and the fellowship of sharing in his sufferings, becoming like him in his death, and so, somehow, to attain to the resurrection from the dead."[33] [Philippians 3:10-11] Clearly Paul wanted to identify with Jesus' suffering, death and resurrection. But this was not about whether God would provide resurrection for him at the end of life; instead Paul desired the "spiritual crucifixion and resurrection" of his Soul-Self while he was on earth. In other words, <u>St. Paul was moving through the experience of Jesus' pain and new life so as to be gifted into the state of "unity" with God</u>. He expressed a similar conviction in Galatians, "I have been crucified with Christ and I no longer live, but Christ lives in me. The life I live in the body, I live by faith in the Son of God, who loved me and gave himself for me."[34] [Galatians 2:20] Some Christians near the end of their earthly lives may have so surrendered their mind, heart and will as to spiritually bond with Jesus; they have been moved through the "Dark Night of the Spirit."

REVISITING THE "DARK NIGHT OF THE SOUL"

In conclusion, the "Dark Night of the Soul" is experienced by Christians who have traveled the Spiritual Road for quite a while. It is experienced in spiritual struggle, dryness in prayer and the seeming absence of God. Its purpose is the purification of Christians to be able to morph into "oneness" with God. The "Dark Night of the Soul" includes two parts: the "Dark Night of the Senses" is about the purification of sensate ways of connecting with God; the "Dark Night of the Spirit" releases the intellectual concepts as well as the feeling-memories of past happening or future imaginations. The human will is also surrendered so as to complete the spiritual process that Jesus modeled.

Christians may have the temptation to withdraw from the world while they go through the "Dark Nights." However, since they are still charged to love God and neighbor as self, they still must live and function in the world. How are they to live? Consider the analogy: Your long time spouse whom you deeply love slips into a coma. She does not respond to you in any conceivable way. To remain faithful to her, you visit her every day, talk to her (even hear the words she would return to you) every day. You even water the plants that she loved so much to honor her and you always tell others how much you love her. You willingly love her because of who she is and has always been – Your Perfect Love.

SUMMARY OF THE ILLUMINATIVE WAY

The Illuminative Way is long – as have been these chapters. It typically covers at least thirty years of Christians' lives and therefore includes a variety of life events and challenges. These years involve growing into a personal identity, gaining skills and convictions, as well as entering into long-term relationships that can include friends, spouse, family and work associates. As the years continue, people begin to see a potential ending of their lives and influences so they initiate ways to build and pass on what they have accumulated.

In conjunction with these life events, people also go through spiritual transitions which center around a growing relationship with the divine. Christians learn and gain skills, which includes a better understanding of what God intends. This leads to "Clarifications" which are deeper and/or more refined knowledge that can lead to wisdom. The "Learnings" and "Clarifications" both enable Christians to become deeply devoted to God and the ways of God. Accordingly, they enjoy an enriching relationship with God, share this freely and eagerly participate in all things spiritual, which includes a more consistent and affective prayer life. "Mission and Generativity" provide the practical application of faith into the world. This may include caring for others, being an evangel, building a congregation, teaching or any other way that extends Christian faith into the world. The "Dark Night of the Spirit" occurs near the end of the Illuminative Way. It is a period of time, sometimes quite extended, of purifying individual Christians until they have totally surrendered all of themselves.

The processes of these years are not linear. Life has so many twists and turns – externally and internally – so predicting the process of spiritual growth is not an exact science. On the other hand, enough similarities exists that allow for a sketch of life to be made; and furthermore, the anticipated end-results are the same – to live the best that is possible and respond to God accordingly. Understanding this sketch hopefully helps Christians to cooperate with what God is doing.

The Christian path has been described as the "training of the human will" to be in line with God's Will. In other words, if Christians are to do God's Will, which is not an innate or automatic propensity, then they need to re-form their human wills. Accordingly, this process requires the increase of understanding and personal strength which will need to be surrendered; and the process usually takes quite a long time. This roughly corresponds to the natural developmental process that psychologists call Individualization, which God uses to draw people into a loving relationship. **In the broadest brush stroke, Christian maturity is about gaining skills in order to acquire the strength of individual personal will so as to be able to surrender that human will to God.**[35] Christians are to give up all that they have come to know that makes up themselves. As a result, all that Christians have left is to "will" to be with God. The majority of this process takes place during the Illuminative Way although it can carry over into the Unitive Way. It is a long, challenging time that hopefully leads into marvelous moments of unity with God and even into a period of living so connected with the divine that it can be described as "oneness."

CHAPTER 11

The Unitive Way

"The Unitive Way is the way of those who are in the state of the perfect, that is, those who have their minds so drawn away from all temporal things that they enjoy great peace, who are neither agitated by various desires nor moved by any great extent by passion, and who have their minds chiefly fixed on God and their attention turned, either always or very frequently, to Him. It is the union with God by love and the actual experience and exercise of that love."[1]

Essentially, no words can elucidate the condition and circumstances of the Unitive **Way**. Words are only symbols that people have to approximate reality. However, they are all people have to express feelings and clarify understandings. In truth, the Unitive Way is mostly indiscernible except to echo St. Teresa, "One can say no more – insofar as can be understood – than that the soul, I mean the spirit, is made one with God."[2]

A number of contemporary spiritual authors have laudably considered St. John's "Dark Nights" and the "Unitive Way" by interpreting his technical material; and I would refer people to those works for full explanations. However, I simply want to place the "Unitive Way" in the Spiritual Road process with enough details to be initially useful for spiritual helpers. So, mindful of St. Teresa's disclaimer, but so that spiritual helpers might have something with which to begin, I will attempt an intuitive sketch of the Unitive Way with the following topics:

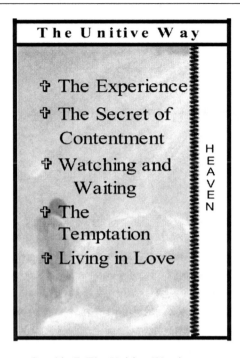

Graphic 7: The Unitive Way is a
deep maturing of Christian faith in
which complete surrender and
God's workings are necessary for it to occur.

THE EXPERIENCE

The groom is a little nervous; the bride is beautifully adorned. The candles are lighted to the soft sounds of stringed music. Family and friends chatter excitedly as they fill the pews of this familiar church setting. The minister is sincerely honored to officiate at this much anticipated wedding ceremony. The entrance music begins to play. The groom sees his bride who seems as beautiful as the first day he saw her. He smiles broadly and she glows in return. They are so happy! They have thought about this ceremony and have earnestly desired to pronounce their "I will" vows to each other. They love all who have come to share this glorious day with them. They will enjoy the festivities and visiting that will follow. Mostly, they will relish this event and revel in its splendor and meaning. However, despite it all, they share a single focus for which they can hardly wait: to go home, cuddle in each other's arms in silence, with nothing they have to do for each other but just be there together. They love everyone and their attention; but to go away unto themselves and hold each other in an everlasting embrace is the only way they can imagine to culminate who they are … on this day of their fiftieth year marriage renewal celebration.

Analogously, this event expresses the feeling and singleness of the "Experience" of the Unitive Way. All that Christians want to do is spend time wrapped in an experience that Jesus called "oneness." It is the consummation of an entire life lived moving toward God; and it came into fruition when God permeated, probably impregnated is better, the human soul. A new life has been conceived and is growing, but yet to be born. It is some form of angelic being within the womb of the temporal-spatial world that will be born into a numensphere yet to be revealed – no wonder "one can say no more" about what is really happening.

Involved is the condition wherein God and humans are "in" each other via the same way that God and Jesus abide in each other. **God brings a newness which causes a total "being-set" change within Christians**. The Apostle Paul attempted to say how this was happening within him: "I have been crucified with Christ and I no longer live, but Christ lives in me. The life I live in the body, I live by faith in the Son of God, who loved me and gave himself for me."[3] [Galatians 2:20] Since Paul was writing, of course, he was not crucified, like dead. In fact, his explanation hardly makes sense, except to others who have had a similar experience. It has been referred to as "spiritual crucifixion." Voluntary hypnosis, perhaps, can approximately clarify how one can live, speak and act within another. Truly, with the surrender of the human will in the "Dark Night of the Spirit," God's Holy Spirit abides internally but without dissolving the person.

Abiding and embracing is part of the new "being-set" condition in which Christians reside. When Christians are immersed in the Unitive Way, there is no other place to be – nothing of the past really matters and the future cannot be imagined to be better than this moment. To fully and perfectly "abide" in the embrace of this Presence of God is eternal life – the eternal now. It is to "know" God, as much as is humanly possible, which is eternal life.[4] [John 17:3]

Christian helpers, of course, need to discern whether or not people are moving toward or on the Unitive Way. St. John of the Cross writes much about this discernment which can be summarized via three criteria. First, a Christian "finds no consolation in things of God, nor in any created thing either."[5] In other words, God does not seem to bless Christians very often anymore; and nothing in their spiritual life tends to excite Christians. They might lament, "I just can't seem to do it anymore." Careful attention needs to be given to make sure that clinical depression is not happening or that sliding into sinful apathy is occurring. This is discerned with the below second and third criteria. Second, after a period of time when Christians attempt to renew their "zeal" for God and "joy" for life, they come to realize that they don't actually want to re-establish their former prayers and spiritual actions. This unconscionable insight feels like "betrayal" for which Christians are sorrowful. Spiritual helpers might simply ask, "If you were really, really honest with yourself, would you say that you don't want to do it any longer?" Discernment needs to be given that such an attitude is not about laziness. Third, these Christians yearn so deeply to be with God, enthralled by God, wrapped in God's warmth and love, understood to the core of their being, assured and affirmed by their perfect Lover. While they are not exactly sure how to obtain this state of being, their sincere and singleness of desiring God is absolute.[6] <u>Finally</u>, spiritual helpers very often must assist Unitive Way Christians to understand that they are still on the right path to God – because they cannot see it themselves and even feel like they are going the wrong way.

While this Unitive "new way of being" typically does not occur until after going through the process of spiritual growth described in the previous chapters, nevertheless, occasional experiences during life do occur that anticipate and approximate the Unitive Way. Perhaps this foretaste of Heaven is God's way of luring Christians onward. These pre-Unitive Way moments involve true joy, beautiful love, perfect peace or genuine faith – **they are always God-given, unexpected and beyond ability to completely explain**. But since they are commonly experienced, people identify and validate them for each other. The welcomed birth of a baby, an extraordinarily beautiful vista or sunset, prayer that transports believers into an alternate state of consciousness in which only God is there, a visionary moment of clarity and perfect understanding as with John's Revelation, the embrace of lovers that melts together as one and so forth. In each of these, people simply and purely want to stay there forever! Of course, that is their desire; God is surrounding them.

Accordingly, such experiences can cause some confusion. For example, the Unitive Way contains much of what is part of the Purgative Way – trust, surrender, the amazement of who God is and how could God ever consider being "with me." The contemporary Christian band, Casting Crowns, clearly wrote "Who am I?" for Purgative Way Christians. However, the sentiment and some of the words could easily be on the lips of those in Union: "Who am I, that the Lord of all the earth would care to know my name?" and it is "not because of who I am, but because of what you've done." It's "not because of what I've done but because of who you are."[7] All of these sentiments cause Christians to trust God, surrender all that they are and be mesmerized by the perfection of God. Yet, there is one huge difference – the Unitive Way Christians are totally giving themselves again. Even with the full experience of having lived through all the struggles of life, they would give themselves in the same way. Couples participating in a fiftieth year renewal of marriage vows ceremony do so fully mindful that it means they would do it all over again, including all the ups and downs.

In addition to the scripture about St. Paul being crucified with Christ, other passages refer to this part of the Christian pathway. For example, when Paul discusses the visions and revelations that God gives, he talks about knowing a man who was "caught up to the third heaven." Paul doesn't describe the details of this experience nor does he want to belabor whether this was an external or internal occurrence, but simply notes that this man was in "paradise" where he heard "inexpressible things" that he was not permitted to repeat.[8] [II Corinthians 12:1-4] This is a Unitive Way experience. Also, the writer of II

Peter indicates that "participation in the divine nature" is possible.[9] [II Peter 1:4-7] The progression he suggests reflects the transitions made along the Spiritual Road: a beginning faith is purified with goodness, knowledge and self-control (along the Purgative Way); this is enriched via perseverance and godliness extended to others (in the Illuminative Way); these are finally culminated in pure love (via the Unitive Way).

Describing this "Experience" can also be enhanced using the opening words to an old song. "Over the river and through the woods to Grandmother's house we go. The horse knows the way to carry the sleigh through white and drifting snow." "Going to Grandma's house" is the comparison that I use to describe this segment of the Spiritual Road, which is in contrast to the labored preparation of the Pre-Christian Way, the struggle of the Purgative Way and the speed of the Illuminative Way. On the Unitive Way, Christians take a slower, unhindered pace – actually they don't drive or direct the course; the horse does and they are just along for the ride. They are enwrapped in the "memory-vision" of being at Grandma's which is a mystical, joyous place filled with love and grace and goodness. Christians are not exactly sure when they will arrive, but just being on the way brings all the wonderful numinousness that floods their souls with a peace that passes understanding. They just rest in, absorb and enjoy the moment whatever it includes. They abide in God – that is the good news.

In summary, the "Experience" of the Unitive Way brings Christians to abide in and live through divine love with a deep satisfaction of all that is. As a result, they have a new "being-set" approach to life – all that really matters is being with God; in those perfect moments that are so incredibly difficult to explain. A calmness, wisdom and focus pervade all of their loving actions. They have learned the secret of spiritual contentment.

THE SECRET OF CONTENTMENT

The apostle Paul, in chains awaiting a death sentence, pens some of the most encouraging affirmations of the Christian faith in his letter to the Philippians. The reflection and conclusion on his life are instructive for the process of coming to the Unitive Way and being in that state. "I know what it is to be in need, and I know what it is to have plenty. I have learned the secret of being content in any and every situation, whether well fed or hungry, whether living in plenty or in want."[10] [Philippians 4:12] The frame of reference for Paul's satisfaction in God is elucidated in the difficulties he went through.

"I have worked much harder, been in prison more frequently, been flogged more severely, and been exposed to death again and again. Five times I received from the Jews the forty lashes minus one. Three times I was beaten with rods, once I was stoned, three times I was shipwrecked, I spent a night and a day in the open sea, I have been constantly on the move. I have been in danger from rivers, in danger from bandits, in danger from my own countrymen, in danger from Gentiles; in danger in the city, in danger in the country, in danger at sea; and in danger from false brothers. I have labored and toiled and have often gone without sleep; I have known hunger and thirst and have often gone without food; I have been cold and naked. Besides everything else, I face daily the pressure of my concern for all the churches.[11] [II Corinthians 11:23-28]

In my first solo pastorate, one of my "if it ain't broke don't fix it" elders approached me after a sermon focused on the crucifixion of Jesus. He said, "I don't like all this talk about suffering and death; can't we just get right to the resurrection?" Today, I can still feel my jaw drop in amazement the same way it did that day as I responded, "How do you think that we get to the resurrection?"

Can we obtain the full maturity of Christ-likeness without going through all of what Jesus went through? Paul didn't think so. "Now if we are children, then we are heirs – heirs of God and co-heirs with Christ, <u>if indeed we share in his sufferings</u> in order that we may also share in his glory."[12] [Romans 8:17] **Christians are united with God, in part, by going through what the divine experienced and experiences – suffering and distress**. What we call pain in life is designed to be opportunity for God – no wonder Paul advised us to "rejoice in our sufferings."[13] [Romans 5:3] Nevertheless, when it comes to trouble, people do get to choose – to push away from God or draw closer to God. **However, the blessing of difficulty, if divinely viewed, leads to contentment; and thus to complete loving surrender to God**.

I ask: Can anyone truly appreciate the goodness of God without knowing the awfulness that comes via life's negative experiences? I think not. Without the experience of cold, people can never appreciate hot. A lukewarm life cannot bring gratitude for the fire of God. Is the "light and momentary trouble"[14] [II Corinthians 4:17] of repeated bouts of devastating cancers or a living with a deteriorating neuromuscular disease worth being embraced by God for eternity? For some people it is; for most it is not – at least until they realize who they are and to whom they belong.

The process evolves somewhat like this: People come to understand, consciously or unconsciously, that they are will-directed Soul-Selves, who come from God and belong to God; but who can freely choose to respond to God or not. Through this world and its events, God lovingly desires to create "angelic beings" to be in unity and perfect communion with God for eternity. For this purpose, via the vehicle of Christianity, God continuously invites people (beginning with the knowledge of God and salvation in Jesus) to the full maturity of Christ-likeness – the completion of the Spiritual Road process. Somewhere along the way, Christians come to identify that they are more than their mind, feelings and actions; and in their pursuit of God surrender all that they are including their intellect, memory and will.[15] This is epitomized in the prayer, attributed to St. Ignatius:

144

Take, Lord, and receive all my liberty,
my memory, my understanding,
and my entire will,
All I have and call my own.
You have given all to me.
To you, Lord, I return it.
Everything is yours; do with it what you will.
Give me only your love and your grace,
that is enough for me.[16]

Until people come to <u>loving</u> surrender through a complete and voluntary response to God, God cannot come (because it would be an irrevocable violation of God's basic nature to do so) and "abide" in Christians – and consequently bring them to "abide" in God. The ultimate loving surrender of the Unitive Way means that people give up all of this life to be with God – the pleasures, the accuracy, the earthly approximations of God and even the right to have and/or manage their own lives. <u>The struggles and difficulties of life actually help them to do this</u>.

If people experience a "good and perfect" life, they do not easily come to understand that ultimately they are not in control. On the other hand, life's trials can facilitate the conviction, "I may not know what the future holds; but I know who holds the future – and God loves me and wants the best for me." This could actually be the mantra and the prayerful approach for Unitive Way Christians. If and when people genuinely have this conviction, they move closer to the new "being-set" attitude of contentment that is characteristic of the Unitive Way. Jesus' comment about how hard it is for a "rich man to enter into the Kingdom of God"[17] [Luke 18:18-25] was much less about his wealth than it was about whether he would be able to choose to surrender himself to God – and therefore be able to experience "oneness." Life was too easy for him to get to this conviction. Interestingly, Jesus "caused" pain for this rich young ruler by not affirming that he could get what he wanted (without complete surrender) – he wasn't in charge.

The journey into the Unitive Way takes Christians through the life experiences of want and plenty. Whether they arrive is determined by whether they come to know the "secret of being content." **Unitive Way Christians have a balance and in that perspective they seem to live effortlessly**. When Christians are concerned about the things, people and situations in life, there is no contentment in them. On the other hand, neither apathy nor slothfulness brings contentment. Healthy "concern for others" has its place in the spiritual life since it helps establish godly values in the Soul-Self and build the Community of God. However, at this point on the Unitive Way, "excessive" concern ONLY keeps God from working within Christians.

On the Unitive Way, Christians are fully alive because they are full of God. On the other parts of the Spiritual Road, Christians can also be characterized as being alive – but on the Purgative Way, they are alive with an anxiousness to get it right and on the Illuminative Way they are alive to understand how to make a real difference. **On the Unitive Way, Christians are fully alive, not only because God is embedded in them, but also because of an attitude of spiritual contentment**.

Life is about coming to experience and appreciate who humans are in relationship with God. When that happens, the Soul-Self denies itself in humble surrender to God. That is the secret of contentment – it happens on the Unitive Way.

WATCHING AND WAITING

The beautiful "Experience" of the Unitive Way brings peace, aliveness, contentment – all initiated through the "incarnation" of divine love given. For various reasons, Christians do not often stay very long on this part of the Spiritual Road mostly because life gets in the way.

When Christians exercise divine love, they cannot do it for too long. Analogously, using muscles strenuously during physical exercise causes lactic acid pain which results in the tearing down of muscle tissue. Rest is needed to repair the "damage" after which the muscle will be stronger and have greater endurance. This same "body building" process likewise occurs in the Soul-Self – "The Experience" with God is exhausting to the Soul-Self. Consequently, Christians need to "watch and wait" and not fall into temptation. They need to rest their muscles in order to be able to run again. Most people are not very patient and want to do something – even when doing something is counterproductive. However, rest is not doing "nothing" – instead it is allowing God's healing to occur in muscles and in the Soul-Self! Do athletes trust that healing is happening during their fallow days? Broken bones knit together when not stressed. A Soul-Self does the same. "But, doctor, when will I be ready to run? How long do I have to wait?" Of course, the unwanted answer is when healing has finished … at an unknown time. As runners tell me, there is nothing more wonderfully exhilarating and refreshing than pushing through the pain to be transported into that euphoric "running zone." They long for those moments. But for now in the waiting, the exhilaration of the Unitive Way "Experience" is gone – although God is still working.

Some classic examples can help illustrate how God is still at work in these Unitive Way Christians' lives. Each analogy has strengths and limitations; they most certainly apply to Christians differently according to their particular life circumstances and personalities.

St. John of the Cross used the illustration of <u>the burning log</u> throughout his writings. People are a log in the fireplace and God is the fire. As the fire enters the log, the log changes – the burning reveals cracks, expels bugs, blackens the log and makes it smells

146

badly. Eventually the log becomes aglow – "it possesses the properties and performs the actions of fire."[18] The log is as much like God as a log can be.

The biblical image comes in the form of <u>metal that is purified in fire</u> in order to burn the doss away so that all that is left is precious silver or gold. God is the one who activates this process. God will be like a refiner's fire … "He will sit as a refiner and purifier of silver; he will purify the Levites and refine them like gold and silver. Then the Lord will have men who will bring offerings in righteousness."[19] [Malachi 3:3] This metaphor deemphasizes the difficulty of the process by focusing on the end result that God has in mind for Christians – pure and precious.

Thomas Green likens this process to <u>floating in a river</u>, instead of swimming. Christians are carried by the current toward the ocean of God. They are moving and making progress. However, they are not actively moving toward a self-determined goal. On the other hand, Christians must sustain the position conducive to floating, which is neither to be limp in indifference and nor engage in rigid, powerful swimming. This image is particularly helpful in regard to how Christians cooperate in the process but without getting into the flow of God's work.[20]

I prefer the image of <u>God as a blacksmith and Christians as a solid block of iron</u> – not unlike the biblical metaphor of the Potter and the clay.[21] [Jeremiah 18:4; Isaiah 64:8] God thrusts Christians into the fire and keeps them there until they are white hot and pliable. Then God puts people on the anvil and beats them into the shape God wants. Then Christians are immersed in the cold water to solidify what they have become. This process is repeated and repeated until God is done. This analogy includes both the pain of the "Dark Night" and the formation by God's hand.

All of these examples make clear that God is doing the work that needs to be done. In fact, if Christians attempt to do anything, it is almost one-hundred per cent guaranteed to be a hindrance to God's Unitive Way work.

In this book, I have intentionally limited discussion about prayer, not because it is unimportant since it is absolutely essential, but mostly because prayer has been the primary way to gage spiritual progress – and I wanted to focus on other ways to value and evaluate the spiritual life. However, at this point, **some prayer discussion is needed. The reason is not because Christians need to pray more or better. In fact, they must pray differently than ever before – God must be "allowed" to pray for Christians**. Accordingly, <u>Unitive Way praying is simply about "spending time" with God</u>. It includes the same kind of non-will directed living that constitutes the Unitive Way as a whole. In other words, instead of telling God anything, <u>prayer becomes non-focused, open-ended attentiveness</u>. Centering prayer is more suited to Unitive Way spirituality although it also can be too prearranged.

Unitive Way praying at its best is just "watching and waiting" – it seems nothing like the ways Christians were taught to pray. In fact, when it comes to prayer, Christians are especially in "weakness" at this place on the Spiritual Road. Nothing that Christians can say or do via former prayer forms can have any positive effect on strengthening and increasing their personal relationship with God; ONLY God can do that. However, God WILL NOT do anything without permission! Actually, "spending time" in prayer IS permission – it is when the Holy Spirit works. "The Spirit helps us in our weakness. We do not know what we ought to pray for, but the Spirit himself intercedes for us with groans that words cannot express."[22] [Romans 8:26] Unitive Way praying is about the "person" of God infusing Christians. Constance FitzGerald refers to this as "someone" not something actively transforming Christians via the person of Jesus as the divine Word or Wisdom of God.[23]

Henri Nouwen's definition of prayer is classic for this stage of the Spiritual Road – prayer is "spending useless time before the Lord." The scripture that encourages this approach is "Be still, and know that I am God"[24] [Psalm 46:10] as well as "Be still before the Lord and wait patiently for him."[25] [Psalm 37:7] **Christians prayerfully spend "dedicated" time with God that seems to be without purpose, defuse, unstructured and open.** Consequently, there is inclination and need for quiet and calm in prayer and in daily living; and even in the midst of a crowd Unitive Way Christians have particularly tranquil and composed demeanors. Life is prayer, really – if prayer is life.

Since Unitive Way Christians offer non-descript prayers that are not about answers, guidance or direction, they need strength to pray in the midst of their spiritual darkness, trusting that God is present and working. They may wish to ask others to pray for them for this purpose; specifically, spiritual helpers can be of invaluable service if they would do this for those who are ready for or moving into the Unitive Way.

On the Unitive Way, while the wedding celebration and the subsequent togetherness "Experience" are the culmination of the Unitive Way, much of Christians' time is spent differently – in watching and waiting. Wait while the log burns. Float while as the river runs. Move while the Potter forms the clay. Take shape while the blacksmith forms the white-hot molten iron bar. Let God be God. Most of the time, all that Unitive Way Christians feel is the burning, the endless floating, being pushed and formed by an unknowable, uncontrollable force. They know that they know that they know God is working and that is enough – so in contentment they wait.

THE TEMPTATION

When I was working, I often longed to retire so that I could spend more time in prayer than my busy life would allow. I longed for non-programmed hours in which to contemplate God. I wanted to focus on all the spiritual subjects and read everything on my long book list. Now that I am retired, after a brief euphoric time, prayer and spiritual reading is simply hard. Oh it is certainly easy enough to do; it's hard because I don't get out of it what I had imagined I would. It can be boring. It mostly is empty, non-responsive and even melancholy. Now I noticed that in those years before retirement that my prayers less and less often resulted in the "feelings of answered prayer" or divine insights in which I would receive clarity on a problem or action I needed to take. I was sure that I was just getting older, more tired and too stressed to have "good prayer times." But I was wrong; my prayers and spiritual life was JUST as God planned.

Why didn't anyone tell me that my Christian spirituality would become so ladened? They probably did; I just had other plans. **All of the ways that I had "prayed"** – scriptural studying that enriched my thoughts of God, insightful journaling, active meditation with playful interaction with Jesus, dreams where God clearly directed my life and certainly corrected my behaviors, even passive contemplation where I flowed where God wanted me and occasionally receiving a "vision" and one confirmable "pre-cognition" prayer – **were intensely wonderful!!!** God still comes in such ways, occasionally and certainly not on demand; and I truly desire those moments. The problem is that I can no longer "make them happen" as if I ever could; but **I thought that if I tried hard enough or practiced better or learned a fresh approach, I would get the end result of bringing the "presence of God" into my life. That is "The Temptation!"**

The really "bad" news for Christians is that during this "Watching and Waiting" of the Unitive Way, "The Experience" of God is mostly unnoticeable – obscure at best. God seems absent again! It is just like Christians have "slipped" backward. They may or may not have. **The other "Temptation" is that if God is not going to show up, then I'm not going to either**. There is something seemingly unfair about putting in lots of effort without getting anything in return. That is how the "Watching and Waiting" seems. Thus, "The Temptation" is to attempt to recreate the former experiences of God or to simply stop – both are sin, doing that which is against what God desires.

What is needed?
"Then in fellowship sweet we will sit at His feet,
Or we'll walk by His side in the way;
What He says we will do, where He sends we will go;
Never fear, only trust and obey.
Trust and obey, for there's no other way
To be happy in Jesus, but to trust and obey."[26]

Christians are to trust that God is still caring, still loving and still working – even though they rarely notice it. Christians are to continue to live as they have done in the previous years. They need to reaffirm and reassert the lessons of the "Dark Nights" – to not actively seek God with the senses and to surrender mind, heart and will from their efforts of pursuing God. I pray more today than I have ever prayed at any former time in my life – I also pray that I continue to give up having to get a good feeling or confirmation from God that comes from my efforts. **More importantly, the entire purpose of the "Unitive Way" is to be united into who God is – but only God can do that.** Christians need to be pliable, patient and willing – stay out of God's way. As God unites, Christians abide.

While it is not wrong to characterize the goal of the Spiritual Road as to go to Heaven, **Christians have to be "like" God so that they can be <u>with</u> God. Only God can actually make this happen,** but Christians have a whole lot of "cooperating" to do – as God does the work of transforming Christians. Eddie Esponisa wrote "Change My Heart, O God" because of the need to overcome sinfulness. However, the feeling of the Unitive Way's voluntary surrender so that God can completely change the Soul-Self is included:

Change my heart, O God,
Make it ever true.
Change my heart, O God,
May I be like You.
You are the Potter,
I am the clay;
Mold me and make me,
This is what I pray.[27]

OK. So, if Christians are to become "like" God, what are they to do? The answer is given in the question: "What does God think, feel and do?" Because God's very nature is love, God thinks, feels and acts in pure love. God does not love for <u>any personal benefit</u> – neither to help others, nor because it is right or to accomplish a purpose, but God loves ONLY because that is who God is. In other words, to be God, God must love, is love and will always love – regardless of the circumstances or the results. **If there is a "task" for Unitive Way Christians, it is to love as purely as God loves – to be in the "unity zone."**

LIVING IN LOVE

Living in love has been the rallying call of Christians from the beginning of their life of faith – but not like this! It is living in nothing but love; nothing but God! Now, there is no concern for what Christians did in the past to be loving or the need to repeat any particular understanding, service or prayer. There is no apprehension about having any particular plan of action that could do the most good, bring the best truth or comfort the fullest. In fact, none of the ways that <u>Christians themselves</u> can love are helpful. <u>All of the ways</u> that God loves through them are exceptionally good!

If I learned anything from my association with twelve step group participants, who are typically caught in the past and manipulate the future, it is to just "do the next right thing." It's simple. Yes, but it is also profound. What is straight ahead? What is obvious? What is the next step? Is that living in love? Then, don't think about it; don't act on emotions; don't consider how others will feel about it; don't remember doing that before; and don't plan it. Just do it – lovingly, quietly, and gently.

The apostle Paul is not considering suicide but just acquiescing with whatever God wants when he wrote: "For to me, to live is Christ and to die is gain. If I am to go on living in the body, this will mean fruitful labor for me. Yet what shall I choose? I do not know! I am torn between the two: I desire to depart and be with Christ, which is better by far; but it is more necessary for you that I remain in the body."[28] [Philippians 1:21-24] He will willingly do whatever comes next; because he knows that God is directing the next step in his life – he will just do it "Living in Love."

During the Unitive Way how do Christians actually function in life? Basically the same way they have grown to live – only with a different attitude and approach to life. <u>In their spiritual life</u>: while they desire to be immersed a state of "oneness" with God, they cannot create it. The best they can do is put themselves in the situation and state of mind where it is possible for God to grace them with "eternal embrace." <u>In the rest of life</u>: they simply approach whatever is next, approximating the love that God has for the world. It is not possible to express that which is beyond words, but let me make some suggestions anyway. "Living in Love" like God is:

- ✟ Effortless
- ✟ Floating
- ✟ Non-anxious presence
- ✟ Simplicity
- ✟ Childlike (not childish or all about me – but trusting)
- ✟ Graceful
- ✟ Forgiving
- ✟ Gentle
- ✟ Smiling
- ✟ Peace-filled

The goal of the Christian life and the Unitive Way is to grow into the maturity of Christ and experience the "oneness" of God. In the process, Christians love like God loves and as a result allow God to affect the world. "Living in Love" is not some form of particular behavior that Christians need to learn – at least that has not already been received. Instead, it is true contentment and trust that God is the one who leads. Christians love because they follow. Christians follow because they love.

Reading the Maps

Ihave spent eleven chapters providing some theory and many details about how people grow spiritually in the Christian faith. I hope that this spiritual map has been helpful in identifying the "X" of people's location along the roadway. I trust that the insights might become foresights for what might be ahead, both for spiritual helpers and for those they assist. **I anticipate that spiritual helpers will be able to use "The Spiritual Road" chart for the purpose of reading this spiritual map**. However, the Christian spiritual overview is only one of many maps that provide synopses of human beings. In the following three chapters, I am going to outline some additional maps. I suggest that overlaying these various maps is indispensible for assisting the Christian spiritual journey because how people grow in psycho-social ways directly affects how or even whether they grow spiritually.

This line of thinking debunks one of the unspoken assumptions that people make about Christianity. **People often believe that they only have to become a Christian and then all they have to do is live life the best they can and God will make their lives good**. Accepting this half truth is the cause of a lot of problems. God truly desires to, and can, make people's lives better, but they need to cooperate. In truth, **Christian people must mature spiritually and as they do, God can be more effectively involved**. If they do not, then life becomes more difficult than it needs to be. If they do not, they cannot employ a re-mastered Christianity to manage their lives. If they do not, then their faith will seem irrelevant, useless and even boring.

In addition, Christian people also need to mature psycho-socially. If they do not, then their arrested development blocks or limits the flow of God's power into their lives. God most certainly wants to intervene, but with human free will affirmed as necessary for loving divine-human relationships, people's choices can obstruct the process. Maintaining unforgiveness, for example, blocks God's forgiveness as strongly supported both scripturally and experientially.[1] As a further analogy, a fourteen-year-olds puppy love is beautiful; but a love that idealizes the other and focuses on the self's own attributes (feelings and looks) will not sustain the life of any thirty-four-year-olds family relationship. Accordingly, human love that does not mature with the changes in life spills over into a love of God that is likewise self-centered. As a result, people's limitations affect both life and faith.

Since both spiritual and psycho-social maturity are important for growing divine-human relationships, having a Christian faith that matures and parallels the movement of each stage of human development is the ideal. God needs to be at the heart and center of all life; and personal lives as well as Christian faiths are designed to mature so that this happens. Thus, the interfacing of God and events all through life can help to assure such mutual developments; and <u>overlaying spiritual and psycho-social developmental maps can assist in this Christian spiritual growth</u>.

CHAPTER 12

Understanding the Process ... Developmentally

I commence this chapter with an overview of the process of spiritual development. Spirituality begins with a realization or even a pre-cognitive recognition of God. I have called this "belief in God" which may or may not be clearly understood or rationally expressed. As people begin to apply this belief in real-life practical ways, I have called this having "faith" (which may or may not include a commitment to Jesus Christ). In other words, belief plus application equals faith. The goal of having a faith that is consistent and authentic I have called "concentric faith." Finally, change from one way of understanding God (and/or its application) to another is "spiritual growth." The classical transitions in Christian faith that people grow through have been labeled the Purgative, Illuminative and Unitive Ways. To this, I have added the Pre-Christian Way because spiritual faith happens prior to accepting Jesus as Savior. This is the process of Christian spiritual faith which develops over time as illustrated below.

Newborns do not comprehend God in an intellectual way simply because they do not have the ability to do so. However, babies do experience the trauma of unknown life, warmth versus cold, a mother's familiar heart-beat and the satisfaction of being nourished. Newborns respond to this "God experience" with a coo or a smile which is rewarded with more of the same. The psalmist affirms infants unacknowledged faith experience, claiming that a sense of trust in God was its result.[2] [Psalm 22:9-10] This faith (belief, application and consistency) will change and grow as life happens – when hungry and no food is provided, crying and no one comes, or when a child bites the baby. Consequently, the newborn's "God understanding" changes.

And the change continues. Infants initially need lots of love and care – then they typically thrive and grow somewhat effortlessly. However, things change. Most parents have experienced the "no" of the "terrible twos." Most parents have suffered through the phase of a child's incessantly asking "why" to every answer given. Many parents have struggled through the "rebellion of youth." These life experiences alter or at least influence people's perception of God.

This understanding of spiritual faith and growth may seem quite simplistic until people comprehend that the process of belief, application and consistency happens repeatedly. **In**

addition to spiritual growth, human development also includes increasing intellectual understandings, emotional quotients, transitions in moral and ethical abilities as well as stages of knowing and valuing in regard to faith assessments. Consequently, spiritual growth becomes even more complex and multifaceted as people experience these developmental transitions and assimilate what they experience along the way.

In this chapter, I want to encourage spiritual helpers to embrace spiritual developmental growth as a lifelong process, which may be most effective after middle age. Also, because spiritual helpers always consider people's life circumstances, unconsciously at the very least, I suggest that intentionally including personal and social developmental understandings can enhance spiritual assistance.

A number of years ago, I watched a film that documented how children think differently at different times in their development. As they grew and matured, their thinking and ability to reason changed. I don't remember exactly the age of the children but in a social science experiment children were asked to decide which pencil was the longest. When the same length pencils were placed exactly side by side, the children would say that they were the same length. However, when the same length pencils were positioned so that one was ahead of the other, the children would always say that the pencil closest to the end of the table was the longest. I was shocked and impacted to realize that people sometimes cannot learn what spiritual helpers think they <u>should</u> learn.

Today, I simply ask church educators and insistently-passionate pastors, "Would you try to teach calculus to a first grader? Would you expect a third grader to be able to learn quantum physics?" Of course, people answer "no" because they realize that children do not have the ability to understand those topics. The same is true for people when it comes to spiritual growth – at different times in the lives of both children and adults, they can only absorb the spiritual growth that their developmental abilities will allow.[3]

Often within the Christian churches, leaders focus on teaching children in order to help them grow in faith. Sometimes the goal is to nurture children so that they become Christians and are baptized. This is the beginning of formal Christian faith but it is far from the end of the spiritual developmental process. Adult lives change too; and adult faith changes accordingly. When spiritual leaders stop instructing children after baptism or fail to assist adults into new forms of belief, application and consistencies of their faith, churches often end up full of faith-stunted people. As each new or important life event unfolds, these folks typically struggle to understand what God is doing in their lives and how to respond. Growing faith, as well as personal maturity, greatly assists their ability to do so.

While it is clear that children think less maturely than most adults, adults also function at various stages from other adults. Indeed, **adults also participate in a development process of spiritual growth and psycho-social maturity**. One of the great tragedies of the Christian Church is that so many adults stop going to "Sunday school" about the same time that they graduate from high school. Carl Jung has been noted that the second half of life is the spiritual half of life.[4] <u>Actually, adults have the tools and the maturity to effectively learn and grow spiritually – far more than children</u>. While children may be "the future of the church," they don't have much of a future when adults do not participate in an intentional spiritual growth process.

While the New Testament rarely focuses on children, it does understand the importance of growing spiritually as an adult. <u>Faith growth not only has a process but also has a purpose</u>. The subject of Ephesians 4 is that God's Spirit has given a variety of spiritual gifts to strengthen the fellowship of believers. The plan – that the church "may be built up" – assumes that it is not fully constructed. The purpose for individual Christians is stated as maturity in Christ, which assumes that they still have to grow and develop. <u>The conclusion is that Christian faith takes developmental growth</u>.

> But to each one of us grace has been given as Christ apportioned it. It was he who gave some to be apostles, some to be prophets, some to be evangelists, and some to be pastors and teachers, to prepare God's people for works of service, so that the body of Christ may be built up until we all reach unity in the faith and in the knowledge of the Son of God and become mature, attaining to the whole measure of the fullness of Christ.[5] [Ephesians 4:7, 11-13]

On the same subject but in a different letter, the apostle Paul reinforces this teaching about the process of spiritual growth, "When I was a child, I talked like a child, I thought like a child, I reasoned like a child. When I became a man (or woman), I put childish ways behind me."[6] [I Corinthians 13:9-12]

The Bible often preaches what people need to do without describing how to do it. **While the goal is new life in Christ that matures into applied action in the world, the process for becoming that kind of person is not always clearly stated.** <u>Part of the reason, I am convinced, is that faith is to be exactly that – faith – not a step by step manual</u>. The process of becoming Christ-like <u>must</u> rely on God's Spirit [I Corinthians 2:10-16],[7] not on following a rule book. If people had such a rigid procedure to follow, given human tendencies they would quickly make the rules into an idol – like the stereotypical biblical Pharisees, today's leaders would legislate all of the details.

In addition, spiritual maturity does not function in such a linear manner. Biblical ontology[8] postulates that humans are all created in the "image and likeness of God." In other words, people have the spirit of God within them, at least latently; yet from the beginning people do not typically act like the divine is guiding their lives. However, at the moment of personal conversion, God's Spirit is "reborn" and people receive the ability to understand what the Spirit of God teaches even if they don't know how to use it. In computer terminology, people have the program of "Godly Growth" in their central processing unit which they cannot use without an activation code, after which they have to learn to use all of the intricacies of the program – effectively learning to use the mind of Christ.

In other words, <u>God is part and parcel of the spiritual growth process – it is not a purely natural course of action which people can do by themselves</u>. But they need to learn to connect with this Spirit and use it in order to grow spiritually – people learn how to do this developmentally. I often describe this procedure as an angel who has been placed on people's right shoulder to whisper God's advice into one of their ears (while other messages are spoken into their left ear.) As people begin to understand and accept what God wants, they increasingly gain the ability to apply it in their lives. They grow spiritually. The way that scripture describes this is:

> We have not received the spirit of the world but the Spirit who is from God, that we may understand what God has freely given us. This is what we speak, not in words taught us by human wisdom but in words taught by the Spirit, expressing spiritual truths in spiritual words. The man without the Spirit does not accept the things that come from the Spirit of God, for they are foolishness to him, and he cannot understand them, because they are spiritually discerned. ... We have the mind of Christ.[9] [I Corinthians 2:12-14, 16b]

Furthermore, the lack of biblical details on how to grow spiritually is also because the biblical writers did not have the availability of developmental understanding and helpful language to express it. Clearly, the sciences of sociology and psychology that are used to help explain how people think and interact did not exist in biblical times. Nevertheless, what the Bible teaches actually assumes an underlying psychological scheme. Consider the passage in Romans where the Apostle Paul is trying to explain the very real struggle that is going on inside of him. He writes,

> We know that the law is spiritual; but I am unspiritual, sold as a slave to sin. I do not understand what I do. For what I want to do I do not do, but what I hate I do. And if I do what I do not want to do, I agree that the law is good. As it is, it is no longer I myself who do it, but it is sin living in me. I know that nothing good lives in me, that is, in my sinful nature. For I have the desire to do what is good, but I cannot carry it out. For what I do is not the good I want to do; no, the evil I do not want to do — this I keep on doing. Now if I do what I do not want to do, it is no longer I who do it, but it is sin living in me that does it.[10] [Romans 7:14-20]

In the passage, this great scholar and evangelist is not speaking gobble goop or trying to be unclear, he is simply struggling to express what is happening within him since he has no psychological language to articulate such complexities. Assumed in this biblical teaching is the existence of the unconscious mind that sometimes causes people, even Christians, to act in ways they would not if they were fully aware. In addition, understanding the use of the personal will as well as obsessive-compulsive disorders would also help clarify this passage. And yes, it feels like a conflict that happens within people's minds and perhaps in their actions as well.

While I am convinced that God's wisdom is placed in the biblical writings, the writers could only employ the language that they had available. **Overlaying a psychological understanding to what the scriptures are teaching can be extremely helpful especially in the area of spiritual growth.**[11] I recommend, however, that spiritual helpers first be clear about what the biblical writers intend to say before overlaying any psychological commentary.

With or without psychological language, the apostle Paul as well as the writer of Hebrews, when dealing with developmentally-varied Christians, noted that they had to use different approaches.[12] They taught Christians differently according to their ability to grasp what was being said. They spoke at the level of their understanding with what would provide the best possible spiritual growth. They gave milk, not solid food. Indeed, as people grow and change, they deal with life differently. Thus, spiritual helpers need to employ appropriate techniques to help people according to the different phases and abilities of their lives. **While the biblical writers did not have psychological language or social science research available to them, they knew that spiritual growth was developmental.** Thus, in order to best facilitate spiritual growth using current tools is advised. While some spiritual helpers may balk at the idea of employing current social sciences, the biblical writers most certainly would have done so if they had had the opportunity.

While my goal is not to help people know what the disciplines of psychology and sociology say about human development, in order to increase the effectiveness of spiritual guides and to enable Christians to cooperate with what God desires to accomplish, a practical and working knowledge is desirable. In following three chapters, I will summarize the developmental theories of Eric Erikson, Lawrence Kohlberg and James W. Fowler in order to overlay the spiritual road with people's emotional, moral (ethical) and cognitive abilities as well as the ways they make sense of and relate to the divine.[13] As with the overview of the spiritual road, these additional maps are not the territories; also, none is included with the debate and critical evaluation to which each has been subjected. **I am simply going to explore these "psychologies of religious development" in so far as is necessary for overlaying their insights onto the spiritual growth process.**[14] I hope that this information will be helpful for spiritual discernment. However, again, I advise spiritual helpers, "If they are helpful, use them; if not, please don't."

CHAPTER 13

Overlaying the Psycho-Social Map

"We are not human beings having a spiritual experience; we are spiritual beings having a human experience."[1]

I remember entering junior high school and obtaining individual text books. The book for the health and physical education class included information on the makeup of the human body. Students had to count all 206 bones in the human body and check out the circulatory system of veins and arteries. Then, major organs of heart, lung, kidneys and so forth were discussed along with the endocrine system of glands, which, of course, made everyone giggle. The muscles were introduced and the skin revealed what everyone thought was a person. However, what was so fascinating and enlightening was how this picture of the human body was revealed. It began with the skeletal system placed on the book's regular paper page. Then, on see-through plastic, the system of veins and arteries was placed on top of the skeletal system so that both bones and veins/arteries were seen connected together. Then, other transparent pages with organs, glands, muscles and skin were overlaid until the entire human body was formed. It was an extraordinary way to view, interconnect and understand the physique of Homo sapiens and the first time I actually conceived the interrelationship between the parts and the whole person.

One assumption from the opening quotation is that while people are essentially spiritual, they are a composite of the human experience which includes how people develop emotionally and mentally. So, if spiritual helpers are to fully comprehend people, they need to consider all of the human dimensions, coordinated together. Accordingly, in order to fully appreciate the whole creature, each of the various developmental "systems" needs to be overlaid.

I will begin with an overview of the stages of the psycho-social developmental life researched by Erik Erikson who provided the approximate ages to go with the labels used by Sigmund Freud. While the ages can assist in application, they are only estimations and do certainly vary between different people. While each stage begins with minimum ages before which it would be unusual to find people, the challenges of each stage may actually linger into later life. Nevertheless, the ages provide the skeletal backdrop over which to place the various developmental maps.

DEVELOPMENTAL STAGE OF PSYCHO-SOCIAL AND SPIRITUAL GROWTH

Danish-American developmental psychologist **Erik Erikson outlined how all people mature through eight stages that juxtapose two necessary but conflicting psychological attitudes.**[2] In order to successfully navigate through each stage, people must determine how and when to employ these two attitudes. **Erikson claimed that the result was the gaining of a virtue for use during life.** I do not want Erikson's "virtue" to be confused with religious virtues so I will refer to them as the positive "personality qualities" gained at each psycho-social stage. Each of these psychological attitudes as well as the personality qualities are important, even necessary, for healthy spiritual growth to occur. When the polarities are not adequately processed, the challenge they present continues into the next stage and may even linger throughout life; this causes complications until completed. Each attitude and quality learned is needed for the subsequent stages; and what is learned will be retrofitted as life increases in complexity.

In the following descriptions, I will use Freud's age group labels to introduce Erikson's psycho-social stage polarities, which I will illustrate with examples to make clear the resultant personality qualities and correlate the spiritual implications with them. The chart (Graphic 8) will provide the structure for the following explanations.

Psycho-social and Spiritual Development

	0-1.5 yrs (Oral)	1.5-3 yrs (Anal)	3-6 yrs (Phallic/Oedipal)	6-12 yrs (Latency)	12-20 yrs (Adolescence)	20-40 yrs (Young Adult)	40-65 yrs (Middle Adult)	65 yrs + (Mature Adult)
Approximate Age (Freud)								
Stages of Emotional Development (Erickson)	Trust Versus Mistrust	Autonomy Versus Shame & Doubt	Initiative Versus Guilt	Industry Versus Inferiority	Identity Versus Role Confusion	Intimacy Versus Isolation	Generativity Versus Stagnation	Integrity Versus Despair
Positive Personality Quality (virtue)	Hope	Will	Purpose	Competence	Fidelity	Love	Caring	Wisdom
The Spiritual Road	**Pre-Christian Way** ✞ Awareness and Naming of God ✞ Awakening and Need for God ✞ Identification of Sin(s) ✞ Acceptance of Grace ✞ Moments of Decision --Confessional Temptation			**Purgative Way** ✞ Purging of Sins ✞ Adopt Ethical/Moral Standards ✞ Establish Spiritual Disciplines ✞ Basic Trust in God --Dark Night of the Senses		**Illuminative Way** ✞ Learnings ✞ Clarifications ✞ Devotions ✞ Mission and Generativity --Dark Night of the Spirit		**Unitive Way** ✞ Experience ✞ Contentment ✞ Watching and Waiting ✞ Temptation ✞ Living in Love

Graphic 8: Comparison of Erickson's Stages of Psycho-social Development with the Process of Spiritual Growth.

In the Oral Stage, infants up to about eighteen months of age deal with the attitudes of trust and mistrust. Intuitively, infants learn to trust that their basic needs for food, shelter and love will be met. They also begin to discern who or what cannot be trusted. Such intuitive discernment leads infants to have a realistic **hope** that they can move forward in their lives. Hope is the beginning of faith and without it, or if it is suspect, people have great difficulty acquiring and maintaining faith belief.

In the Anal Stage, toddlers up to about three years old contrast autonomy versus shame/doubt. The differentiating of individuals from others is essential for the development of the **personal will** and a beginning sense of identity. Toddlers come to understand that they have choice and can do (some) things for themselves. They can say "no" (and often do) and they can also totally give of themselves. Parents and caregivers who view toddler's expressions of "no" as resistance and being "bad" instead of the need for autonomy often assert restrictive control. Accordingly, the toddlers develop shame about themselves and doubt about their abilities. The use of the human the personal will is essential to the spiritual growth process especially the farther along the spiritual road people travel. With a lot of shame and doubt about their own self and their abilities, people cannot choose to follow God or will do so with an extremely subservient attitude. While such submission is adequate for the Pre-Christian and early Purgative Way stages, greater assertiveness and free choice are needed for more spiritual growth. Thus, the development of the personality quality of the will is spiritually important.

In Freud's Phallic/Oedipal stage, Erickson contrasted initiative and guilt. Preschool children, age three to six, typically initiate and even complete their own simple projects; and **Erickson's personality quality of purpose is the result**. Children are learning what works and what does not, what is right and what leads to undesirable consequences. This learning may begin with toys that won't fall upward, but may also include that saying a "bad word" elicits a timeout. Completing desired tasks brings a sense of accomplishment; failing to do so, even if the tasks are not possible, leads to feelings of inadequacy, including a sense of guilt for "doing it wrong." During this stage, pre-schoolers start learning about structure, order and rules. If they play by the rules and work within the prescribed parameters, they can succeed; they also learn to initiate and lead. If they do not play by the rules and do not succeed, they feel guilty and inadequate. Spiritually, children learn that God created rules and subsequently they feel good about following the rules and being approved as a child of God. Understanding the way things work and using the rules are good; it brings the personal ability of purpose, "I can do it." However, working against the rules brings guilt and sometimes acting out that negativity. Ethics and morals are initiated during the first two of Erikson's stages, if only from an ego-centric point of view. Nevertheless, young children want to avoid punishment as well as being guilty for wrong actions. This inclination leads to the need for God and the identification of sins. God made the world and organized it; going against that immoveable force causes bad things to happen which is felt as being wrong.

The Latency Stage compares the polarities of industry and inferiority in children six to twelve. The crucial personality quality to be gained is competence which emerges from approval. Similar to the previous stage, children need to accomplish tasks and goals in order to feel good about themselves. While the previous stage focuses on the personal start of projects and relationships, this stage is about finishing them. However, the tasks of this stage are more complicated because children are now part of a larger group and they need to accomplish what is determined to be acceptable by the rules (via society and God). In the Latency Stage, children begin to comprehend that they need to adopt these guidelines so as to be able to gain the recognition they desire and need. Since the standards and rules apply to everyone, the group consciousness initiates the ideas of fairness and sharing. Indeed, affirmation for success within the rules is the ideal (although negative behavior also brings "recognition"). Furthermore, the concept of competition is introduced because only so much affirmation and so many awards are available. In order to obtain the basic acceptance and love they need, children may even attempt to emulate and please teachers, parents, "hero/heroines," coaches and God.

The stage of Latency is an energetic and challenging time. In fact, so much proficiency is needed to be gained in so many areas that this stage's tasks are often not limited to the age range designated. What is important is that young children believe they can do some things well and receive approval for them. **Affirmation for what they accomplish develops further industry and self-confidence; ridicule and excessive criticism for their efforts brings feelings of inferiority**.

For healthy spiritual growth to occur, a delicate balance is needed between industry and inferiority. Both a positive sense of self and following the rules are necessary. People need spiritual affirmations; people need to follow spiritual rules (the Law, right from wrong). On the other hand, developing feelings of inferiority are a distinct possibility if affirmations are not received for following the rules or if excessive criticisms are inflicted.

How do people get God's approval? <u>What children learn from this stage is that working hard and being successful can bring approval – Christian blessings; and this is accomplished by industriously following the prescribed rules</u>. This can be inaccurately understood that people can work hard enough to get God's approval. Indeed, God wants people to adopt the rules – not as a way to get to God, but <u>as a way to recognize their need for God</u> and also as a way to say "thank you" to God. On the other hand, typically children do not have enough self-confidence (competence) to feel approved. Thus, keeping the rules is necessary (in order to receive adequate affirmation to feel good enough about themselves).

On the other hand, breaking the rules is disobedience or sinfulness. God is displeased when the Law is broken. <u>However, children also need to be repeatedly told that even when they do wrong (or fail to achieve), they are loveable, capable and acceptable especially if</u>

they have attempted to "play by the rules." This is grace; and without it children (as well as adults) will fall into inferiority because no one can perfectly succeed. Of course, receiving Jesus as savior can help people not fall into inferiority since divine forgiveness provides affirmations even though the rules are broken. Nevertheless, since learning and adopting a moral and ethical standard is an important and necessary psycho-social task, children need to be encouraged to follow the rules, not just rely on grace. As children begin to choose to implement right from wrong (at least measured by the affirmations/rewards they want to receive), they begin to purge their sins – separating what is good from what is bad. Even before becoming Christians (which officially begins the Purgative Way), young children adopt "Christian" values that can be identified later as what God desires.

These spiritual distinctions are difficult to make and nearly impossible to fully communicate to anyone between six and twelve years old. While better understanding may only be received later, attempting to keep the rules (industry), gaining self-confidence (competence) and receiving grace (to counter inferiority) are necessary during this Latency Stage. Without a delicate balance between these principles during Latency, spiritual helpers will probably need to unpack and clarify them with the adults they accompany. For example, while keeping God's rules is pleasing to God, it does not automatically establish a relationship with God. Or regardless of how awful the misdeeds, God has the power and desire to forgive and love.

In the Adolescent stage, approximately ages twelve to twenty although the years are often extended, **the successful dealing with identify versus role confusion brings fidelity. This stage has become popularized as the search for identity**. "It is a quest for a sense of inner consistency and continuity matched by a consistency and continuity in what one means to others."[3] In other words, identity is discovered and reflected from within the context of a group of others. These "teenagers" (and those in their twenties, as well) will attempt to discern "who they are" via their relationships with others and how they fit into the world. In order to do so, they need to acquire skills and will "try on" many different roles in a variety of groups. As such, these youth need to belong or fit into a group from where they receive the necessary identity-development and confirmations.

Throughout the Adolescent stage, people are gradually sculpturing themselves into the people they want to be. They differentiate themselves from others both through the groups with whom they associate and through the personal skills and attitudes they adopt. As such, they begin to move toward independence while still remaining connected to specific groups. For examples, sixteen-year-olds can drive a vehicle but still do not have the means to purchase and maintain it; or twenty-one years old may be able to mostly function like adults but without seeing the path ahead of them. This sense of independence is tested and solidified when people leave their household of origin. They may need to return "to the nest" in order to maintain safety and security as well as encouragement and resources. During this transition which typically includes moving into young adulthood, people make more and more personal choices that distinguish themselves from others including the groups that fostered them. They truly become independent; and they often do so with strong opinions and unambiguous actions designed to defend their positions.

Through a combination of clarity, corroboration and visceral discernment, youth finally feel content with who they are, their friends and where they are heading in life. When youth discover and choose their personal relationship identity, friends and life values, they must do so in opposition to the other possibilities. **Fidelity is the ability to maintain a chosen commitment in spite of competing loyalties**. Accordingly, they become loyal to the group/partner/family/church and the group confirms the loyalty to them. Role confusion results until this niche is found and adopted.

Spiritually speaking, children and youth (even some young adults) may have grown spiritually by mimicking the values of the culture in which they had been reared. During the Adolescent stage, people need to choose their place and purpose, their friends and goals. Since group acceptance and affirmation is necessary for these decisions, participating in various groups may be needed. Thus, Christian spiritual faith and its supportive groups need to be available for youth to see themselves as Christians who belong to Christ as a way of life. Youth groups and church camps provide both the community and the freedom to discern and decide. If Christianity is chosen, after exploration of the options, youth (and emerging young adults) start eliminating whatever is not defined by the group and practicing the skills associated with their choice. In other words, they begin to voluntarily and intentionally move forward with the Purgative Way tasks of intentionally purging sins, adopting moral/ethical standards and establishing spiritual habits. As a result, they feel good about themselves and believe that this spiritual choice will lead them successfully into the future – they have a basic trust in God and God's ways. However, if people are confused about "who they are" and who are their friends and life purpose, they will resist fitting into any group and their spiritual growth becomes dormant.

Erickson did not anticipate the rapid multiplicity of modern life and the effect it would have especially on the transition between the Adolescent and Young Adult stages. Complicated and intelligent people living in a complex environment often require greater skill development and extra time to successfully navigate through the choices of the Adolescent stage; and they can easily carry the unfinished business of a clear and definite identity into the Young Adult stage (intimacy versus isolation). On the other hand, physical development and social exposure attract people to bond together more quickly. This tendency, of course, has potentially disastrous consequences unless youth and emerging young adults have a solid sense of identity. Before youth actually "find themselves," they may couple or marry with multiple broken relationships or divorces occurring. They may "be forced" onto a career path only later to resist when their true skills emerge. They may "be required" to become Christians without having an authentic choice and their "involuntary" action will not grow into a deep love of God. With such scenarios, isolation, instead of intimacy, will result. Indeed, both the psycho-social as well as the spiritual goal is to progress into intimacy which cannot develop without an independent and clear sense of self. Spiritual helpers may need to assist with these Adolescent stage choices and perhaps with the resentments generated – long after they actually occurred.

Erikson's Young Adult stage contrasts intimacy with isolation and aims toward the personality quality of love. This stage is about moving from independence to interdependence; it is about giving of one's self to another person (people and causes) and still maintaining a confident, self-assuredness. Erikson rightly claims that people cannot move into this stage until they have a strong sense of self because they need to give themselves without fear of losing themselves. Accordingly, people can marry without having a strong sense of self but they will not experience intimacy; in fact, they may feel isolated even in relationship.

Typically, people experience a strong desire to share their life with another. Young adults may tend to think of this stage as about "finding someone to love me." However, in order to obtain intimacy (and the accompanying quality of love) they need to "make themselves loveable." **Intimacy is based on non-dependent people.** (The same is true when it comes to intimacy with God.) Thus, young adults need to have the ability to be independent, even from their significant others, in order to successfully give themselves and be truly interdependent. **Compromise and sacrifice are also needed in order to obtain the higher goal of love.** To have a relationship, a spouse, a family or any other shared venture, the attitude of giving of self (without anything necessarily given in return) is essential. If people do not discover other people with whom they can share their lives, they will separate themselves into a sense of isolation.

The "Learnings" and "Clarifications" of the Illuminative Way are likewise about distinctively claiming the Christian faith as an individual. No longer do Christians blindly adhere to doctrines given by their "church family of origin," but they choose what they believe and practice, even if that is the same as what they had already been taught. When they choose to share this freely chosen faith with others, they move into relationships and community – this takes interdependence. The consequence of this psycho-social development is a level of intimacy which becomes love of and for one another in ways that reflect how God has loved. In addition, as Christians come to share the values that God has for the world – they grow into "Devotion." During this process, Christians need to clearly establish their own independent faith and options; and they need to share interdependently with others and make the compromises that are required to do so. Accordingly, different people at different places along this, at least, twenty year Young Adult path are likely to disagree. Learning to love those with whom people disagree is the challenge that helps propel people into Erikson's next stage.

The Middle Adult stage, from approximately age forty through sixty-five, contrasts the challenge between generativity and stagnation; the positive personality

quality desired is caring. This stage can commence earlier than age forty or much later because it is dependent upon whether people sense that their life will end and wonder about what they have accomplished or completed. Accordingly, people want to make sure that what they have done has some meaning and purpose – that it will continue in some way. Typically, the form of generativity is related to the major emphases of people's lives. If family has been the focus, then having and being attentive to grandchildren will seem important. If business has consumed many years, then securing that it will continue in the capable hands of a trusted friend or relative will take precedence. If principles and truths have been the guiding star of people's lives, then they will desire to teach what they know and value to whomever would learn. In other words, generativity can come in any number of ways. If people sense that their lives will cease and do not have or develop a way to pass on to the next generation whatever has been important to them, they will experience stagnation. Stagnation can also take a variety of forms, but it always looks like people have stopped with no energy and are just going through the motions. The psychology is: if people's lives have been worthwhile, they want to leave a legacy regarding whatever has been significant. They care about what has happened to them; but they care even more about what others can glean from them.

Spiritually, Middle Adulthood corresponds to the "Mission and Generativity" part of the Illuminative Way. Christians have developed their relationship with God; they have established and lived by the rules and spiritual habits; and they have questioned and deepened their understanding until they have fallen deeply in love with God. As they review their life of faith, they want to make a lasting difference for God with the time they have left. Accordingly, they desire to touch the world with God's message and practices – it is their mission. As this unfolds, they will also attempt to perpetuate God's will and ways, as they have known them, onto the next generation. If Christians do not obtain "Devotion," they will not care much about paying it forward. As a result, they will die on the spiritual vine and not go to seed – they may do what they have always done waiting lethargically for God to take them to Heaven.

Erikson's last stage, which I call Mature Adulthood, deals with the polarities of ego integrity versus despair. Hopefully, the personality quality to emerge is wisdom. This is to be a time of summation and satisfaction. "What frame do you want to put around the picture of your life?" "Has the journey been worth the effort?" "Have personal goals been achieved?" "Will thinking about it bring a smile or a frown?" All of these kinds of questions are designed to assess whether the ego (the individual) can be evaluated as having honor and validity. This stage can also be about making things right, getting personal affairs in order and dealing with the mistakes made and resentments held. People need to feel that they have done their best. Unless these things are done, the mature adult will slide into despair, which can even cause the physical body functions to deteriorate.

Spiritually, surrender is the key attitude. Ideally, Christians have come into the Unitive Way where a sense of contentment, peaceful waiting and living in loving ways is the norm. Nothing needs to be done; and everything that is done, God does. Since many people do not obtain this unitive spiritual state of being, surrender comes in the simpler form of accepting that God is in charge while trusting in the faith they have acquired. If this does not happen, people will fall into despair, spiritually, thinking that they are lost or doomed. Interestingly, the personality quality of hope that is needed to be gained during infancy is essentially the same trait needed to counter the potential despair at the end of life.

SPIRITUAL APPLICATION OF ERIKSON

"Train a child in the way (s)he should go, and when (s)he is old (s)he will not turn from it."[4] [Proverbs 22:6] Traditionally, this scriptural adage has been used to encourage adults to teach children the correct rules by which to live. In addition, adults also focus on having children become followers of God (or Christians) early in their lives. However, an informed understanding of the Old Testament Hebrew passage paints a revised picture. The phrase "train a child" has extremely strong overtones about being "dedicated" to a project and to give, teach or bestow whatever is needed to bring it to completion. Children need to complete different "training" at different times in their lives. Thus, the phrase "in the way" refers less to giving them the "rules" than it does to providing them whatever they need for each step along the way. **Training of children means to provide whatever is the appropriate mental, emotional and spiritual lessons for the phase of life in which they are**. This also applies to adults who didn't learn the childhood lessons when they were children. A classic, theologically conservative commentary on the Old Testament confirms:

> The instruction of youth, the education of youth, ought to be conformed to the nature of youth; the matter of instruction, the manner of instruction, ought to regulate itself according to the stage of life, and its peculiarities; the method ought to be arranged according to the degree of development which the mental and bodily life of the youth has arrived at.[5]

Indeed, acquiring Erickson's positive personality qualities as well as accomplishing the correlated spiritual tasks deeply embeds them into the human character so that they remain throughout life.

In Erikson's theory, after people adequately gain the ability to discern when and how to use each stage's contrasting psychological attitudes, they obtain a virtue or personality quality. This character quality allows them to grow developmentally into the next stage. I assert that these personality qualities have a direct impact on spiritual growth and development because **how people relate to others directly affects their relationship with God**.

As James writes, "For anyone who does not love his brother, whom he has seen, cannot love God, whom he has not seen."[6]

Ideally, children and adults go through the psycho-social stages in a timely manner. When they do, the task of spiritual helpers is mostly to help others identify God presence and where the promptings of the Holy Spirit are leading. This dual task often includes connecting the current psycho-social quality with their spiritual purpose (i.e., the "independent" tasks of claiming "identity" with the "Clarifications" of faith). On the other hand, spiritual helpers may need to assist adults through unfinished psycho-social issues (or ethical transitions) in order to facilitate their spiritual growth.

Consider these following examples of **how psycho-social development and spiritual growth interconnect** with each other.

If people gain basic trust (versus mistrust), they have hope. If infants trust that their fundamental needs will be met and that their world is mostly safe, they live and thrive. Internally, they "believe" the world is safe – this is the virtue of hope. Infants do not know what the future holds, but they have come to hope in it. This translates to the spiritual affirmation, "I do not know what the future holds, but I know who holds the future." The spiritual application of hope is the most essential of all the personality qualities, both at the beginning and the end of life, because it allows humans to continue toward God in the face of the unknown.

A young Roman Catholic priest taught one of my seminary classes, which was on comparative religions. The reading list was extensive. While I did read through a little of Rudolph Otto[7] and Mircea Eliade,[8] I did not think I did particularly well with the subject although it was fascinating and enlightening. The focus of the classroom interactions was through spirited discussions from which the professor typically brought the conclusion back to one and only one question: "Do you believe in a friendly world and a friendly God?" He asserted that all experiences of the numinous that become religious faith must begin with an affirmative answer to this question. At the time, I thought his approach strange and did not fully appreciate his wisdom. However, today I understand that all faith begins in the virtue of hope which is intuited in whether the world (and therefore the divine) is perceived as "friendly."

People come to the virtue of hope in God because they have experienced the trustworthiness of their world and those who provide its consistent, albeit imperfect, security. Truly, infants who do not experience care and love die; and their ability to grow spiritually depends on the degree of friendly "hope" they experience as their non-rational "understanding" of God, which they carry with them and enhance throughout life and into eternity. In other words, part of the spiritual purpose during childhood, psycho-socially, is to experience the qualities of God through powerful, trusted caregivers. If not accomplished in childhood, spiritual growth is hindered until it is.

For example, early in my ministry I met Cindy, a fairly young woman minister, who came into my office one day to introduce herself. During the collegial conversation, she somehow began talking about the sexual abuse that she had experienced as a young girl and how the effects of the abuse had been causing her great difficulties in her life and ministry. Cindy started quickly retreating from her unregulated sharing as soon as she realized what she had been devolving. When she stopped, I commented, "I might be able to help you with that if you want." She was surprised, but also willing to do whatever would help.

"Cindy," I began. "I need to ask you two questions. First, do you trust me?" "I guess I would not have told you about all my pain so quickly if I didn't. Yes, I trust you." I continued, "Good. And secondly, can you close your eyes and imagine a living picture of Jesus to provide God's healing power?" Cindy immediately stiffened and bristled! With a radical shift in her attitude she said, "I don't think I can do that." Then, she launched into an explanation of her male abuser, how she really resisted getting close to men and that masculine-oriented theology increased these problems.

In an attempt to ease her anxiety I interrupted with assurance, "It's ok. I know this is hard. Just tell me who do you know that best represents the qualities of God?" Cindy relaxed and smiled as she said, "That would be my grandmother. I loved her and she taught me spiritually; in fact, I am in the ministry because of her influence in my life." I responded, "Excellent. Can you imagine her radiant and full of the power of God?" She answered that she could easily do that. Accordingly, I asked her to go back in her faith imagination to the event of her abuse. Then, we invited her saintly grandmother-God to intervene and cast out the evil that had been inflicted on her and lived in her unconscious. We prayed a prayer of gratitude for what God had done in her.

Those moments were exhausting, after which Cindy forced a brief smile, whispered "thanks," excused herself and left. The very next day Cindy bounded back into my office and exuberantly extroverted, "Do you know what you did?" I was caught off guard and wasn't completely sure where she was going with this question so I replied, "Not exactly; but please tell me." Her animation increased when she said, "You totally changed my life! I feel so different; and I'm quite sure I will never be the same again. I haven't stopped thinking about how my grandmother took care of me – like she always did. I've done lots of therapy and I have consistently tried to pray for God to take this pain from me. But nothing helped until yesterday." When she finally finished with a big smile, I simply responded, "You know that was all God, not me?" To which she confirmed, "Of course, I know that; but I have never felt this new. Thank you so much. I'm sorry I've got a meeting but I just had to stop and tell you." As she turned to leave, I answered back, "You are very welcome."

This vignette speaks on many levels but I use it here because <u>Cindy needed the assistance of the most important, powerful and trusted caregiver of her life</u>. The primary masculine caregiver in her life raped her trust leaving her with a negative experience so that neither the traditional male image of God nor Jesus could transmit the divine power she needed. For Cindy, God chose not to come in the form of a burning bush, a talking donkey or a man named Jesus but in the form of a saintly grandmother. Cindy's grandmother exhibited the qualities of the divine that her negative male abusive experience would not allow. God delivered the "hope" Cindy needed through one of God's saints. If Cindy's life was to be filled with Erickson's virtue of hope, she had to access it through the primary trusted caregiver of her life. When hope is lacking as a life-attitude, spiritual helpers might suspect that dealing with early life conflicts can be helpful for spiritual growth.

Erickson's positive personality quality of human personal "will" emerges when people successfully deal with shame/doubt and autonomy. Many adults I guide deal with the inability to decide which, if it occurs repetitively, points to the need for Erickson's autonomous ability to choose for themselves. **Shame and doubt keeps them from doing so. This is supremely a spiritual issue**. Shame-filled people can do what they are told to do; in fact, they are especially good at it. They can say the words that are required, keep the rules that need to be kept and practice the spiritual disciplines of faith. However, they cannot make a freely-formed, independent choice for God – exactly what is necessary in order to respond fully to God's love. **People who feel shame regarding who they are as individuals have this spiritual problem**. This often occurs for people who have been abused, been captive to addiction or prostitution or any other experience that makes them feel less than human. While these people may feel guilty (sometimes for things they are not truly guilty of) their spiritual inability to choose God originates in their toxic shame.

One of the most helpful psychological distinctions that I have learned is between shame and guilt, the subjects in Erickson's second and third stages. Guilt and shame typically run together in the emotional life but need to be considered separately. **Guilt** is primarily about a rule, duty or obligation that has been broken or violated. **Shame**, on the other hand, is not so much about people's actions but about how they perceive themselves, their basic nature.

Shame has a good side; people feel shameful when they have been inappropriate (which comes via their actions, but refers to the type of person they feel they are). For example, people feel shame if they are seen naked in public or say unflattering words about a person who accidently heard them. Shame helps to "enforce" the society's rules by defaming the character of the person; shame establishes the limits that both keep people safe and the culture from becoming chaotic. Shame can become destructive when it becomes people's default character quality; this is called **toxic shame**.[9] The effect is that people basically feel worthless and unable to assert their own desires except to utter, "I can't do it; nobody likes me; nobody wants me; I'm going outside and eat worms."

When toxic shame is the prevailing life-attitude, spiritual helpers might suspect that dealing with early events that shamed those they assist so much that they believe their core nature is a "bad boy" or a "bad girl." Therapy may be needed. However, if such moments have been dealt with in therapy, then simply asking, "Who told you and showed you that you were "bad?" can be helpful. Follow up with, "What does God believe about you?" (Answer: that they are created good; loveable, capable and acceptable.) "Who is right?" Toxic shame inhibits the activation and initiation of the personal will which is needed for spiritual growth. Spiritual helpers counter toxic shame whenever they attribute to God the power to determine who people are created to be.

In chapter nine, I used the example of <u>women who experienced</u> permission and encouragement to participate in <u>the Christian task of "Clarifications."</u> As adolescents such women were disallowed to initiate their own choices (stage 3) and follow through on what they thought important to do (stage 4). They were told what to do and how to do it; and they felt guilty and incompetent. <u>Consequently, they were never able to clarify their own Christian faith</u>. Spiritual helpers can affirm whatever these women choose to initiate to do and believe. Spiritual helpers can applaud the purposes these women have already claimed for their lives and also affirm the competence they have achieved – which the women most likely will not say "out loud." Then, spiritual helpers can proclaim, "God hopes that you will feel ok about choosing how you understand and apply your own personal spiritual faith … if you choose to do so."

Lastly, after people who are latent in one particular psycho-social quality gain this "lost" ability, they can sometimes grow quickly. For example, Augustine of Hippo for decades did not practice the morals and ethics necessary to move forward in Christianity of which he had full knowledge. When he suddenly stopped being a drunkard, a womanizer and all-around rogue, he was catapulted to become one of the Saints of the church. My early life experience was filled with the physical pain of a debilitating disease and I felt very inferior to others even though I was told differently. As a result, I became guarded and cautious typically not opening myself up to new experiences and the feelings associated with them. I limited myself and controlled my world. When I "accidently" became a skilled gymnast, I gained the virtue of "competence" I was lacking. Accordingly, I gained enough confidence to allow myself to experience the "unknown." This is to say that I understood Christianity long before I would allow myself to have a personal experience of God. As I started to complete my psycho-social unfinished business, I came to feel the mystery and tremendousness of God and was fascinated that God loved me so much. In my competence, I gave my life to Christ and became committed to spiritual growth.

<u>Spiritual helpers who understand the relationship of psycho-social development to spiritual growth can be invaluable to those they accompany</u>.

CHAPTER 14

Overlaying the Moral/Ethical Map

Building upon the psychological theory and research of Jean Piaget,[1] Lawrence Kohlberg developed his "Stages of Moral Development."[2] **What Kohlberg demonstrated is that people grow developmentally in their ability to think and make moral/ethical decisions.** In other words, people make moral and ethical choices based on the particular level of reasoning ability that they possess; and they are unable to function at any more mature stage. Kohlberg's theory is concerned with what kind of reasoning people use to make their decisions, not about whether their choices are moral or not. On the other hand, Christianity is concerned about morality and ethical choices.

MORAL/ETHICAL DEVELOPMENT AND SPIRITUAL GROWTH

The Christian Spiritual Road is primarily concerned with people's relationship with God. However, **effective spiritual growth always has an application dimension to it as what people believe takes form in the world. Many of these applications are moral and ethical in nature**. Thus, Christian spiritual growth is directly impacted by people's moral and ethical reasoning ability. While the Bible illustrates different moral/ethical ways to live, it does not outline any moral/ethical pattern of growth. Nevertheless, Christians grow developmentally in morals and ethics. In fact, as people progress through the stages of moral/ethical capabilities, they actually move closer to the way God makes these choices. However, expecting lesser-developed Christians to make mature ethical decisions is inappropriate, unhealthy and graceless. Since Christians (as well as faith communities) never fully obtain the divine level and are never perfect, tolerant understanding with gentle encouragement of less mature decisions is desirable. What is important is that people continue to grow spiritually and function ethically and morally at the highest level that they can.

Especially during the Pre-Christian and Purgative Ways, people are establishing and adopting Christian moral and ethical values, which further develop as people grow. Adopting moral and ethical values is absolutely necessary since it sets both behavioral limits that provide protection and also institutes the projected goals for the Holy Community that God is designing. However, Christians, even good Christians, will only act according to the level of moral development they have acquired.[3] For example, a simple Christian ethical principle could be stated as: "Hurting other people is morally wrong." However, people will understand (interpret) this Christian dictate differently at different times in their lives (even if they "should be able to" comprehend it as God intended it to be understood.) After considering each of Kohlberg's stages of moral/ethical development, I will provide an example of how people might interpret this Christian ethic at that particular moral/ethical stage. The chart (Graphic 9) overviews Kohlberg's theory and compares it with the process of spiritual growth.

Ethical/ Moral Development and Spiritual Growth

	0-1.5 yrs (Oral)	1.5-3 yrs (Anal)	3-6 yrs (Phallic/Oedipal)	6-12 yrs (Latency)	12-20 yrs (Adolescence)	20-40 yrs (Young Adult)	40-65 yrs (Adult)	65 yrs + (Mature Adult)
Approximate Age (Freud)	0-1.5 yrs (Oral)	1.5-3 yrs (Anal)	3-6 yrs (Phallic/Oedipal)	6-12 yrs (Latency)	12-20 yrs (Adolescence)	20-40 yrs (Young Adult)	40-65 yrs (Adult)	65 yrs + (Mature Adult)
Kohlberg's Moral/ Ethical Reasoning	Pre-Conventional			Conventional		Post-Conventional		Transcendent
Stages		Stage 1 Personal	Stage2 Instrumental	Stage 3 Expected	Stage 4 Legal	Stage 5 Agreement	Stage 6 Multi-Group Consensus	Stage 7 Absolute
Based On		Obedience and Punishment	Self-Interest (Mutual)	Desire to Be Approved Of	Social Law and Order	Individual Covenants	Principles Determined / Applied Cross-Culturally	Eternal Good
Example		"If I do it, I get a whipping."	"How do I benefit from this?" Or "It's not fair (personally)!"	"If that is what everyone else does?"	"Everyone needs to maintain the system of rules."	"If we agree, the rules are good."	"We must consider all perspectives as if all people must live by that decision."	"What would God do?"
Justice Issue		Punishment and Reward.	Equally good for me.	Disapproval is Unacceptable.	Law is God.	Majority Rules.	Principled Consensus	Eternal
The Spiritual Road	**Pre-Christian Way** ✢ Awareness and Naming of God ✢ Awakening and Need for God ✢ Identification of Sin(s) ✢ Acceptance of Grace ✢ Moments of Decision --Confessional Temptation			**Purgative Way** ✢ Purging of Sins ✢ Adopt Ethical/Moral Standards ✢ Establish Spiritual Disciplines ✢ Basic Trust in God --Dark Night of the Senses		**Illuminative Way** ✢ Learnings ✢ Clarifications ✢ Devotions ✢ Mission and Generativity --Dark Night of the Spirit		**Unitive Way** ✢ Experience ✢ Contentment ✢ Watching and Waiting ✢ Temptation ✢ Living in Love

Graphic 9: Comparison of Kohlberg's Ethical/Moral Development with the Spiritual Growth Process.

Kohlberg originally categorized his researched data into three major groups, each containing two stages: pre-conventional (egocentric-centered), conventional (society-based) and post-conventional (comprehensive principle-oriented). Later he suggested the addition of a fourth group or seventh stage, Transcendental Morality, which was associated more directly with spiritual ideals.[4] He also noted that a "transitional" phase between stages four and five may be needed. This modification corresponds with the fourth stage, Individuative-Reflective, of Fowler's Faith Development Theory. Both researchers indicate the struggle to emerge from the conventional/society values into post-conventional/individually with its independently chosen standards. In my experience, this rite of passage is the most difficult to transverse; and the guidance of spiritual helpers is crucial during this time.

Pre-Conventional, Stage One – **The morality and ethics of people, mostly children, during this stage is directly related to the reward or punishment, either real or perceived, that they believe they will receive**. Their evaluation has a personal and immediate orientation – it is all about them. The moral reasoning is: "It is bad to hurt others because I will receive punishment in return." Or, "It is good to take advantage of others because of the rewards I will get." Also, when observing others who are being punished, stage one people conclude that those other people must actually be bad (whether that is accurate or not). For example, when people at this stage view television news reports of accused individuals, they believe they are actually guilty of the offense, even before a trial. These conclusions are internalized spiritually as, "If I hurt others, God will punish me." God punishes bad people and rewards good people. In Genesis, Cain killed his brother Able [Genesis 4:1-16].[5] When Cain's offering to God was not rewarded, he decided to eliminate the competition in order to get what he desired. This was reasoning with Pre-Conventional, Stage One morals. Cain gets punished for his bad behavior; but he also gets taught to master his basic sinful impulse to take what he wants. He was encouraged to move onto the ethical stage two.

Pre-Conventional, Stage Two – **The morality and ethics of people during this stage sustains a strong self-interest orientation while acknowledging that others exist**. Thus, people "learn" to share but always want to make sure that they get what they think they deserve. Their primary rationale (in addition to avoiding punishment) is to receive God's blessings or a trip to Heaven. "I do not hurt other people and do good things to them so that I can go to Heaven." People at this stage often have strong reactions to real or perceived unfairness saying, "It's not fair!" However, the concern is not for others but for the lack of receiving their personal reward. At the very least, stage two people want others to get the punishment that they would expect. "An eye for an eye and a tooth for a tooth"[6] [Exodus 21:23-24] ethical stance prevails at this stage.

Both Pre-Conventional stages one and two ethics/morals can easily extend past the chart's approximate age-ten limit. This is especially true if children have been abused, neglected or not acquired Erikson's qualities of trust, autonomy and initiative. They will not have an adequate sense of self and still crave personal attention, which will be seen in their actions in the world and particularly in their ethical accusations regarding others. Adults, who carry this need into later life, will be limited in their spiritual growth and development – they may have little concern for others (that doesn't personally benefit them) and they will not come to deeply love God or God's ways, only avoid negative consequences. Spiritual helpers may need to assist those they accompany both in a strengthening of self as well as moving into the level of Conventional morals and ethics.

Conventional, Stage Three – **The morality and ethics of people during this stage is motivated by acceptance and approval**, which begins in middle adolescence. This stance is typical for teenagers but can easily be maintained into adulthood. Accordingly, people desire to do what everyone else does and thinks is okay. They begin to accept the standards of society or the group with whom they are associated because they will be determined a "good person." People at this stage assert the desire for everyone to get along and "be good." They support the Golden Rule to "do to others what you would have them do to you"[7] [Matthew 7:12] at least until the rule doesn't prop up the inclination of those they are with at the time. People at this stage are incessantly seeking to know what everyone else thinks so that they can fit into the group. People are always asking "What do you think?" so as to tally an opinion poll in order to chose the "right" side. Such mental juggling can also occur in regard to Christianity versus other belief systems. Consequently, having double standards and flipping between them is the norm because their ethic is contingent on whom they are with at the time. In support of Christian spiritually, they would echo, "We agree that we should not hurt you as long as you don't hurt us." However, when perceived injury occurs, stage three people would assert that the injured parties have the right (given by the majority) to return hurt.

A consistently articulated view of society, or the ethics promoted by the Christian community, is extremely helpful for encouraging people in this stage. In other words, strong-assertive preaching of Christian values that oppose other views is very supportive. People in stage three, typically agree with what authorities conclude and do what others in the group have concluded is correct. In the church, one request for baptism/confirmation leads to numerous others because people need to be accepted and part of the group; and baptism brings official acceptance into the Christian faith. Strongly-stated opinions from authoritative leaders have great import. In addition, the rules of the faith become more important to learn and sustain. Following the rules, and being part of a church that has homogeneous rules, means people will be accepted by others and God as well. Going outside the accepted group with its ethical/moral standards is difficult for people at this stage.

Conventional, Stage Four – The morality and ethics of people during this stage is a continuation and expansion of stage three. While people want to fit in, **they have become more convinced of the need for a solid standard of morals and ethics in order to main-**

177

tain the status quo. They progressively develop a trust in the system as well as a "basic trust" in God as they apply what they believe to the life they live. **These people often strongly promote the society's standards, unexamined, and have a sense of loyalty to them**. Stage four people maintain that moral and ethical rules are necessary for people to live together well. Thus, **law and order** is required and everyone must abide by the rules so that this society can be maintained. "I don't hurt others because the society would fall apart if I did; AND I (or my designated enforcers) will not allow you to hurt others for the same reason (even if I have to hurt you to make you do that)." Spiritually, Christians with this standard of morals and ethics would affirm, "If the Bible (or the elected leaders) says it, I will do it (without evaluating its accuracy in order to be accepted and maintain a solid society for God.)" An example of this ethic biblically stated is:

> Everyone must submit himself to the governing authorities, for there is no authority except that which God has established. The authorities that exist have been established by God. Consequently, he who rebels against the authority is rebelling against what God has instituted, and those who do so will bring judgment on themselves. For rulers hold no terror for those who do right, but for those who do wrong. Do you want to be free from fear of the one in authority? Then do what is right and he will commend you. For he is God's servant to do you good. But if you do wrong, be afraid, for he does not bear the sword for nothing. He is God's servant, an agent of wrath to bring punishment on the wrongdoer.[8] [Romans 13:1-4]

While Conventional stages three and four are primarily developed during adolescence, either level of morality and ethics is often extended long into adulthood, especially for people who have children and promote these standards to them. Unless moral and ethical values are personally examined, people will not move into the Post-Conventional stages. As noted above, Kohlberg indicated the likelihood of a "transitional" period between the conventional and post-conventional stages during which people struggle with what values to accept and which to reject. This transition typically requires moving away from the current conventional authority into an association with an alternative authority, which as a "non-anxious presence" allows for new decisions. Spiritually, Christians also travel through this time of personal discovery. This transition begins as Christians become aware of options beyond the traditional faith they have been taught and are allowed to discern what is acceptable to them.

Post-Conventional, Stage Five – **The morality and ethics of people during this stage is social contract driven**. In other words, people need to agree upon the moral and ethical rules. In stage four, obeying rules themselves make the society good. In stage five, common agreement authorizes the rules as acceptable. While this approach typically includes examination of the legitimacy of the rules themselves, the goal is to support and improve the social order. Thus, if the current laws do not support the common good, then they need to be changed. <u>While stage five people understand that a variety of opinions exist, morality and ethics are often determined by what is the greatest good for the greatest number of people</u> – a utilitarian ethical form. Coming to a majority conclusion is essential; and details of behavior and consequences are delineated in laws and documents. Ideally, democracy is based on stage five principles (assuming that everyone's opinion is heard and that those making the conclusions do it for the common good). This stage of moral/ethical reasoning is necessary for successful agreement between different individuals and groups.

The Christian ethical assertion at stage five would be: "I don't hurt you because we have both agreed we won't hurt each other; and it is the best decision for all concerned." On the other hand, a passionate game of jinx, where first seeing a particular object means one person gets to hit another, demonstrates that people can hurt others when they are right, because of the previously agreed upon rules. Spiritually, Christians have examined and accepted the morals and ethics to which they have become committed. When groups of Christians have similar values, they can agree to be a Christian community or even work together ecumenically. **A variety of life experiences is an important ingredient during this stage as is considering the needs of those beyond people's own group**. <u>As those in stage five experience different people and options, they have the opportunity to reflect on and perhaps adopt a new or revised ethical and moral stance</u>. In fact, officially authorized interactions with others, such as mission trips or working with disadvantaged people, can initiate such considerations. Jesus' parable of the Good Samaritan[9] [Luke 10:25-37] has the effect of teaching stage five morals/ethics by re-defining "who is my neighbor" – not just someone within an individual's own group, but any person in need.

Christians in stage five are typically on the Illuminative Way engaging in Learnings, Clarifications, Devotion and Mission. How they treat others becomes more based on freely-chosen principles, rather than just the unexamined application of the rules. Accordingly, Christians are more inclined to consider alternative suggestions from sources beyond their own tradition when applying their faith's ethics and morals. However, whatever mutual agreement is obtained becomes the rule to be followed. Such mediated social contracts are most often recorded for the purpose of confirmation and verification. The Apostle Paul's extended discussion of integrating non-Jews into Christianity and having the Council of Jerusalem agree upon its guidelines is an example of stage five ethics.[10] [Acts 15:1-35]

<u>Post-Conventional, Stage Six</u> – This stage extends the "beyond the conventional society" reasoning. Laws, morals and ethics need to consider everyone involved, including the desires of other societies. They also acknowledge that what is good for one person may be harmful to another. **After an evaluation in which people consider what they would do if they were the other person/group and believed in what they do, then informed consensus building can result in the moral/ethical action taken**. People are enlightened by their own laws and principles as well as those of others; but they are not duty bound.

Conclusions are based on the results of all cases and perspectives in order to arrive at the best case scenario, which makes stage six reasoning very complex. This often develops into an emphasis on the importance of universal human rights. While stage six ethics have a utilitarian emphasis (what is good for all), it also combines consideration of what is the intended good of the action from the perspective of the other individuals.

Spiritually, Christians have become mature and wise enough to consider other alternatives, even from other religious traditions. Their life experience has broadened their perspectives to accept the fact that truth, morally and ethically, can be gleaned from beyond what they have already learned it to be. What is most important is that they view life and people as God would. Their highest priority is to obtain what is just and right, regardless of their particular religious tradition's point of view. When considering the ethical principle "It is wrong to hurt others," stage six people might object that the stage four's "authorized hurting of others" stance in order to maintain the rules of society (or even the revised laws of stage five) is unacceptable. Stage six Christians might argue that hurting is hurting, that killing is killing, whether it is authorized or not; and hurting/killing is against God's law. They would biblically affirm, "We must obey God, not men."[11] [Acts 5:29] They would say, "Let us, as much as possible, do no harm to anyone (after we have all understood what is hurtful to each person/group)."

Even though the following passage from Romans is immediately followed by a clear stage four ethical dictate, it approximates a stage six morality – considering all including enemies, doing good, while allowing retribution via God's ultimate moral/ethical evaluation to take place.

Do not repay anyone evil for evil. Be careful to do what is right in the eyes of everybody. If it is possible, as far as it depends on you, live at peace with everyone. Do not take revenge, my friends, but leave room for God's wrath, for it is written: 'It is mine to avenge; I will repay,' says the Lord. On the contrary: 'If your enemy is hungry, feed him; if he is thirsty, give him something to drink. In doing this, you will heap burning coals on his head.'[12] [Romans 12:17-21]

Transcendent, Stage Seven – Kohlberg theorized this stage without having research to support it. However, **in a perfect world where all creatures would live together in peace and harmony, only God's perfect implementation of morals and ethics can exist**. When it comes to the morality of not hurting others, sometimes self-sacrifice is the highest, stage seven, level of action. However, it is neither a rule nor a duty nor an agreed upon conclusion. The action is often complex and even non-rational within the finite-limits of human perspective. Stage seven ethics includes extreme humility, self-sacrifice and what would seem unreasonable to people in former stages. As a parable and approximation, the book The Five People You Will Meet in Heaven[13] might illustrate the moral and ethical unfolding of stage seven. Therein, five people do not understand the connection they have to each other as they (God) work out justice in a complex manner until all the "unfairness" is understood as the only righteous way. In real life, this approach is only seen occasionally as with the Nickel Mines, Pennsylvanian Amish elders' act of forgiveness in which they publicly forgave a man who murdered some of their school age children.[14] This stage seven ethic is a "turn the other cheek"[15] [Matthew 5:39] and "go the extra mile"[16] [Matthew 5:41] and "do good to those who hate you"[17] [Luke 6:27-28] approach even though it does not "make sense." Also, the apostle Paul counseled the Philippian Christians to adopt an ethic that closely resembled the actions of Jesus on their behalf. This would be a transcendent stage seven ethic.

Each of you should look not only to your own interests, but also to the interests of others. Your attitude should be the same as that of Christ Jesus: Who, being in very nature God, did not consider equality with God something to be grasped, but made himself nothing, taking the very nature of a servant, being made in human likeness. And being found in appearance as a man, he humbled himself and became obedient to death – even death on a cross![18] [Philippians 2:4-8]

THE ETHICAL GUIDANCE OF SPIRITUAL HELPERS

Ethics deal with whether human conduct is right or wrong. **Ethical systems are based on one of two questions: either "What should I do?" or "What kind of person do I want to be?"** I will refer to these as <u>action-based</u> and <u>character-based</u>.

<u>In action-based systems</u>, people determine their actions according to what is best for them (personal), what is according to the rules (duty or deontic) or what is best for all concerned (utilitarianism or teleological). <u>In character-based systems</u>, people determine their actions based on "What will make me a better person?" (Virtue-development) While some people would like to relegate the Bible and Christianity to a deontological system – one in which God sets and enforces all the rules – it is not a totally rule-based system since growing into the character of God (Christ-likeness) and even negotiating with God to change the principles are inherent.[19] In fact, all of the views from each ethical system are included in the scriptures. In coordination with Kohlberg's research and moral development theory, Christians move through personal-based (Pre-Conventional) ethical decisions into adopting rule-based behavior (Conventional) and then into assessing and choosing ethics that are good for all – first based on group mutual happiness and moving to multicultural universal principles (Post-Conventional).

<u>If the goal of Christianity is focused on correct behavior</u>, then the process becomes that people move out of selfishness to understanding the basic rules into the ability to evaluate and revise those rules. Nevertheless, the complexity of determining universal principles is

so involved and complicated that people conclude that only something transcendent can understand how to perfectly do that (Transcendent, Stage 7) – Christians call this God.

While part of the goal of Christianity is right behavior, the other part which I consider the primary goal, mostly because it initiates and sustains the behavioral goal, is growing into oneness with God – which means that human character must become akin to God's character. **Thus, the character-based ethical system is at least as important for Christians as is what is right/wrong.** For Christians, the question of "What kind of person do I want to be?" becomes "What decision will help me align (abide) with God?" Being one with God, of course, would also mean that people's actions would be ethically right. It is highly unlikely for people to move into a character-based ethical system orientation until they have at least obtained Erickson's Conventional, stage four. (They also need to be on the Illuminative Way and have obtained Erickson's personality qualities necessary for such exploration).

According to where people are along the developmental road, spiritual helpers need to assist differently – always enabling people to more mature behavior. In addition, spiritual helpers, via Spiritual Road conversation, can also encourage growing into the character and oneness with God – developing a personal virtue-based system of ethics. Indeed, God-logic does not always reflect human reasoning and people must grow into the mind of Christ. "My ways are not your ways."[20] [Isaiah 55:8-9]

I have often heard people I accompany say, **"It's a justice issue!"** While I am not an expert ethicist, I am quite sure that different Christians were applying the word "justice" in a variety of ways. Some people were simply saying, "If I do the deed, I get the punishment. But I will do it because I *need* to do it." (Stage one) Some people were venting that they did not get the piece of the pie that they thought they deserved. (Stage two) Some people affirmed that everyone should get the same as everyone else using the "What's good for the goose is good for the gander" thinking. (Stage three) Still other people assert that if it is the law of society, it is just. Thus, they got the proper justice. (Stage four) Stage five folks may cry "It's a justice issue" because they don't believe that everyone was heard and that the conclusion did not have the good of everyone in mind. (Stage five) In addition, some people may want to broaden the perspective. Without "walking a mile in the other person's shoes," justice cannot be obtained. They are concerned to arrive at a more universal conclusion approximating absolute good for all people in all times and places. (Stage six)

Spiritual helpers would be advised to reflect on the moral and ethical stage of those they accompany in order to assist them along the Spiritual Road. Each stage obtained is movement toward the perspective of the divine. While Christians must live according to ethics and morals (at the very least because they need to apply what they believe), they are also in process of growing into the ability to evaluate as God would. Until then, justice belongs to God. Perhaps, that is why the oldest and wisest of the saints often say nothing or at least do not quickly rush to judgment.

CHAPTER 15

Overlaying the Faith Development Map

In 1981 James W. Fowler[1] fashioned "Faith Development Theory," which is an affective-cognitive-structural form of understanding and valuing faith. Fowler describes it as: "These (complex interplay of factors that form the stages of faith) include biological maturation, emotional and cognitive development, psychosocial experience, and the role of religiocultural symbols, meanings, and practices."[2] Simply put, **people can only comprehend God and faith concepts that their level of maturity will allow**. Maturity includes: their rational abilities (Piaget and Kohlberg), their emotional development (Erikson) and their spiritual experiences (the place on the Spiritual Road). Fowler adds to these developmental understandings so as to identify how people experience faith. Regarding Fowler's theory, obtaining a stage of faith any earlier than the suggested age to do so would be unusual. Also, people do not necessarily move to the next level and may continue at any stage throughout their lives. Furthermore, while Fowler as a social scientist clearly notes that his research is religiously generic in nature and is not about any particular beliefs that people have, it can easily be applied to Christian spiritual growth and development.

People at each stage have distinguishable patterns of thinking, experiencing and behaving. They also operate spiritually in particular ways. However, <u>people are not required to advance to a "higher" stage in order to be a good Christian</u>. If they progress, they will function with more complex ways of thinking, experiencing and behaving which will make their faith multifaceted. Nevertheless,

> To identify a person's stage or stage transition does not imply that his or her spiritual life is better, more faithful, or desirable than anyone else's, whether in that stage or another. Faith development theory is not intended to be used, nor should it ever be used, as a measure of "how good a Christian," (may be).[3]

In other words, spiritual helpers should never use the stages to judge the "validity, sincerity, value, or effectiveness" of people's faith. For example, just because twenty-five-year-old Christians (at Synthetic-Conventional Faith) see no value in other religious traditions that fifty-five-year-olds do (at Conjunctive Faith), does not make their faith expressions wrong.

After overlaying the previous emotional and ethical/moral maps, concluding with Fowler's faith development theory will return the reader to the subject of spiritual growth and development, the purpose of the book, only with greater insights. While the Spiritual Road map focuses on spiritual relationship development, Fowler's Stages of Faith help summarize how people typically receive and respond to the experience of faith. In other words, **people understand God according to their personal abilities, through which they evaluate experiences and manage the details of their personal spiritual faith**.

I will begin by briefly summarizing each stage of faith and providing some correlation to the personal faith steps along the spiritual road. The chart (Graphic 10) is provided as a guide to this discussion. Afterward, I will reflect on three ways to apply the theory: How people conceive God as well as what experiences encourage and discourage faith. Finally, I will conclude with a couple of vignettes to illustrate how spiritual helpers might employ the maps.

Faith Development Theory and Spiritual Growth

Age (Freud)	0-1.5 yrs (Oral)	1.5-3 yrs (Anal)	3-6 yrs (Phallic/ Oedipal)	6-12 yrs (Latency)	12-20 yrs (Adolescence)	20-40 yrs (Young Adult)	40-65 yrs (Adult)	65 yrs + (Mature Adult)
Stages of Faith Valuing and Knowing (Fowler)	Primal Faith I know via un-differentiated sense experience. I value the symbiotic relationships	Intuitive-Projective Faith Understanding the existence of personal wills and expectations of others. Imaginative, inconsistent "short story" forms of knowing. I value clear-cut representations of good and evil. I value power.		Mythic-Literal Faith I know via an emerging logic to see cause and effect as concrete literal meaning. I value our common story and shared experience.	Synthetic-Conventional Faith I know via what is reflected when I, without examination, model others. By abstract thinking I can project values and beliefs. I value roles as they reflect who I am and our together life.	Individuative-Reflective Faith I know via critical examination. I seek to understand, accept or reject previously adopted faith, values/belief. I value a fully understandable and freely chosen self.	Conjunctive Faith Symbols and experience express truth beyond my critically made systems. I discover my map was not the territory. I value truth (even paradoxes) in all places.	Universalizing Faith I am no longer the center of knowing or valuing. I am transformed and drawn by God's perspectives. I value whatever is and what will be.
The Spiritual Road	**Pre-Christian Way** ✤ Awareness and Naming of God ✤ Awakening and Need for God ✤ Identification of Sin(s) ✤ Acceptance of Grace ✤ Moments of Decision --Confessional Temptation			**Purgative Way** ✤ Purging of Sins ✤ Adopt Ethical/Moral Standards ✤ Establish Spiritual Disciplines ✤ Basic Trust in God --Dark Night of the Senses		**Illuminative Way** ✤ Learnings ✤ Clarifications ✤ Devotions ✤ Mission and Generativity --Dark Night of the Spirit		**Unitive Way** ✤ Experience ✤ Contentment ✤ Watching and Waiting ✤ Temptation ✤ Living in Love

Graphic 10: Comparison of Fowler's Faith Development Theory with the process of personal spiritual growth.

Stage Zero, Primal or Undifferentiated – Originally, James Fowler proposed six stages of faith that began at age two. He has subsequently added a pre-stage zero to reflect that **spiritual faith, albeit non-rationally, begins at birth**. Building upon the insights of Erickson, this stage focuses on how the quality of care given to an infant translates into the type of "God" they experience. The best possible scenario is to be able to adopt the attitude that there is a friendly God with a friendly world in which to live. Accordingly, the concept of God takes on the form of the one who takes care of "me." The basic trust gained during this stage is the embryo of basic faith.

Stage One, Intuitive-Projective – As children gain language and mobility, they begin to interact with the "unprotected" world in which they experience confusion and concern. These children, ages two through six, struggle to obtain a beginning sense of autonomy and initiative; however, they also tend toward shame, doubt and guilt. If children are severely restricted, rejected and told how wrong they are, they as a result can intuit being power-less and unworthy. The autonomy they gain in their ability to do basic tasks provides them some control and safety. Imagination, story, role playing, symbol and fantasy are used to do so. During the "intuitive-projective" stage, children typically process internally via the imagination, which is projected as their worldview in order to obtain this "knowledge" and assurance – real-life accuracy is not easy for them to discern at this stage.

Religious stories of good versus evil where good wins can be used to help children manage their world. **God and God's representatives are the super heroes/heroines who magically conquer all and affirm their world as ok**. Additionally, adults become surro-gates that model the divine for children at this stage of faith. So, adults who exhibit strong negativity transmit a harsh image of the divine for children during these years, which can easily carry on through life. During this stage, the imaginary spirit world is the medium though which to enter the reality of faith; and that ability can be employed effectively at any age, especially during times of mysterious uncertainty. The power of the imagination has been harnessed to help in conquering cancer as well as to enable professional athletes to overcome deficiencies. Indeed, imagination is one of the first ways that people access the positive power of God, which remains deep-seeded in people's consciousness. Since words are originally pictures, the imagination is the primary vehicle of communicating with God. The nightmare vignette below indicates how people can spiritually assist young children through use of stage one faith abilities. This "faith imagination" approach is also effective and legitimate especially whenever adults are dealing with situations that seem beyond their control or are dealing with shame, doubt, guilt, fear or uncertainty. Spiritual helpers are advised to use "faith imagination" with adults because it touches people in ways that rationality cannot.

By age two to six years of age, the imaginative function of the brain is the primary tool for faith expression. For example, most children have "bad dreams." In our household I was the official parental dream interpreter. "Daddy, I had a bad dream." were words that often awakened me in the middle of the night. "Ok." I would say. "I'll be right there." So, I would get up and go sit on the side of our three-year-old son's bed and ask him to describe what happened. At the moment of crisis, danger or disturbing change in his dream, I would ask him to see Jesus come into his nightmare and simply say, "Tell me what happens." Well, Jesus is divine and all the most powerful three-headed monsters in the world were no match for him. After the words, "I feel better now," I would sometimes speak the prayer, "Thank you Jesus for your help." The result, of course, was the ability to go back to sleep but much more than that: the image of Jesus conveyed the powerful truth that God was able to handle his worst problems and touch him in a personal way. This is spiritual awareness appropriated in a personal way. It is REAL Christian faith, a stage one "intuitive-projective" faith in action.

Stage Two, Mythic-Literal – At this time of life, children experience faith in a mythic-literal way although the same schema can be carried into the teenage and adult years. Their world is concrete and literal. Experiences and events are explained by life narratives in order to construct meaning. **The stories that children (and adults) repeat determine how they understand their world and how God works in it for them**. When spiritual helpers say, "Tell me your story," they will receive the foundational propositions of people's theology which reflects their personal spiritual faith. If the stories never change by reexamination or forgiveness, if they are not reframed with deeper introspective truths, then people's faiths are likely to remain the same. In order to make such transition, people have to deal with the conflicts and contradictions in the mythic paradigms which they have adopted to literally be the "rules" of their lives.

Children are in the midst of bringing structure and logic into their understanding of the world. As such, they self-devise a world based on "how things are supposed to work" that brings predictability and dependability. **Consequently, God becomes the cosmic designer, controller and ruler over all things**. "God is often constructed on the model of a consistent and caring, but just, ruler or parent."[4] However, when their worldview of God does not adhere to immediate payoffs that reflect their personal sense of justice, these mythic-literal stage people either have to change their expectations (i.e., God doesn't work like that.) or reject God. Fowler talks about these "eleven-year-old atheists." They are the people who seriously ask, "Why do bad things happen to good people?"

While "mythic-literal" children have feelings and attitudes (impulses) and are exploring (recognizing, interpreting and managing) them, they do not step outside of themselves in self-assessment. Internal feelings and attitudes do not occur as guiding principles in these children who are mostly self-absorbed. Because girls tend to mature earlier than boys, they more quickly function relationally and become concerned about the feelings in others and in themselves.[5] Nevertheless, **typically God is not felt as personal, but above all and out there**. "They do not construct God in particularly personal terms, or attribute to God highly differentiated internal emotions and interpersonal sensitivities."[6] Accordingly, stage two people cannot internalize an authentic "personal relationship with Christ." To do so, Christians must have obtained a lower level of anxiety with a maturing trust in God, have reframed their spiritually perceived inconsistencies and have likely gone through a Dark Night of the Senses. Mythic-literal people can experience God as friendly just not as friend. Instead, **the spiritual faith of stage two people is based on following the rules to the best of their ability in order to participate in a world where faith makes sense to them and has order**.

Stage Three, Synthetic-Conventional – Fowler uses the terms "synthetic" and "conventional" to indicate **faiths that merge into communally-held, socially-acceptable forms**. Previously at stage two, people "constructed and adopted" a spiritual understanding that made sense to their own personal structure of the world. During stage three, people become aware that other people have different understandings and that the society (or group in which they are included) have a prescribed way of being. Consequently, major transitions, which include spiritual transformations, take place in the lives of teenagers during this time. They must learn about and amalgamate into the group in order to be accepted. **Spiritually, this is faith by imitation**. In other words, "I want to be like who I think you are so you will like me." This mantra applies both to other people and also to God.

Stage three people gain the ability to think about their own thoughts (self-reflection) and wonder what others are thinking about them (external perspective). Researchers have summarized this "mutual interpersonal perspective taking" as: "I see you seeing me; I see the me I think you see." and also "You see you according to me; you see the you you think I see."[7] Accordingly, **peer pressure and peer affirmations become the primary determining dynamics in life and faith**. In fact, the self-focused perspective of the previous stage now becomes dependent on the approval of others in the "synthetic-conventional" stage.

Because teenagers, as well as adults, at this stage want to fit in and feel accepted, they need to be part of a group and will emulate the qualities of that group. People in this stage are so focused on getting approval from other people that they will often seek everyone else's opinions in order to take a straw poll so as to make their conclusions. Ethical questions are often evaluated in terms of the harm the actions might do to relationships or what others might say about the decisions. Often, churches have a large contingent of stage three people. In fact, the culture of the church affirms that "everyone believes the same" and "you don't need to think about what that faith claims." Accordingly, most people remain with stage three spiritual values in a group that encourages them to stay at that same level of faith understanding.

Spiritually, this propensity for approval and acceptance causes people to emulate the officially defined beliefs of the group. **Their faith and its actions are not examined but assimilated**. So, if a church (and its leaders) models a high Christian standard of values and behaviors, then Christians will adopt those attitudes and actions. The opposite is also true. This same need for approval and acceptance means that **Christians will mirror who they think (that is, what they are taught) God is (loyal, loving, and supportive during crisis) and wants them to be**; and they will attempt to embody and live this persona. **Spiritually, stage three people crave a God (and God's representatives) who knows them and values them deeply**. And when Christians faithfully follow the rules, God can be experienced as companion or friendly parent who affirms their worth and helps them through their struggles.

This manner of spiritual thinking rarely changes until some major difficulty with a spiritual authority, a group, a set of beliefs or life tragedy – which cannot be reconciled or ignored – shatters it. This is a form of the Dark Night of the Senses, in which faith and its practice cannot be maintained as people have always thought they should be.

Even during such a crisis of faith, <u>most stage three people will go to great lengths to not disapprove or disagree with their church (at least on substantive matters) because it would potentially bring disapproval of them by the group</u>. So, when church people are disagreeable typically regarding unimportant issues, I suspect that they are either dissatisfied with their stage of faith but won't admit it to themselves for fear of retribution or they are feeling threatened that "their stage three church" might change. Thus, when people exhibited complaining behavior or began to ask questions, I understood that the teachable moment was at hand. When I was in pastoral ministry, I would invite these people into personal conversation. If no change in their personal faith was desired, then I could focus them on the Christian values of caring about others, bearing the failings of the weak and doing all things in love. On the other hand, if these people were at the critical juncture of spiritual growth, they were free to explore all faith topics and options with an emphasis on making their own independent free choices. Until people do the hard work of thinking on their own, they will likely either feel badly but maintain association with the group or reject faith as being unreliable, unreasonable or impractical. A non-judgmental, third-person objective perspective is exactly what is needed to assist the transition they seek.

Spiritual helpers always have a choice to make regarding those they assist: "Do I help this person be the best 'stage #' they can be?" or "Do I assist them to move into the next stage?" Of course, the answer doesn't have anything to do with the spiritual helper's desire but with whether people seem ready or ask for help.

How do spiritual helpers assist stage three folks? Since they put an extremely high value on the teaching of authority figures, especially within their own preferred group, <u>whatever spiritual helpers say will be taken to heart</u> and have a powerful impact. So, be cautious about what is said. Harsh words feel like a guillotine beheading. Permission given can be license to sin. Weigh words carefully.

If people are firmly in stage three and show no signs of wanting to move to stage four, do not push because they are not ready and will actually become resentful. <u>Stage three folks need to complete their current Spiritual Road tasks</u>. Most likely, these people are still on the Purgative Way, so they may need to finish purging personal sins or establishing good spiritual habits. So, assist them to do so. If they are on the Illuminative Way, they will have avoided "Clarifications," but they may be seeking deeper "Learnings" to fit into their life experiences. Now because they want to stay at stage three, these learning, even revised or expanded ones, need to fit within the authorized teachings of the accepted group. Thus, referring people to whatever source is authoritative is an excellent way to keep them where they choose to be but also to allow them deeper understandings. For example, if a particular creed or catechism supports their faith claim, use it but also help them explore what others from within their own group has said about that creed or catechism. While this is supportive, it may also sow seeds of alternative faith understandings. The same is true when it comes to scripture as an authority. Using cross referenced passages for comparison will broaden their learning but from within what is sanctioned. Heading stage three Christians to commentaries (authorized ones, of course) can also do the same deepening of the spiritual faith. Some stage three people may have skipped to "Mission and Generativity." Helping them to process what they want to do and why they choose to do it is important.

Stage three people may be in or heading for a Dark Night of the Senses, which is God's authorized spiritual crisis basically designed to help Christians know that they need to let go because they don't have all the answers. Accordingly, spiritual helpers can invite people to explain what they believe, asking for details and applications. They can also pose questions designed to enlighten the inadequacy or incompleteness of their current stage three faith thinking. They may also question any inconsistencies or contradictions in a non-obtrusive, uncritical way so as to allow the kind of introspective thinking needed in order to move farther along the Spiritual Road. These "Clarifications" questions are designed to increase faith not destroy it. However, the process may feel destructive so be ready with a lot of encouragement and affirmation.

As a personal observation: I believe that part of the decline in main line or non-doctrinal denominations is because of inadequate ways of dealing with stage three Christians who are ready to move to stage four. Those Christians who are ready to re-evaluate their faith understanding need a stage five "pastor of spiritual direction" to accompany them through the transition and to focus them with specialized programs and ministries that are "authorized" by the church but allow for their emerging new set of faith values. Their faith application will typically take them outside of the congregation, even into marginally-church kinds of activities. An alternative approach, which will sustain the organization but without helping stage three Christians to move to stage four, is to emphasize conformity while attracting new believers.

Indeed, serving "synthetic-conventional" faith Christians is a challenge. Great discernment, deep trusting relationships and personal conversations are needed. Adding these time-consuming tasks to the job of the typical pastor would be burdensome. Nonetheless, Christians, who are ready to move forward along the Spiritual Road, require such personal and sustained contract. Spiritual helpers, assisting busy church leaders, are especially needed.

Stage Four, Individuative-Reflective – As the story goes, a young woman was preparing ham for a family dinner. Her young daughter watched her as she cut about two inches off the end of the ham, threw it in the garbage and put the large portion into the oven pot. "Mom, why did you cut off the end of the ham?" Mom responded, "I guess that is because my mother always did it that way." When the little girl's grandmother came over for dinner, she asked, "Grandma, mom said you always cut off the end of the ham before cooking it. Why do you do that?" "Oh, my dear," replied her grandmother. "You don't have to do that. I just didn't have a larger pot so I had to cut off the end." Re-evaluating precious, long-held conventional ways of thinking can be very painful, but also liberating.

This stage is aptly named because through **critical reflection people make personal (re)decisions which separates them from the traditional and conventional ways of thinking and acting.** Fowler notes that two qualities are necessary in order to embark on this part of the faith journey: the ability to think critically and an independent self who does not need the approval of the group. My experience dictates that these qualities are actually nurtured and nourished via other people who strongly affirm that it is ok for people to question and become a new person. Because the struggle to break free of stage three conventions can be extremely painful as group affirmation and acceptance are withdrawn, mentors are extremely valuable for stage four Christians. However, with such support the "Individuative-reflective" stage of faith is quite exhilarating and freeing!

Furthermore, without grounded mentors, people are likely to "throw out the baby with the bath water." **The task of this stage of faith is for people to claim their own personal spiritual faith which requires critical examination of what they have been taught.** The tendency, in an act of individual assertion, is to jettison all of what they have been given. However, just because mom believed it doesn't mean that the son should reject it. This endeavor needs to become about discovering the truth behind the symbols and the meanings behind the actions. The key to this stage of faith is examination not rejection, action not reaction. Left to their own devices, people generally do the latter.

Stage four Christians become independent in so many ways during this time of life. As discussed at length in the Illuminative Way chapters, unless people become independent, they cannot freely and fully give of themselves or voluntarily surrender to God. While this transition may at times look like the rebellion of youth, it is instead a movement toward oneness with God. In addition, God no longer seems "out there" but instead resides within people and may be identified as the apostle Paul's "Christ within."

Spiritual helpers who assist people during this process are advised to take people "off the leash," let them explore and re-decide. There is so much to learn and clarify. Spiritual helpers can assist the process by occasionally asking stage four people to summarize what they think they have learned and/or the changes they have made. They can also be spiritual growth motivating by asking these Christians <u>how God was involved in making</u> <u>these changes happen</u>. Connecting their changes both to God's desire for them and God's assistance for them allows them to stay within the parameters of faith while developing independence at the same time. A similar technique would include having them describe themselves without the roles or labels like son, pastor, husband that might be imposed upon them. In addition, asking people to explain their faith without using any traditional religious terminology can be very effective in helping them claim their own faith expression.

   <u>Stage four faith development is heavily loaded with reason and mental analysis</u>. In fact, **the spiritual faith that people rationally determine to be accurate becomes the only acceptable faith to them**. Since stage four Christians are distinguishing themselves from others and from tradition, they may be insistent and argumentative. It is part of the process. However, ALL spiritual helpers especially pastors, who are at stage four need to have professional mentors to help temper their decree-oriented enthusiasm. Or more clearly stated: someone needs to stop stage four church leaders from imposing their views on others. As Christians grow through stage four, they claim their own personal faith and become deeply committed, which is exactly what God desires. This "Devotion" brings them one step closer to unity with God but also to the Dark Night of the Senses.

   Stage Five, Conjunctive – The conjunctive stage of faith occurs not before mid-life. Conjunctive faith includes the ability to interconnect a variety of life/faith experiences and becomes open to integrating additional ones. The collectiveness of stage five is the polar opposite of stage four's self-differentiation that is needed to become an independent person. This stage five radical change of perspective sometimes results from a mid-life crisis, a spiritual Dark Night, dealing with pain or existential anxiety. When such issues have been processed to a satisfactory conclusion, they result in self-reflection with awareness that life is coming to an end and that there really is something beyond this earthly existence. <u>This stage indicates the dynamic</u> <u>transition from the personal attitude of independence to interdependence</u> – noted in changing prayer forms and ethical attitudes as well as being comfortable as an individual while in the midst of a committed marriage relationship. The focus on getting answers, proving worth and establishing self all fade – in the big picture they are now deemed so inconsequential.

   Whereas stage four has a strong emphasis on rationality and figuring things out, <u>people</u> <u>in stage five people increasingly come to realize the futility of such mental effort. They have</u> <u>also gleaned truths from sources not included in their former understanding with different</u> <u>perspectives that are not easily reconciled</u>. For example, men who spent a lifetime becoming a "man's man" will discover that they have undeniable feminine qualities within them that are crying to be released. This realization at least causes an acceptance of the conflicting data or even a redefining of what a real man is. Christians may come to realize the presence of the Divine and spiritual truths in other religious traditions or even other religions; and they assert that justice must extend beyond their own culture and include everyone if true justice is to be obtained. They feel the need to conjoin these truths, which were formerly separated by strict dogmatic assertions. No longer does everything have to fit because it doesn't. No longer does everything have to be understood because there is too much to collate even if all truth could be known. At best, the incompatible and the unknowable are embraced as the path to God. This stage five faith thinking initiates the ability to have a broad perspective that allows people to consolidate, in spite of the inability to perfectly reconcile, different understandings. More significant principles overshadow the factual details and issues of right versus wrong. These people understand that a mutual working relationship is more important than concluding who is correct – even if they have to sacrifice for this greater good. This makes conjunctive faith people good mediators and arbitrators in life and within faith communities.

Stage five faith thinking initiates the ability to live within Christian mysteries. Grace predominates over law. Resurrection assures crucifixion. Weakness perfects power. Love conquers hate. Conjunctive faith-thinking Christians begin to regularly live with such seeming contradictions guiding their thoughts and actions. This indicates the philosophical concept of the "coincidence of opposites."[8] Simplifying this complex premise, hot cannot exist without cold and in perfect balance warmth is experienced but only for a moment because the entire process is in motion. In other words, the precise balance between thought and action is being, between past and future is the present or between human and divine is Christ. **In the spiritual life, people appreciate the importance of both "the individual" and the community, solitude and involvement, prayer and action, human and divine; and they implicitly seek to equally value and participate in all**. God is experienced via the perfect mix between the respect of an elder and the kiss of a lover. Overall, there is a co-creating for and with God in the work of faith – not because Christians have become so good, but because Jesus has bestowed friendship and granted the keys to the kingdom. **Stage five conjunctive Christians, as equally as possible, embrace the polarities because they intuit that unity with God is received in that moment**.

Stage Six, Universalizing Faith – Building upon stage five's appreciation of the opposites, people now move beyond focusing on either of the perspectives and are **committed to total participation in the vision of God**. The individual self and the human will are surrendered to the wisdom and the importance of divine purposes. According to Fowler very few people get to this stage of knowing and valuing. Some examples might include: Jesus, Moses, Buddha, Mohammed, Gandhi, Nelson Mandela, Martin Luther King, Jr. and Mother Theresa. Stage six people understand opposite positions and issues but they are not fighting against, nor are they fighting for any of them; they are working cooperatively with – not for their own good, or even the good of others, but for the good of God.

I believe that people do not actually live at stage six. Instead, they have moments, even periods of time, in which they visit. Consequently, more people than Fowler suggested actually have stage six experiences of faith. The cynical adage states, "How can I fly with eagles up there when I have to live with turkeys down here." While people have moments when they soar above in numinous moments in God's frame of mind, the humanity of the world pulls them back down. These are "Unitive Way" moments. I specifically remember a two-week spiritual direction intensive retreat in which God's Spirit transformed people into their best selves and the entire event into a beautiful loving faith community. If the reader has had such an experience nothing more needs to be said; if not, then nothing more can be said. The point of the illustration is that when I came home with the strong intention of living differently, I could not make it work within the structure of the world in which I lived. The emotional and spiritual crash I felt was profound! The higher level of consciousness that God had given on retreat was a foretaste of the divine will and ways.

Accordingly, stage six "universalizing" people are growing to think, feel and act as God thinks, feels and acts. Stage six Christians may not be able to go to the cross like Jesus, but they are beginning to want to do so because this radical way to change the world and even themselves is beginning to grasp hold of them. The paradox of dying in order to live makes no human logical sense but it is starting to seem obvious when directed by an internally-conveyed divine logic.

In order to be more fully alive, stage six Christians tend to identify and embrace the disadvantaged, the destitute and the maltreated. However, they are no longer under the illusion that they can change the condition or the situation of the world. Instead, <u>they knowingly or unconsciously desire to participate in the suffering of others</u> – God has merged into their being to cause this movement toward unity. Paul Tillich, the great analytic and systematic thinker, recognized this mystical inclination:

> God, as manifest in the Christ on the Cross, totally participates in the dying of a child, in the condemnation of a criminal, in the disintegration of a mind, in starvation and famine, and even in the human rejection of Himself. There is no human condition into which the divine presence does not penetrate. This is what the Cross, the most extreme of all human conditions tells us.[9]

Because stage six Christians have surrendered striving and even given their own personal will, <u>God has come to be a guest within them</u> – even if just for fleeting moments. During that time, they are imbued with God's ultimate expression of love – the crucifixion. The expression of this act in the world is to suffer along with it and for it.

IDENTIFYING AND ENCOURAGING FAITH DEVELOPMENT

The chart (Graphic 11) summarizes how people typically experience God at each stage in faith development; and it also indicates what life experiences enable or hinder such valuing and knowing. Spiritual helpers may use this chart to encourage what is needed or supplement what was missing in people's lives in order to allow them to continue in the process of spiritual growth and development.

Faith Development Theory and Life Experience

Age (Freud)	0-1.5 yrs (Oral)	1.5-3 yrs (Anal)	3-6 yrs (Phallic/ Oedipal)	6-12 yrs (Latency)	12-20 yrs (Adolescence)	20-40 yrs (Young Adult)	40-65 yrs (Adult)	65 yrs + (Mature Adult)
Stages of Faith (Fowler)	Primal Faith	Intuitive-Projective Faith		Mythic-Literal Faith	Synthetic-Conventional Faith	Individuative-Reflective Faith	Conjunctive Faith	Universalizing Faith
Type of God	One who takes care of me.	An almighty miracle worker. A deeply felt powerful magical "person" who become a rule giver and limit-setter of what is good and evil.		Stern, powerful, but a just parent. A Benevolent Dictator.	A friendly Spirit/ Person who knows me better than I know myself.	A God who is known through the analyzed conclusion of my beliefs.	God who shares tasks; and befriends but in un-analyzable even mystical ways.	The Eternal Lover who merges people into union and draws all things to the Omega point.
Experience that Allow Belief	I am fed, nurtured and held. I see me on your face.	I sense you are with me in this wonderful, surprising world we live in. Gaining a sense of control and ability. Autonomy and Initiative.		Having mutual concern, fairness and consistency. Quick pay-offs needed. Industry.	Significant others who bring me into contact with God. I believe what the church/ others believe. Identity.	Mentors and equals who allow freedom and expression. Personal bonds that mediate love.	The chance to be a mentor or leader to share and build.	God's Grace alone brings this stage. It de-centers and connects me.
Experience that Leads to Unbelief	I am not cared for.	When I sense the world as powerful or painful and you do not affirm for me that I am ok as I am, I am uncertain and not acceptable. Shame, Doubt and Guilt.		Inconsistent/ delayed rewards and punishments. Inferiority.	Rejection and unacceptance. Unresolved identity crisis. Role Confusion.	Being told what to believe that doesn't make sense; punished for disbelief.	Separation from community or no opportunity to produce something worthwhile.	Inability or unwillingness to relinquish personal will and true Soul-Self to God.

Graphic 11: How life experiences can enable or hindered personal spiritual development.

195

The divine thing about God is that God fully knows and values all whom God has created regardless of people's stage of faith development. Spiritual helpers must do the same. In addition, because it is part and parcel to the very nature of God, God encourages all whom God has created to grow in faith and love toward oneness with God. Spiritual helpers are advised to do the same.

USING THE OVERLAID MAPS

The developmental maps of Erickson, Kohlberg and Fowler have been presented, not because they perfectly describe the territory – they don't, but merely as additional ways to approximate where people are located on their journeys. Hopefully, using them will assist to confirm for spiritual helpers what particular assistance might be offered. Nevertheless, if they are not helpful, please don't use them. **Below, I have included an extended example in which I have employed these theories as part of the process of spiritual guidance**.

Martha Lou desired a closer relationship with God. This was an emotional issue; it was not about coming to faith which she had consistently maintained throughout her entire life. She had a solid mature theology which had been built on an intellectual foundation. She knew what she believed. She just couldn't feel any closeness, any real connection with God. She desperately wanted to and was ready to do whatever it took to have that relationship. For example, she believed in grace as the unearned, undeserved love (forgiveness, acceptance) of God and she quite regularly helped others to receive that grace and feel it. She just did not feel it herself.

Martha Lou was approaching retirement. She had become a Christian at an early age. Although a struggle, she had adopted morals and ethics. She had established a great set of spiritual disciplines. She had moved into the Illuminative Way with great questions that assisted her in the "Learnings" and "Clarifications" of her faith. She was fully engaged in "Mission and Generativity" as she was both a humble servant and a spiritual mother to many women. However, Martha Lou was missing the emotional content of "Devotions," which had nothing to do with her faith commitment to God through her Savior, Jesus. Nevertheless, she was stuck, seemingly unable to become affective in her relationship with God.

Martha Lou consistently lived her faith. When I suggested that she pray regularly, she had no trouble maintain that discipline. In fact, she easily moved from meditative prayer to active contemplative prayer. Her prayer even became passive contemplation where she could be open for God's instruction to be given. However, even those moments where received as teaching, not devotion. Accordingly, Martha Lou "retreated" to active contemplation where she was more in control of this interactive form of praying. In addition, Martha Lou had a personal prayer partner and they shared with and prayed for each other. Basically, Martha Lou had a rather solid expression of faithfulness – desirable by many – but her dilemma was very real. She deeply wanted a close relationship with God and she wanted to feel it.

Traditional spiritual guides could easily accompany someone like Martha Lou because she had all the right answers and did all of the right things, faithfully. Nevertheless, she wanted to and needed to grow in her personal spiritual faith. Martha Lou would be a perfect candidate for spiritual direction so as to process where God was noticed in her life and discern how to cooperate with that awareness. However, this traditional approach would only help Martha Lou so much.

Overlaying the other developmental maps would be the spiritual key. Two major life events had hindered her full spiritual growth. First, between the ages of three to sixteen, Martha Lou had been devastated by serious and repeated sexual and emotional abuse within her family of origin. Second, while Martha Lou may have been in love briefly she never moved into the emotional intimacy of a marriage even though she now was a grandmother. Importantly, Martha Lou had spent years in psychotherapy and had made dramatic progress in her healing as evidenced by her ability to function well in life and how she greatly affected the lives of others.

People, like Martha Lou, who experience abuse that begins during Erikson's stage two, "autonomy versus shame and doubt," often develop a deep sense of shame which John Bradshaw calls "toxic shame." Shame is a healthy personality quality when it limits the blurting out of demeaning comments or running around naked in public. However, when shame becomes toxic, people have the basic deep-seated belief that they are neither loveable nor acceptable. Martha Lou's shame was so invasive that she would drag past emotional events into her present condition and use them to negatively interpret her life. Essentially, she would keep silent or withdraw, but internally Martha Lou would consistently evaluate herself as old, ugly and undesirable. She understood herself as totally unacceptable – God could not even love her! Intellectually, she knew that was not true, but because she was essentially shamed to the core, she could not feel God's love.

In addition, Martha Lou had not had a committed heterosexual marriage relationship in which she would have been loved just as she was, warts and all, by a "significant other." In truth, her toxic shame often sabotaged the possibility of such intimacy; instead, Martha Lou would slide into isolation at least in her interior life. An undeniable, insistent, unconditional love that comes from beyond individuals is necessary to induce the intimacy that Martha Lou needed. Martha Lou had come to believe, validated via her life experiences, that she was so unlovable that she could not feel emotionally connected for very long at a time.

At one particular session, Martha Lou's emotional reaction to a particular situation was much stronger than seemed appropriate, which is always a clue that some important issue needs to be addressed. The quick summary is that a particular individual was being treated unfairly by a Para-religious group and rejected because of her gender. Martha Lou had championed this woman and strongly supported her. Now, Martha Lou accurately and intellectually challenged the religious establishment with well-crafted arguments based on the highest Christian principles. Nevertheless, the board censored her and then removed her from her voluntary position. Martha Lou was furious. She, like Jesus, was disconcerted about the injustice but her reactions contained a much stronger anger. Martha Lou was focused like a laser on how unfair the treatment was as well as on how it took away this woman's rights and abilities and "treated her like she was dirt." Martha Lou wanted to "present her case" to be "justified." After I thought she had vented enough, I interjected, "I agree! You are right! They reacted wrongly! But, Martha Lou, you might consider that this issue is more about you than it is about her." Being the sharp-witted person she was Martha Lou stopped and suddenly changed. She initially made some cutting, smart-alecky comment which was what she would do when she didn't really want to admit a truth; then reflected. "Are you suggesting that this has something to do with my victimization by abuse?" I didn't say anything, nor did I need to. She continued, "I was treated harshly and it destroyed my life. Yes, I think that if somehow I could get this woman to be loved and accepted for whom she is that I would be ok as well." I smiled and slowly nodded my head.

Martha Lou was firmly in Kohlberg's Post-Conventional stage six, intellectually. Her ethics were principle-based and mindful of a multitude of perspectives for the good of all. However, Martha Lou's was emotionally reacting with a Pre-Conventional Stage Two scream, "It's not fair!" Martha Lou re-experienced being abused and her objection was less about the other woman than about her true personal need for acceptance. This moral dilemma further elucidated how the early abusive events in Martha Lou's life were hindering her further emotional, moral and spiritual growth.

What is the spiritual prescription for Martha Lou? While further therapy might be helpful for Martha Lou, it would not accomplish her self-diagnosed spiritual desire for a closer relationship with God. While Martha Lou had traveled far along the spiritual road, the emotional holes in her personality had come to limit her ability to move into "Devotion." Besides the conventional approach of a spiritual helper, I could assist Martha Lou in the following ways.

First and foremost, I would not allow Martha Lou to put herself down and therefore reinforce her toxic shame. I would help her to assert that her past experiences do not determine her present or God's future desires for her. Thus, strongly objecting to her "that's the way it used to be so that's the way it's always going to be" thinking was necessary. I would reinforce this countering of toxic shame with confirming scripture references which Martha Lou would declare as valid, at least intellectually. For example, Psalm 8's translation personalized that God had intentionally created Martha Lou just a "little lower than the angels."

Second, Martha Lou upon beginning most spiritual direction sessions would regularly say, "You know, I don't want to be here and would rather just run for the door right now." More than anything, Martha Lou needed the freedom to be autonomous – to develop Erikson's personality quality of "Will" in the "autonomy versus shame and doubt" stage. Accordingly, I would matter-of-factly say, "It's ok. You are free to leave anytime." Then I would playfully add, "Besides, you are bigger than I am, closer to the door and I'm handicapped." Martha Lou needed to feel safe and in charge, even more than most people.

Third, my entire approach was to establish a "relationship bridge" so that Martha Lou might decide to walk across it into God's waiting arms. I choose to consistently offer a boundary-appropriate authentic, warm loving relationship toward Martha Lou. I always looked for how I could see and affirm the best in her, even when she would not believe it; I would do this especially during closing prayer. Because this was a male agape bridge, it was also healing for her former abuse as well as an invitation to move closer to God, who Martha Lou professed as male.

Fourth, I would find ways to offer grace. Martha Lou would set the schedule for spiritual direction, or change it, whenever she chose. When she sabotaged, unconsciously, the spiritual direction relationship by bouncing her check, I suggested that she collect "quarters" between sessions and that would be the designated amount for her session. Martha Lou needed to be graced. (Limiting the payment was not a big deal for me since I had been significantly graced – given what I didn't deserve or earn – throughout my life. I certainly see it as thanking those who gave to me and it paying forward as well.) Experiencing grace in human forms communicates unconditional love; and it is felt not just understood.

Fifth, what I have done naturally for Martha Lou was confirmed by her comment, "I like how you bring everything back around to God. I don't think that way." Whatever Martha Lou experienced during her life, I would help her understand how God was involved in it. For example, when she was absorbed into a particular song during worship and felt affirmed to tears, I asked, "Do you not understand that you were allowing God to touch you intimately?" Of course, Martha Lou didn't naturally think those thoughts, but neither could she deny the truth of what she felt. Thus, identifying God and the associated feelings in her life experiences helped her have a closer relationship with God.

Sixth, such emotional life experiences would invite Martha Lou to allow God to be invited to enter into her unconscious. Because such permission would seem too risky and too intimate, even invasive, Martha Lou would likely resist. However, God indeed desires to change Martha Lou at her core with what can come only from God – salvation (healing, forgiveness, grace and love).

Overlaying the psycho-social developmental maps (Erikson, Kohlberg and Fowler) on top of the spiritual road map helped to clarify Martha Lou's spiritual progress but more importantly identify what was needed for her to move forward. Spiritual helpers, especially for those they accompany who do not respond to the more traditional approach, can gain insights by considering the entire person via the various developmental understandings. After spiritual helpers do such analysis, they are advised to spend significant uninterrupted time listening for God's Holy Spirit to provide additions or corrections to their thinking. Neither clarity nor analysis ultimately has lasting effects. Only love changes people and that happens via God and in relationships.

Tools for the Journey

W hen heading out for a cross country road trip that includes using secondary sight-seeing roads, people first need to know where they are going or they will not necessarily get there. Travelers also need comprehensive maps with all the options needed to figure where they are along the path and where to find what they need. However, it is more than helpful to take along emergency items and necessary provisions.

Spiritual helpers need the same kind of "emergency" supplies when assisting others on their Spiritual Road trip. <u>Chapters sixteen through twenty-one include some of these necessities.</u> Sometimes folks just need a drink of water, other times they are out of gas, and then, of course, there are times when the engine starts to make a "funny" sound that indicates trouble. Road signs along the way are helpful but some lead to dead ends. In addition, how do people deal with the endless miles of highway monotony? And finally some travelers may actually not want to go where they say they want to go and may in reality try to sabotage themselves from arriving.

<u>Prayer</u> is nourishment, like a cup of cool water. When people are close to being out of gas, they can bet that <u>forgiveness</u> is likely required to continue. Engine trouble is painful; but what kind of dilemma – simple or tragic – is happening? "Dealing with Pain" helps assess the value of <u>pain</u> and the action required to reduce or eliminate it. My particular favorite "Tool for the Journey" is the signs we read along the way – especially those <u>words</u> that become so internalized that they significantly retard progress. Two other less practical, more specialized tools are needed to deal with two more difficult situations – how to deal with <u>loneliness</u> and <u>the unconscious</u>. These conditions occur especially while traveling through barren and arid regions – often after a long time on the road.

I hope the reader will find this emergency kit helpful for guiding those on the journey. Use of the following tools has assisted me personally but also proved to be insightful for others as well. Before opening the following tool kit, please entertain a word about tools themselves. Many spiritual guides have considered them suspect – and for good reasons; **the tools can <u>easily</u> be idolized as "the way" helpers are supposed to do spiritual direction – they can become a substitute for the real relationship-accompanying that <u>IS</u> spiritual companionship.** Part of the discussion regarding why spiritual direction and therapy should never be mixed revolves around this concern. Very truly, spiritual guidance is not about problems that need to be fixed!!!

The Spiritual Road is absolutely about a relationship with God that can ONLY be strengthened in that relationship AND made real (realized, purified, illuminated or unified) when two or three are gathered in Jesus' name because he is THEN (through the presence of the Holy Spirit) present in the midst of that relationship. On the other hand, issues that need mending do arise while helping others to grow spiritually. And if helpers haven't heard it said, they most certainly have not have been listening – people ask, "How do I do that?" For example, folks note: "My prayers are not working. Do I need to pray differently; if so, how do I change the way I pray?" Others have said: "I thought that I had forgiven but obviously I have not. What am I missing? How do I do that?" In great numbers, I have heard the lament, "I really want to follow God and God's ways and have been sincerely praying for that so why do I repeatedly and dramatically fail to change?" Of course, people ask, "Is God punishing me? The Bible tells me "yes" in some places and "no" in others. How do I know what is true and what to do about it?"

There are simple and spiritually sensitive ways to assist others with these concerns. God absolutely knows what people need; but suggesting that people leave a spiritual direction session and just pray about their quandary may not be what is best for them. Accordingly, <u>I have collected the following practical tools in this section for options to be considered when helping others grow spiritually.</u>

Spiritual growth is absolutely the responsibility of those being helped so they need to choose what to do or not do. However, if they do not have a tool to help, they have no choice to make. Whether to offer the use of any particular tool is the responsibility of the spiritual guide, who needs clear divine guidance about whether to do so. Since the spiritual guidance relationship is about discerning together what God wants for the person being helped, then sharing that insight is paramount. So, have the tool box close at hand – God will be pleased if you do.

CHAPTER 16

Prayer Forms

Prayer is any intentional contact with God. Prayer can be words or deeds, internal or external, but it cannot be accidental. Prayer must be intentional in whatever form – thinking, feeling or willing (to be in God's presence). The great and wondrous news is that God always honors and uses prayer to help people grow spiritually – it is the loving thing to do and so God, who is pure love, cannot do otherwise. In order to illustrate the importance of prayer I want to continue a vignette from chapter nine, "The Illuminative Way: The Process" in the section of "Clarifications" about DeShawn who after doing a dramatic monologue of Judas Iscariot had new insights into his Christian faith.

After the "Clarifications" had been worked through, DeShawn's spiritual director continued. "DeShawn, it is really great that you have had such insights about having a little of Judas' tendencies inside of you and that you feel really uncomfortable about that. Sometimes we have new thoughts that actually change the way we think about our faith. Our emotions can humbly take on a little healthy shame for behaving in that former way. And we can even make amends or fix the error of our ways. However, there is still one thing that is missing that makes all the difference. Do you know what it is?"

DeShawn reviewed his former thoughts but could not verbalize what was still needed; and asked his director about what he was referring. "It is so simple that you just overlooked what was necessary," replied his director. "We need to bring our insights into prayer. You see, God can give us new thoughts; God can enable us to feel regret; and God can actually fix the world to be as God intends. But God cannot, because God will not, do one thing. God will not make us admit our wrong ways or confess our sins. That would be manipulating us and disrespecting who we are. It is the opposite of true love – and contrary to the very nature of God. So, we must admit to God, not just know, feel and change our mistake. Our spiritual relationship with God does not improve or grow stronger simply by changing our lives. However, the divine-human connection grows spiritually when we surrender to the fact that God is divine and we as humans need God. And we do this through sincere prayer."

"So you are saying that we can feel badly about what we have done, change our way of thinking and even make amends – and none of that matters?" asked DeShawn. "Oh, no," clarified the director. "All of that matters a lot! And we need to do those things. But what God wants most is our voluntary response. In fact, without admitting that we need God our relationship with God does not get stronger. Actually, we can change our thinking, feel badly and make amends without it having anything to do with God. Those actions, of course, are all about us making ourselves better and that we don't need God to do it. Surrendering as a creature is the only thing that God will not do for us. So, we truly need to offer to God all of our new insights and necessary corrections. They are the means for growing spiritually. Prayer is the way to grow in our personal spiritual relationship with God." DeShawn understood and committed himself to pray about this change.

Throughout the centuries and transversing culture, language and trends, God has used prayer for the purpose of drawing people into the depth of a divine-human loving relationship. God has been able to do this with or without people understanding the function of prayer; and God will continue to do so far into eternity. On the other hand, <u>if people have insights into how different prayer forms support and strengthen the relationship they desire, then they and God would actually combine efforts</u>; remembering that they are only cooperating in the work that God is accomplishing within them.

Different prayer is for different people at different times in their lives. <u>Understanding the various prayer forms and spiritual development is important for making informed suggestions as spiritual helpers.</u> Many scholars have written in detail about prayer, as well as the function and process of praying. I am not going to try to improve on such excellent works. Instead, **my purpose is to provide an overview summary of the types of "Prayer Forms" that are available (but not all of the individual styles within each) in coordination with where spiritual travelers are along the Spiritual Road.** This knowledge-tool may be employed to assist people to go further on the journey. For example, when changing a spark plug, using a wrench instead of a pair of pliers is recommended. In other words, pray-ers might get the job done with passive meditation but active contemplation might be more effective in deepening their relationship with God. Using pliers might actually get the spark plug changed, but trying to do so by using a hammer, I don't recommend. Accordingly, pray-ers sticking to a "Formal Prayer" form will probably not receive an affective relationship with the divine.

I spent about ten years on a certification team that helped nurture seminary students through the process of education and into a status of ordination. I gained a reputation from students about being the person who always asked the "hardest questions" in which I still take some delight. The questions were not so hard but they were absolutely about the students' relationship with God and their spiritual growth or lack of it. I guess that qualifies as "hard." While meeting with a particular student, I felt led to ask if she had considered participating in spiritual direction. The team received a curt and abrasive response, "Why, all a spiritual director will do is say, 'Light a candle and go pray about it.'" I was not intimidated, but was shocked, by the comment. Then after reflection, I was heartbroken that spiritual direction, which deals with prayer, had such an inept reputation. It certainly was not how I pronounced benediction on those I helped spiritually.

Occasionally, Christians get stuck in a rut on the Spiritual Road because they need a different form of prayer. Also, particular forms of prayer most easily coincide with certain parts of the Spiritual Road journey. Hopefully, considering the following "Prayer Forms" will enable spiritual helpers to discern which is "best" suited for what individuals need. Formal, meditative, contemplative and soul prayers – all most likely take place throughout the course in Christians' lives, yet one form is typically more appropriate and helpful at different stages of spiritual growth.

Having made that assertion, I need to affirm that <u>prayer, like the spiritual life, cannot be adequately described as a perfectly logical, step by step sequential formula</u>. Nevertheless, prayer "*is* a process, and it *is* going somewhere."[1] Different forms can be described BECAUSE different forms are experienced and practiced! Also, these forms of prayer have a "direction." For certain, they are not always experienced in precisely the progression I will describe. **However, they do generally move from authority-directed praying, to person-directed praying, to interactive praying to God-infused praying**. <u>But even this progression is not always the rule since any form can be and is experienced at various times throughout the spiritual life</u>. Nevertheless, I believe that spiritual helpers and those they accompany can greatly benefit from guidelines.

<u>Please, if these guiding principles do not seem to fit in a particular situation, discard them</u>! Also, just because people do not fit the pattern, do not believe it is the spiritual helper's job to make it work for them. Instead, listen carefully to the description of their experience. And always trust what people say at least until what they explain contradicts what they previously stated. Their spiritual life is not the spiritual life of the helper; and helpers are not responsible to make sure that other people "get it right." In fact, some errors made by spiritual travelers on their own can become the best spiritual growth lessons they can ever learn. Primarily, understand the value that the experience has for their relationship with God. Honor that and help them build on it. For these purposes, I offer the following guidelines that I have come to understand as a typical progression in forms of prayer that guide Christians into deeper relationship with the divine. Allowing people to understand what has happened to them in their prayers as well as enabling them to move to an alternative form of prayer may be exactly what they need for their own spiritual health and wholeness.

DEFINING "PRAYER FORMS"

Throughout the centuries, prayer has been defined and described in so many different ways; and much confusion is the result. In spite of the fact that various forms have gotten blurred, prayer remains about coming into relationship with God. Most people, however, have no problem understanding about the common practice of reciting a prayer that everyone knows by whatever name it is given; I call these "Formal Prayers." On the other hand, a lot of discussion has occurred about the Christian practices of meditation and contemplation – what is what, how to do them and whether they are even legitimate forms of prayer. Accordingly, various writers, including the masters and saints, have assigned various names and differing descriptions to each. Although I would love to use the scripture to figure out the differences, it is not very helpful since biblical writers were not attempting precise delineations and sometimes even wrote about prayer poetically or metaphorically. In addition, what I have called "Unitive Prayers" also has accumulated debate, but that may be primarily because those prayers are exceptionally difficult to explain adequately.

This chapter on "Prayer Forms" is written to assist the reader to understand the general pattern that Christians employ while using prayer as they travel the Spiritual Road. The definitions of the prayer forms that I have used are based on the manner in which the person praying approaches prayer. The pattern typically moves from external, to mental, to affective to will-directed praying. In their attitude toward prayer, people begin as dependent, move to independent, to interdependent and to surrendered praying. And as mentioned above, they also move from authority-directed praying, to person-directed praying, to interactive praying to God-infused praying. So, whatever ways that the reader has learned to categorize prayer, please consider the intent, which is to facilitate spiritual helpers to discern by listening to the descriptions of what is actually happening as people pray.

These forms of prayer include:

- ✠ Formal Prayers
- ✠ Meditative Prayers
- ✠ Contemplative Prayers
- ✠ Unitive Prayers

In supplement to these four forms of prayer, they each can be further delineated into either active or passive approaches. This distinction is not so needed for "Formal Prayers" as it is for the other forms. Simply put, active approaches are pray-er initiated; in passive forms of prayer, the pray-er receives from God who makes the first move. A chart (Graphic 12) that describes and integrates "Prayer Forms" with the Spiritual Road has been provided.

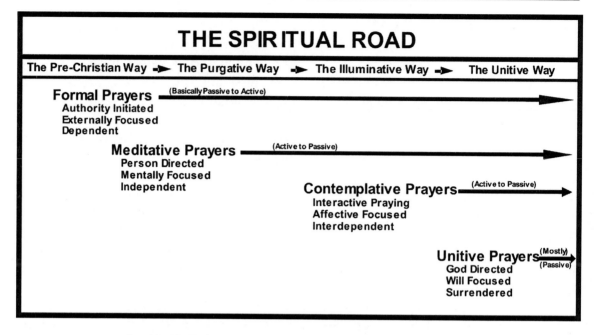

Graphic 12: Each "Prayer Form" typically begins during a particular stage of spiritual growth and would be unusual to occur any earlier.

FORMAL PRAYERS

"Formal Prayers" are official and often pre-written prayers – even pre-authorized as many of the prayers in the early church were. As such, "Formal Prayers" are initiated by an authority, which God uses to draw people into a relationship even before they recognize that is what is happening. These official prayers can come from the authority of mom or the highest representative of the church. As such, through official representatives God initiates these prayers, which make them passive in approach. On the other hand, when people, devoid of an official setting, choose to pray "Formal Prayers," those prayers would be deemed as active. In other words, when a person attends worship (mass, meeting or service) and they speak aloud the Lord's Prayer when it is started, they do so "passively." However, at another time when people decide to pray and they use the Lord's Prayer to do so, they have an "active" approach to using this authorized prayer. In addition, via "Formal Prayers" much teaching and training occurs, which is especially necessary in order to grow spiritually through the "Pre-Christian Way" and the "Purgative Way." On the other hand, Christians during all stages of spiritual growth benefit from "Formal Prayers."

Remembering my definition of prayer as **any intentional contact with God** means that worship itself is prayer and it is full of "Formal Prayers." Worshippers are brought into contact with God where they can experience spiritual growth in the process. The more

206

the liturgical or ceremonial the style of worship, the more likely it is to contain "Formal Prayers" which can include any responses, songs, benedictions or written prayers that are repeatedly used. "Formal Prayers" also have the unidentified purpose of bonding people into common faith affirmations, which they all profess. **While "Formal Prayers" is routine and habitual, through them people actually name God, are aware of God, feel the need for God, identify sin, accept grace and are led to decide for God.** Perhaps, the reader recognized those qualities as those needed during the "Pre-Christian Way" part of the Spiritual Road that I outlined in chapter six.

Many examples exist and include all taught and formally spoken prayers like the Serenity Prayer, Hail Mary, Prayer of St. Jude, any table Grace and so forth. The "Now I lay me down to sleep" prayer[2] at bedtime is an example of "Formal Prayers" and so is the request from the Apostles for Jesus to teach them how to pray, when he responded with "The Lord's Prayer."[3] In addition, creeds, responses, the doxology or other hymns/songs, scripture readings even kneeling and signs of the cross can all be designated as "Formal Prayers" – which may be spoken aloud, silently or tactilely. Portions of scripture like Psalm 23 or "I can do all things through Christ who strengthens me"[4] [Philippians 4:13] or the Trinitarian response "In the name of the Father, Son and Holy Spirit" or the Mizpah[5] [Genesis 31:49] can be used as "Formal Prayers."

One of my favorite stories about "Formal Prayers" took place in a hospital room. One young girl needed to have her tonsils taken out. As I arrived at this routine surgery, this girl and her sister were delighted to see me – they both had regularly participated in Sunday school and Vacation Bible School with me. The adults present were cordial and appreciative that I had taken the time to come. We visited for a while and then quite unceremoniously I simply turned both of my hands' palms upward and slightly to the side. Immediately, both girls became animated and alert as they moved to mimic me – joining hands to form a circle. The adults, who were occasional church attendees, had no idea what was happening. The action I performed was a regularly experienced, unspoken invitation to prayer – via my formal action these girls immediately came into the Presence of God. While the praying itself was not formal, the simple action of hands extended and joined communicated not only that God was there but also that those who turned their hands upward wanted to respond. "Formal Prayers" are powerful (at least in regard to the effort given proportional to the results received). I dare say that both of those girls will always respond to hands turned upward and outward as an invitation to pray.

Spiritual helpers who accompany people at the beginning of the faith journey would be advised to assist them in learning as many formal or authorized prayers as possible, even using them when meeting together. In many ways, "Formal Prayers" are the foundational building blocks of Christianity. Because of their commonality, they connect Christians to each other as well as individuals between different branches of the faith. "Formal Prayers" instruct and therefore initiate faith growth in beginners; they also sustain the continuity of faithfulness throughout life; and at the end of life I pray that I will be able to at least turn my palms upward with my last breath.

MEDITATIVE PRAYERS

The word "meditation" means "to think about." Accordingly, **"Meditative Prayers" are praying with the mind**; which is primarily active in approach but may also be passive. **Any form of intentional thinking about God as well as the things of God is "Meditative Prayers."** My definition certainly enlarges prayer to include some very non-traditional forms of being in contact with God. Absolutely, thinking about God is not the same as God; nonetheless God uses meditation to enhance the God-human relationship. In such "praying with the mind," people are learning information that helps them to make a decision for and grow toward Christianity – of course, God is very interested and supportive of this methodology. In other words, when people think about God, God is confirming that prayerfulness, even if it never seems that God is active or present in the midst of such meditations.

I cannot even begin to list all of the ways that people can engage in "Meditative Prayers." **Most spoken prayers and publically issued prayers are "Meditative Prayers" because they are thinking about God**. Typically, prayers in this venue have the purpose of confirming what the community believes, which also can be spiritual growth for those who are just coming into belief or do not know just what to believe. Whenever people wonder about creation and are intentionally thinking about God, they are practicing "Meditative Prayers." Whenever people consider where God is in a certain situation or what God is teaching through particular events, they are participating in "Meditative Prayers." In order to support faith beginners, spiritual helpers might simply name the beginners' God-thinking activity as prayer, which lends greater value to it. I often comment: "You know if you just put 'Dear God' before and 'Amen' after what you just said, it would be a perfect prayer." However, I already know it is prayer the way it is. Such thinking not only brings people to greater knowledge of God and spiritual things, but it also can increase their personal faith relationship with God. The psalmist says as much: "I remember the days of long ago; I meditate on all your works and consider what your hands have done. I spread out my hands to you; my soul thirsts for you like a parched land. Selah."[6] [Psalm 143:5-6] Just thinking about God moved the psalmist to drink eagerly of what God provided.

All forms of spiritual reading and Bible study are also "Meditative Prayers." Gaining spiritual information and thinking about it helps to clarify between God's ways and not God's ways, to purge sins, adopt ethical and moral standards, establish spiritual habits and basically to trust more in God. Perhaps, the reader recognized those qualities as the ones needed during the "Purgative Way" part of the Spiritual Road that I outlined in chapter seven. Thus prayer, especially "Meditative Prayers," becomes important when on that part of the faith journey. All of the ways that Christians attempt to "think about" God increases their strength of faith and thus their relationship with God. The phrase "saying your prayers" is very accurate and appropriate for those on the "Purgative Way;" and it should never be condemned as not "real" prayer. By the very nature of rational activity, people are typically very "active" in their approach to do something ... to do prayer. <u>This is an active approach toward "Meditative Prayers."</u> On the other hand, people may be studying a passage of scripture for understanding, but then stop attempting to learn, start pondering and receive new thoughts about what they have been reading. The same progression may occur when actively listening to a homily or sermon; Christians relax and God enters the thoughts with new concepts that enhance the spiritual relationship. As a result, God comes into the process which allows people's thinking to put together information and draw conclusions that were neither obvious nor on the written page. <u>These are passive "Meditative Prayers"</u> because people are in the process of receiving, whether they know it or not, from God.

As a spiritual helper of people practicing "Meditative Prayers," I may suggest that they focus on a particular spiritual book, biblical passage or all the biblical words on a certain topic. Whatever they learn will increase their faith and relationship with God especially in conversation about what it all meant. I may ask people to summarize what they have read or to make a good/evil or pro/con list. Using their own comparison and discernment helps them to solidify their faith and shed light on who God is.

When listening to those Christians on the "Purgative Way" (and even some on the "Pre-Christian Way"), I ask if they ever stop and just ponder while in active "Meditative Prayers" or study. And if they do so, especially spontaneously, I may discern that they are ready to make the transition from active to passive "Meditative Prayers." Accordingly, I might recommend that they intentionally "wander and ponder" to see what new thoughts God gives them. In addition, Christians farther along the Spiritual Road may be struggling with a certain topic like service, Holy Spirit or forgiveness. Often, I will suggest "Meditative Prayers" on that subject, which would include as much information from scriptural passages (or occasionally a very good book) as they can hold at one time in their minds. In my experience, this biblical "thinking about" approach will surround them with God and God's truths. Because they are farther along the Spiritual Road, they typically will process the information quickly, moving onto letting God talk and even having conversation with God about it all. Clarity almost always emerges – although they still may not like what they learn nor be willing to follow through to action.

Especially for Christians traveling the "Purgative Way" part of the Spiritual Road, "Meditative Prayers" is the primary way that they get to know God and thus build their personal faith relationship with God. Interestingly, they often think that they are just going to church, studying the Bible, praying together and helping others; and they are, but they are also in prayer. At this point on the Spiritual Road and <u>through the use of "Meditative Prayers," growing spiritually is hard work</u> and it takes consistent, strong effort to do so. Thus, there may be a lot of starting and stopping and starting again, which is not about unfaithfulness or sinfulness; it is just hard work. In the process, however, God is teaching them about who God is and drawing them nearer. With the developing common language, values, understandings and goals, God will be able to draw these Christians even closer, close enough for them to not just talk, but listen carefully, discerningly and in ways that begin to change their spiritual nature as they grow into the maturity of Christ Jesus.

CONTEMPLATIVE PRAYERS

In one sense, "Meditative Prayers" are included in "Contemplative Prayers" because Christians have to "think about" God in the process of praying. In fact, Christians who are practicing passive "Meditative Prayers" could easily be determined to be doing contemplation. A clear-cut distinction between Christian meditation and Christian contemplation is complicated to determine; they seem to overlap and do. The lines are blurry. That nebulousness is ok since spiritual helpers do not need to firmly categorize in order to mentor others. Some clear guidelines about "Contemplative Prayers" are all that is needed.

As Christians mature, they start asking honest questions and listening for new insights that clarify their faith and bring them to a much deeper commitment, which they "pay forward" in terms of mission and generativity. They also desire a deeper faith that is integrated into living. The reader might recognize these qualities as those which occur on the "Illuminative Way" summarized in chapter eight. Consequently, their prayers change. Or perhaps because their prayers change, their faith grows deeper. **Corresponding to this part of the spiritual journey, active "Contemplative Prayers" are interactive, interdependent and affective**.

Interactive – A primary characteristic of "Contemplative Prayers," which is consistently different than in "Formal Prayers" or "Meditative Prayers," **is listening for the revelation and wisdom of God**. While Christians may still have a tendency to "tell" God what they need, the insightful "Learnings" and "Clarifications" with which God has enriched and deepened their faith as applied to life has convinced them that they need to receive from God; "Devotion" begins. So they listen more. When consistent "listening" is added to praying, Christians' prayers become interactive. In this talking-listening interchange, Christians are seeking God's Will which they desire to put into action in their lives. **"Contemplative Prayers" are interactive in regard to this conversational dialogue**.

Interdependent – Christians, however, have put in copious amounts of work to develop the faith they have – in personal change, study, prayer, service and so forth. Especially toward the beginning of the "Illuminative Way," Christians are moving from automatically accepting traditional beliefs and practices toward independently claiming their own expression of faithfulness. They are committed to Christianity but need to make it their own. And even though Christians are convinced that God has so much more to provide for them, they still "need" to assert their own independent opinion in dialogue. Accordingly, "Contemplative Prayers" have also been called "Discursive Meditation." "In discursive meditation, mind and imagination and other faculties are actively employed in an effort to understand our relationship with God. The word discursive comes from the word discourse and refers to having a conversation."[7]

Christians not only interactively listen to God in "Contemplative Prayers" but they also express themselves independently as well. Tevye, the poor Jewish milkman, in the 1964 musical "Fiddler on the Roof"[8] is a wonderfully comedic example of talking back to God while being totally committed to God. Abram seriously negotiated with God for fewer and fewer "good men" required so that God would not destroy Sodom.[9] [Genesis 18:22-26] Even Jesus demonstrates a form of independent conversation in his John 17 prayer; he asks God to protect his Apostles but not to take them out of the world.[10] [John 17:15] **Because Christians know their need for God, but choose to express themselves at the same time, interdependence is a characteristic of "Contemplative Prayers."** Psycho-socially, people need to grow developmentally into independence which Christians achieve spiritually via prayer that is conversation with an "equal." In fact, spiritual helpers may be thrust into such discussion. I find that practicing spiritual guidance with those Christians at this particular junction often means consciously engaging in spirited and challenging debate. This interchange must be for the good of the pray-ers and not prompted by the helpers' reaction to some comment that was made. On the other hand, Christians who do not achieve such independence will often be hindered from moving into praying contemplatively.

This quality of interdependence represents how the pray-er approaches active "Contemplative Prayers" – they have become independent and approach God with a strong sense of self who "deserves" to be respected. In reality, God the Creator is not dependent upon those God has created, except in the fact that the God wants humans to voluntarily respond to God's invitation for relationship. However, in the final analysis, <u>God knows the need for Christians to engage in authentic, even adversarial, conversations in order to grow spiritually</u>. Later, Christians will recognize and confess their arrogance; God will simply affirm, "It's ok; you were just going through a phase."

Affective – As Christians move along the "Illuminative Way," they gain a depth of commitment that engages the total person – especially the emotions. **The passion and zeal for God, as well as how Christians feel that God has interacted in their lives comes to the surface and is often strongly expressed in prayer**. "Contemplative Prayers" have also been called "Prayers of the Heart." Many of the Psalms exhibit this characteristic; accordingly Christians can use them as examples of "Contemplative Prayers." The affective quality of "Contemplative Prayers" is needed in order to love God with the heart; and love is only effectively communicated through dialogue and emotional interaction. Actually, a deep spiritual relationship with God is not possible without affectivity; but as expressed in chapter nine, God responds to Christians with reciprocated love only when God knows they are ready, which happens after increased "Learnings" and "Clarifications" bring a certain level of commitment and God adopts Christians into the family business. That is indeed a memorable and emotional time of life.

As a right-handed and predominantly left-brained Christian, the affective quality of "Contemplative Prayers" has not been easy. However, without question, the affective moments I have experienced totally bonded the faith I held and opened my relationship with God to previously unimaginable dimensions. Without the affective, I would not have known that, at least for me, the Holy Spirit is feminine in nature. I would not have connected the "I love you's" of my wife with God's communication and grace. I would not have accessed the spiritual connection between polio and my spiritual purpose in life. In short, with the affective part of my "Contemplative Prayers" I made a transition into a totally different person – one that I hope increasingly reflects a deeper maturity in Christ. As Christians' faith becomes deeper and more devoted, their transition into Christ-likeness develops naturally, if they allow it; this can be especially evidenced in "Contemplative Prayers."

Illuminative Way Christians easily, spontaneously and consistently pray "Contemplative Prayers." However, spiritual helpers still can assist them with their prayers by making sure that all three qualities (interactive, interdependent, and affective) are present. Pray-ers who only listen do not develop a strong sense of self (which is needed in order to be able to surrender later). Pray-ers who primarily assert themselves do not learn what God wants them to receive, because they do not listen often enough. Pray-ers who do not have emotional intercourse do not fall into God's loving arms, which neither just listening nor asserting can attain. <u>Having a balance between the interactive, interdependent and affective in "Contemplative Prayers" is extremely helpful.</u>

In addition to the three qualities, "Contemplative Prayers" can also be understood to have active and passive approaches. Again, active is pray-er initiated; and passive is God instigated. Because "Contemplative Prayers" are non-rational (not anti-rational) in nature, they make use of other functions of the brain – especially the intuitive, imaginative and sensate dimensions. Active "Contemplative Prayers" employ these in order to move into dialogue with the divine. Passive "Contemplative Prayers" occur when God directs the interchange. <u>I am going to explore the active-passive difference and the transition by high-lighting two particular forms of "Contemplative Prayers" that were developed by St. Ignatius of Loyola – the Spiritual Exercises and the Examen.</u>[11]

The <u>Examen of Conscience</u> is typically an end of the day, heart-felt review of how a Christian lived and where God was present/absent during the day. Accordingly, the Examen begins by thinking about the day, which is active "Meditative Prayers." It may move to passive "Meditative Prayers" in which God causes Christians to think about information other than the intended subject. The Examen is to conclude with active "Contemplative Prayers" which takes the form of a personal conversation with Jesus that focuses on gratitude for what was good and confession of what was sinful. This "Just a Little Talk with Jesus" makes life all right again and deepens Christians' spiritual relationship with God. The same emotional and conversational style of "Contemplative Prayers" is captured in the classical hymn "In the Garden"[12] as well as in the friendly, upbeat chorus of Cleavant Derricks' gospel song "Just a Little Talk with Jesus."

Now let us have a little talk with Jesus.
Let us tell Him all about our troubles.
He will hear our faintest cry
And He will answer by and by.
Now when you feel a little prayer wheel turning,
Then you'll know a little fire is burning.
You will find a little talk with Jesus makes it right.[13]

The Spiritual Exercises actually begins with active "Meditative Prayers" and moves through passive "Meditative Prayers" to arrive at active "Contemplative Prayers." During the Exercises, Christians are invited to think about a subject, for example an event in the life of Jesus. These active "Meditative Prayers" may lead to allowing God, through the Christian's rational thought process, to provide new insights, which is passive "Meditative Prayers." However, the Exercises are especially designed for Christians to have an extended conversation with Jesus for the purpose of receiving divine teaching and the practical application of it for their lives. (While doing the Exercises, Christians will often put emphasis on one particular "Prayer Form" that corresponds to where they are on the Spiritual Road.) The conversational style at the conclusion of the Exercises corresponds to classic "Contemplative Prayers;" it is active because the pray-er initiated the dialogue. Such prayerful conditions may allow pray-ers to enter into a relaxed, open and receptive state of being through which God begins to further communicate on subjects other than what was on the agenda. This becomes passive "Contemplative Prayers" because God initiates the communications and its content.

As spiritual helpers recognize that those they assist are ready to move into a more contemplative style of praying, they may make certain suggestions. A recommendation to journal how Christians feel about a particular topic that includes a written heart-felt prayer would be helpful. Also, some Christians who journal conversational prayers with Jesus have prayed "Contemplative Prayers" using this technique; writing with the non-dominate hand has been understood as passive – penning words that come from beyond themselves. Teaching the Lectio Divina form of prayer, especially with an emphasis on the Oratio part of it which is supposed to be an authentic emotional response to the Spirit-given topic, will assist Christians to be affective. The structured nature of Lectio is suited for moving Purgative Way Christians, who particularly need order and clarity. In addition, since the first two parts of the Lectio prayer are very much like Bible study, moving Christians toward interactive and affective prayer can be easy. For example, writing an emotional responsive prayer may be a post-Bible study homework assignment. Christians may convey interest in the Psalms or scripture that has passionate expression. Inviting them to paraphrase the passage in their own words applied to their own situation will assist them into moving from meditation to contemplation. Of course, a very simply but exquisitely effective technique to help Christians is to invite them to put their own name in a portion of scripture. At a "Moment of Decision" using John 3:16 in this way is valuable; however, doing so in the transition between meditation and contemplation enables Christians to launch into a very personal and affective response to what God has done for them.

The transition from "Meditative Prayers" to "Contemplative Prayers" moves Christians from using the rational function of their brains to use of the imaginative, intuitive and sensate parts of it. Imagination as well as intuition is well suited for interaction with something beyond self. In the Spiritual Exercises, Christians are asked to immerse themselves in a particular event of Jesus' life – to use all the senses in order to be fully present in the story. Imagination and intuition are best suited for this intent. Imagination and intuition also allow people to identify with others, even understand "how they feel." Compassion and empathy for others develop from the use of imagination and intuition. The rational function of the brain can deduce what others are going through, but without the emotions being engaged. **Imagination and intuition are necessary for quality personal relationships – including a spiritual relationship with God**. Can people experience what another person feels? No, because no one can be in the same place at the same time – at least in this level of consciousness. However, absolutely, people can and do experience the same kind of feelings that others are also experiencing. This ability to identify the feelings of another and experience similar ones is essential to all affective communication. "Contemplative Prayer" is affective communication between humans and God. These "prayers of the heart" require the use of the imaginative and intuitive functions of the brain so that Christians can identify with God – even "feel" what God "feels."

In addition, **active "Contemplative Prayers" can be experienced through the use of "guided imagery" which uses imagination, intuition and sense impressions as well**. Through biblical-oriented "guided imagery" Christians immerse themselves into a scripture story such as the woman at the well or blind Bartimeus.[14] [John 4:5-42; Mark 10:46-52] As they merge into the story and the presence of Jesus, they "experience" the interconnectedness, emotional content and conversational style that makes it active "Contemplative Prayers." While Christians employ these "Contemplative Prayers" actively by bringing the effort and topic of the conversation, they can also become passive.

For a number of years, I consistently engaged in "guided imagery" as part of my morning prayer-time. In this venue, I would relax until I, in my "faith imagination," went to a safe place where I met Jesus and gave him permission to do whatever he chose to say or do; and I followed. These self "guided imagery" times of prayer yielded innumerable corrections to my character, to which I most certainly would have never voluntarily proposed. I also gained some incredible insights into life and faith, as well as guidance for how to spend my daily efforts. However of greatest importance, I gained an immeasurable increase in my personal spiritual relationship with Jesus via these "Contemplative Prayers" which were primarily passive in design because God led them.

The purpose for both active and passive "Contemplative Prayers" is to enter into dialogue with the divine – however, it is not to be confused with intellectual study of the Holy Word. Some Christians have vehemently opposed "guided imagery" as demonic, witchcraft and the practice of magic – doctrine that is based on St. Jerome's mistranslation of the Bible, which has been replicated in the King James Version and subsequent English translations. Christianity is indeed indebted to Morton Kelsey for uncovering this mistake and other writers who continue to disclose the truth.[15]

Note: "guided imagery" should NEVER take place of solid scripture study which is designed to elucidate God's Word given through the written word. Such Bible study, which is active "Meditative Prayers," needs to be done in order to develop the clarity between right and wrong as well as the strong ethic/moral standards and establishment of spiritual disciplines that connect Christians into a basic trust of God. UNTIL these Purgative Way qualities are strongly underway, "guided imagery" is not recommended! (Freely entering into the "Spirit World" which includes both divine and demonic is unhealthy and potentially dangerous without a strong Christian foundation.) **However, for mature Christians who have journeyed onto the Illuminative Way, the use of "guided imagery" and other forms of passive "Contemplative Prayers" is strongly advisable because it allows them to be instructed by God in ways that enhances the loving spiritual relationship that God desires.** The precedent for the significant value of passive contemplative forms of prayer is contained in the tenth chapter of Acts, which is discussed below. However, these revelations and insights MUST be tested via scriptural understandings, the history and tradition of Christianity and through mature Christian individuals (for example, the Spiritual Exercises are always to be conducted via continual, regular debriefing with a spiritual director).

Some dreams can also be rightly considered as "Contemplative Prayers" as they are passive in nature because the dreamer is not in control; and God delivers the message. The specific biblical theology, or understanding, of dreams is spoken on the lips of Elihu in the book of Job.

God does speak – now one way, now another – though people may not perceive it. In a dream, in a vision of the night, when deep sleep falls upon people as they slumber in their beds, God may speak in their ears, and [in this case] terrify them with warnings, to turn people aside from wrongdoings, and keep them from pride; to preserve their soul from the Pit, their life from perishing by the sword.... then people pray to God, and find favor with God, people see God's face and shout for joy. People are restored by God to their righteous state.[16] [Job 33:14-18, 26]

The Apostle Peter was the recipient of a God-initiated, passive "Contemplative Prayer" that totally and completely changed the course of Christianity.[17] In fact, the vast majority of Christians reading this book would not even be Christians without this event. **And the conversion came in the form of a dream**. Please read and study the Word so as to be informed as to how God uses the Holy Spirit to communicate divine truth that was not contained in the written word. This transformation came through passive "Contemplative Prayers." Similar divine insights can also be received through, those yet to be discussed, "Unitive Prayers." In synopsis of Acts 10:1-48, Christianity began within Judaism as those Jews who believed that the Messiah had been sent by God in the form of Jesus of Nazareth. Thus, all who received the savior had to be Jewish first. The dream that God gave to Peter, which was interpreted by the Holy Spirit, confirmed in the experience of Cornelius and affirmed by the council of the church at Jerusalem [Acts 15:1-35], allowed non-Jews to become Christians without being Jewish.

When working with Christians who are clearly in the Illuminative Way and using "Contemplative Prayers," I typically invite them to share any dream that seems to be strongly experienced.[18] Occasionally their dream will be a form of passive "Contemplative Prayers" through which God has provided instruction to which they have not yet responded. Having such dreams may also be an invitation for these Christians to spend more time in "quiet prayer" so that God might initiate passive "Contemplative Prayers" for them. Teresa of Avila called "Contemplative Prayer" the "Prayer of Quiet" which I deem applies most directly to the passive approach. <u>Indeed, when mature Christians are open to the Holy Spirit's instruction, especially as it comes in passive "Contemplative Prayers" and "Unitive Prayers," God increases the trust and depth of relationship as well as instruction in the life and faith</u>.

USING DIFFERENT "PRAYER FORMS"

While moving from one "Prayer Form" to another can assist or confirm spiritual growth, the particular "Prayer Form" that Christians use is essentially not important. In fact, **different "Prayer Forms" can be employed on any given subject**. As an illustration, I have included the following example of how intercessory prayers can draw on any "Prayer Form."

Intercessory prayer is basically when one prays for another. Christians pray a lot for others but they use different "forms" of intercessory prayer. Of course, "<u>Formal</u>

Prayers" are spoken in worship; they are offered on behalf of "all the people." When individuals pray for others what are they doing? Some pray-ers are asking God to intercede or heal another person or group of people. Because these prayers are thinking about others, they are meditative in nature. Because people initiate the prayer with their minds – it is an active meditative form of prayer. On other occasions, Christians may be "thinking about" the same person or group of people but without actually directing their thoughts; during such "thinking about" prayer times, they allow their minds to freely associate and receive information about their subject that they have not thought of before. This is a passive meditative form of prayer. Those who help others spiritually might ask, "How did you manage to think those thoughts you have never had before? Was God using your brains to communicate with you?" Also, spiritual helpers might like to suggest that active meditative pray-ers try to think about the person of their concern "passively" – without directing their thoughts. What happens in this transition is that the pray-ers' relationship with God changes in the midst of their praying for others. Basically, active "Meditative Prayers" talk to God whereas passive "Meditative Prayers" invite God to use the minds of the people who are praying. The form of prayer becomes more two way communication but with pray-ers still "in charge" of their prayers.

While intercessory prayers most naturally fall into the mediation form of prayer, they can also be prayed in a contemplative form of prayer. Contemplative praying can be practiced by actively entering into a biblical story. Likewise, intercessory "Contemplative Prayers" might be done by entering the situation of the person being prayed for or by imagining the person being completely healed. This kind of praying is "active" in nature because pray-ers are directing the interaction – pray-ers willingly enter into the situation of another in order to "bring God" into it or pray-ers actively "see" the person being prayed for as experiencing God's healing.

Contemplative forms of praying can become "passive" in nature. After pray-ers, for example, finish being immersed in a biblical story, they are invited into a conversation with Jesus who instructs them about what to learn and how to apply this biblical truth into their own life. Intercessory passive "Contemplative Prayers" may occur when pray-ers lift another person into the presence of God to sense what God wants to do with this person – at which point God may or may not respond. Devout Christian healers, such as Edgar Cayce, have demonstrated the ability to enter into a "passive" state of prayer in order to receive from the divine on behalf of others.[19] Mature Christians, who can enter into passive "Contemplative Prayers" and with whom God chooses to engage, can receive from God information and power that makes a difference in the lives of others. The words of James 5:16 affirm, "The prayer of a righteous (person) man is powerful and effective."[20]

In the contemplative form of prayer, Christians are fully engaged "from the heart" in an open dialogue with God. What happens in the active "Contemplative Prayers" is that people who pray initiate the direction of the imaginative and intuitive functions of their brains in order to connect with God for a particular hope or outcome. In the active contemplative form of prayer, the prayer relationship has its basis in "mutual" interchange, talking and listening with heart and mind engaged, but for a specific purpose or result. Active "Contemplative Prayers" might be considered in terms of an interpersonal human relationship that is entered into on a "friendly" basis. On a romantic date or even in business collaboration, free flowing give and take exists but with the desired conclusion still in mind. On the other hand, passive "Contemplative Prayers" utilizes any and all abilities to fully attend to God but with the simple desire to hear and respond to what God has to say. Also, the transition that occurs between active and passive contemplative forms of prayer may be analogous to a friendship conversation – one friend who lets another say whatever as long as that friend gets to do the same versus a wise and trusted friend to whom people would go, not to dump all of what they are experiencing, but to listen and absorb the wisdom the friend has to give.

Intercessory prayers are primarily meditative or contemplative in nature. However, if God chooses, pray-ers might have a "Unitive Prayers" experience regarding the person of their concern. Active "Unitive Prayers" means intentionally emptying the mind and heart so that God can fill it. This is often done, via Centering Prayer, with a word or phrase that re-focuses the pray-er when the mind wanders or the hearts feels distracted. Using the name or symbolic word that represents the person being interceded for as that centering word is a way to make intercessory praying "Unitive Prayers." God provides a "Unitive" moment when people are open and non-focused. So, when people see another person who has died and have an overwhelming sense of ok-ness about them, that experience can be understood as a "Unitive Prayers" in which God is answering the previously expressed concern. The same can be noted about some powerfully moving, crystal clear dreams regarding a particular person or situation about whom those pray-ers have been praying.

INTERMITTENT DRYNESS

Somewhere past the midpoint in the Illuminative Way, after Christians have experienced "Devotion" and an increasingly beautiful loving relationship with God, those consolations begin to cease. **Consolations** are the blessings or confirmations via the good feelings that come from time spent in relationship with God, especially in prayer. The content of consolation-gratification varies from person to person and from time of life to time in life. However, consolations, although personally experienced, are best understood as something that God gives. Accordingly, **the expression of consolations comes in forms of truth, beauty, oneness and goodness, which are the four basic categories in which God can be received.**[21] Thus, Christians may experience a life-opening insight or clarity, being overcome by powerful emotions or sensing incredible beauty; they may feel a profound sense of connectedness or harmony in life or with people; they may also experience a deep stillness, perfect peace, or overwhelming joy or being loved in an indescribable manner. These are from God and may even be God, experienced in a finite way. **"Intermittent Dryness" is a spiritual condition, not the lack of it, when God is withdrawing these consolations**.

As expressed in chapters eight and nine, God withdraws, not to punish, but to purify. In fact, God does not withdraw affirmations, confirmations and blessings all at once – which is what happens when severe sin has been committed. Instead, **God's goodness comes and goes in an ebb and flow manner – but so that Christians do not know where and when to predict what will happen.** "The dryness is sporadic, there are times when God is close and we are consoled, and times when he seems far away. The important point is that we don't seem to be able to do anything to control the water or devotion – he is teaching us to let him be 'the Boss.'"[22]

"Intermittent Dryness" applies to the totality of Christians' relationship with God but especially in prayer. Prayer used to be something that Christians looked forward to. They could count on God's blessings, consolations and good feelings to occur regardless of how crazy and awful the circumstances of the world around them. Accordingly, Christians desire the former "great moments" of being with God and even try to make them happen – but they can't. Christians suppose that they are really seeking God. However, they will only know that when all consolations are taken away. Thus, pray-ers must continue to pray even without positive results. **Instead of seeking the blessings of God, they must come to seek the God of blessings**. This process corresponds to the "Dark Night of the Senses" and the "Dark Night of the Spirit" in which the imagination, intuition, intellect, memory and human will are surrendered so that God's Will can be dominate and all that remains. The insight to seek God and not the consolations is affirmed in the classic hymn "My Goal is God Himself" which is so universal that it has also been popularized with a contemporary Christian music sound:

> My goal is God Himself, not joy, nor peace,
> Nor even blessing, but Himself, my God;
> 'Tis His to lead me there—not mine, but His—
> At any cost, dear Lord, by any road.[23]

The experience of "Intermittent Dryness," which can last for an extended length of time, is an extraordinarily helpless and frustrating time in the spiritual life! Thankfully, Christians have grown spiritually to such a degree that they can only conceive that God has their best interest at heart. But even though Christians deeply believe that God wants the best for them, they often question themselves and their faith. Although it is not entirely clear whether the Psalmist believed he had sinned and God's blessings had been recalled or whether he was experiencing the "Intermittent Dryness" of God, the feelings expressed are clear. "Do not cast me from your presence or take your Holy Spirit from me. Restore to me the joy of your salvation and grant me a willing spirit, to sustain me."[24] [Psalm 51:11-12]

As "Intermittent Dryness" proceeds, Christians, who have been accustomed to such ease in their spiritual lives, can be tempted to abandon prayer altogether, at least the contemplative and personal "Prayers of the Heart." Or, as mentioned above, they may believe they have sinned or displeased God, which is exactly the opposite of what has happened. On the other hand, Christians may tend to ignore or deny that they rarely "feel God anymore." To say so publically would cause them to face ridicule and condemnation of being bad or having lost their faith – when only the opposite is true!

Those kinds of accusations actually formed the "media frenzy" responses to Mother Teresa's official biography as her years of not sensing God were evaluated, by those who were ignorant, as unfaithfulness.[25] Nevertheless, <u>admitting to this dry and dark condition is exactly what is needed, at least to God and one significant spiritual person, because it is an act of surrender of self</u>. **Christian helpers, who suspect that "Intermittent Dryness" is occurring, would be supportive to mention the possibility to those they assist.** This conversation can dispel the myth that people project on good Christian folks – they need to "be perfect" and have it all together. Because they have played that role for years, having been the rock of Christ himself and the pillars of the church, the temptation of spiritual pride to maintain that facade is great. To have a spiritual helper to validate the experience can be extremely freeing and allow them to do what is needed at this point along the Spiritual Road. Christians in the midst of "Intermittent Dryness" need to be helpless even in prayer, especially in prayer. They need to surrender all of their confidence and all of their abilities of having "God on demand." Christians especially at the end of the Spiritual Road must deny themselves. It is when the paradoxical truth of the Christian faith may be the clearest, "For whoever wants to save his (or her) life will lose it, but whoever loses his (or her) life for me and for the gospel will save it."[26] [Mark 8:35]

Spiritual helpers, reading the signs in an objective way, have an exceptionally important task to perform for God's Community – assisting those mature Christians who have started to experience dryness in their Christian life and prayers. Spiritual helpers need to let Christians know, especially since they rarely figure it out for themselves, what is happening AND strongly encourage them to continue to pray – regardless of the seeming lack of results. <u>Without prayer and other expressions of faithfulness, God will simply wait – in the shadows</u>. However, as Christians continue to pray, suddenly without notice God's giant consolation comes – even in forms that cannot be explained because of its revelation quality. The prayers of union with God have begun.

UNITIVE PRAYERS

Since I have only limited experience with "Unitive Prayers" personally, I have to rely on what others have said. <u>The most important thing I can say is that "Unitive Prayers" are real and have a powerful effect</u>. **"Unitive Prayers" are characterized by peace, content-ment, aliveness and togetherness that may best be described as "abiding" in God.** This overwhelming sense of connection to and within the holiness of God is "Unitive Prayers." It is a condition that Jesus interprets as oneness. **"Unitive Prayers" are totally and completely God-given. Period**.

In biblical times, marriage began with the bride preparing in her own residence; the groom in his. This would often occur over an extended timeframe which was climaxed when the groom would come to the bride's house to escort her to the wedding and their new home together. The precise timing of this unitive moment was not known. The bride could only be ready for the groom's arrival so that they could abide together in a new place. This is about as good of "Unitive Prayers" analogy, although archaic, that I can express. All that Christians (the bride) can do is to be promised to God (the bridegroom), ready for the moment of God's arrival and be swept away in loving embrace at an unknown time. However, the timing of the event is not completely "unknown." The two must have knowledge of each other (or each other's families), have worked and lived together (in the course of growing up), have liked each other and made a commitment to the marriage and the desire to abide together – although arranged marriages would eliminate some of these conditions.

In a similar fashion, "Unitive Prayers" developmentally occur in Christians' lives – after a time of getting acquainted, deciding for each other, being together in common life activities until the "moment of marriage" – which has often been a phrase used to describe "Unitive Prayers." In other words, <u>Christians must have done some things before "Unitive Prayers" can developmentally occur</u> as previously outlined in the sections on the "Dark Night of the Senses" and "Dark Night of the Spirit."[27] Christians need to surrender the use of the senses to facilitate praying; Christians need to do the same with imagination, intuition, memory and intellect. Finally, Christians must consciously and voluntarily surrender their will.

In the Christian mystical tradition, "Unitive Prayers" are often listed as a type of "Contemplative Prayers;" but because of their qualitative difference and uncommonness, other people, including me, have given them a separate category. <u>"Unitive Prayers" can begin via an active approach as a natural extension of passive "Contemplative Prayers."</u> For example, passive "Contemplative Prayers" might begin by using relaxation to enter into a prayerful state where Christians might allow a "spiritual guide" like Christ, Mary the mother of Jesus, ball of Holy Light to lead and teach whatever God desires. Putting oneself into such a "kataphatic"[28] receptive state of prayer is a way of inducing "Unitive Prayers" to occur. While people cannot make "Unitive Prayers" happen, because by definition they are God-given, this would be considered an "active" approach since people intentionally move toward such a prayer experience. **In order to step out in faith desiring "Unitive Prayers," Christians need to spend "dedicated" time with God that seems to have no purpose, defuse, unstructured and open**.

The use of centering prayer, an "apophatic" receptive state of prayer, is another way to actively invite a unitive prayer experience. **Centering prayer is a style that seeks to hopefully dismiss all psychological functions of the brain in order to enter a calm, quiet and peaceful state which can "induce" prayers of union**. This "without images" approach to "Unitive Prayers" has been called "contrived contemplation" because of its active approach and is often suggested for Christians along the "Unitive Way" as the best way to pray. However, Christians cannot make "Unitive Prayers" happen – via either kataphatic or apophatic approaches – because they are instigated by God!

Spending non-directed, open-ended, unstructured time in a prayerful attitude is giving God permission to do whatever; this is considered a passive approach to these prayers of union because people are not trying to make them happen. As always, God may or may not provide "Unitive Prayers" for these Christians. However, if they happen in this spontaneous, non-person contrived manner, they have been called "infused or higher contemplation." This experience has also been called "a gaze of faith" or "a silent love" because the "Soul-Self" (that which God originally created) without finite interference is centered on God. Indeed, "Unitive Prayers" uniquely expose Christians to the truth of being "in the world ... but not of the world."[29] [John 17:18; John 17:15]

The experiences of "Unitive Prayers" have been further clarified as happening in various degrees: beginning with the above described simple union to ecstatic union to transforming union with God. Almost all "Unitive Prayers" are very short in duration. During the simple "Unitive Prayers" Christians are conscious, but without any anxiety or stress. There is a sense of being embraced in the loving presence of God but without being able to identify much of what has occurred. The result is a peacefulness and calmness. During the ecstatic and transformative "Unitive Prayers" experience, people will move into a temporary trance-like state where they lose touch with bodily sensations, thinking and awareness of specific surroundings. No understanding is known; but upon "awakening" Christians have an incredulous serenity and some sense of inner healing. **"Unitive Prayers" experiences do not alter Christians' ability to function in the world, except that they do so with dramatically enlarged sense of freedom from worry and they may exhibit a kind of wisdom that comes from already knowing the final outcome – and it is excellent. In addition, Christians operate with increased humility which causes them to become more other-centered and compassionate.**

As I think about describing one of my simple "Unitive Prayers" experiences, it seems so non-extraordinary in the outer circumstances, but so transformative, internally and spiritually, that I am at a loss for words to communicate.

Late one evening in 1995 I was sitting on a large roll of carpet alone in the dark and gazing out a large full-length window on the Milky Way and a multitude of stars that shined against a black velvet sky. The next day the carpet, the crowning touch to years of bringing a Christian retreat center into being, would be put down. I was tired, prayerful and grateful. Suddenly, I was completely overcome with emotion and gently whispered prayer. In the next frame of time, upon reflection, I had lost all sense of where I was and only later realized that my constitution had changed, my resolve, my commitment, my purpose … my soul was different. While spiritual growth and development had for ten years been a passion of mine, from that time it has been my "infused" purpose.

In review, "Unitive Prayers" is, in essence, to love God with the Soul as the Great Commandment teaches. However, what is most important is the surrender so that God can finish the work of salvation and transformation that humans cannot do for themselves and which cannot occur until they are out of God's way. **"Unitive Prayers" make possible the real work of spiritual growth which only God can do – making God and individuals one as Jesus and God were one**. Truly, "Unitive Prayers" provide God's Holy Spirit the opportunity and permission to bring about this oneness.

THE PRAYER GARDEN

In the sixteenth century, Teresa of Avila, who thankfully and finally was recognized in 1970 by the Roman Catholic Church as the FIRST WOMAN "Doctor of the Church,"[30] analogized the process of prayer. Her picture portrayal has now become classic. St. Teresa deals with prayer after a person's confirmation into the faith. All Christians, regardless of their branch of Christianity or particular denomination, are somewhere in Teresa's description. Because every praying Christian would be enhanced to know about her work, I want to include this brief summary and allude to how "Prayer Forms" interface with Teresa's Prayer Garden.

In St. Teresa's metaphor on praying, she says that the **human soul is God's Garden**.[31] When people begin a relationship with God (at their confession/confirmation of faith), God entrusts people with the garden – designating them as assistant gardeners. God owns the garden, has cleared it of weeds and has planted flowers in this garden. **All people need to do is get water to the plants so that they will grow**. Prayer is to Christians as water is to the plants. Prayer and water allow for growth; and the act of prayer/watering also provide good feelings, which are called consolations or affirmations.

As important as watering is, the goal is to have the flowers blossom and spread their fragrances. <u>Flowers are the virtues which grow in Christians because of their contact (prayer) with God</u>. As the flowers (the virtues of Christians) blossom and spread fragrance, God is attracted to the garden – God comes to take delight in the goodness that God has created. I believe God also comes to share the experience of being together – that's what lovers do. As Christians move forward on the Spiritual Road, the flowers grow with greater ease. They also grow bigger and healthier so that the increased numbers of blossoms multiply the power of the fragrance, which is carried far beyond Christians own little plot of the world. For this all to happen, Christians need to water in order to nourish and mature the flowers. **How do Christians get the water to the garden?**

According to Teresa, four ways of watering describe four "degrees" or forms of prayer. "The first degree is meditation; the other three are deepening dimensions of contemplation in which the person's sense of autonomous effort in prayer is increasingly replaced by a feeling of God's deep and obscure divine activity."[32] However, I would like to re-title the last form, or degree, as "Unitive Prayers." **Teresa's four ways to water** are: 1) Getting water from a well with a bucket and carrying it to the garden. 2) Getting water from a "waterwheel and aqueducts" (or in modern terms from a pump or with some mechanical assistance) and then directing it to the garden. 3) Getting water from a river that runs through the garden (or from a natural spring that suddenly emerges) so as to be able to channel the water with natural irrigation. 4) Getting water through heavy rains that covers the garden and goes to the roots without any effort on the part of the gardener.

Bucket – Using a bucket to get water from a deep well and then carrying it to a garden is hard, inefficient work! **Teresa's watering-by-bucket form of prayer corresponds to active "Meditative Prayers."** Thinking about God and godly things is mediation. It is to love God with the mind. This is a hard job. People cannot love what they do not know – bucket praying is coming to the knowledge of and contact with God. It actually begins on the Pre-Christian Way although Teresa's analogy only includes Christians who have begun the "Purgative Way."

By my definition of prayer, learning and thinking about God is meditation. Whenever people are intentionally doing godly things, understanding the person of Jesus, reading religious books, studying the scriptures, making lists of scriptural promises, keeping records of answered prayers, saying the same form of prayers repeatedly (even in one's own words) as well as meaningful pre-authorized prayers, they are "experiencing God" – which is watering the garden. People do not have to be in precise "conversation" with God (or colloquy) in order to grow flowers (Christian virtues) in their garden. However, the amount of water people obtain is extremely limited and gained with great effort.

Nevertheless, the flowers do get some water. People, through their meditative work and with a little help from God, obtain some "good feelings" or consolations. And more importantly, the watering does cause the flowers to spout, which is to say that Christians' virtues begin to emerge. The process is kind of like a natural ability or talent that people finally figure out that they actually have. It was there all the time but it took some effort to believe it was really true, to accept it as theirs and begin to use it. Finding God via bucket praying is not unlike that. Christians gain spiritual strength by the bucket-carrying that they do, are able to make more trips to the well and increasingly spill less water on their way to the

Prayer Garden. Accordingly, Christians begin to believe that the consolations are coming from their own efforts; it seems they are doing it all by themselves. When such confidence is gained, God will provide corrective action to renew and strengthen "basic trust" in God. Accordingly, Teresa refers to a devastating dry spell when no water comes from the well after which God's grace not only restores the water but the idea of waterwheel praying as well.

Waterwheel and Aqueducts – When the water starts to return, Christians conceive the idea of getting the water to the Prayer Garden in a different manner. **Teresa has in mind turning a crank connected to a waterwheel that brings up water and places it into some kind of trough.** Watering still takes work, but much less effort is needed to get even more consolations, which actually, according to Teresa, come from God but are "felt" by Christians.

The waterwheel time of prayer typically occurs as part of the Illuminative Way during which heart-felt prayers become prominent. Life and prayer become more of an interaction with God as well as expressing of emotions and personal, internal thoughts with God. Christians also sense more affirmations from God, gain insights for their beliefs, clarifications of faith and deep devotions with the person of God; they are also motivated into mission/ministry actions. The spiritual life, the work of watering, is so much easier that God seems so much closer and Christians are more fully alive. They are not just thinking about God but have come into the presence of God.

As applied to the spiritual life, the term "recollection," which has active and passive forms, refers to paying "attention to the presence of God in the soul."[33] While Teresa employs the term "passive recollection" and the "Prayer of Quiet" to describe her water-wheel form of praying, it more precisely points to what I have called passive "Meditative Prayers" which can quickly stir into active "Contemplative Prayers."

In passive "Meditative Prayers" Christians stop directing their rational thoughts and allow God to re-mind them. For example, they may "involuntarily" hear the scripture coming to them, "Be still and know that I am God"[34] [Psalm 46:10] which may propel them into a contemplative listening form of prayer. Active "Contemplative Prayers" are different – using the imaginative, intuitive and sensate functions of the brain – they use less mental concentration, are quieter and more open to God's leading (listening to God). Active "Contemplative Prayers" are focused but open. They are like "brainstorming" on a particular issue, but are open to all and every option that is presented – that God gives.

Turning a crank to get water takes effort; orienting the flow of water takes work – although less than before. Corresponding to prayer, some "work" is required in passive "Meditative Prayers" and active "Contemplative Prayers." As Christians move into contemplation – interactive, interdependent and affective prayers – they experience grace upon grace, consolation added to consolation, joyfulness in excess. All of these plentiful blessings of water cause the flowers to produce a multitude of buds. This enjoyable time in

Christian life allows virtues to abound easily and brings great anticipation of a beautiful garden. Christians are in touch with God as they sense the garden's loveliness which they have "created."

River through the Garden – Teresa uses the analogy of a river in the midst of the garden. **What is important to this analogy is that the water soaks the ground and the roots of the plants so that manual watering is rarely needed**. I find it a little strange that a river would suddenly appear in a garden and it does not explain the ebb and flow of the water that exists during this "degree" – water from an underground spring that bubbles to the surface might be a better description. Nevertheless, Christians don't have to go and get the water or experience of God. Christians may have to occasionally irrigate the flowers; but it seems hardly like work. God is everywhere and in everything.

The water-springing-forth prayer corresponds to passive "Contemplative Prayers" in which Christians mostly receive from God; passive "Contemplative Prayers" are open and unfocused. In the external spiritual life, Christians may serve the poor but are much more greatly blessed by the face of Christ they see in others – God comes to them without actively seeking God. In fact, Christians' former way of praying (of going to get the water) seems pretty much useless. God can make the flowers bloom, the Christian virtues, with almost no striving for them – God doesn't seem to need Christians' efforts to make the flowers bloom, to develop Christian virtues. During this time, interfacing with the experience of the "Dark Nights," the spring water comes and goes; Christians never know exactly what they will get or when they will get it. At first, they are truly stressed and worried about the need for water. However in time, they come to trust that water will come and the flowers will continue to bloom.

With the root-watered consolations, the garden extraordinarily flourishes with colorful blossoms everywhere. Christian virtues flower galore. God is attracted to the fragrances and comes to enjoy them with Christians. Being in the Prayer Garden is no longer about the work but residing in the fruits of the labor. All Christians want to do is to listen for the footsteps of God coming into the garden, hoping for a gentle holy breeze to blow the aromatic fragrance scents far and wide.

Heavy Rain – The Prayer Garden of the Soul abounds totally in God's grace-filled showers of blessings. It grows without effort on the part of Christians – but it would not grow without the voluntary presence of Christians being in the garden with God. Corresponding to "Unitive Prayers," Christians simply abide in the virtues that God has created with the experience of God's rain washing all over them. The Rain of God becomes the Reign of God. The virtues continue to blossom; and the wind of the Holy Spirit spreads fragrances afar and even may cause the flowers "go to seed."

SUMMARIZING "PRAYER FORMS"

As a rule, Christian spiritual faith develops over time and in coordination with human psycho-social development. Prayer likewise takes on different forms as spiritual growth occurs. I have summarized the spiritual process of prayer as typically beginning with "Formal Prayers" that move into all kinds of "Meditative Prayers" that make transition into "Contemplative Prayers" and may be transported into "Unitive Prayers." There are various individual types within each "Prayer Form." Also, each form can be approached in an active or passive manner. The active approach means that people initiate the prayer; and the passive approach means that God instigates it. As a general pattern, prayers typically move from more active to less active and from less passive to more passive in nature throughout the entire process of a prayer life.

The above information on "Prayer Forms" is complex; but it can also be summarized in simple ways: **Formal Prayers are given; Meditative Prayers are thought; Contemplative Prayers are felt; and Unitive Prayers are received.** In his trilogy work on prayer, Thomas Green[35] describes the process as prayers of knowing that move into the prayers of loving which become prayers of truly loving. The transition can also be noted as moving from head to heart to spirit/soul – loving God with all of the mind, heart and soul.

In its contemporary style, Lectio Divina,[36] the Holy Word prayer, is divided into four sections that roughly correspond to the four "Prayer Forms." Lectio is the word from scripture or subject of the prayer (which should be given from outside of one's self via the Holy Spirit, but can be given from any outside source). Meditatio is the thinking about the subject in a manner that moves from active to passive approaches. Oratio is the heartfelt conversation regarding this "thought about" subject. Contemplatio corresponds to the quieting of the mind and heart so as to be able to receive whatever God wants to provide. However, the rural southern Protestant preacher probably summarized it best when he said, "I reads myself full; I thinks myself clear; I prays myself hot; and I lets myself cool – and God is always there!"

Shortly after graduation from theological seminary in the mid 1970s, I attended a large event with multiple workshops designed for lay people. One of my well-liked seminary professors was leading a group on prayer which I decided to attend. When I got to the first session, I recognized another recent seminary alumnus. Somewhere during the workshop, we decided to "gang up" on the leader asking exceptionally difficult questions and pointing out seeming contradictions regarding prayer. Unflappable the professor graciously responded to each of our objections until, I assumed, he figured out the game we were playing. At that point, he addressed us, **"I don't have all the answers to the subject of prayer but one thing I know is that when it comes to whether I should pray or not pray, I would rather be wrong than not pray at all."** I felt the weight of his plea and dropped to my knees and have been there ever since.

CHAPTER 17

CPR for New Life[1]

W hile working with a spiritual directee regarding the issue of forgiveness, she asked me to explain the biblical concepts of confession and repentance; as I did, I added penance into the conversation. After detailing the subject for a while, I suddenly blurted out, "You know, when we are dying, we need CPR for new life! Unforgiveness leads to spiritual death; and we need Confession-Penance-Repentance for a new or renewed spiritual life." Such spontaneous, from out of nowhere clarity happens far too often to me that I would claim to have thought of that (or even intuited it) on my own. So, I credit God with it.

Without question, unforgiveness is the most crucial issue in life – and in the lives of Christians! When Christians' cars run out of gas on the Spiritual Road, they had better check the forgiveness meter because it is on "Empty." When it comes to forgiveness: "If you say no, you won't go!" **Forgiveness is the attitude and action of repairing or correcting a mistake that has been made or a rule which has been broken that violates the integrity of a relationship.** Forgiving is a process that includes the elements of confession, penance and repentance. While Cardio-Pulmonary Resuscitation can provide new life for hearts that have stopped, Confession-Penance-Repentance can do the same for the breath of life spiritually.

This chapter is about helping others to fill up their faith gas tank which happens when they forgive well. However, I first need to provide a brief overview of the biblical concept of forgiveness and how CPR fits into it before dealing with the practical aspects that spiritual helpers can use.

DIVINE-HUMAN FORGIVENESS

Biblically speaking, there are basically two different types of forgiveness – divine-human forgiveness and interpersonal forgiveness. Certainly, they are related but have essential differences. The major difference is that divine-human forgiveness is initiated and offered effortlessly by God and is seamlessly woven into the fabric of life. On the other hand, people have extreme difficulty forgiving other people, even when they know it is right and necessary.

Divine-human forgiveness is initially about coming to Christian faith. It concerns the grace (love, forgiveness and salvation) that God offers and how humans need to respond in order to receive it. The Bible is quite clear about this process of forgiveness. While God offers this forgiveness, people do not have to accept it; and in order to accept the forgiveness that God offers these Pre-Christian Way people have come spiritually to the "Moment of Decision." Accordingly, God establishes a fledging spiritual relationship, which people have no ability to make happen. Forgiveness has occurred and reconciliation has begun. This signifies the beginning of the Purgative Way.

God also determines what is needed for the continuation of this reconciled relationship (i.e., terms of the trust). Accordingly, God requires the purging of sins as a way of confirming that Christians mean what they have said. Purgative Way Christians are not sinless, except in the sense that God's forgiveness has been entrusted to them (i.e., an inheritance held in a trust until a certain time). In addition, God requires that they will subsequently "work out their salvation" and grow spiritually into a healthy divine-human relationship that ultimately manifests itself in a sense of oneness. **Initially, confession, penance and repentance are needed to receive God's offer of salvation. However, CPR is also necessary during the process of purging of sins which takes multiple applications in order to finally be free of perpetual and persistent sinful behaviors. In addition, CPR is important for those Christians coming to new enlightenments in the Illuminative Way as well as any time the divine-human relationship needs to be re-started.**

If Christians stop participating in the process of forgiveness, God's forgiveness is still offered; however, the divine-human relationship is "put on hold" – it stops growing and like all relationships over time it will deteriorate. Analogously, Christians decided to travel the Spiritual Road but have car trouble – a stalled engine, running out of gas, and so forth. Sometimes people just don't know what is wrong – the "stupid engine just won't start!" Ultimately it is not about how long a person is stopped on the side of the road, but whether they want to get re-started or not. Nevertheless, as long as Christians still want to be on the way, God is faithful and true to the forgiveness God has offered (which is completely awarded at the end of the journey). However, re-starting the divine-human relationship, just like starting it, takes CPR.

Regarding this divine-human redemption, the Old Testament uses the Garden of Eden story to illustrate the disobedience that Adam and Eve exhibited by violating the one rule that God insisted that they keep – and the relationship was broken. This mistake changed the ontological condition between God and humans from being in harmony to one that was in need of forgiveness, followed by reconciliation. God initiated the offer of repairing the relationship through the covenantal agreement between God and the Hebrew people (through both Abram and Moses). Since humans broke the divine-human relationship, it is their responsibility to "make amends" – to re-establish the relationship by demonstrating that they will remain faithful to the holy agreement and promise. Christians often characterize this by keeping the rules, for example the Ten Commandments, until the reparation evolves via the prophet Micah's summary of what is needed to stay in God's graces – "to act justly and to love mercy and to walk humbly with your God."[2] [Micah 6:8]

Some people would depict the Old Testament laws as a way to "earn" God's forgiveness. However, it is much more accurate to say that God forgives fully and faithfully to all who ask for it. In return, **it is essential for people to show "good faith" in the form of clear conversation, public practices and an amended attitude –** clear conversation in terms of unambiguous confession, public practices in terms of real-life changes regarding what was confessed and an amended attitude in terms of a totally opposite approach to the sin confessed. When restoring the divine-human covenantal relationship became distorted to become something that people could "earn and deserve," God sent Jesus to re-establish the process of forgiveness, which can also become distorted by "works salvation." The God-established Old Testament "agreement for relationship" as well as the receiving of Jesus for the forgiveness of sin has the same purpose – to bring people into relationship with God. God offers the forgiveness and people can do nothing to get God to do that nor do they deserve such kindness. People have the choice of whether to accept the offer or not. **CPR is the process of receiving God's forgiveness, for coming to Christian faith and for the purging of sins.** As a Christian, I am convinced that Jesus is the clearest and best way into God's good graces and becoming a Christian is open to all without prerequisites. However, accepting Jesus is only the beginning of showing "good faith" that maintains the divine-human relationship.

INTERPERSONAL FORGIVENESS

Part of what God requires for the continuation of the divine-human reconciled relationship is "To be holy as I (God) am holy."[3] [Leviticus 19:2] In other words, humans are to develop the qualities and attitudes of God. **The primary God-quality that humans are to emulate is love, which cannot exist without an attitude of forgiveness!** "Forgive us our debts, **AS** we also have forgiven our debtors."[4] [Matthew 6:12; Luke 11:4a] Interpersonal forgiveness is putting the "shoe on the other foot" because humans, taking on the role of God, are to forgive others. God's forgiveness is the pebble that is dropped into the water that ripples outward to everywhere. Accordingly, humans are to exhibit the kind of forgiveness with each other that God exemplifies. **CPR is the procedure for responding to the offer of both types of forgiveness – divine-human and interpersonal.** In large part, offering forgiveness to other people is about sustaining the newly reconciled spiritual relationship that God has given. (It is the penance and repentance of divine-human forgiveness.) In addition, offering forgiveness to others includes God's intention for the world.

In my experience, Christians most consistently neglect to include in their mindset what was assumed in the Old Testament and absolutely by Jesus. **God's intention for the world**

is to create a Holy Community! The strong emphasis among many Christians, to their determent, is on the salvation of individuals in order to be in relationship with God. However, God does not have in mind saved individuals floating on separate clouds in Heaven. The Kingdom of God is the Community of God – gathered together from every nation united and praising around the heavenly throne of God.[5] [Revelation 7:9-15]

When people have problems with unforgiveness, I half jokingly ask, "Who do you think is going to be your cloud-mate when you get to heaven? You will be stuck on that cloud with that person for eternity until you get it worked out. So you might as well start now." My tongue in cheek retort actually begs the question of whether unforgiving people get to heaven. Some days, I really don't like it that Jesus was so unequivocally clear on this subject. "If you forgive men (people) when they sin against you, your heavenly Father will also forgive you. But if you do not forgive men (people) their sins, your Father will not forgive your sins."[6] [Matthew 15:16] How can this be? How can God be so harsh?

Understanding this spiritual law of forgiveness is truly very simple, and has little to do with God. Since the beginning, God has been attempting to have the ideal, divine environment in which all humans and God can co-exist in a long-term loving relationship! I call it Holy Community which is based on perfect, eternal loving relationships. Such a community cannot perfectly exist when even one party willfully continues to sin against another. People who refuse to forgive automatically **exclude themselves** from God's Will and also from the Holy Community of the forgiven that God desires. In addition, when people go against this Holy Community, they oppose God and what God wants – and are automatically in need of forgiveness. **God will not forgive those who continuously and willfully disagree with God's intention for the world**.

God understands that coming to abide in God on God's terms takes humans a long time! Indeed, God waits for humans to become willing to accept the conditions needed to live in the presence of God for eternity; and interpersonal forgiveness is the key indicator to this willingness. The practical pastor John was extremely clear when he stated: "If anyone says, 'I love God,' yet hates his (her) brother (or sister), he (or she) is a liar. For anyone who does not love his (her) brother (or sister), whom he (she) has seen, cannot love God, whom he (she) has not seen."[7] [I John 4:20]

Interpersonal forgiveness is the key to building the Community of God – it is also essential for staying in God's "good graces." So it is no wonder that unforgiveness is like an empty gas tank on the Spiritual Road. Helping others onto the forgiveness process, to fill their spiritual gas tank, may be the most important form of spiritual assistance that can be offered. God honors the process of CPR which is why it is so powerful, especially for interpersonal forgiveness. Nevertheless, people in unforgiveness, especially those who have been seriously injured, can be extremely reluctant to forgive – part of that may include **a misunderstanding of what forgiveness is, what it is not and actually what is required**. So, spiritual helpers, who are aware of any unforgiveness in those they accompany, can be a God-send just to provide the following information to assist others to keep going on their Heavenly journey. It is worth the extended time and effort it takes to do so because forgiveness is a most important spiritual quality to practice and often takes a long time to implement fully.

DEFINING CONFESSION, PENANCE AND REPENTANCE

It is prudent to begin with some definitions of confession, penance and repentance before launching into the process of forgiveness. In some ways, these terms can be summarized as clear conversation, public practices and an amended attitude; but the roots go deeper as well.

Confession comes from the Greek word, ὁμολογέω (homologos); but the Greek preposition, ἐx (ex or ek), is often connected to this basic word when used in the New Testament. This optional prefix is very significant because it helps to define the intention of "confession." The basic word ὁμολογέω **literally means "to speak one thing" that is, "to assent, agree with, confess, declare or admit."** The preposition ἐx (which is connected to the front of the word ὁμολογέω making the translation ἐxὁμολογέω (exhomologos) in some cases; it means "out from" or "out to." Thus, confession means to "declare the same that the other says." With the prepositional emphasis of ἐx added, confession means to get the declaration (either to admit or to profess) out from within the person.

The scripture also teaches the need to speak confession out loud: "For it is with your heart that you believe and are justified, and <u>it is with your mouth that you confess</u> and are saved."[8] [Romans 10:10] This is not unlike the earlier chapter "Making It Real" – keeping belief (or confession) inside is limiting and does not allow for continued spiritual growth. In fact, external action is necessary to confirm internal thinking; practice also increases the skill or ability to be able to repeat the actions that will enable a total "repentance" change.

Penance is the action that goes with what was confessed. Thus, penance is "doing the opposite of the sin" – and the penance needs to be directly related to what is being corrected. For example, if I have said something unflattering about my brother, then my penance needs to be about intentionally saying something nice about him. If I have stolen from my brother, then my penance begins with making restitution (making us even) but concludes when I have given back more than I took from him. Penance can also be understood as the ninth step in Alcoholics Anonymous of "making amends." AA includes, and I believe correctly, that penance or amends should not be made where to do so would create further harm. Going to a person to apology, when they have explicitly and strongly stated not to be visited, is not good penance because it is sin.

While the word "penance" is not included in the Bible (except when imprecisely inserted in some English translations for the Greek word for "repent"), the idea and practice of it most certainly is. When people were healed, saved spiritually (forgiven) or made whole[9] by Jesus, many times they were required to perform certain actions. This was the penance needed to complete the forgiving/healing process. The specific penance typically fluctuates because it has to fit the situation as evidenced in these three biblical examples.

First, the woman at the well[10] [John 4:4-42] confessed Jesus as Savior after he told her "everything she ever did" which included having five former husbands and currently working on breaking up another marriage. She would have offended numerous people in her hometown of Sychar. Her trust level with her village-mates was nil – they could not believe anything she said. She needed to re-establish that trust with concrete results. Her penance was to go back to Sychar, where she had caused so much interpersonal damage and live differently – not breaking relationships but healing them. She did this with inviting people to witness Jesus. However, her larger penance was still to take place – she had mucho apologies to offer and broken relationships that extended throughout her little town to attempt to repair. She had a whole new attitude to live. She was spiritually "made whole" at the well but her penance required her to follow through with interpersonal forgiveness.

Secondly, a leper came to Jesus seeking to be healed.[11] [Mark 1:40-45] In Jesus' day, leprosy was a long-term, progressive disease, and like certain other skin diseases, was not acceptable in Judaism under the Levitical code. As a result of having this disease, lepers were considered ritually unclean and unacceptable. That meant they could not participate in the religious or cultural rituals and celebrations of their day. They were isolated from society. In fact, they were required to wear a bell or make a warning announcement, "Leper," as they traveled from place to place so people could avoid them. In addition, it was assumed that physical disease was the result of unrepentant sin.

Boldly, this leper came to Jesus and pleaded, "If you choose, you can make me clean." This statement of belief was a weak form of confession and turned out to be only a selfish desire instead of including the follow through action that was needed for complete healing/forgiveness. Nevertheless, Jesus reached out, physically touched him, and said, "Be made clean." Now, Jesus did not always touch the people he healed, but this man's spiritual rejection and social isolation required personal contact.

Now when this leper was healed, imagine the jolt of excitement and joy that went through him. Most people would probably react similar to this man's enthusiasm. At this very ecstatic moment the scripture tells us, Jesus clearly and sternly warns this former leper: first to "say nothing to anyone" and second to "go, show yourself to the priest and offer for your cleansing what Moses commanded, as a testimony to them." Superficially, people might think that Jesus was concerned about his fame and healing ability spreading; but that was going to happen no matter what. Instead, Jesus was actually concerned about the total healing of this leper – physically, emotionally, socially, and spiritually.

The initial penance that Jesus required was that this man should take seriously what had just happened to him – keeping silent helps that to occur. The primary penance was for him to go show himself to the priest who, in those days, had the power to officially proclaim him healed and be re-instated into society. It was an act of forgiveness toward the religion and the people who had made his life such a living hell. Showing himself to the priest would not have changed the state of his renewed physical body; but it would have reconnected him both to the society and to its religious faith. It would have also changed him internally. If he blamed God for his physical condition, which often happened, he would also have had opportunity to recant. However, he did exactly the opposite of what Jesus required. Truly, Jesus' purpose was never just physical healing in and of itself; but to affect forgiveness, initiate reconciliation and to bring glory to God.

Third, consider <u>the woman who touched the hem of Jesus' garment</u> and was immediately healed from the intermittent flood of blood that had lasted twelve years.[12] [Luke 8:40-48] Her "confession" was in her action. She believed the same that Jesus did that she could be healed and the touch provided immediate σῴζω (sozo) for her. Healed! End of story! No, Jesus required penance from her. Penance; what was she required to do? In biblical times, this flood of blood would have condemned this woman to be unclean, shunned and condemned to hide in the shadows of society. Her self-worth would have been mostly non-existent. She had repeatedly tried to find healing but no one could help; via the context of the rest of the story it can be safely assume that she felt unworthy of being healed and blamed herself. Her penance was that she would come out of hiding, show herself and be affirmed. That seems pretty good penance, but it would have been excruciatingly difficult for her. After loudly demanding that the person who was healed be identified, this woman timidly crept forward and crashed to her knees at Jesus' feet. What did Jesus do? He gently, lifted her to her feet, showed her to everyone and affirmed her as completely as possible by saying, "Woman, your faith has made you well; go in peace." She was good. She was ok. She was valued. Now she could believe it about herself. Where was the forgiveness in this story? She needed to forgive herself – forgiveness that required action to complete.

While penance takes different forms, its purpose remains the same – to continue and complete the process begun with confession. Accordingly, penance is to enable forgiveness toward others, God or the person doing the penance. **Penance takes the form of action** – it puts the walk in the talk, the follow through in the intention, and the work in the faith. If confession fully transforms, it includes acting differently. However, most people need to be encouraged to take tangible steps in the opposite direction of the way they had been going. <u>After a confession occurs, mutually agreeing on some appropriate penance is one of the most important tasks that spiritual helpers do.</u> In order to be most helpful, when spiritual helpers consider what penance would assist the forgiveness process, they need to reflect on what action would counter the former way of living.

Repentance is a complete change of mind; a 180 degree about-face turn. Consider the root word "repent" from which repentance is derived. "Repent" comes from the Greek word, μετανοέω (metanoeo), which is a compound word of μετα (meta), which means "after" or "with" and νοέω (noeo), which means "to understand" or "to think."[13] The implication of the Greek is that time is needed in order to change one's mind. Thus, "repent" infers a new way of approaching the world – this occurs after thinking and with a new understanding. **"To repent" implies a complete attitudinal adjustment to one's mindset**. While this might be obtained quickly, life experience indicates that changing one's individual attitudes takes a considerable length of time – especially when re-adopting God's will over human will. "Repentance" comes from the similar Greek word μετανοίας (metanoias) from which the English word "metamorphous" is derived. People know that the change of a caterpillar into a butterfly takes a considerable amount of time. Not everyone knows that without the struggle to get out of the cocoon (repeated confession and penance), the butterfly cannot emerge healthy. Indeed, the "change of mind," required by repentance, also takes time. But once it happens, a fundamental transition has occurred – persistent-sin has been replaced by a forgiveness mindset.

THE FORGIVENESS PPROCESS

FORGIVENESS is at the center of the Christian faith – both as divine-human dissolving of sin/separation and also as interpersonal forgiving. Divine-human forgiveness is taught clearly in the scriptures as something God initiates and to which humans need to respond with surrender and willingness. God forgives quickly and perfectly; humans take time to fully respond. So often, I hear from new Christians or others being critical of them, "I can't be a Christian; I told God I wouldn't do that; and then I did it again!" The fact that these Christians are lamenting their inconsistency between intention and action means that their fledgling Christian faith remains valid. They need to understand that their change happens over time – **forgiveness takes confession and penance, repeated until repentance occurs**. That's what God wants instead of the excessive guilt that inhibits further progress that is often exacerbated the inappropriate criticisms of unhelpful bystanders.

Some people are convinced that they have failed God; their particular need is to be forgiven by God but resist receiving it. These folks are particularly difficult to guide because they have put up their own self-made road blocks which stop their moving forward on the Spiritual Road. I have found that these impediments often come in the words that Christians continuously use to reinforce those beliefs. (I have committed an entire chapter "Words Can Sometimes" to discussing such words.) Assisting these people also resides in discovering what has authority for them – which must be stronger than their own personal unwillingness. If scripture has value, exploring the nature of God as loving and faithful to forgive can be effective such as: "If we confess our sins, he (God) is faithful and just and will forgive us our sins and purify us from all unrighteousness."[14] [I John 1:9] This truth about God can be coupled with the great value that God has placed upon human beings exhibited in passages such as Psalm 8:3-6,[15] Jeremiah 29:11[16] and Psalm 103:10-13.[17] If people in need of forgiveness strongly value authority figures, those mentors may simply conclude that those they help are indeed worthy of forgiveness; and then they will believe and receive it. In addition, people may value "success stories" of other people who have demonstrated how receiving God's forgiveness has totally changed their lives. Sharing or reading the life stories of such people can provide courage and initiative. Often the inhibiting guilt resides because of past events which may need therapy to provide insight. However, since God's power is not limited by time, casting out the evil and providing divine healing/forgiveness to those past events may be exactly the power greater than themselves that these guilty individuals need.

On the other hand, such individuals may not be guilty of failing God at all even though they believe they have. Accordingly, they have a false sense of guilt, or pseudo-guilt. In this case, they have nothing to be forgiven for – and thus cannot be forgiven. Helping these individuals to be very specific about their sin and then exposing this "sin" to the light of truth is necessary. If it is a valid failure, then CPR will relieve the guilt. If nothing has been truly violated or broken, then the perceived "sin" is a false. The person who believes they have failed God now has a choice. "Do you want to live a lie or not?" and "Do you believe that God is strong enough to remove your guilt or not?" In some cases, my original spiritual mentor's words ring true, "That person is not ready to get free; help them to deeply feel their pain. When they hurt badly enough, they will be ready to change." I still dislike the truth of his assertion!

Similar dynamics happen with interpersonal forgiveness. Sensitive Christians come to the point of saying/praying, "I forgive" that person with the good intention of accomplishing the purpose of forgiveness. Often, they feel guilty because they believe that they "should" be able to forgive – but the feelings so easily return. They may believe, or have been taught, that forgiveness happens with a single phrase, "I'm sorry." God can forgive humans in this way; but typically humans cannot forgive other people with such ease and simplicity. <u>Forgiving is a process and takes time to happen</u>.

Sometimes, both the reluctance to even try to forgive interpersonally and the guilt from not being successful at doing it can be addressed by simply understanding what forgiveness is not. Spiritual helpers who assist others to become clear about what is and what is not included in forgiveness will most likely enable the process.

WHAT FORGIVENSS DOES NOT MEAN

✟ Forgiveness Does NOT Mean Forgetting

People often quote the old adage, "Forgive and forget." However, <u>forgiving someone does not mean that people need to forget the wrong that another person did</u>. Forgiveness has nothing to do with forgetting. For example, what would happen if a person burned their fingers on the stove, and then forgot that hurt? Remembering the pain helps people not to repeat the event. An important part of forgiveness is remembering and dealing with what has happened. While the pain inflicted may never be forgotten, <u>forgiveness allows people to put the pain in a place where it doesn't continue to hurt them</u>.

✞ Forgiveness is NOT Condoning the Offender's Behavior

<u>By forgiving, people are not saying that what the offender did was acceptable or unimportant, or "not so bad</u>." It was bad, it did hurt, and it was wrong! People are not declaring the offender "not guilty" or absolving them of the wrong. (That is God's job.) Forgiving does not mean removing responsibility for what the offender has done. <u>There is nothing about genuine forgiveness that precludes holding people accountable for their actions</u>.

✞ Forgiveness is NOT Reconciliation

<u>Forgiveness does not mean people have to meet face-to-face with the person who wronged them. Forgiveness and reconciliation are two different processes</u>. People accomplish forgiveness on their own. Reconciliation requires the participation of the offender. Forgiveness and reconciliation are often intertwined in Christian teaching; but if separately taught would actually enable both to be more easily accomplished. Forgiveness happens prior to reconciliation; but requiring reconciliation often causes forgiveness to be immediately discontinued.

✞ Forgiveness is NOT a Clear-cut, One-time Decision

Forgiveness cannot be forced, and <u>it is a process</u>. Experience and research both confirm that this is true. Perhaps a better way to look at forgiveness is as two ends of a continuum, with people moving, often not in a linear fashion, between unforgiveness and forgiveness over time. Where are people in the process? Can the progress be evaluated? Spiritual helpers may want to ask those they help with forgiveness to indicate where they would place themselves on the "Forgiveness continuum." If the spiritual helper would do the same, some productive and affirming discussion could follow.

WHAT FORGIVENESS DOES MEAN

✞ Forgiveness is a Unilateral Process

<u>Forgiveness is something people do alone</u>. Forgiveness involves working through the feelings of what occurred and giving validity to "the loss" – i.e., uncovering and understanding. It is a process that involves freeing people from the emotional effects of what

was done to them as well as getting free of the hurt, bitterness, and resentment. This is a spiritual process because until the negative emotions are exposed, people cannot ask God to either remove those emotions or seek forgiveness.

The offender does not need to cooperate or even be aware of this process. Reconciliation requires two people; forgiveness does not. Forgiveness does not depend on what the other person does or doesn't do. When injured people put conditions on when they will forgive, such as when the offending person has done or said something in particular, injured people have not completed confession. While they may have started the forgiveness process, their emotions are still controlling them.

✟ Forgiveness Involves "Letting Go"

Forgiveness is not as much about releasing the injurer as about freeing the injured. Letting go is the act of emptying the acid that eats its own container – negative emotions destroy individuals. To forgive literally means "to give up" — to give up hatred, revenge, and punishment, to give up being the judge, jury and executioner. It is a change of perspective. In the final analysis, the most important issue becomes not about the number of times someone hurt a person or whether that offender deserves forgiveness. What is most life-giving becomes about not being held captive by the strong negative emotions that neither injured people nor God like.

The motive of injured people now becomes to move their lives past bitter obsession. Forgiveness is about THEIR healing. It is a way of getting poison out of their system. While the act of "letting go" must be repeatedly done, the choice comes through an initial act of the people's will to do so.

✟ Forgiveness is Canceling the Debt

When someone wrongs another, people feel as though the offender has taken something that belonged to them – their peace, joy, happiness, property, integrity – and that the offender now "owes them." After people have released or are no longer focused on their own emotions, they can consider canceling the debt "owed" to them. When people forgive, they simply release this debt. It's no longer "you've hurt me and you've got to pay." People don't pretend the debt never existed, they just forgive it. As such, they say, "You no longer owe me anything."

INTEGRATING CHRISTIAN TEACHING AND PSYCHOLOGICAL RESEARCH

Clearly, the Bible teaches that forgiveness is necessary; but provides non-systematic instruction about how interpersonal forgiveness is obtained. Since the mid-1980s the science of psychology has done significant research on forgiveness that confirms biblical teachings and also integrates it into an understandable step by step pattern. Putting these two sources together greatly enhances the ability of people to effectively participate in Christian interpersonal forgiveness.

The Christian teaching on forgiveness includes Confession, Penance and Repentance. **Psychological research** outlines four phases to the forgiveness process – Uncovering, Decision, Work and Deepening. Both the biblical teaching and the psychological instruction can be overlaid and integrated with greater effectiveness.

THE CHRISTIAN "ACT OF CONFESSION" – is speaking the exact nature of our wrongful attitude and/or behavior to a significant spiritual person who is mature, non-judgmental, "righteous" and skilled at dispensing God's presence. Confession is "saying the same thing" that God states or what the rule maintains; and it does so by getting it "out of" the person confessing.

When I was in my first or second year of pastoral ministry, a young Hispanic man wandered into the church and asked if he could talk with me. Jose had much on his mind including some things he had done wrong for which he was sorry. When he finished, he uttered some transforming words, not for himself but for me when he said, "Thanks, Father, for hearing my confession." I don't believe my surprise showed. I was not a Roman Catholic priest and I did not even pre-consider that what I was doing was "receiving confession" – but I was. How I had responded and my praying with Jose must have seemed to him like "absolution" – in reality, it was. Because of that experience whenever someone has asked to talk with me, I have seriously considered that I might be dealing with a confession. Thus, I look at what I do in those times as both divine and imminently important. Spiritual helpers would be advised to be prepared for those times when someone says, "Can we talk?"

What brings a person to need confession? What is happening in confession and how does it fit into the process of forgiving?

At some point, one person hurts or wrongs another; and the result is a break in whatever connection they have which may be either very personal or as part of the human community. This inflicted action often, though not always, causes negative emotions such as disgust, sadness, anxiety, anger, rage or even self-inflicted destructiveness. Emotions are spontaneous and natural; and emotions, even negative ones, are not bad. **What people who are affected do with the emotions determines whether confession is needed or not**. At times, emotions need to be "validated" which means to affirm that they are real, normal and natural to feel. Validation is especially necessary for people who hold their feelings inside or who tend to be over-responsible for others. However, validation of feelings is not permission to return the hurt or pain that is felt. When such reciprocated action occurs or is anticipated, confession is needed. In other words, **being angry is ok; acting because of that anger is not**. The Bible clearly teaches, "Be angry; but do not sin."[18] [Ephesians

4:26] Thus, emotions cannot be confessed; but acting negatively because of those emotions needs to be.

When people act, or want to act, on the negative emotions that arise because of wrong done to them, they have chosen to sin, to give retribution of an eye for an eye or worse. Jesus teaches, "But I tell to you, do not resist …"[19] [Matthew 5:39] Confession is agreeing with God that retribution is wrong; it is also agreeing with God that any returned negativity was wrong and hurtful. The act of confession is getting it out – casting it away, giving it to God. Confession is the acknowledgement that people have already or want to "payback" and "get even" with the person who wronged them. Forgiveness is the releasing of the power of these negative emotional reactions and their consequences.

The emphasis of the Protestant Reformation rightly was the return of the responsibility of Christians' faith from the clergy to the laity. One of the many practices that the Protestant Reformation rejected from the Roman Catholic Church was the sacrament of confession. However, this was the proverbial throwing out the baby with the bath water. While Protestants don't go to confession, they (and numerous Catholics) have turned to therapy and pastoral counselors to confess. On the other hand, some of these Christians would like to believe that confession only needs to happen between "me and God." I am suspicious that such confession does not qualify as getting it "out of" themselves that the biblical Greek word indicates is required. It most certainly removes any kind of accountability so as to be able to follow through with the forgiveness process, which needs support and encouragement.

Furthermore, **confession is not just about saying "I'm sorry" but also about receiving affirmation from God** – that the confession has been heard and that the "forgiveness process" has begun. In the history of Christianity, this action has been called "absolution." If this is understood to mean that "Your sins are forgiven and everything is ok," then, that is simply wrong and perhaps heresy. If absolution is understood to be: "I have heard you and affirm that God has heard you and that you have started the process of forgiveness," then that is essential. In fact, **spiritual helpers must never underestimate the importance of confession and the extreme value of absolution that they would pronounce**. There is real power in that combination – because God is in it!

Additionally, many people talk about what is bothering them but do not understand what they are doing. Informal confession often happens in everyday conversation. Spiritual helpers, who hear such admissions, can provide a gallon worth of gas for a disabled vehicle by saying, "That sounds like a confession to me. Is that what you intend?" This question can potentially begin discussion about the first step in making effective forgiveness as well as what it takes to finish the process. The question is actually not as intrusive as it sounds because most people, making such innuendos, are actually ready to confess.

I cannot begin to express the extreme important of offering to have such conversation. Bringing up of a half-hearted "confessing moment" is like a tea kettle letting off steam and whistling a signal. There is a moment of opportunity when the time is right for tea to be made. What happens in most daily dialogue of this type is that people are temporarily relieved – having catharsis but without doing anything constructive with the released emotional pressure. Accordingly, the pressure in the tea kettle, because the emotional fire is still on, will rebuild over time and the process will be repeated later. Well-meaning friends who listen to others vent, or even commiserate with them, without identifying the conversation as confession are not helping, and may be hindering the forgiveness process. However, if people take the opportunity to confess the wrong they have done or planned (be sure to distinguish between emotions and actions), then spiritual helpers need to declare that God no longer holds this against them assuming that they continue in the interpersonal forgiveness process. Such absolution is important because it needs to come from "beyond the person confessing."

I estimate that the need for forgiveness is about ninety-five per cent of all spiritual problems. When people are stuck in their spiritual life or when they come for counseling and the conversation doesn't seem to be productive, quite spontaneously I might ask, "Where do you need to offer forgiveness in your life?" So many times, the result will be a flood of tears followed by a productive confession. Such confession is the beginning of forgiveness because it acknowledges the negative emotions held onto and recognizes that holding onto them is undesirable. In psychological research, this is called the Uncovering Phase.

Uncovering Phase

During the Uncovering Phase individuals become aware of the emotional pain that has resulted from a deep, unjust injury. <u>Characteristically, feelings of hurt or anger or even hatred may be present</u>. Expressing these feelings is not sin; acting on the feelings and harboring them is sinful. As these negative emotions are confronted and the injury is honestly understood, individuals may experience considerable emotional distress. However, as the anger and other negative emotions are brought out into the open, then healing and forgiveness can begin to occur. Some people may not even understand that they have been offended or the extent of their pain until permission is given for them to feel it. According to psychological researchers, the Uncovering Phase includes the following practical actions which are related and best understood if charted from left to right for each identified injury.

1) **Recognize the Injury**. This may include writing a list of the actions that cause the hurts that people have felt. For example, Jane would feel hurt when her spouse lied about his actions. Jane actually denied (or wouldn't acknowledge) feeling hurt because of the "greater" good of keeping the marriage together.

2) **Describe the Effect**. Follow the identified action with a description of what happened and how it emotionally affected the person injured. For example, the spouse avoided

particular subjects until Jane "caught" him in inconsistency. She felt let down, frustrated and angry. Jane has a right to acknowledge her feelings.

3) **Indicate the Response**. Because of the emotions felt, what action was the result? For example, Jane loudly and continuously yelled at the spouse even to the point of "preaching" at him. She inflicted revenge via the tone of her voice with condemnation, even invoking the power of God to do so. Degrading and punishing the spouse was more important than resolving the issue or changing the spouse's behavior. Her emotions become sinful with these actions. Understanding her responses or reactions does not absolve her husband of what he had done; however, it can separate what he did from what Jane needs to do for her own spiritual growth and wholeness.

The purpose of the Uncovering Phase is to express the injury and its emotional pain as well as to understand why it is so painful. The Uncovering Phase may also need to include setting boundaries to protect the person offended from further harm. This boundary setting is not only for physical protection but also to allow continuation of the forgiveness process since the strong emotions that have been uncovered can easily deter further progress. While uncovering can certainly take place in therapy, spiritual helpers are better suited to encourage the process to continue to its forgiveness conclusion.

In coordination with the Christian "Act of Confession," verbal prayer is often an important summation of these uncovered or acknowledged truths. Such prayers, often prayed by spiritual helpers, would include the acknowledgement that God has heard this conversation which included understanding the fact that the person had been hurt unjustly and also that the person had negative feelings on which s/he would like to have acted or had already taken action. It would further include request for protection, physically and emotionally, for the person injured as he or she moves forward into the Decision Phase.

Decision Phase

In psychological research, **the Decision Phase includes understanding of how holding onto unforgiveness is hurting offended people and not allowing them to become the people they want to be**. Their emphasis on the event and their feelings has put their life on hold. Injured people are invited to understand that such destructiveness inflicted on themselves is unfair to them; they also need to understand that God is not pleased with their hurting themselves – even though God is patient, their focus on the injury and their unforgiveness block the flow of God's healing and forgiveness to them.

For example: Unforgiveness may cause them to have physiological stress or high blood pressure; or cause them to be overly cautious or distrusting; or cause them to adopt self-destructive habits like drinking too much alcohol; or cause them to inflict frustration on the innocent people around them. This is easily evidenced when the emotional reaction to a simple accident is much stronger than the event would normally elicit. For example, if a person starts yelling and throwing things because a three-year-old unintentionally spilled a glass of milk, the emotional expression is too strong. With such insights, **individuals begin to realize that to continue to focus on the injury or the person who offended them does not bring about the desired justice or change the past but actually perpetuates their own pain.** It is valid for Jane to "blame" her husband for his actions; but it is not appropriate for her to blame him for "making her mad" and causing her to lose control.

The Uncovering Phase plus the Decision Phase need to be included as part of the Christian "Act of Confession." Both spiritual helpers and injured people often try to rush this phase in the forgiveness process, which is not helpful. Actually injuries, especially if they happened long ago, are multi-layered and take an extended time to uncover. The Decision Phase culminates as offended individuals begin to understand that their decision to forgive, which is not trivial or easy, will bring healing and positive change to their lives. Accordingly, offended people learn what forgiveness is and become willing to do it.

At this point in the forgiveness process, people need to make an official "Declaration of Forgiveness" which is best done in writing. This certification does NOT provide closure for the forgiveness process but essentially concludes the "confession" part of it. When I sense that people have gotten to this point in the process, I have found it helpful to suggest that they complete a "Declaration of Forgiveness" form (Graphic 13), which I have reformatted from somewhere.

Declaration of Forgiveness

I _____ (your name) do hereby declare that on _____ (today's date) I have decided to completely forgive _____ (name of person who hurt you) for

_____
(description of the offense). I give up my right to old feelings I have held and cancel the debt against him/her including the repeating of unfavorable characterizations of this person and stories about what was done to me.

*Signed*_____

Graphic 13: The Declaration of Forgiveness is a written statement which concludes a time of confession and initiates the work phase of the forgiveness process.

After completing the form, I offer a prayer of celebration for the help that God has provided to this point and provide encouragement to continue to move forward into a new future with a new life.

The Decision Phase must be followed by specific actions in order to be effective. Accordingly, the offended person needs to continue the process of forgiving the person who injured them with practical steps. In psychological research this is called the Work Phase; it also is the Christian "Act of Penance."

Work Phase

In the Work Phase, forgiving individuals begin the practical real-life work of forgiving the injurer. This phase includes new ways of thinking and acting toward the injurer. It is putting into practice what has been uncovered, learned and decided, which have been included in the Christian "Act of Confession."

The Work Phase is like trying to actually do any complex new thing that has been learned. After reading a driver's manual (even taking a driver's education course) or watching a gourmet television show (even participating in the class), then it's time to try it alone. Putting into action without assistance is always difficult and prone to mistakes. After uncovering, learning and deciding have been completed, be sure that the strong feelings, "impure thoughts" and inappropriate actions will return. Or after confession and beginning penance, Christians will be tempted to be unloving, even mean, or go back to former behaviors. In truth, **going through confession and penance in a cyclical process is normal and necessary in order to move into the Christian "Act of Repentance."** Since inconsistency and regression are to be expected, spiritual helpers need to be reassuring of those attempting to change. Willful backsliding is sin which must be condemned and confessed; unintentional slippage is must be confessed but not condemned. Discernment is needed. Do people want to be traveling the Spiritual Road or going their own way? If they are on the road, then Paul's affirmation applies, "Therefore, there is now no condemnation for those who are in Christ Jesus."[20] [Romans 8:1]

The Work Phase makes practical the decision, "The pain stops here; not to be perpetuated." **Thus, the Work Phase includes whatever actions confirm the confessional decision to let go of the need for revenge, cancel the debt and generally give up trying to change offender**. At its best the Work Phase employs a plan so that injured people go off "autopilot" and become intentional about continuing the forgiveness process.

In some ways, completing the "Declaration of Forgiveness" is action – and ties the Decision and Work Phases together. In order to begin the work, the psychological researchers suggest that a person might write a letter to the offender, detailing the issue and their feelings, write "Cancelled" across it, and destroy it without sending it. This is to be the final word. After such a letter is destroyed, forgiving people agree to no longer describe the offender in undesirable terms. **They commit to stop characterizing the offender as an awful human being and re-telling the story of the offense.** At the very least, recovering people choose to not say anything, reminding themselves that the injurer no longer owes them any debt and that voluntarily re-ingesting the negative emotions will only make them sick. When friends ask about the problem, person or issue, forgiving people can say, "I have chosen not to speak about that any longer and I would appreciate if you could help me keep that promise."

Completing a "Declaration of Forgiveness" like the one above for each significant offense to be forgiven is good, practical action. Forgiving people might do so for their personal use and post it where they will see it every day. This action allows people to remember the specific date when they tangibly and concretely cancelled the debt; and enables them to remember and participate in the process of forgiving. Also, reading or praying their declaration out loud in the presence of the person holding them accountable is recommended. While full forgiveness has not yet been realized, injured individuals have decided to explore forgiveness and have taken the initial steps in the direction of full forgiveness. The Christian "Act of Penance" reflects this same process.

THE CHRISTIAN "ACT OF PENANCE" – is intentionally behaving in positive ways that are the exact opposite of what has been confessed about an offender or issue. In other words, the penance needs to be directly connected to the offense. For example: if I confess anger toward my father, then I will agree to act (i.e., words and/or behaviors) in some particular non-angry manner toward him. I do not have to do this in his presence, just do it publicly. Or if I come to understand that I have been punishing myself (by imposing guilt) instead of recognizing abusive words spoken against me, I need specific acts of affirming my worth. Or if I, as a recovering alcoholic, went to a bar to drink, I need to call my sponsor and confess what I did and agree to attend specific number of AA meetings. While saying three "Hail Mary" prayers might bring a person in contact with God, it is not an appropriate penance in these cases. The same would be true if people decided to spend more time reading their Bible.

In other words, individuals agree to do some positive action that is the opposite of what they did wrong. I have discovered that structuring a penance in a particular three-focused way is best. The intended actions need to be specific (or limited), obtainable and measurable. Using the above example, it is best that my penance not be stated "to love my father." That is the correct approach; but it is unclear what I am to do. In addition, being totally loving is mostly unobtainable and cannot be measured whether it happened. Instead, a better formulated penance would be to telephone my father to inquire how he is, one day a week for a month. This is action; it is the opposite of my negative emotions; and it is specific enough to know when it has been accomplished. Celebrate its completion; and renew its practice or design a new penance.

When it comes to seeking revenge, Jesus corrects the old instruction saying, "But I tell you to love your enemies and pray for those who persecute you."[21] [Matthew 5:44] Different Greek words used in the New Testament are all translated as "love" in English. Each Greek word has different meanings or emphases.[22] The word that Jesus used in this passage is ἀγαπᾶτε (agapate) which is a form of the word "agape." This "kind of love" does not mean that a person must have a romantic attitude toward the offender. Agape love requires a decision, not a warm-fuzzy feeling. Agape is the kind of love that God has toward people when they sin – people like you and me. God does not like what was done but chooses to want the best for people. What is needed to "love" an enemy or a person who has injured others is an attitude of "unconditional positive regard." This kind of love begins from the thought, "I do not wish you harm; and it would be ok with me if good things happen to you." The Christian "Act of Penance" maintains the same approach.

Christian Confession and the Decision Phase are just talk, although they include good and helpful talk. Penance is walking the walk. When people's emotions and actions coincide, full forgiveness can occur. Penance is a positive action step in matching talk and walk. Truly, penance is an important way to test whether forgiveness is moving forward and people actually have cancelled the debt as well as foregoing negative thoughts, feelings or intentions toward the injurer.

Deepening Phase

In the psychological research, forgiveness is determined to be mostly complete when it reaches the Deepening Phase. **Forgiving individuals begin to realize that they are gaining emotional relief from the process of forgiving their injurer. They also are not regularly remembering the injury made against them**. Importantly, similar situations do not propel them back into the emotions of the original offense. For example: if my father yells at my sister, I do not automatically feel yelled at nor have personal feelings of anger; nor do I wish to cause him harm. This change is part of the Deepening Phase of forgiveness.

During this time, injured individuals may strive to understand why injurers acted as they did – not to excuse the hurt but only to see injurers as members of the human community. Sometimes, empathy or compassion may result from the new perspective (i.e., his father abused him, so he abused others.)

Forgiving individuals may even find meaning in their suffering. For example: individuals may gain personal strength as well as sensitivity toward helping others facing similar situations. Or the emotional relief and new found meaning may lead to increased compassion for self and others. Or individuals may discover a new purpose in life and an active concern for their community. After penance is firmly underway, Christian helpers might choose to recommend that injured individuals, especially if they are in the generativity part of their lives, volunteer with an organization that helps people who have experienced similar traumas. In helping others, people will be reminded how God and the courage to forgive have brought them to this place in their lives. As they share how they came to realize the importance of CPR and how it has given them new life, they will become even stronger. Thus, **forgivers discover the paradox of forgiveness: as people give to others the gifts of mercy, generosity, and agape love, they themselves are healed**.

In the Deepening Phase, people begin to see forgiveness from an even larger perspective – how it was even available for them and what it can do for the life of the world. They recognize how participating in forgiveness is actively building the Community of God – paying forward the forgiveness that God through Jesus commissioned from the cross.

People remind themselves that they have been forgiven and desire to do the same. They take increased personal responsibility for their own need to forgive and desire to help the wider community of people to do the same. As a result, a sense of humility is developed in the way that they treat others – becoming more considerate, more tolerate, less controlling and less judgmental. Their entire attitude is so completely altered from when they were first injured. Indeed, the Deepening Phase dovetails into the meaning of the Christian "Act of Repentance."

THE CHRISTIAN "ACT OF REPENTANCE" – is a 180 degree mental and attitudinal change toward all other similar persons, events and issues. **Repentance is a complete change of mind and heart which comes from repeated confession and penance.** Repentance is mostly unconscious and automatic; not so much a task that Christians accomplish as something they grow into. Repentance is a new mindset which is evidenced in the way people respond to situations that formerly caused them to sin or become unforgiving. Often their responses are completely opposite in nature. For example, people who have experienced verbal abuse from their parents will respond differently to loud, harsh criticism from their stressed supervisor. After CPR people do not react to the "parental anger" but actually express appreciation for whatever might improve their character (while requesting that the tone of the conversation be softer). The purpose of their life has deepened to be less concerned with self and more with whatever would make the world community better.

Instead of overcoming evil with evil, people respond with the tenor of the New Testament teaching, "Do not be overcome by evil, but overcome evil with good."[23] [Romans 12:21] Individuals begin to live life totally opposite of the way that they originally did before beginning the process of forgiveness. This is repentance. People who have moved into repentance value the peace prayer attributed to St. Francis and may benefit from memorizing it.[24]

Lord, make me an instrument of your peace.
Where there is hatred, let me sow love.
Where there is injury, pardon.
Where there is doubt, faith.

Where there is despair, hope.
Where there is darkness, light.
Where there is sadness, joy.
O Divine Master,
Grant that I may not so much seek to be consoled, as to console;
To be understood, as to understand;
To be loved, as to love.
For it is in giving that we receive.
It is in pardoning that we are pardoned,
And it is in dying that we are born to Eternal Life. Amen.

SIGNS OF GENUINE FORGIVENESS

From confessing and continuous releasing of negative emotions plus the increased willingness and positive actions of penance, the Christian reality of repentance can occur. CPR provides new life. After moving through the phases of uncovering, decision, work and deepening, **how do people know when forgiveness has taken place?** The following includes some of the signs that the Christian "Act of Repentance" has occurred.

✞ When the memory of the offense or the offender no longer causes negative emotional reactions or inappropriate behaviors in the person who was hurt, the process of forgiveness has been finished. Certainly, forgiving does not mean forgetting because remembering helps people not to repeat the past. On the other hand, **forgiveness is complete when the POWER has gone out of the memory**. When the memory of the event, or similar circumstances, does not propel people into the negative emotions and actions they previously experienced, healing has occurred. (After CPR has been completed, Unitive Way Christians may pray to even forget the memory of being injured as a way to allow God to become one with them.)

✞ Forgiveness is noticed with an increase in more neutral or genuinely positive attitudes, especially toward the person or situation forgiven. Also, there is a greater life capacity to give and receive love, and experience gratitude.

✞ Forgiveness is evidenced when an attitude of "unconditional positive regard" toward the offender is offered. This is a secular definition of Christian agape love.

✞ The ability to use anger constructively also comes with a forgiving attitude. People can use anger to initiate and sustain constructive activity (facilitate justice, protect self, engage in conflict resolution). They are no longer controlled by anger or fearful of its expression.

✞ An ability to easily ask for forgiveness from others and to give forgiveness, even when the other refuses to forgive, is a deepened outcome of having done CPR.

As evidenced by the lives of those individuals who have moved into repentance, the process of forgiveness certainly provides new life. It is the kind of new life that God has conceived to be the basis of the Holy Community. Spiritual helpers can provide no greater assistance than to facilitate confession, penance and repentance whether that occurs as part of the divine-human process of forgiveness or through interpersonal forgiveness. However, in the final analysis, forgiveness must happen at the heart level and be both given and received with open child-like genuineness. So, perhaps forgiveness is best expressed in the words of Palmy in his Veggie Tales' "The Forgiveness Song."

You know that in love we can forgive
It is the only way to live
Obey God and see that we can live in harmony!
Since God has forgiven us, it's true
You forgive, I'll forgive you
I'm gonna start to show forgiveness from my heart![25]

CHAPTER 18

Dealing with Pain

"Pain is a holy angel who shows us treasures that would otherwise remain forever hidden."[1]

M any people have been among the unfortunate ones to be on vacation or a road trip only to hear their vehicle start to make a funny-sounding noise that seems to originate in the engine. Then the engine light on the dashboard flashes, followed by sputtering and chugging with just enough time to pull off road to a disgruntled halt. Engine trouble, especially in the middle of an unpopulated countryside, is a sick in the stomach feeling! **Pain is the engine problem of the Spiritual Road; pain stops spiritual growth, but later facilities its development.** Everyone has to deal with it; and no one gets to avoid it. In this scenario, people have two basic difficulties: what is wrong with the engine (so they can get it fixed) and addressing the peripheral issues, which range from "Why me?" to "Where do I go to the bathroom or where can I get something to eat?"

The subject of pain is extremely complex. People, delayed on the side of the road, need to have their vehicle's engine repaired so they can get moving again. However, they frequently get stuck talking about other, often very personal, "painful issues." While spiritual helpers rightly want to assist people in fixing their engine, they likely will have to be diverted first by those peripheral concerns. Thus, in order to work with people dealing with pain, some key questions need consideration: How do people experience pain? Where does pain come from? Does pain have a purpose? How can people use pain for spiritual growth?

HOW DO PEOPLE EXPERIENCE PAIN?

Pain in life can be physical, psychological or spiritual. **The discussion of pain in this chapter begins by centering on the external and mental/emotional distress that people experience.** Typically, the spiritual implications of pain are mostly inaccessible until after the physical and psychic issues have been dealt with.

Life is full of episodes that stop people in their tracks. Whether the moment involves a trip to the hospital or a chronic disease, criticism or divorce, or an unwanted divine insight or unanswered prayer – pain rules the moment. Pain is a primary motivator. When pain occurs, people pay attention. **Pain informs people that something is wrong. In that sense, pain is good – although it does not feel good!** I estimate that over ninety per cent of people who would have sought private conversation with me were motivated by the physical or emotional pain they were experiencing. What they often did not realize was that their pain was often also spiritual – in the sense that it was a way that God was attempting to communicate with them and direct their lives. However, considering the spiritual implications of pain is getting way ahead of the story.

Prior to engaging with people, spiritual helpers would be advised to answer the question, **"When you have a tooth ache, about what do you think?"** Everyone knows that the answer is "the tooth ache." When people are in pain, they just want the pain to stop!!! However, before they are willing to "get their tooth fixed," they may need to or want to process why the pain is happening to them. They may want to talk about when they first noticed the hurt, how they always brush their teeth or what happens when they eat ice cream – before they are ready to get the tooth fixed. (They will be much less interested in talking about eating too many sweets, having healthy eating habits or the need to have the tooth extracted.) Accordingly, **the job of the spiritual helper is not to take a person's pain away but simply offer to help.** Until people are ready to release their hold on their pain, they will mount all kinds of resistance to getting on the road again. Supporting and embracing people as they go through their painful physical or emotional issues is sometimes the only, and the best, that spiritual helpers can do.

However, after listening a long time in order to understand the context and the pain, I often ask the above rhetorical "tooth ache" question to invited people to **validate their pain** – whatever it is. So many Christians discount their own pain often because they believe either that others are more important or that they don't deserve the concern of others. Thus at some point, I will invited Christians to conclude that their pain is real and that they deserve to concentrate on it. However, I primarily ask this "tooth ache" question because dealing with pain is necessary in order to move forward in life or to progress along the Spiritual Road. After summarizing, "Your pain is real; it affects your life; you deserve to be relieved; and there is hope that you can feel better," people may be ready to take care of the tooth.

On the other hand, **spiritual helpers need to determine how long and to what degree talking about the pain is helpful.** While processing and validating pain is important; sometimes people may be wallowing in their pain, just feeling the emotions ad nauseam. Long-lasting conversation may also be a symptom of the unwillingness to do the hard work that is ahead. Nevertheless, with such therapeutic listening and perhaps some practical suggestions designed to relieve the pain, **in time people's pain will be lessened to the point**

of considering the spiritual implications of it. Ideally, this process can be done in one half hour, but in reality it takes a number of hours over weeks, even months, to complete – and the deeper the pain, the longer it takes. While taking the time to validate the pain, spiritual helpers need to discern where the pain originates.

WHERE DOES PAIN COME FROM?

Triage is the process of sorting in order to determine what type of action is needed and what priority/treatment is required. Triage often refers to sorting and prioritizing people, especially after a disaster, in regards to medical care. **In the art of spiritual guidance, discernment is similar to medical triage**. For a quick <u>overview examination of the topic of pain</u>, I have developed a **"Spiritual Growth Triage Chart"** which I have divided into two sections: the first considers the sources of pain (Graphic 14) and the second deals with the responses to pain if it is discerned as "coming from God" or being "used by God." (Graphic 15) This second section also integrates the understanding of the purpose of pain with the concepts of spiritual darkness (Confessional Temptation, Dark Night of the Senses and Dark Night of the Spirit) described in chapters six through eleven.

The experience of "anxiety, discomfort, distress or pain" has different sources. The source of pain can be externally inflicted, internally felt, from the devil or God. <u>Spiritual helpers need to listen insightfully and ask appropriate questions in order to help discern the source of pain because the helping approach varies according to the source.</u>

If people do not experience pain, then they are not alive, are a purified saint or have a serious mental illness or rare physical condition. If people experience pain, most will automatically start talking about their pain and where it originated. However, if they do not, then simply asking, "When did you start feeling this way?" or "What happened?" will get a flood of information. Clergy often listen to these answers when visiting people in hospitals or in other stressful circumstances. **Discerning the source of pain is an important part of the spiritual guidance process and determines what kind of follow-up conversations would be appropriate to have.**

First, consider whether the pain has a cause that is external to the person. I separate external pain into <u>two sources: from "natural" circumstances and from other people/ groups of people</u>. Pain may be the result of circumstances like natural disasters or accidents.[2] An accident is an accident; natural is natural – the source is not attempting to communicate with people. <u>And in my opinion, a loving God does not, and does not need to, cause natural disasters in order to change individual lives or affect the course of the world.</u>[3] In addition, God does not cause pain in others in order to get someone else's attention. In the normal course of living, people experience enough pain individually which God can use to encourage change. **While the pain of the external circumstances is very real and potentially has caused great life difficulties, my recommended spiritual guidance**

conclusion is that **God does not use all-sweeping community pain to communicate with individuals about their individual lives – and there is nothing in particular to do except to communicate that conviction about God.** Thus, compassion and empathy with the people affected are helpful to provide until they have worked through the tragedy, regained enough strength and are able to get back on the Spiritual Road. It is like an arrested engine that just needed to cool down so that it could be restarted.

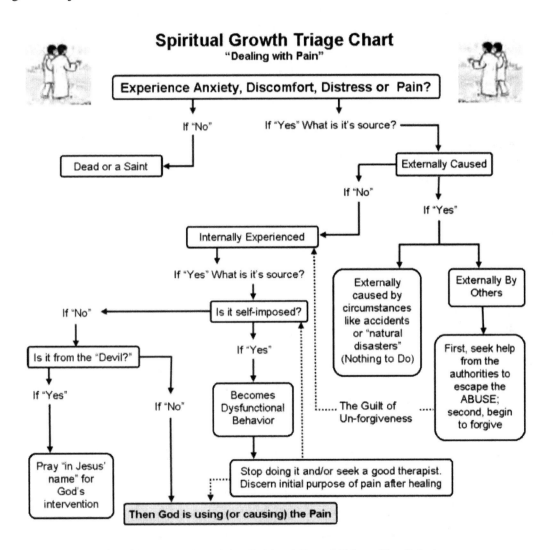

Graphic 14: This portion of the "Spiritual Growth Triage Chart" deal with identifying the source of pain.

On the other hand, **external pain that is inflicted by other people or groups of people is abuse and needs an immediately response**. <u>In order to stop the pain, appropriate authorities need to be contacted and protective boundaries need to be established</u>. While spiritual helpers can and should offer support, many specialized care-givers are better trained to provide emotional support, legal counsel, physical care and so forth. **The primarily spiritual task during the immediacy of abuse-inflicted pain is to do whatever God would do in order to provide safety for the "child of God." Do whatever intervention is needed.** <u>Begin by asking the rhetorical question, "Does God want you to experience such mistreatment?" This may be necessary in order to stimulate people to accept some new limits and take protective action</u>. Assist them in making appropriate tangible changes. Take their hand and walk them to the shelter; or telephone the police and hand the phone to them. In this way, spiritual helpers are acting as representatives of God, who does not want people to be abused. Accompany abused people until they are safely in the arms of an appropriate helping professional. By doing so, the spiritual helper becomes a valued and trustworthy person. Later, when the inflicted external pain needs to be processed, they will know who can be consulted to deal with the emotions.

Almost always, people will need to process how they feel about intentionally hurtful actions or abuse. Doing so will often require the kind of instruction and insight which spiritual guidance can typically facilitate. However, <u>such spiritual conversation is unlikely to occur until after the threatening situation has been made safe</u>. Accordingly, spiritual helpers often deal with the external pain inflicted via others after a significant period of time has elapsed – <u>sometimes years later</u>. Just because it is history, does not make it any less important to re-consider – especially with the goal of restarting the spiritual engine that has been immobile along the side of the highway.

When the opportunity to work with these people arises, spiritual helpers will, of course, affirm that the external physical or psychological pain inflicted by other people was real and not the fault of the person affected. However, <u>external pain needs to be differentiated from the internal feelings</u> that people experience from such abuse. Spiritual helpers might do so like this: "Yes. What happened was wrong and intentionally full of hurt. I understand that you feel angry (or depressed, and so forth.); however, other people who have had a similar experience may feel totally different. <u>These are your feelings and your experience; and what you do with them is your choice</u>. **They are not caused by the external source.**" For example, the accusation "He made me feel this way"[4] is internally feeling the abusive experience which cannot be realized or processed because blame is being assessed. While one person may have unfairly criticized someone, the criticism is not the pain that stops the spiritual trek; it is the holding onto the condemnation of the abuser. In addition, abused people can also be reluctant to revisit the painful time in their lives. Having conversation about how the former mistreatment continues to affect people today gives relevance for the need to deal with it. Externally inflicted pain may have ended, but the feelings that lead to behaviors of caution, resistance, inability, displaced anger and so forth can erupt in the present – not to mention the latent guilt of unforgiveness that is likely to surface.

In summary, people who experience externally inflicted pain need safety and boundaries in order to stop the pain. After completed, they may be ready to process the internal pain they feel, which must be a separate issue from the abuse inflicted upon them. If and when they are ready to do so, spiritual helpers can assist them in discerning whether God was teaching/guiding them or not. However, before helping people deal with the negative emotions they feel, spiritual helpers need to make some additional assessments about this internally experienced pain.

Truly, internally experienced pain can emerge from within people as a result of external events. However, internally experienced pain can also be felt because the demonic is causing it. In addition, internally experienced pain can become serious dysfunctional behavior. In each case, people are holding onto the pain – "imposing" it upon themselves. Nevertheless, until people are safe from further external pain, spiritual helpers should not attempt to deal with the internal emotions. Until the devil has been ruled out and dysfunctional behaviors have been changed, spiritual progress is highly unlikely.

THE DEVIL DID MAKE ME DO IT

Internally experienced pain can be caused by the demonic. Spiritual helpers are prudent to consider this option before launching into dealing with the negative emotions. Understanding the devil as working to bring about all human pain has been called "demonic oppression." Spiritual helpers are advised to consider that which borders on "demonic possession" as the source of pain. This possibility can be discerned through observed behaviors. For example, perpetual lying is a clue to people who may be captured by this evil. Descriptions of atrocious and sadistic actions are another. Excessively enraged images, visions or dreams are another. A long series of bizarre and unexpected events can be suspected to be influence by the devil. While any of these symptoms may also indicate deep psychiatric problems, most likely the people affected will be treated with confinement or disabling medication, which will not connect them with the divine. Spiritual helpers, who may not be comfortable or feel knowledgeable enough, may wish to refer or have a consultant available. In thirty plus years of providing spiritual assistance, I have experienced the demonic possession in only three situations – although every time was unforgettable. In each, the power of God invoked, as specifically as the facts inferred, was adequate to relieve the chaos.

In dealing with the demonic, first remember that God is more powerful. If the affected people are Christians, then that power has been poured into them and is available. Spiritual helpers need to evoke it by praying aloud that God deliver the person from this affliction in the power of "Jesus' name!" Please, do not discount employing God's power in its simplicity. Casting God's pure light into the internal darkness is truly effective because the demons cannot remain in the same vicinity as the active presence of God. God is still the most powerful means to cast out the foe. Perhaps it goes without saying but spiritual helpers are re-establishing the relationship with God for such individuals. In addition to this spiritual action, spiritual helpers may also need to contact other professionals for further assistance.

If internally experienced pain is not from the devil, then it is pain held onto by the person. It has become "self-imposed internal pain," which may or may not have been done intentionally. Self-imposed internal pain is a generic term for held negative emotions. Experiencing negative emotions in painful circumstances is normal; and it often protects people and serves to defuse negative events. Nevertheless, **internal pain held over an extended length of time becomes self-destructive**; it builds walls and inflames passive-aggressive behavior – it becomes "imposed pain" that is harmful. Internally experienced pain that is held for too long develops into dysfunctional attitudes and behaviors. By whatever means, this conduct must be stopped before dealing effectively with the meaning of pain.

Internal pain is like the skin of the body which provides protection from getting sick. Spiritual helpers should never take the pain away; but be available when the person in pain "wants" to (correction … becomes willing to) let it go. I ask people in pain if they are in or have been in therapy, in recovery or have seen a physician because without having that kind of help to reduce pain, the counsel that spiritual helpers have to give will not be heard. On the other hand, since I have enough therapy training, for non-complex psychological conditions I might begin with a therapeutic conversation but be poised to move into spiritual guidance – because that is why the person came to see me in the first place.

IT WORKS IF YOU WORK IT

This imposed internal pain may be turned into self-destructive attitudes or behaviors, which must be stopped before moving forward with spiritual guidance. This intervention may make use of professional therapy, a strong act of the personal will or God's intercession. Alcoholism, uncontrollable rage, severe depression, drug addiction, continuous lawlessness, obsessive attitudes or compulsions as well as significant lack of self-esteem are some symptoms of pain that is being intensified by self-infliction until the person's actions have become dysfunctional. In addition, people experiencing criticism may adopt an angry life-attitude or become inept with a severe lack of self confidence. All of the above conditions are engine problems that stop spiritual movement. Every time I encounter these situations, I hear the words of Cliff Custer, one of my first spiritual guides, "Blame, guilt and inadequacy will stop the flow of God's power into your life."

Any pain is bad enough, but pain gathered and caressed totally overwhelms people. Any tooth ache puts the focus on the hurt; but a mouth full of decaying teeth is all-consuming. Any stopped engine is frustrating; but a flaming motor is heart breaking. When people are surrounded by imposed internal pain that has become dysfunctional behaviors or attitudes, they cannot think about God for long and maintaining a growing spiritual relationship is out of the question. Thus, dealing with the dysfunction is of paramount importance. However, even after the behaviors have been changed, people will typically have the tendency to return to them.

While a congregational minister in a Chicago-area, I had the privilege of working with numerous Christians who were struggling through drug or alcohol recovery. During this time, I helped many of these folks to cross the "church boundary" and re-affirm their relapsed commitment to Jesus as Lord and Savior. I graciously accompanied each person through this process of spiritual growth. I even married recovering addicts – however, I did so only with a firm commitment that the couple would participate in regular marriage counseling for at least six months after their wedding. This covenant anticipated that the additional stress of marriage would propel them into old habits, which it did. I remember well when those people would relapse and their spiritual growth would come to a sudden stop. Make no mistake; each person was dealing with internally imposed pain through which God was teaching them. However, no spiritual progress could be made until they "got sober again." The same can be said for those who are workaholics, relationship addicts, the intimacy challenged or any other dysfunctional behaviors. These well-practiced dispositions are so embedded that even after being redeemed they can suddenly return, displacing healthy living. In fact, Christians can be quite far along the Illuminative Way when this abrupt regression into sinful behavior will occur – it is often identified as a mid-life crisis.

Most people have a "signature sin" that will be their default, especially when stressors arise, times get rough and pain emerges. A "signature sin" is whatever inappropriate action or attitude keeps returning. These have the strong possibility of becoming internal pain that becomes dysfunction. "Once my tendency; always my tendency" is my personal mantra that keeps me aware of lurking dysfunction in my life. Of course, the process of Confession-Penance-Repentance is the prescribed spiritual prescription for reoccurring sins. However, while CPR is the spiritual remedy to remove the sinfulness, understanding what God is communication through the returning pain and cooperation with what God is teaching can actually stop the signature sin from returning. Thus, spiritual helpers can be of significant aid when they assist people in recognizing their default tendency. Indeed, the vast majority of issues and spiritual concerns can be related to signature sins. I find this true for nearly one hundred per cent of the people I guide spiritually. Thus, being sensitized and aware of one's signature sin pushes people to maintain reliance upon God and keeps that relationship growing.

Summarizing, in considering the sources of pain, spiritual helpers (as well as those they accompany) are trying to discern if the pain comes from God by eliminating alternative sources. First, investigate if the pain is <u>inflicted externally</u>. If from natural or accidental disasters, affirm that God cares but did not cause the pain. Pain inflicted by others must be stopped and safety restored. People may experience <u>internal pain</u> from external sources. However before dealing with this option, further discernment is required. Scrutinize if the internally-felt pain comes <u>from the devil</u>; if so, use God's power to dispel the evil. Also, this internal pain may be held so as to become internalized and self-imposed until it develops into <u>dysfunctional attitudes or behaviors</u>, which must be changed for spiritual growth to begin or continue. After the demonic or the dysfunction has been removed and the internally-felt emotions remain, they can be used to understand what God is communicating in regard to what is needed for spiritual growth. However, for many people the question still remains can pain legitimately be used as an indicator that points to spiritual direction?

DOES PAIN HAVE A PURPOSE?

Is the experience of pain just the result of random acts of senseless hurtfulness? Or if pain has a purpose, does that mean that God (or life) intended to hurt people who move in a particular direction? In other words, do people's actions elicit reward and punishment? Those are huge mostly unanswerable questions.

Nevertheless, spiritual helpers will be asked such questions by those people who are experiencing pain in their lives. <u>Even though no definitive answer can be given</u> people "deserve" a thoughtful discussion, which clearly needs to reflect where people are along the Spiritual Road. Beginners in the faith will often ask what the Bible says about pain and punishment. Others may choose to argue or disapprove of the seeming unfairness that they feel coming from God. Alternative understandings may be presented. While the topic will not result in a final conclusion, talking about the questions that people have actually can release them to deal with the pain. So, <u>I have included some thoughts regarding the purpose of pain along with my best working assumption in order to encourage people to dealing with their pain</u>.

Taken at face value, <u>the Bible clearly teaches that everyone will experience pain and for a purpose</u>. Jesus claims that the poor will always exist and that people will feel pain and difficulty that will eventually turn to joy.[5] [Matthew 26:11; John 16:20] The book of Hebrews teaches "Our fathers disciplined us for a little while as they thought best; but God disciplines us for our good, that we may share in his holiness."[6] [Hebrews 12:10] The Bible provides the illustration of "good" Christians, Anaias and Sapphira, falling dead because of selfish, blatant lies that threatened the community of God.[7] [Acts 5:1-10] St. Paul dealt with the "thorn in the flesh" that was used by God to remind him of God's all-sufficient grace.[8]

[II Corinthians 12:7-9] Not to mention all the Old Testament incidents of severely negative consequences for acts of sin. In addition, people are predisposed to believe, or at least question, whether God is punishing them or not. These examples are enough to answer that question for those who need the written word to be authoritative, clear and precise. However, they are not enough for those Christians who struggle with scriptures that have multiple variant readings and include some obvious mistranslations – one example which is included in this chapter. Nevertheless, while God's word of truth is included in the Bible (at least in my belief), it still takes work and discernment to receive it.

Even if Christians had a pristine and original version of the Bible, some people would assert that a God whose very nature is love and who has the power to do otherwise would not cause injury and pain. Some theologians (and Christians) want to disregard or even disallow reward and punishment from the divine scheme of things, making that claim based on how much Jesus was all about grace and that God will finally redeem all people. Ultimately, their conclusion ends up being that bad things just happen. That premise seems a bit too stoic and theistic for a God whose essential nature is rooted in love.

Let us acknowledge that understanding the complete balance and implementation between obtaining the justice of the law and the liberation of grace is one of the divine Mysteries. Even after making that admission, both life and scripture indicate that certain actions lead toward pain and that other actions lead toward reward – although there is not a vending machine correlation between actions and their consequences. The dilemma is how to deal with both the life experiences that point to God's radical justice and those that point to God's unmitigated grace. **Perhaps the only accurate way to respond is with the standard of personal life experience and at the same time including all data points beyond one's familiarity**, especially with the details that do not fit into one's mental system. When this is obtained, people live via their own experience while still being open to the possibilities that have happened to others, even if they are not understood.

Thus, this author's fundamental assumption is that whether God uses or allows pain to discipline or persuade people in particular directions, God does that with the goal of drawing people to God's self in the spirit of perfect love and for people's best interest. In some ways those suppositions infer that God cannot punish but could discipline – a concept which removes the idea of God intentionally inflicting pain for the purpose of being hurtful. Also, while rewards can come, but do not always have to come, from certain actions, when all is said and done God will reward people in the end – when the mystery of balancing justice and grace will be revealed.

Perhaps this author is well-able to speak to the subject of pain and in particular to the conclusion that pain has purpose that comes from God. At age four years old, I did not earn nor deserve the effects of a neuromuscular disease, which totally altered the way I have lived my entire life. I will soon celebrate sixty years of moving through life with atrophied legs, leg braces and walking sticks. I did not say struggle, but celebrate – because God has made me who I am because of the affliction. <u>My disabling experience has caused me to say that God did not cause the pain of my life for punishment, but most certainly God has used it to draw me into a deep personal relationship as well as to glorify God and assist others</u>. Clearly, other people in similar circumstances have said the opposite, which leads me to conclude that **it is not about the pain but how people respond to it**. And yes, in some of my more "inhuman" moments, I have lamented that I have had to struggle with such "unfairness" and deal with consistent physical pain and its accompanying emotional and social discord. I have great sympathy and compassion for my brothers and sisters who experience physical disabilities; but I have an even greater prayer focus that they will allow God's touch upon them.

Now if someone had harangued me when I was a young person that God had caused my painful condition, my life would undoubtedly turned out differently than as a person who has dedicated it to God. I'm sure that I would have resisted (I was not ready to process the internal pain at that time.) However, I received wonderful support and encouragement, especially during my early years of recovery, from an entire cadre of people who helped me grow in strength and stature and in faith of God. I also received great guidance with helpful attitudes instilled in me which I got from my parents and others, such as: you are not any different than anyone else, if there is a will (your will) there is a way (which you will find) and you need to persevere to become as good as you can be. All of this assistance translated into "God is on your side and wants the best for you." That is my prayer for all who experience pain, especially the kind that hurts abominably, until the day when they have the personal strength to receive the connection between God and their pain.

Rev. Cliff Custer is an ordained, spirit-filled Presbyterian minister, who specializes in emotional and spiritual healing workshops. When I was an associate minister in my first congregation, I met Cliff who was brought into the congregation for a special event and returned for two consecutive years. People were touched, healed and changed. I was cerebral and suspicious. But when those people maintained their new life and continued to grow spiritually, I became softer and curious. After the third year's workshop, I asked Cliff, "I have seen you touch people and give them new life; I want to know what you think about me." Surprisingly, he avoided any answer to my inquiry and walked away. I chased him down the hall and literally cornered him and insistently repeated my demand. He looked through me and noted, "Ok. If you really want to know what I think, I will tell you. ... The spiritual dimension of a physical disease such as polio is best described as when two strong-willed people lock horns; the person who loses the struggle has the disease. Your left side is affected and it is the feminine side of the body. Do you ever have any conflicts with the strong-willed women in your life?" Did I ever – from the beginning and all along the way! Cliff asked me a couple of informational questions and then he began to describe the kind of young child I must have been; and he asked if that was correct. Since I had a (God-graced) memory block of my early polio years, I did not know. However, I immediately wrote down the questions, went to my parent's home on my next day off. <u>Every one</u> of Cliff's assertions was absolutely accurate! In some ways I felt like the Samaritan woman at the well when she proclaimed about Jesus, "He told me everything I ever did."[9] [John 4:39] I also elicited other information that confirmed his assessment of me. Fortunately, before he left I had asked him, "If this is the case, what am I to do?" I knew from his teachings that inner healing was all about faithfully following God. He clearly spoke, "It is simple. You are to love the strong-willed women in your life." I have taken the medicine of this spiritual prescription for decades and as a result I have become softer so much so that most of the women I accompany in spiritual direction have had severe abuse in their background. I have intentionally become their advocate and in many ways build male relationship bridges for them. I do it for them; but God continues to heal me in the process.

Does God cause or allow pain in order to instruct people? There is no satisfactory answer to this question that will be acceptable to all. <u>People's understandings of God and interpretations of life experiences significantly influence the answer</u>. In addition, where people are in the process of spiritual growth is a determining factor. <u>In the beginning of the Spiritual Road, Christians emphasize the sovereignty of God and need God to be in control even if that means God causes pain</u>. I remember well the event of a parishioner's close family member being tragically killed in an automobile accident. I comforted, "This was not God's will." However, immediately I was told by this Purgative Way Christian, "Don't tell me that! I need to believe that God is in charge." <u>Later in the spiritual journey as Christians move into independence, they will emphasize their free choice and are not likely to want God to impose pain, but may allow the belief that God uses pain</u>. Further down the spiritual road, Unitive Way Christians really do not even care to focus on this debatable question because not only do they live most of life in spiritual pain (dryness of prayer, the absence of God, consequences of their signature sins, etc.) but all of their energy is focused on being with God.

As I write, I experience periodic physical pain. When I do, I am not happy, have difficulty in many areas of daily life and often cannot even think about writing, at least for very long. So, I stop and release the control I am attempting to have over my life; and I deliberately abide with God for awhile. Now, I am certainly not a "feel sorry for me" kind of guy; but I use this to illustrate how pain is a gentle, or not so gentle, reminder of where I am and what I need in my spiritual life. The pain corresponds to my spiritual need to reduce my control over life, to be pruned to limit my activities and focus on God as God prepares me for the Unitive Way.

In review, when people experience significant pain, their engine stops and they need help to get it diagnosed and repaired so they can get back on the road again. Spiritual helpers and others are needed to ease the pain since people, at first, cannot think of anything, including God, except the pain and the problem. Eventually, the pain may lessen enough for them to talk about the possible meaning of their pain. The spiritual help they receive and what they conclude determines the spiritual growth and development in their relationship with God. **Dealing with the pain means to solve, dissolve, resolve or accept it as well as to find God's meaning or purpose in it**. Specifically, working with physical or psychological pain is like dealing with any problems; some can be solved, or they may just go away as the process unfolds; and they also may be resolved as the person takes action. However, at times the pain may just have to be accepted. In addition, God's meaning and purpose needs to be discovered which often cannot be accomplished until after the problem has been addressed.

When people are ready and have processed the meaning of their pain, their spiritual progress can be as rewarding as it is powerful. The roar of an engine that has been in disrepair for a long time is indeed a joyous sound! **Spiritual helpers validate the experience, enhance personal strength, initiate a forgiving course of action and assist in implementing the lessons learned into daily life. Why? To get Christians back on the Spiritual Road in order to glorify God and grow into oneness with God**. It is easy to forget this ultimate purpose when in the midst of the long recovery from pain. However, when people are ready, they can understand that God is using or has caused this pain for their benefit. Indeed, it is an awakening that totally changes the orientation of living. It is an awakening that God facilitates and people receive; and it is expressed beautifully in these verses of the contemporary Christian song "Awakening."[10]

> Is this love or madness
> Is this cruelty or grace
> You have given this dry season
> I'm thirsting for the reason
> You have brought me to this place.
> This is death and living
> I am empty and fulfilled
> And all that's left for me
> Is the abundance that I see when I
> Open my eyes to your will.

HOW CAN PEOPLE USE PAIN FOR SPIRITUAL GROWTH?

God created life and God can use life to lure people in the direction God wants them to go. The same is true about pain. God can use it. **I totally believe that God's basic nature is pure love. This means that God can only love and want the best for everyone. Thus, if God uses pain, it has to be for good**. It is the conclusion of the long biblical story of Joseph, who endured much pain and was ready to inflict revenge because of it. However, God taught him until he realized, "You intended to harm me, but God intended it for good to accomplish what is now being done, the saving of many lives."[11] [Genesis 50:20] I believe that God, if God chooses, can take pain away or remove the offending infection – and God does do that. However, removing pain is not God's highest priority for humanity: bringing people into loving relationship with God and creating the Holy Community is. Those priorities last eternally; pain is finite and limited, even if it does not feel that way.

When "Dealing with Pain" there are two problems: relieving the pain itself, which may take professional medical or therapeutic care, and concluding what spiritual redirection the pain is inviting people to adopt, which usually takes the assistance of spiritual helpers. I am totally convinced that most people, even the smartest, do not realize what they do to themselves – it takes someone with a different perspective to see what is happening. This is simply and easily demonstrated with the now classic Jo-Hari Window.[12] Yet, when people understand and decide to change, they can begin to relieve the pain. Fortunately, careful, empathetic listening practiced by a comforting, non-anxious presence (which can be the Holy Spirit delivered) can help people repair and re-start their spiritual engine. A stopped engine indicates a problem in the way Christians are relating with others, self or God. How to repair the vehicle depends on where people are along the Spiritual Road.

As discussed above, pain comes from different sources. First, the externally-inflicted and all-consuming pain (via Devil or dysfunction) must be significantly reduced before people are ready to deal with the pain. **Afterward if people are still holding onto (or remembering) anxiety, discomfort, distress or internal pain, then God is using the pain for the good of people.** Spiritual directors for centuries have understood this truth, which Bruce Wilkinson illustrated using the teaching of Jesus in John 15:1-16 about the vine and the branches in his book Secrets of the Vine: Breaking Through to Abundance.[13] He was able to make this biblical passage effective for spiritual guidance because he clarified the process of grape growing (which Jesus and his apostles would have indigenously known) and corrected a traditional biblical translation of the Greek (and therefore its interpretation). I have included implications from Wilkinson's research and writing in the second part of my "Spiritual Growth Triage Chart," which deals with understanding how God uses pain. Accordingly, once internally-felt pain is verified to be used (or caused) by God, a series of questions can be used to determine how to respond.

NO GAIN BRINGS PAIN

In John 15:1-16, Jesus compares himself to a grape vine, his followers to the branches of the vine, and God to the gardener or vine grower. The scripture describes the relationship between each; and it also overviews the spiritual purpose of the disciples' lives. First, recognize that in this teaching-analogy Jesus is speaking to believers, those who have accepted him as Messiah and savior, as indicated in verse two when he refers to "every branch in me." Jesus is the vine and Christians are the branches connected to him. What Jesus is teaching does not apply to non-believers. Second, the vine grower wants the greatest possible harvest from the grapes. Wilkinson coins three "Secrets of the Vine" that helps people to know what God wants, helps them to live more effectively without so much pain and to better co-operate with God in providing a great grape harvest. Accordingly, each principle includes instructions that helps build the Community of God (to "do good") and strengthen individuals' relationship with God ("to become one").

When habitual pain is experienced, people might consider whether God is attempting to move them in a different direction. **The first question to ask regarding the internally-felt pain is: Do people have persistent sin in their lives?** If they do, then people need confession, penance and repentance to repair their engine. This sin-related pain can occur on the Pre-Christian Way because people have not accepted the relationship God offers. Thus, spiritual helpers need to lead them to accept Jesus as Savior (a form of CPR) for the pain to subside. (However, remember that Jesus' teaching is for those people who are already followers.) The sin-related pain can also occur on the Purgative Way, after becoming a Christian; in this case, pain-reduction also requires CPR but for a different purpose. The internally-felt pain feels much the same in either case; however, the reasons for it are different and potentially very important.

The pain felt by Pre-Christian Way folks indicates that there has been no true, official heart-felt acceptance of God. **This pain felt by Purgative Way Christians occurs after people have become Christians and because they are not changing their lives in accordance with their commitment. The Purgative Way pain does not mean that a person is not a Christian.** They absolutely are in relationship with God through Jesus Christ – but they are not growing so God gets involved to help. Purgative Ways Christians fight sinful tendencies – it is their primary "job." In addressing these Christians, the writer of Hebrews teaches, "In your struggle against sin, …you have forgotten that word of encouragement that addresses you as sons: 'My son, do not make light of the Lord's discipline, and do not lose heart when he rebukes you, because the Lord disciplines those he loves, and he punishes everyone he accepts as a son.'"[14] [Hebrews 12:4-6; Proverbs 3:11-12] Distinguishing the difference between Christians in pain and non-Christians in pain can be very important. The difference is between being in the family or not as well as being condemned or not. The real difference is in how Christians in pain look at themselves. I have met so many "backsliding" Christians who feel so reviled that they have no ability left to move forward. God does not want them to feel put down; in fact the opposite is true. **God desires these Purgative Way Christians to be lifted up!** Spiritual helpers provide one of the greatest services when they help Christians in pain to understand that God has not rejected them. Affirm for them, "Therefore, there is now no condemnation for those who are in Christ Jesus."[15] [Romans 8:1] Then deal with the purpose of the pain they feel.

As discussed in chapter seven, the Purgative Way is focused on sin-removal and establishing spiritual basics. **As followers of Christ do this, they begin to both do good things for God and also grow closer in their relationship with God – biblically speaking, "producing some good fruit."** Signs of this process are evidenced in increased ethical/ moral behavior, following scripture/spiritual teachings, a beginning trust in God as well as a diminishing influence of sin in their lives. Hopefully, by means of the natural process of spiritual growth, Christians mature and begin to produce good fruit for God – and in a timely fashion. However, **when this does not happen in a developmentally acceptable manner, Christians experience pain and stop traveling farther on the Spiritual Road.** This painful experience is not about being non-Christian but about the need to have a concentric faith – their actions are not growing to coincide with what they have said they believe.

Following the teaching of John 15:2a, Bruce Wilkinson notes that God intervenes to discipline Christians by correcting and lifting them up. This secret was revealed to Rev. Wilkinson only after two different revelations happened. The first insight happened on the day that he was invited to tour a vineyard. And the second revelation occurred with some good Bible study.

Bruce Wilkinson recalls the time when he went to the vineyard and the man giving the tour explained,

"New branches have a natural tendency to trail down and grow along the ground. But they don't bear fruit down there. When branches grow along the ground, the leaves get coated in dust. When it rains, they get muddy and mildewed. The branch becomes sick and useless."

Now Bruce Wilkinson in his agricultural ignorance suggests that those branches ought to be cut off and thrown away.

"Oh no!" exclaimed the tour guide. "The branch is much too valuable for that. We go through the vineyard with a bucket of water looking for those branches. We lift them up and wash them off. Then we tie them up to the trellis. Pretty soon they're thriving."[16]

Now as any Indiana tomato grower knows. You don't get any tomatoes if you cut off every tomato branch that grows on the ground and gets muddy. Instead, you tie them up to the tomato stake where the fresh rain can wash them off, and the air and sun can get to them.

The second insight that Bruce Wilkinson received involved some good, ground breaking Bible study.[17] The Greek word "αἴρει" (Transliterated as "airo" and pronounced

265

– ah'-ee-ro) is the verb used in John 15:2a. Unfortunately, it has most often been translated as "cuts off;" and has been rendered, "He (the vine grower) <u>cuts off</u> every branch in me that bears no fruit …"

The same Greek word "αἴρει" (airo) is used in other New Testament passages but with a different translation. Consider the passage in Matthew 9:6 where Jesus heals a man who was lying on a mattress and then says to him, "Airo your bed and walk." The translation is not "cut off" your bed and walk, but it is take up, or lift up, your bed and walk. Likewise, after the feeding of the 5000 people in Matthew 14:20, the translation is: "the disciples "airo-ed" twelve basketfuls of broken pieces." They did not "cut off" the leftover food, but collected it or picked it up. **Thus, if Christians use a Bible that translates the Greek word "αἴρει" in John 15:2a as "<u>cuts off</u>," they might wish to use "airo's" legitimate, alternative translation "lifts up."** Then the verse reads, "The vine grower <u>lifts up</u> every branch in me that bears no fruit." (Christians might want to write that translation in the margin of their Bible so they won't forget it.) **Accordingly, Christians are not being condemned but disciplined in loved**.

Now if I am a new Christian branch growing from Jesus – my savior vine, I will tend to fall down to the ground and get all dirty. When it rains, I get muddy. When the sun comes out, I get baked until I'm stuck in the mud. Then, God comes along and with strong loving hands takes hold of me and lifts me up and cleans me off. But oh how very much it hurts, being ripped from the strong-hold of the mud. Oh how much it hurts, when my diseased leaves with their open sores and cuts are washed clean. And oh how much it hurts when I am tied up with strong cords to the trellis that hold me up to the healing of the sun. But oh how good it hurts to be lifted out of sin by the one who only wants me to get well and bear much fruit.

<u>Pain sometimes is the indicator that God is trying to get Christians to do something different. And if there is persistent sin in Christians' lives, they can be sure that God is trying to move them away from that sin and lift them up so they can be fruitful</u>. **When such pain occurs spiritual helpers need to ask: "Do Christians have persistent sin as an active part of their attitudes or behaviors?"** If the answer is "Yes," then CPR is necessary. Spiritual helpers need to, and God always gives people a choice. They may either continue to grow in their downward way; or they may wish to cooperate with God's effort to lift them up.

NOTE: **Do not easily dismiss pain as <u>not</u> being caused by persistent sin; it may be hidden in the passing of time**. <u>Sin-removal typically begins with obvious, tangible negative behaviors. However, sin-removal definitely includes internal attitudes that are easily hidden from public observation</u>, such as prejudices of all types, unspoken envy, veiled resentments and so forth. These unresolved attitudes may have become concealed dysfunctions like internet pornography, unethical business practices, child abuse and so forth.

Such internal sins and hidden practices may surface long after Christians have purged the obvious external actions.

Spiritual helpers may notice that those they accompany feel "stuck" or "trapped" or express being "down" with no particular reason. By the prompting of the Spirit or an intuitive hunch, I may ask, "As far back as you can remember, when did you feel this same way?" If emotional distress accompanies the answer, then I would follow with "Carrying that experience must have been an awful burden." Or "How have you hidden such an emotional memory for so long?" Or "How has that experience changed your life?" Or "Have you forgiven?" Even long-term Christians can hold "unfinished business" for a long time. **Spiritual helpers need to be aware of latent feelings and attitudes because they are internally-felt pain and they stop the Spiritual Road travel.**

Indeed, engine problems bring pain – being stopped along the side of the Spiritual Road. God has gotten Christians' attention and needs something to be repaired in order to continue. However, if an engine is broken for a long time, its gasoline will evaporate. It will be out of gas – which is a problem of unforgiveness. When negative emotions are held onto for too long or turned into sinful actions, people have run out of gas and have a broken engine. Thus, people need to get gas back in their tank and repair the engine as well – they need to forgive and also take care of the internal pain. To take care of the pain means to solve, dissolve, resolve or accept it as well as to find God's meaning or purpose in it.

LET GO AND LET GOD, REALLY

As Christians are signaled onto the superhighway of the Illuminative Way, they are eager and excited about learning, growing and bettering themselves spiritually. Instead of struggling to find God, they are living for God and God's Holy Community. They are definite and committed to the Christian Way; and they want to make a difference in their lives and in their world. They consistently and earnestly express love for neighbor and love of God. The learning, the clarifications and applications are insightful and exhilarating. Indeed, the Illuminative Way is full of wonderful opportunities to do good things – and the possibilities seem endless. Consequently, the pain that Illuminative Way Christians feel is often quite different.

During the first part of the Illuminative Way, the Christian life is typically quite enjoyable and enriching. **At some point, however, things start to change** and people begin to ask, "Why does my life not seem satisfying?" "Why do things not go smoothly?" "Why does my prayer time not seem as meaningful as it used to be?" "How come I am more anxious and worried about things?" Christians may even, in secret, question their salvation, what they believe or God. At the same time, they see how different (holy) they have become. They look at all the great things they do for others and at church – and give God so much credit for it all. Yet, they experience a gnawing anxiety or a painful angst. If

Christians do not experience this pain naturally, some external event will likely occur and elicit internally-felt negative emotions. Either through natural attrition or a surprise event, their sense of uneasiness does not match what they believe or who they have become. This disconnect is painful.

Up until this time, Christians have learned that experiencing anxiety, discomfort, distress or pain meant that they had persistent sin in their lives – but now they lament, "For the life of me, I thought I was doing good; what am I doing wrong?" **So often maturing Christians experience this pain and feel that they must be bad; and they feel so guilty that they tend to not talk about the pain**. They just figure that they have to try harder to do more good and sin less. If there is ever a perfect rationale for solid Christians to have a spiritual director who engages them in very personal spiritual conversation, this is it. Numerous Christians have stopped on the side of the road thinking they have done something, unknowingly, wrong. **The real reason for the pain is that they have done so much right!** What is happening?

If they were grape branches, they would have already resisted the temptation of trailing down into the mud and are thriving on the trellis, basking in the sun and growing some clusters of grapes as well. They have become thriving branches attached to the grape vine, Jesus. They are growing so vigorously that they have started shooting off in all different directions; it takes lots of time and energy to do that. Being a soccer mom or a baseball dad; an endearing spouse and a loving parent or a world adored grandparent; a Sunday school teacher and a local community politician; a club officer, a valuable volunteer and successful at work are all good things. And although Christians glorify God with a few clusters of grapes here and there, all of the activities and possessions of their lives zap their time and energy. They have become really, really, really beautiful healthy wax-green grape leaves! But that is not their ultimate and divinely-created purpose.

So, what is the pain the branch feels? It is being pruned! When such rapid and diverse growth occurs, Christians can be sure that the gardener is on the way to prune some of those leaves; the purpose is to pour more oomph into growing grapes for God. Indeed, left to itself a grape plant will always favor the new growth of beautiful leaves instead of producing more grapes.[18] Thus, the good gardener prunes so that the life-generating energy of the vine will be used to grow more grapes. Or as Jesus says, "I am the true vine, and my Father is the gardener. ... (and) every branch that does bear fruit he prunes so that it will be even more fruitful."[19] [John 15:1a, 2b]

Pruning means to reduce or remove plant parts for a purpose. That purpose for the grape plant is to produce more and better grapes; for those who are in Christ, the purpose is always about having a greater harvest for God. But just like the grape plant, people, left on their own, also will always favor looking good instead of becoming good. Christians will constantly grow more and more beautiful leaves, which correspond to obtaining and accomplishing many good things in life. **Accordingly, the vine grower needs Christians**

to focus their energy into producing more and better grapes – that is, good works and good words that glorify God as well as a deeper relationship with God. Accordingly, Dr. Wilkinson adopted his second secret of the vine: "If your life bears some fruit, God will intervene to prune you" so that you will bear more fruit.[20]

So... "Why does this painful dissatisfaction happen?" **This painful dissatisfaction is a way in which God is inviting Christians to cooperate with the spiritual pruning process. Actually, the pain occurs when Christians are not cooperating**. At first, the angst comes to encourage Christians to release and relinquish some activities and practices. Mature Christians are often doing so many good things that it becomes painful to juggle all of the good that is happening – this can be a sign that pruning is required. Often, long-term Christians want to keep on doing all that they are doing, not simply because they want to control but because they feel so guilty when they "retire" from all their activity. They do not realize that God has invited them to release and relinquish to the next generation; but they might feel the discord between ideas that different generations create. In such cases, personal spiritual direction could prove exceptionally helpful to both the individuals and the community. Hopefully, Christians get the message and cooperate with God's pruning of their lives. If not, the pain will increase internally or with external life events.

Jerry was past middle age and a long-term Christian. Recently, he experienced an extreme foundationally-shattering event that threatened some of what he held most dear – he had an explosive argument with his much loved wife and she with him. In everyday language, the stress of life got the best of him and he got very angry. Some people would ask, "What's the problem? These events happen all the time." Not to Jerry! One of his greatest fears was that he would do something to hurt his marriage and go through another devastating divorce. So, he had been a very compliant husband who was also over-responsible and had great difficulty saying "no." As a Christian, he functioned in much the same way: always willing to help everyone with a "taking care of everything" style of leadership and feeling excessively guilty when things didn't go as planned. His career behavior was not any different – in fact, his last evaluation criticized that he was always doing the work that others left undone.

For quite a while, God had been inviting Jerry to cooperate in the pruning process. However, Jerry would not learn to say "No, thank you" to all the activities in his life. He refused to utter "Enough is enough." Consequently, his self-made pressure cooker personality erupted inflicting his latent anger on those around him; in addition, his greatest fear was unleashed into his life. To Jerry's credit, he is extremely smart and pretty much knows what is happening to him. To his discredit, his rationalizing intelligence gets in the way of his putting into practice what he knows. Jerry needs to prioritize, decide and let go – not only for himself and those around him, but also for strengthening his spiritual relationship with God. His activities are getting in the way of the Christian that God wants to make of him.

Spiritual helpers need to discern if the pain that Christians are experiencing is because they are doing too much (either internally or externally). If so, then pruning is needed; and sometimes sharing the knowledge of the spiritual pruning process can assist Christians to cooperate in what God is doing. If they do, then their engine will re-start and they can get back on the Spiritual Road.

<u>**Pruning is always about deciding, prioritizing and letting go. Christians are called to release and relinquish**</u>. Pruning is a cutting away for a good purpose. Interestingly, the word "decide" comes from the root word "cido" which means "to cut" and from the prefix "de" which means "away from." Just like the word "incision" means "to cut into" **the word "decide" means "to cut away."** Christian pruning is difficult. <u>Even if Christians realize that certain practices need to be released, deciding is hard; and it is especially painful when choosing between good things.</u> When Christians realize that God wants them to prune, what do they cut? It all looks so good. Discernment is advised in order to decide what to cut. However, the issue is not so much about what to cut as it is about cutting. Actually, an extended discernment process can become avoidance of doing the cutting. Indeed, the fear of cutting the "wrong" things will extend the pain that only action can relieve.

In addition, when Christians stop being "attached" to the beauty of the leaves that they see in their lives and focus on the purpose for which they have been created, then they will cut. With too many Christian things, they lose Christ. With multiple ways to point to God, they don't have time to be in that relationship with God. Additionally, <u>when Christians realize that they did not create the good things in their lives – God did – and remember that God wants them to cut them away, then they can decided and let go</u>. On the other hand, pruning is not primarily about having less responsibility but about putting focused energy into selected areas of life.

Indeed, diverse Christian lives can touch lots of different folks; however, growing into Christ-likeness or into oneness with God is not about the things, or even the effectiveness, of Christianity, it is about God. Christians easily gain a healthy pride about the godly things in their lives – but they are still just things. Thus, Christians need to be pruned in order to be prepared for what God ultimately desires: abiding with God eternally. Throughout life and particularly through pruning, God is methodically preparing Christians for eternity, loving them, even with pain, step by step. The contemporary Christian song "Love by Degree" describes the cutting and cooperating during this phase of Christians' lives.

> When you try my heart like silver
> And test my soul with fire
> When you cut away the beauty
> Of the treasures I desire
> One by one I lay them down
> Through the working of your hand

(Chorus)
And if it takes my whole life through
And if it breaks my heart in two
But if it makes me more like you
Lord, let it be in me
Love by degree[21]

A NOTE OF WARNING: If Christians need pruning, but resist pruning – they resist God. If Christians resist God, they are behaving sinfully and therefore God will discipline them... again. In an alternative scenario, if Christians need pruning, but think they have just not gotten it right again (thinking that they must have been sinning), they will put themselves into a cycle of feeling guilty when they are not guilty – and the pain never leaves. In a "perverted" sort of way this pattern becomes their perpetual sin, which, of course, needs CPR in order for them to spiritually grow again.

STAY IN LOVE

To this point, spiritual helpers have guided Christians to assess that no persistent sin existed and no forgiveness was needed. They also discerned that much releasing with a deepening focus was required and practice has been adopted. Yet the pain in those they accompany still exists. Why? What is happening? God has them exactly where God needs them to be. They are to do nothing different – just abide as deeply as they can. Nothing is wrong and nothing needs to be fixed. The pain indicates that God has done and is doing spiritual surgery; the pain is the recuperation into a new self – with a new heart and a transformed spirit. Recovery from spiritual surgery is painful with nothing to be done except what the Great Physician instructs. Healing, which is God's job, can best be completed if people do not get in the way by doing too much or taking their spiritual growth into their own hands. On the other hand, Christians may desire to know more about how the healing process works. However, exploring the details of this Dark Night will not make it happen any faster nor reduce the pain.

In his grape vine analogy Jesus teaches, "Remain (abide) in me, and I will (abide) remain in you."[22] [John 15:4] The verb form used in this sentence is the imperative which makes it a command or at the very least insistent instruction. What is being accomplished is detailed in the chapters on the Unitive Way and the Dark Night. Christians are to do what they are able to do, no more and no less. **The task for Christians, if they have a task, is to stay in relationship and simply be aware of when Jesus comes and abides with them IN THE LIFE THEY HAVE.** Christians are to continue to live their life pointing to God, enduring the pain, while God transforms them. **This is "abiding."** "Abiding" means to remain or rest in the presence of another; it is the level of intimacy that the Bible calls "oneness." Nevertheless, it is God who determines when and how deeply Christians will abide in oneness with Christ Jesus.

There is a television commercial that promotes buying of diamonds.[23] It contains only music except for the closing phrase "A diamond is forever." It begins with a thirty-ish couple rapidly walking, side by side with arms swinging, down a path through a park. Also walking this same path ahead of them is a couple in their eighties. This older couple is intentionally walking slowly, holding hands, and have a beautiful look of peace and contentment on their glowing faces. As the thirty-ish couple approaches the older couple, they separate – one to the right and one to the left – in order to go around. When they come back together, they slow down a bit and reach for each other's hands. Smiling they look into each other's eyes as if to say, "That's the goal isn't it? To abide in each other's holy presence – in peace, in contentment, in love."

This "abiding" in Christ takes on deep meaning and importance. It is the testing of faith at the highest level – similar to what the apostles' experienced. If Christians are worthy to be intimately joined in oneness with God, then they must be able to endure as he did the darkness of the cross when all seemed lost. At this "abiding" time in Christians' lives, the phrase "it is your cross to bear" actually applies; however, earlier in the spiritual journey "endure the pain" is absolutely the wrong spiritual guidance to give – not to mention that it can provide irreparable harm. When Christians endure this Unitive Way pain, they are spiritually simulating in their contemporary lives what Jesus went through. In addition, part of the Unitive Way pain emerges as the feeling of the "absence of God" which is also similar to what the apostles experienced. At the end of his life, Jesus told his followers that they would experience his absence for a while. Then later when they would see him, no one would be able to take their joy away from them.[24] [John 16:22] Christians are faithfully remaining in the presence of the one who has loved them most perfectly – regardless of internal feelings and outward circumstances – with trust and love. Christians still deeply desire God; they have purified their lives; and they have lived faithfully. Now is the time simply to practice trust, to stay the course, to hold the line... to abide and stay in love.

PAIN AND THE SPIRITUAL JOURNEY

After Christians have said that they choose to live for God and be united eternal with God, God will do whatever is necessary to enable that to happen – and that includes using pain. Accordingly, pain can be an indicator of what God is encouraging. Assuming that God is using (or causing) the pain in a Christian's life, then using the second half of the "Spiritual Growth Triage Chart" (Graphic 15) is appropriate. This chapter on "Dealing with Pain" has focused on the physical and psychological pain that stops Christians temporarily from traveling the Spiritual Road. In addition, the experience of spiritual darkness that typically occurs at the end of each of the Three Ways is also very painful. I have included how these Dark Nights integrate into the pain discussed in this chapter.

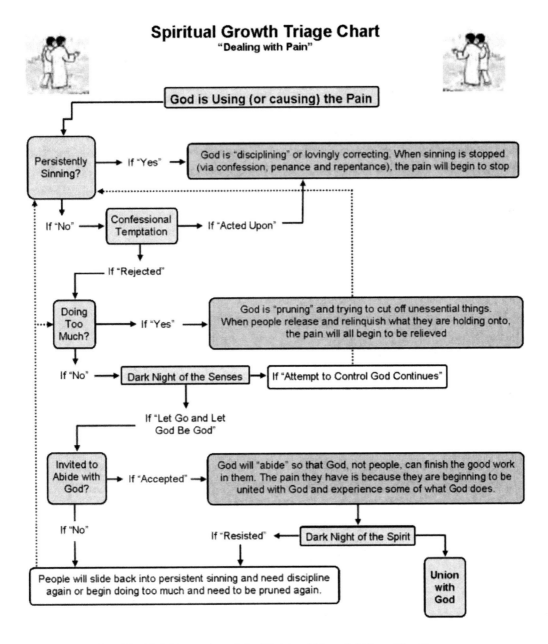

Graphic 15: This portion of the "Spiritual Growth Triage Chart" how God is using pain to encourage spiritual growth.

If pain is determined to be used (or caused) by God for the good of people, first ask (discover) whether Christians have persistent sin in their lives. If "yes," then God is disciplining or lovingly correcting them. The process of confession, penance and repentance is needed and will begin to reduce the pain. Persistent sin is characteristic of the Pre-Christian Way. However, it often significantly re-occurs during the "Purging of Sins" process of the Purgative Way – until Christians adopt spiritual habits and mature into a basic trust of God.

If the answer is "no" persistent sin is present, then the pain has a different purpose. First, consider if Confessional Temptation, which typically occurs at the end of the Pre-Christian Way around the time of baptism but can happen later, is causing the pain. Confessional Temptation occurs when there is an enticement to not follow through on the original spiritual commitment. Christians are tempted to return to their former lives and/or compromise their faith and what it takes to be truly faithful. Confessional Temptation is removed by renewing commitment and seeking God to dispel the temptation. Acting on this Confessional Temptation will, of course, lead to persistent sin and increased pain.

If the pain is neither from persistent sin nor from Confessional Temptation, then consider if Christians are "doing too much." If the answer is "yes," the pain is about "releasing and relinquishing" some activities and practices in order to focus on God and what God desires. God is pruning these non-essentials. Accordingly, Christians need to cooperate by letting go and following God with increased singleness – and the pain will begin to subside.

If Christians have already greatly reduced life and oriented themselves toward God, they may be in the midst of the pain of the Dark Night of the Senses. This spiritual crisis will often mask as doubt or uncertainty, but it is truly about getting God to behave the way Christians have come to believe God should. For example, when praying in a particular manner will not elicit God's answer; or when serving the poor will not always bring God's blessings. The Dark Night of the Senses requires Christians to stop attempting to control their spiritual lives with sensate techniques – it is a letting go of tangible-finite ways to access God, which have become ways to "control" God. These learned spiritual attitudes need to be relinquished and released. The proper spiritual response is surrender, accepting that God cannot be controlled by whatever sensate behaviors Christians attempt. Refusing to let God be God will, of course, leads to Pharisaic sinfulness requiring CPR.

If Christians are neither participating in excessive activities nor obsessing on how to get God's favor, consider if Christians just need to "abide." In this Unitive Way time, God is inviting Christians to be satisfied with their spirituality – to rest in God and the Community of God. This time of "abiding" is an invitation to continue doing what they are doing faithfully. Their pain is connecting them with God; it is spiritual crucifixion. The pain of Good Friday is not relieved until Easter Sunday. This pain will move into the Dark Night of the Spirit, which God uses to unite Christians into oneness. Of course, any time during "Abiding," Christians can stop resting in God and return to persistent sin or doing too much. Accordingly, increased pain will return to guide Christians back onto the Spiritual Road.

In summary, this chapter is primarily for spiritual helpers so that they can assist travelers whose vehicles have stopped along the side of the Spiritual Road. Pain in Christians' lives will cause this engine trouble. But the problem is not pain; it is discerning the source of the pain in order to know what to do. While pain can come from different sources, once the personally experienced pain has been determined as being used (or caused) by God, then what God is attempting to communicate can be discerned according to where Christians are in the process of spiritual growth. Christians do not actually have to understand what God is doing in order to make progress. People will naturally move away from the pain and eventually toward God. Nevertheless, understanding what God is doing can certainly help people to cooperate with the working of the Holy Spirit. Hopefully, employing the process can facilitate spiritual helpers to keep Christians traveling the Spiritual Road.

THE FINISHING ANAOLGY

Jamie Rickert's piercing to the soul ballad "New Wine"[25] inspired this finishing analogy.

Lord, do I believe
That you're tearing from my hands the things I am dying to hold
And you're pouring me out 'till I'm empty, 'till I'm empty
And there is nothing inside anymore, Father, but you
Father, I do.
And the fresh new wine is so raw when it's young
Brings tears to the eyes and it burns on the tongue
And it carries the cries of the grapes that are ripped from the vine.
And the flesh has been torn from my back and my bone
My hide has been cut; my hide has been sown
For my Father has need of a new skin
Because he's making new wine

For decades now, Christian branches have been tied to a trellis, healthy and growing good grapes. They have been sapping up all of the spirit-energy that Jesus could give them from the vine. They have been saying to the vine grower, "Please prune me; I don't need these leaves, take them." Accordingly, Christians have produced more and better clusters of grapes. And now Christians are soaking up all of the fresh air and basking in the warmth of the sun longing to produce the greatest harvest that they can for God. However, the purpose of the Christian grape plant is not just to produce grapes – in Jesus' day it was to provide wine. How does this happen? The vine grower can use the same life-giving Spirit-energy that flows through both the vine and the branches into the grapes.

When the vine grower decides to rip the grapes from the vine, toss them into the wine vat and then stomp the juice out, Christians and Jesus begin to be mingled as one. And when the mixture is bottled into the new wine skin, Christians begin to feel it happening. They begin to experience the joy-filled, effervescent energy of the Spirit that occurs when they have become one with Christ. It is such a glorious moment that it is truly impossible to describe. Indeed, the vine grower has grape expectations for Christians. Thus, when God chooses to make wine and when Christians are ready, they will be graced with those moments of abiding in Jesus Christ, the Lord, where there is no pain and joy is savored forever. Amen.

CHAPTER 19

Words Can Sometimes …

"Words can sometimes, in moments of grace, attain the quality of deeds.[1]

When I was in seminary, I needed to take a course that fit into my tight schedule and the only one available was "Gestalt Therapy," which was taught by a local Christian psychiatrist. The course on gestalt therapy did not focus on the abrasive, even abusive, techniques that are often association with that particular therapy style. Instead, the direction was toward being aware of what was obvious and helping to bring it into the spotlight.

One day in class, the professor asked, "Do you know what a banana tastes like?" My classmates and I responded that of course we did. Unceremoniously, the professor brought out a bunch of bananas and proceeded to cut them into slices. After distributing a piece to each of us, he instructed, "I want you to taste only the outside of this banana slice and tell me what you experience." The banana's circumference had an almost bitter taste and a raspy-bland sensation. "Now," began the therapist. "Please, bite into the banana and tell me what the center of it tastes like." It was creamy-soft and incredibly sweet! I had never noticed the difference in taste or texture.

Our teacher was not particularly hungry or amicably providing the class with refreshments; he had an important point to make which I vividly recall after nearly forty years. Awareness is key! I learned a copious amount of transformative information from the class that has directly impacted my approach to spiritual guidance. I learned how to help people recall the details of an event so that they could enter into them and even experience what was previously unnoticed. Also, besides the teaching to remember the very first topics that were spoken when beginning a session because they would be related to the primary issue for the day, he also instructed to be aware of continuous words that were uttered, usually unknowingly.

What happens when people are not aware of the most obvious words they use repeatedly?

Travelers have gone down a road and encountered slip-covered signs with alternate messages like "detour" or "flagger ahead" or "stay in your lane." The official direction signs are temporarily covered to alert drivers of the unusual. However, occasionally, highway department workers have neglected to remove the "detour" signs and travelers are diverted through the countryside where the twists and turns are reminiscent of original Daniel Boone trails that seem to have no rhyme or reason for their directionless-ness. Words are signs. Words spoken become the signs that people follow, including misplaced detouring words. **When Christians repeat certain words or phrases, they can be misguided from the Spiritual Road and their relationship with God.** Indeed, repetitive words can "attain the quality of deeds" as they direct the course of action.

Like me, many people grew up with the childhood adage: "Sticks and stones can break my bones, but words will never hurt me." Well to set the record straight, that is not true! **Words are powerful and can hurt abominably!** People cannot always do something about the words that bullies and abusers use; but they certainly can be in charge of the damaging words that they say to themselves – especially if spiritual helpers enable them to become aware. Accordingly, spiritual helpers, who regularly accompany people, are advised to listen with their German Sheppard ears peaked and ready to hear the words that are continuously spoken. These words or phrases are directing the course of travel – some of them to dead ends. As most spiritual directors affirm, awareness is the beginning of all spiritual growth! Sometimes change can occur by just bringing to the travelers attention, "Is that the sign you want to follow? I think it may be leading you the wrong way."

Through the rest of this chapter, **I will list some of the typical words or phrases that Christians have unwittingly followed that send them in the wrong direction** and how to unveil God's original or intended signs so that travelers can get back on the Spiritual Road. <u>The tool of re-hanging and pointing to the proper spiritual sign is one of the most helpful and non-abrasive ways to assist spiritual travelers.</u> Almost always, these restrictive phrases influence a huge portion of people's daily activities. In fact, many people would rightly claim this tool is psychologically based. However more significantly, **the use of these words restrains God's movement in people's lives.** While this information is not particularly profound, when offered and applied into the lives of those who were unaware of what they were telling themselves, it will make all the difference in their world.

"I CAN'T"

When a dozen scouts were sent to the land of Canaan, which God had unconditionally promised was to belong to the people of Israel, the majority returned with horror stories of the extreme danger that existed there. However, Caleb focused on the goodness and the possibilities that God had in store for those who were not petrified by fear.[2] [Numbers 13:1-33] The "cannot" fear won the day. As a result, the people of Israel were again disobedient and wandered much longer in the wilderness. The same happens in the spiritual lives of those who perpetually say "I can't!" Relating the Old Testament story can provide the analogy that those who say "I can't do that" are likely to wander aimlessly for a long time.

Except in cases of obvious physical restrain **"I can't" means "I won't."** In my experience, over ninety-nine per cent of the time, "I can't" needs to be translated. Accordingly, I first draw attention to the fact that people have repeatedly spoken "I can't" by asking, "Do you know how many times you have said 'I can't' today?" They may or may not respond with a number. However, I will approximate a quantity, purposefully with a high estimate. Then, I will categorically inform people (a gestalt therapy technique) that the word "can't" doesn't exist, but that it has an alternative meaning. I will ask, "Do you know what it means?" And follow with the question, "Do you want to know what it means?" (This approach is intentionally very specific in its attempt to "evoke the will.") If they answer "no," I suggest we continue with what they were saying. If they answer "yes," then I respond, "It means 'I won't.' <u>Why don't you substitute 'I won't' for 'I can't' in what you were just saying and see how it sounds</u>?"

For example, people may say, "I can't tell him how I feel." Or "I can't do" that particular thing. Having them to translate their words to say: "I won't tell him how I feel." or "I won't do" that particular action puts the words into a totally different context. When they do, the results are often dramatic. **People realize that they have been refusing, not unable.** When people become aware that with the phrase "I can't" they are actually choosing to refuse or decline, then they can decide what they want to do. Their decision can become a free and clear choice, instead of obliviously heading in a direction they do not desire to go. The assistance that spiritual helpers can give is to guide people to become aware of how the words they are speaking are "deciding for them." God is neither consulted nor involved in such actions – awareness allows Christians to seek God's counsel.

Sally, a faithful Christian, was in the midst of difficult situation and seemed unable to make it any different. One day, she revealed that such conundrums tended to happen often to her and then she mimicked her typical prayer, "God, you know the situation I am in. I need your help. But I can't do it …" In truth, Sally actually knew what God wanted her to do, but she resisted, hoping that God would take charge. After the above "I can't" discussion, Sally realized that she was "unwilling to act." As she interpreted the words of her prayer, she said it was like "slamming the door in God's face!" Her willing unfaithfulness, as is typical, was related to fear. However, once Sally claimed that God was inviting her to act and that she was refusing to do so, she could address her "fear of failure." The conclusion became: Failing is the best thing that willing Christians can do – because they can learn! Not trying is the worst thing that unwilling Christians can do because they are failing to grow spiritually. They are feeling guilty, hiding and sinning against God.

Substituting "I won't" for "I can't" is always about engaging the personal will and making a clear choice. Freely and consciously choosing is a spiritual issue because, for

Christians, it includes consulting God. Relationship with God is based on personal choice to respond to God's Love and to build God's Holy Community.

In addition, how Christians act toward others determines whether or not the Holy Community is strengthened. When Christians choose to reject others or refuse to do what God desires, the Community of God is not built. By saying phrases like "I can't help" or "I can't forgive" or "I can't tell them they were wrong," Christians are making unaware "choices" against strengthening the community that God wants. God allows people to say "I won't." However, if they are unaware of the choices they are making, they never understand that they are following the wrong road signs. **Thus, the phrase "I can't" functionally detours Christians off the Spiritual Road; and they don't even know they are going the wrong direction**.

"I DON'T KNOW" ... "I DON'T BELIEVE IT"

Endlessly repeating "I don't know" will make people think of themselves as intellectually-challenged. Many people who use this phrase have been told that they are "stupid." The phrase "I don't know" keeps them not only from claiming what they know but also from increasing in knowledge. After helping people become aware of their repetition, I ask, "Do you believe that you are incapable of learning? Do you want to tell yourself that you are stupid? Saying 'I don't know' before you have tried is doing exactly that." I may even inquire, "Who told you that you were stupid?" At this point, I will usually assert, in the most specific ways as I can, how I know they are smart and capable. I will also affirm for them that "God don't make junk!" And I unequivocally tell them, "God made you loveable, capable and acceptable. I need to you know that about yourself." (Of course, people sometimes are ignorant of information, which is much different than being unable to know. Making this distinction may be necessary.) As conversation continues, people may begin to ramble out the phrase "I don't kn…" but stop themselves mid-word, smile and note, "I started to do it again, didn't I?" To such dramatic improvement, I will affirm, "You and I both know you did."

Occasionally, people who obliviously reiterate "I don't know" are doing so to keep themselves from claiming what they actually do know – a kind of self-imposed defense mechanism. If I suspect that this is the case, I will inquiry, "What is it that you don't want to let yourself know?" In those circumstances, what people do not want to admit is often exactly what God is attempting to communicate and inviting them to adopt. So, I might follow with the query, "What is it that God wants you to know about yourself?" In this case, their automatically spoken "I don't know" resists what God's teaching and is a form of disobedience.

A good portion of the Christian life is based on knowledge – especially when it comes to knowing and doing God's will. Accordingly, if people keep themselves from knowing, then they are limiting their spiritual progress. Jesus affirmed, "The truth will set you free."[3] [John 8:32] But when people keep themselves from knowing the truth or accepting the truth of God, they become unable or unwilling to follow where God leads.

"I don't believe it" is a related phrase that also provides such limitations. While this phrase is typically exclaimed about a surprise, it can have a similar effect to the above not knowing expression. **Repeatedly proclaiming "I don't believe it" encourages people to not accept the truth that is immediately before them**, even though it is obvious. Accordingly, when people become practiced at "not believing" tangible, sensate data, faith mysteries become increasingly difficult to accept. Spiritual helpers might encourage "I don't believe" people to express their surprise and/or delight instead of their inability to have "faith."

"I SHOULD" or "SHOULD NOT"

One of the most common limiting phrases that people declare is, "I should do that." I routinely respond with the antidote, "You can if you choose." In a situation where private conversation is possible, I might say, **"Using the word 'should' means you are following a rule** (that you don't want to observe)? Whose rule are you obeying?" Various explanations follow for the use of the word "should."

Some Christians who are repeating "should" are trying to talk themselves into doing what God (or the Bible) wants them to do. They may need more information or encouragement – but they have not decided to do so. Thus, the task of the spiritual helper is to accompany them through making a decision saying, "It sounds like you are wrestling with that subject. Would you like to figure out what is the best choice for you?" Where Christians are along the Spiritual Road is paramount to the guidance to be given. If people are on the Pre-Christian or Purgative Way, they need rules because the structure keeps them safe, secure and growing spiritually. To keep Christians on that part of the road, a person of authority may only need to say, "I recommend that you do it." Other people may only be seeking a deeper understanding of the rule they are already following. However, Christians who are beginning the Illuminative Way may need to question the previously-given rule, make it their own or even rebel against it. Spiritual helpers are advised to do whatever will keep them moving forward.

Some people may utter "should" as a form of unconscious resistance – they don't really want to do it but someone or something told them they are required to obey. When people feel obligated, without any choice, they rarely, or begrudgingly, agree to do whatever the "rule" necessitates. Even after they agree externally to follow the rule, internally they are already figuring out ways to not do so.

Thus, when working with mature adult Christians, spiritual helpers are advised to begin by getting those people to understand that their "should" is a rule and also to identify the source of the rule-giver. Sometimes Christians do not actually object to the rule but to the choice-less doing what they were told to do. Talking about the rule-provided obligation can assist them in making a choice – to do or not do it. On the other hand, a "should or should not" may be an objection to the authoritative person who gave the rule. In the process of psycho-social developmental people in their twenties are breaking free of the authorities so that they can become individualized. Sometimes simply because "mom" or the "pastor" gave them a rule is reason why they resist it. In such cases, Christians need to be freed from those authorities so they can make their own choice. So, I may say, "If you blindly obey your mother's rule, then she is in charge of your life. Do you want to give her the power to do that? Of course, not. But you know, just because she told you to do something is not a good reason to reject the rule which may very good for you. You are free to choose; and God needs you to be free to choose."

Rules, as foundations not obligations, have their place in Christianity – they bring people to Christ and they enable people to follow faithfully. However, the phrase "I should become a Christian" may indicate that a rule or a rule-giver is inhibiting the action. The apostle Paul affirms that the Law (the holy "should") brings people to the personal knowledge of being sinful[4] – which affords people the choice of accepting Jesus as Savior or not [Romans 3:20b]. The preaching of the rule itself cannot make that happen; but becoming a Christian and following Christ need to be about choice. Thus, people need to personally appropriate the rules. Mindlessly saying "I should" can certainly indicate that people are resisting – following a sign that does not lead toward God. Identifying the rule and the rule-giver may free people to choose.

Spiritual helpers need to be aware of when the "should" is helping the process of Christian spiritual growth and when it is repelling people away. Either way enabling people to make a decision about the "should" or "should not" in their vocabulary is paramount.

"BUT" … "MAYBE" … "PERHAPS" … "I THINK"

Spiritual travelers who use these kinds of words repetitively keep themselves from clarity or making any decision. These words typically introduce alternatives and objections which have a limiting or qualifying effect and hinder people from being assertive individuals. Such repetitive qualifiers prevent people from making choices. In fact, when people employ such words or phrases, they resist accepting or agreeing with everyone – including God.

These words, spoken either intentionally or unconsciously, keep people stuck. When people "refuse" to choose, they cannot intentionally move forward in their thinking or in their lives. Using such words may be a form of "protection" that defends against dealing with internally-felt pain of a past event. On the other hand, some people may refuse to take a stand because they do not want to have to defend their position or be accused of being wrong. Regardless whether the internal motivation comes from fear, pain or genuine uncertainty, repeating these limiting or qualifying words maintains the status quo.

Spiritual helpers who experience such contrarians can be helpful by simply drawing attention to the fact that they seem to be refusing to make a decision. Truly, some people may not be ready or willing to move forward in their lives. And that certainly is a valid choice that can be made. Spiritual helpers may assist them to say, "I do not want to make a decision about that right now." On the other hand, some people may be unaware of the stop-gap words they are uttering. Spiritual helpers can encourage assist them by saying, "God loves you and will not reject you. I will accept whatever you say. Just say something definite." God does not desire people to be trapped. Remaining stuck, especially with self-imposed words, is limiting God and refusing to let God to work in their lives. Instead, God wants people to move forward in their personal relationship with God and in their lives.

Daniel was a fifty-five-year-old ordained minister, who had not officially served a congregation for eight years due to a family tragedy, personal illness and being released from a distressing congregation. He was victimized by external life pain and a mostly dysfunctional congregation who when their pastor couldn't serve, jettisoned him. Daniel was in the process of seeking to serve as leader in a congregation. While the recovery both physically and emotionally had not been easy, Daniel was making good progress.

One day during a spiritual direction session, Daniel's very first word in multiple sentences was "But." His spiritual director brought awareness to this fact and Daniel immediately attempted to stop that habit because he realized that it was inappropriate. However, the underlying purpose of this objecting word was still to emerge. Shortly after ending the use of the word "But," Daniel started to accuse his guide of being critical and exacting. He stopped in mid-thought when he realized that they had previously talked through this issue to include that the guide was absolutely on his side and the guide's questions were only in an attempt to completely understand what Daniel was experiencing. As the conversation turned to all that Daniel was doing to secure a new pastoral position, Daniel erupted and broke into a flood of tears, "It feels like God is punishing me!!!" Comfort and consolation was the only appropriate response.

The pain that Daniel experienced came from both external circumstances as well as being externally-inflicted by others. However, he had internalized it and comingled it with a long-held sense of insecurity and feelings of inadequacy that he had previously seemed to have overcome. Daniel was verbal, intelligent and pretty angry albeit with a smile. His "but" enabled him in this resistance and kept him from "facing" his pain. <u>The use of "but" provided a legitimate way to object intellectually, but limited his ability to face the underlying emotional and spiritual issues</u>. Until Daniel stopped objecting, he would not move forward into the love of God, the affirmations of his spiritual helper or his own freely made choices.

In order to move forward with their lives, people need to stop leading with their "but." The same is true for other excessively used words such as "maybe," "perhaps" and "I think" that qualify, limit and object. Often, simply drawing attention to the use of such words will allow people to follow the correct road sign and start heading in the right direction. At the very least, spiritual helpers can help people be clear that they are <u>choosing</u> to object to everything. Making a choice, any choice, means people are beginning to be unstuck. While these words of delimitation may indicate a deeper problem, the invitation to be definitive can be helpful.

"H/SHE MADE ME FEEL/THINK/DO IT"

"He made me feel angry" or "She hurt me" are examples of misplaced emotions that shift the responsibility for them. They totally change the focus and make it nearly impossible to grow spiritually. The first sentence, "He made me feel angry," is easier to understand than the second sentence, "She hurt me," which effectively hides the feelings under a layer of "justifiably" external-inflicted pain. These types of sentences are such an epidemic in common ever day conversation that dealing with them in that context is nearly impossible. However, within the parameters of spiritual guidance, they most certainly need direct attention.

The structure and dynamics of the above sentences claim that emotions have been imposed which makes other people or circumstances the cause of this action. **People do not like to admit to negative emotions (and sometimes even positive ones) so they use words that deflect their origin and the responsibility for them**. "He made me mad" claims that some male caused a negative feeling and that emotion suddenly materialized within the person making the claim. When emotions are not at fever pitch, basic clarifying questions can help: "Who feels mad?" and "Who is responsible for that feeling?" Indeed, as a result of a particular event initiated by someone else, I may feel mad … but they did not cause that feeling to occur in me. Simple evidence of this unpopular conclusion is that someone else experiencing the same event may have a totally different feeling or response.

Emotions belong to the people who feel them and they are ultimately responsible with whatever they do with them. The tragedy of "He made me mad" is that people have transferred their personal feeling onto someone else AND with it the ability to do anything about that feeling. They have given away their own power to do whatever they might choose to do with that emotion. As long as this condition exists, they will be trapped, unable to change – only blame others. **The sign of "blame" is the wrong road sign to follow in order to remain on the Spiritual Road**. Blame, akin to unforgiveness, stops the flow of God's power into people's lives.

<u>Spiritual helpers who assist others to take back their emotions and to take responsibility for them are pointing the direction to God</u>. When people regain this personal power, God

can assist in deciding what to do with those feelings. In this process, spiritual helpers need to affirm that emotions are indicators that something is wrong and in themselves are neither good nor bad. It is ok to have the feeling; but what is done with that feeling may not be. I like the unequivocal translation of Ephesians 4:26a "Be angry; but do not sin."[5] In addition, when people reclaim their emotions, they are accepting the truth about themselves. Since truth is a quality of God, people are more aligned with God.

"YOU" and "THEY"

During spiritual conversation when people are describing the consequences of thoughts, feelings or actions, they may begin to use the words "you" or "they." For example: "When you get mad, you get all red in the face and say things that you regret and inflict damage that affects your relationships." Talking about someone else is usually easier than talking about one's self. In addition, such deflection makes what is said impersonal. Substituting the word "I" in place of the words "you" or "they" changes the emphasis, makes it personal and inherently provides the possibility that change can occur.

People who are not prone to action or who are thinkers may tend to use "you" or "they" in an unconscious way to avoid action or feeling what is internal. Reminding people to use the first person singular language of "I" can help them to be able to take the action that God wants them to take or to process the feelings that will eventually cause harm or sin.

"IF ONLY" and "WHAT IF"

People who continuously use the phrase "if only such and such had not happened" are hoping that the past would change. Clearly, by definition, the past cannot be changed and endlessly wishing that the past would have been different is neither productive nor helpful. However, when people use lots of "if only" phrases, something about their past is bothersome. Helping them to identify what that is can be helpful. Ask: "What is it about the past that makes it difficult for you to live freely in the present?" This question hopefully brings forth a hidden subject that either contains unprocessed emotions or needs to be acknowledged as unchangeable. Without addressing such issues, spiritual travelers will remain stuck following signs that do not lead forward.

People who continuously use the phrase "what if such and such might happen" want to plan for every possible option. People who have this desire are typically afraid of something ... the unknown, failure, displeasing and so forth. As a result, they want to anticipate or control all possible consequences. They may not realize that to be the case, but it is usually true. Thus, helping them to see the futility and impossibility of the task they have set out for themselves by using "what if" may move them forward. The spiritual issue of "what if" is attempting to "be like God" and know everything like God knows. To know everything that God knows is not the way to God ... following faithfully is.

"I HAVE NO CHOICE"

A very difficult phrase to counter is "I have no choice" because it is often spoken in situations where no "good" choice is an option. Nevertheless, **asserting choice is essential for spiritual movement – it keeps people from feeling trapped and limits their ability to blame others**. A physician may assert, "You have no choice but to have the surgery." However, people do have the choice to die. It may not be as good of choice for a twenty-eight-year-old as it is for an eighty-eight-year-old ... but the choice needs to be affirmed and a decision clearly made.

Some people in the midst of a stressful situation may not be able to identify their choices. Spiritual helpers can patiently assist them to sort and clarify. Even if the conclusions would not be altered, the process can be affirming and assertive for people. When people make a full-knowledge choice, they gain a sense of freedom and strength, which can actually assist them for better consequences. For example, research confirms that people who placate to surgery have a more difficult recovery process than those who have a healthy anxiety but have chosen to proceed with it.

In addition, making a choice, even a limited one, places the responsibility where it belongs ... with the person affected. If "the doctor (or pastor) told me I had to do it," they can be blamed and the blamer's individual spiritual growth comes to a halt. Spiritual helpers keep people on the spiritual path when they encourage and assist people to make clear and free choices. Affirming that people have a choice, even though none of the options are positive, is a spiritual practice that honors the soul-self that God has created. Even surrender is a choice.

"I FEEL SO GUILTY"

When people are truly guilty, the only revitalization is to be forgiven and proclaimed so. The process of confession-penance-repentance followed by absolution accomplishes this purpose. Obtaining this from other people is important; but it is essential to receive forgiveness from God. The process for forgiveness is elucidated in chapter seventeen. **However, when the phrase "I feel guilty" comes forth repeatedly in spiritual conversation, then spiritual helpers need to suspect that the people are not truly guilty, even though they absolutely feel guilt. They have pseudo-guilt, which is a major spiritual problem.**

Real guilt comes when people have broken a rule or violated a trust. Thus, the easy way to determine true guilt from pseudo-guilt is to ask, "What law have you broken?" If a rule can be identified, then CPR is needed. If, however, people have not broken the rules, they ARE NOT guilty, they only FEEL guilty. **It is an offense for which they cannot be forgiven**. Thus, pseudo-guilt continues endlessly, causing a multitude of spiritual issues, until it is released. Typically, those who experience pseudo-guilt are on the Purgative Way and respond positively to authority figures. Thus, spiritual helpers are advised to categorically proclaim: "You are not guilty" of whatever has been perceived to be violated.

Sometimes people suffering from the condition of pseudo-guilt do not believe that either they deserve to be forgiven or that God is actually able to do so. Some faith traditions that specialize in the purging of sins have a culture in which Christians can become oversensitive to the task of purging sins and see sin everywhere. The confessor of Martin Luther told him in no uncertain terms to not return unless he had something more to confess than "broken pencils" and after he had read the book of Romans. As a result, Luther became famous for emphasizing the phrase that people are saved by "faith alone," which is better translated that people are saved by God's grace through faith alone.

The spiritual prescription for this state of mind is to strongly proclaim the love of God for people and deemphasize their sinfulness. Spiritual helpers might ask, "Is the love of God stronger or weaker than the sin you have?" The follow up question is, "So, God is able to forgive whatever you have done?" Then, move to the conviction, "Will you believe that, right now?" **When Christians accept that the grace of God can remove their sins (and have asked) but still feel guilty, they suffer from pseudo-guilt**. Thus, spiritual helpers can inquire, "If God has taken your sin and guilty away, what could be the reason you still have it? Could it be that you have not release it even though God is trying to take it away?" Of course, this attempt to release the pseudo-guilt can "make people feel guiltier" which indicates that they are in charge of the guilt, not God or the spiritual helper.

Pseudo-guilt creates a dysfunctional relationship with God. It inadvertently takes God's power away. It destroys people's ability to approach God. Pre-Christian Way people need the "Identification of Sin;" but if they do so without the "Acceptance of Grace," they can become trapped in guilt that they will not let be taken away. Spiritual helpers need to discern whether the emphasis is best placed on sin or grace, guilt or forgiveness, depending on the circumstances and the personality of each individual.

"I DON'T CARE"

Occasionally in spiritual conversation, people will respond with "I don't care" to the request to state an opinion or to make a choice. However, people who say this really do care and often have an opinion; they just do not make a choice. Their motivation may vary between believing that others are more important or thinking that they are not significant enough/deserving enough to have what they desire. Accordingly, they do not choose and consequently feel like a prisoner in their own life. Eventually, they feel trapped, hurt and angry which gets unconsciously released on those around them, most often in passive-aggressive ways. Then, of course, they feel guilty about their actions, withhold their choices and reiterate, "I don't care." And the cycle repeats.

<u>Spiritual helpers need to affirm that the choice of those they accompany does matter and that they want to hear what it is</u>. After making such a sincere request, silence is best. Wait until the person speaks may take a long time since they are accustomed to defaulting to the words of others. <u>Spiritual helpers who do so are modeling that God wants to hear what these folks think and feel</u>.

CONCLUSION

Dealing with these words or phrases may bring to the surface major life issues that require the assistance of a psychotherapist. The role of the spiritual helper, in listening carefully, is to help identify repetitive ways that Christians in unawareness follow the wrong road signs. The goal is to be able to point the way back onto the Spiritual Road whether spiritual helpers do that or other professionals are needed.

A chart (Graphic 16) can quickly summarize repeated words that debilitate, the effect they have, the alternative or words to substitute as well as the change that will result.

Repeated Word	Effect	Alternative	Change
I can't	Claims inability or impotence	Substitute "I won't"	Evokes personal will/ strength so choice can be made
I don't know; I don't believe it	Makes people feel intellectually challenged	Stop speaking the phrases	Allows people to claim what they know and gain ability to learn
I should; I should not	Following an unconscious rule	Identify the "rule-giver"	Makes free to choose whether to accept/ follow that rule
But; maybe; perhaps; I think	Places automatic limitations or qualifications on actions or what is thought	Stop automatic use of words. Live in the present moment trusting God (and self) to protect and be in charge.	Opens the range of possibilities and alternatives
S/he made me angry (feel)	Blames others for one's own feelings	Substitute "I feel" for "made me feel"	Restores personal responsibility for one's own emotions and thus the ability to change them
You; They	Deflection makes what is said impersonal	Substitute the word "I"	Personalizes and allows for change to occur
If only; What if	Living in the past or future that inhibits current movement	Identify past or future hurt/fear that is not real in the present moment	Stress reduced and movement enabled when past is released and future is open
I have no choice	Feeling trapped or hopeless	Affirm individual choice (even if options are limited)	Restores sense of control and freedom
I feel so guilty (if it is pseudo-guilt)	Endless cycle of guilt feelings	Identify that no rule has been violated	Release from self-imposed punishment
I don't care	Refusing to make a choice	Affirm that personal options matter and give permission and time	People become alive to personal preference

Graphic 16: These repetitive words and phrases hinder progress in the spiritual journey. Alternatives bring change.

Words, especially the ones people continuously say to themselves, can strongly influence what they believe or feel and how they live. **All of the self-repetitive words or phrases highlighted in this chapter, because they are used to refuse clarity, limit God from bringing truth into people's lives**. When this happens, people need to change which is always about making a new choice. Thus, working with Christians to strengthen their ability to clearly choose has been much of the focus of this chapter. However, making people strong assertive individuals is NOT the ultimate goal the Christian life. On the other hand, having a strong sense of self is essential in order to surrender to God – to freely and fully acknowledge God as the Creator, Redeemer and Sustainer. Whenever people use unhelpful words and phrases that they mindlessly repeat, they are following the wrong signs that cause them to wander off the Spiritual Road. Spiritual helpers can draw attention to people's delimiting words and invite them to make choices. Nevertheless, whether they do so or not must always be their choice.

CHAPTER 20

"That's What the Lonely Is For"

When traveling the Spiritual Road, people can end up on the inside lane of a round-about and endlessly circle; or they can be speeding down a superhighway for the longest stretches of time without any changes. The result is a feeling of exhaustion for doing the same things over and over, even good things. From this sense of monotony questions arise about "Why am I doing this?" or "What is the purpose of it all?" or "Why do I seem to be going nowhere fast?" Regardless of the level of activity in which Christians participate, a mostly indescribable and indiscernible feeling invades like a blob monster and covers over all. Some people have called it melancholy, the blahs or a sense of loneliness. Whatever the description, this condition causes a serious spiritual problem about which spiritual helpers need to be aware, especially because travelers do not always recognize what is happening.

The spiritual problem is: Christians believe that all of the good ways <u>they are striving</u> to live will fulfill their relationship with God. Yet in the midst of living, they feel a vague, but persistent anxiety. **Christians long for something that keeps eluding them**. This uneasy feeling, described above, is actually a clue that they are on a spiritual growing edge.

This chapter's title was inspired by a secular song, "That's What the Lonely Is For"[1] when sung by the Christian group, "GLAD."[2] The song centers on the longing desire that people have which lures them onward to envision unknown dreams and wishes. Picturing people as a castle, this longing is characterized as an empty room – a loneliness feeling in the midst of positive living. The conclusion is that this room has been created and put there on purpose; and when people feel lonely it means that they are being beckoned forward. The chorus affirms:

When I get lonely
That's only a sign some room is empty
And that room is there by design
If I feel hollow
That's just my proof
That there's more for me to follow
That's what the lonely is for.

The "loneliness" can happen at any place along the Spiritual Road although it typically culminates in a sort of Great Loneliness after mid-life – often popularly labeled as a "mid-life crisis." Philosophically, it is identified in the Heidegger Question, "Why is there something rather than nothing?"[3] Or in its more personal form, "Who am I if I were nothing at all?" While the "lonely" always contains an element of anticipatory "non-being," **people experience the "lonely" as the need for someone or something to fill a longing that has crept into their lives**. However, this "lonely" cannot be specified because it is a defused, non-descript emptiness. For example, people might say, "I want something; I just don't know what."

The "lonely" borders on and is often confused with depression or fear, but it is neither. Identifying the "lonely" is often complicated because depression or fear can occur at the same time. Accordingly, **both the psychological malaise and the spiritual condition need to be addressed**. Clinical depression has specific criteria to determine its diagnosis.[4] Fear necessitates a specific phobic object or subject; and people can either flee or fight it. Certainly, spiritual helpers need to consider these options as an issue for those they accompany. However with the "lonely," people experience a hard to nail down feeling of uneasiness which communicates that something is wrong.

As a result of this unidentifiable loneliness, people feel anxious in a general sort of way. In fact, one major difference between fear and anxiety is that fear has an object but anxiety does not. Because the "lonely" is built into the human condition and happens to everyone, philosophical theologians, like Paul Tillich, have labeled it "existential anxiety." Tillich defined it as "the state in which a being is aware of its possible nonbeing."[5] Anxiety accompanies this condition. Even though people rarely say, "I feel like non-being is coming to get me," they do experience a sense of "lonely" anxiousness. **Existential anxiety is not solvable, resolvable or fixable in any traditional or humanly contrived way. But it does have a purpose – to draw people to God. That's what the lonely is for**. One of the most important observations that spiritual helpers can make is to identify that the "lonely" is a God-created state of being that cannot be eliminated, just lived into.

"That's What the Lonely Is For" makes lyrical the state of being that all people, who are spiritually sensitive, experience. The empty room is where God resides within the castle of the Self; and just when people are ready to open the door to that room, God instantly builds another room and moves into that place. Interestingly, St. Teresa of Avila described individual Christians and their journey to God in terms of a castle. Teresa's book, The Interior Castle,[6] is a guide for spiritual development, inspired by her vision of the soul as a crystal globe in the shape of a castle containing seven mansions, which she interpreted as the journey of faith through seven stages, ending with union with God.[7] As illustrated in both Wilcox's song and Teresa's book, people are always lured to discover God, who cannot be captured even in castle-sized people. The "room of loneliness" means that there is more.

During the same monotonous stretches of highway, Christians feel blah, uncertain, and even seemingly depressed. Especially in the case of long-term Christians, this uneasiness is most often not the fault of the church or the preacher … it is the "lonely." **Christians experience uncertainty as they look at the end of earthly life, not being ok with the mistakes they have made and even doubting what they have found most meaningful**. People in this condition may have a few problems in their life but nothing that really needs to be fixed, emotionally or spiritually. Effectively, people feel empty, lonely and a little lost – although as "good" Christians, they are unlikely to admit this. If they have a sense that they are basically ok but still don't know why they feel so unsettled, they need to seek spiritual counsel from someone who understands that what they are experiencing is part of the spiritual condition and not something that needs to be fixed! **When spiritual helpers encounter Christians with long-term or continuous uneasiness that does not seem to have a solution, they would be wise to suspect existential anxiety – a "loneliness" that is drawing people closer to God**.

While a being-lured-toward-God feeling can be experienced all along the Spiritual Road, the "lonely" is primarily identified after mid-life. People can have a "lonely" feeling on the Pre-Christian Way before they come to accept God and receive the gift of God in Jesus Christ – although this is better understood as the "Hound of Heaven"[8] pursuit. In this case, God seeks to get people's attention in order that they might face their need for God. Christians can also have an uneasy uncertainty when they are tempted to return to their previous life – but this is better identified as the Confessional Temptation. In this situation, God allows a sense of the demonic to invite new Christians back to their former lives.

However, the experience of the Dark Night of the Senses most closely resembles the "lonely." This darkness comes as a result of attempting to access, even manipulate, God in ways that had previously worked well in producing positive feelings and effective two-way communication with God in prayer. These no longer happen when they are "supposed" to transpire because God will not allow them "on demand." The Dark Night of the Senses typically begins by making ineffective the practices, the things that Christians do, to connect with God. Some spiritual teachers note that after or as these external practices are being purified, Christians' internal attitudes go through the same process. The "lonely" most closely mimics this needed attitudinal adjustment. As such, these long-term **Christians are not in danger of losing the faith expressions they have; but they have become stagnant or have reached a dead end because of the spiritual approach they have brought to both their lives and their relationship with God**. (Also, if Christians make it to the Dark Night of the Spirit, they have already confronted the "lonely" and know that this darkness is not it.)

Christians who are strongly focused on God will travel naturally through the spiritual stages. When they encounter the Dark Night of the Senses, they will normally

experience a sense of the "lonely." However, the "lonely" will also occur to even those who have not been intentional in following the Christian life; and God gets their attention at least for a while. In addition, some people can go through life without extraordinary pain or major problems. When this occurs, they do not feel the intensity of pain described in chapter eighteen, "Dealing with Pain," that causes reflection and changes in behavior. Pain can bring people to a greater emphasis on God and narrow the focus of their life activities, and even change their attitudes. However, if pain does not bring this fruition, then the "lonely" keeps gnawing a hole in the soul until people know that something is wrong. **Accordingly, the "lonely" is existential – part of being human – and its accompanying anxiety is designed to stop people from speeding through life in order to recognize their potential non-being and pay greater attention to God.**

A traditional example of a man running into existential anxiety comes in the description of the accumulation of multiple "boy toys" – new car, a boat, second home in the Hamptons, and so forth. He buys what he thinks will satisfy his craving and discovers that that the new item does not fill the emptiness; so he purchases the next obsession only to find it does not fulfill him either. Of course, the wealthier the people the longer it takes to conclude that possessions cannot provide the contentment they crave. With such realization, people often turn to "making the world a better place." Their mantra becomes, "It's not what you get but what you give that makes the difference." While this new approach is more laudable, it is most often simply a transfer from the use of physical things to satisfy them into how others remember them for their service or giving; it may also take the form of seeking personal fulfillment via believing that the difference they have made will last. The problem is that **people never become satisfied – either with the things they buy, the accolades they receive or the amount of good they do**. The spiritual guidance question of "When is enough, enough?" receives the answer "It is never enough." People experience what I call an "emotional black hole" which can only be filled via God.

RESPONDING TO THE "LONELY"

In regard to recognizing the "lonely," **I have discovered four primary topics: certainty, guilt, meaning and death**. If spiritual helpers encounter people who are unsuccessfully attempting to deal with these issues, they might suspect that the real problem is the "lonely." Indeed, people cannot fill the emptiness brought on by the "lonely." The spiritual responses to these four issues are: No amount of knowledge can obtain absolute truth; no amount of good can remove underlying guilt; all meaning is situational and changes; and all life ends.

Responding to each of these four typical existential anxiety issues with helpful spiritual guidance is relatively simple. **First**, spiritual helpers need to assist Christians in concluding that the issue is not fixable because it is innate to what it means to be a finite human being;

and advise travelers to stop trying to chase the wind. "Then I applied myself to the under-standing of wisdom, and also of madness and folly, but I learned that this, too, is a chasing after the wind."[9] [Ecclesiastes 1:17] No human effort can ever satisfy the "lonely." **Second**, Christians, employing this kind of surrender, need to do so without any sense of fate or destiny, but in faith as a way to be held "underneath the everlasting arms" of God. Christians must respond with radical trust – to live in God without certainty, guiltlessness, clear meaning or proof of new life. **Third**, Christians need to assert particular God-affirmations to their explicit anxiety-laden concerns. In other words, they need a self-talk statement that avows their faith. "I trust in God for ultimate knowledge, absolute absolution, perfect pur-pose and life after death." In fact, spiritual helpers might ask those they accompany what affirmation comes to mind and use that statement for their manta. **Finally**, spiritual helpers whether they admit it or not have the tendency to want to fix those they accompany – even though they may call it enabling, facilitating or helping. Thus, spiritual helpers must sur-render to this fact in order to recognize and be able to decline to fix existential anxiety in others. Truly, only God knows the absolute truth. Only God can absolve all guilt. Only God determines ultimate meaning. Only God can guarantee new life.

Most assuredly, Christian travelers experiencing existential anxiety can fall into a sense of hopelessness especially when they choose the path of radical surrender. **While iden-tifying the inability to solve this human condition, spiritual helpers are advised to end the discussion with a focus on radical hope!** Accordingly, nurturing the deep-seated hope that is God and fundamental to God's character is extremely important. Even though Christians cannot change the uneasiness that existential anxiety brings, they can be content with hope. Before Mother Teresa would begin performing small acts of kindness that made no foreseeable difference in the big picture poverty of Calcutta, she would spend over an hour each morning connecting with the promises of God and the picture of Jesus; then she would go into the world to find and serve the divine. She did not need to do (or even try to do) great actions because she was assured with the hope that God would work effectively in her small endeavors.

The letter to the Romans is clear that after all of Christians' strivings, it is hope that will not disappoint them because hope is intimately connected with the love that God pours into the very being of Christians.[10] [Romans 5:3-5] In other words, because Christians have received the love of God, then they have also received the hope that is in God. **Hope is part of the very nature of God; and truly, the qualities and character of God will never be dissolved. Indeed, what God loves will be loved. What God hopes for will happen. The will of God shall be accomplished; and on that, Christians can hope** – regardless whether they know the truth, feel guiltless, have ultimate meaning or are at perfect peace with dying. Just because Christians no longer focus on striving to make the Community of God happen by their own efforts does not change the fact that God will continue faithfully make it happen. In fact, without the burden of feeling excessively responsible to succeed,

Christians become more content, even pliable, and God can use them even more effectively. The hope of God enlivened in the human heart is all the cooperation that God needs to do the work.

Hope is real. Hope is the vehicle God uses to sustain Christians through the unknown. While hope cannot be seen, it can be envisioned. Hope comes as God is in charge of birthing the New Creation into being. Thus, imagining the promise of the wolf living with the lamb and the lion lying down with the calf as a little child plays with the poisonous snakes in peacefulness and harmony is a way to allow hope to guide Christians forward.[11] [Isaiah 11:6-9] God will bring all things to perfect completion. The picture of the New Heaven and the New Earth are assured.[12] Holding that vision is a simple and effective way to realize hope. Indeed, "Where there is no vision, the people perish."[13] [Proverbs 29:18] A vision is the preferred picture of the future – God's future. Help travelers see it and live toward it because they are God's children whom God wants to come home. "Dear friends, now we are children of God, and what we will be has not yet been made known. But we know that when he appears, we shall be like him, for we shall see him as he is. Everyone who has this hope in him purifies himself, just as he is pure."[14] [I John 3:2-3] **Spiritual helpers need to leave those in the midst of existential anxiety with hope – hope in the character and promises of God!**

CHASING CERTAINTY

People want to know for sure. People feel anxious when they do not know. **People have existential anxiety when they sense that they are always going to be in a perpetual state of unknowing**.

When I was studying philosophy in college, I noticed the endless progression of thinkers who took what their predecessors had said and provided correction or additions in order to state "the truth." This process of striving for the unobtainable truth has continued throughout human history. Nevertheless, coming to knowledge is not a bad thing. In fact earlier in the Christian life, "Learnings" and Clarifications" are highly recommended as the way to grow in faith. **The problem comes when this pursuit of knowledge becomes either an obsession or an expression of finality**.

Mariette is a mature Christian who owns tens of thousands of religious books which she has read multiple times. Her knowledge and ability to quote scholars and ideas is extremely impressive. Despite nearing retirement, she continues to acquire more volumes, attend more lectures and engage in deep academic conversation ad nauseam. While much understanding has been gained, certainty has not been obtained. Every answer seems to bring additional questions. Consequently, Mariette is very unsatisfied with her ability and her knowledge. She actually knows far more than I could ever hope to forget; but she still wants to know more and obtain truth – although she would likely counter that assertion with an intellectual argument. She is in the midst of existential anxiety viewed in her chasing certainty. It is a very "lonely" place.

On the other hand, **other people strive for perfect precision with rules or systems of clarity** from Christian Fundamentalism to the rigors of science. When Christians try to obtain truth, they rarely see it as a problem – just filling their lives with knowledge to obtain certainty, as well as information and ideas that bring exactness. This laudable beginning-goal can evolve into a strictly followed religious system of rigid rules. Sometimes Christians will go to great effort to build and maintain such a system so as not to be wrong. Jesus objected to the Pharisees' attempts to do this. I am convinced that he did not object primarily because he did not like them (he valued some) or that the rules were bad (he used many). Jesus criticized their approach of trying to contain God within their strict system of knowledge and requirements. Nevertheless, **God is not about to be known until God is ready to be known which does not occur until after Christians have completely stopped trying to know for certain**.

A very intelligent elder in one congregation where I served used a quick analogy to illustrate obtaining truth. He would put a chalk dot on a blackboard to indicate what one person believed was the truth. He would put a second dot on the same plane some distance to the right of the first dot. Then, he would state, "This represents the distance we are from each other's understanding of the truth." Subsequently, this elder would place a third chalk dot far above the first two dots to make a kind of tall acute triangle saying, "This point represents what God knows to be the absolute truth. We are actually closer to each other in our understandings than we are to God or absolute truth."

This analogy can speak to people on different levels. However, for those in the "lonely" chase after certainty, it can assist them to acknowledge that they, even working with others or through the "perfect" system, cannot obtain ultimate truth. Admitting to uncertainty after years of accumulating facts or relying on a particular scheme is not failure, but divine success! It is like taking limited wisdom, laying it down before the throne of God in humble surrender and saying, "I know nothing that makes any real difference. Please bring me into your Truth."

RELIEVING THE GUILT

People want to be good and feel good. People feel anxious when they are going to be caught doing something wrong (even bad). **People have existential anxiety when they sense that they cannot be relieved or released from the guilt they feel, even if they have been forgiven**. (The condition of existential guilt should not be confused with pseudo-guilt or toxic shame. Pseudo-guilt clearly identifies actions and attitudes about which people "feel" guilty, but are not. Toxic shame's assertion of "I am no good" arises from externally inflicted pain, typically in early childhood, which results in a near continuous state of unworthiness. On the other hand, existential guilt is a non-specific state of being that occurs when people compare themselves with God's holiness.)

While I belong to the group of people who believe that God births every person into this world as sinless and created good, I also believe that children inevitably, and often quickly, "fall from grace" so that their existential experience is of being sinful, bad and inadequate. Life is the journey of correcting those feelings and moving back to the original intent of God for people at birth. The overview of the Spiritual Road process includes coming to a saving faith, aligning life with God's ways, developing a solid and strong sense of Self so as to finally surrender it in the Dark Nights. These tasks can only be accomplished in relationship with God – actually, God does the work if and only if we cooperate. Sometimes, Christians attempt to fill the angst of lingering guilt, inadequacy and condemnation by helping others and making the world a better place to live. However, **even after a life has been lived well, a sense of guilt in moments of reflection still remains**.

I remember the elderly woman in my first congregation who came to me stating that she was not sure that she was forgiven. Charlotte had lived life for many decades in faith with Jesus as her savior, close to the church and with actions that confirmed what she believed. Charlotte was probably forty years my senior. I was sensitive to her concern as I led her back through the steps to receive Jesus as savior in order to confirm her forgiveness, which I believe was never in question. After we prayed, she thanked me and said she felt better. However in retrospect considering what I did not know then, I believe Charlotte was experiencing the "lonely" in the form of a sense of existential guilt. The Relieving of Guilt is motivated by an underlying sense that "I am not good enough to be in the presence of God." Neither knowledge nor emotional experience can remove that existentially experienced truth. Given what I know today, I would have led Charlotte to rely fully on God by affirming that expiating her underlying sense of guilt was not beyond the power of God. Christians simply need to lay it down, not strive to remove it.

The Apostle Paul struggled with a physical ailment but also with whether God would remove it or not.[15] [II Corinthians 12:7-9] The implicit spiritual struggle juxtaposes "If I am good, then God will answer my request; and if it is not removed, I must not be good." While clearly this scripture is an example that not all prayers are answered as Christians would desire, it also speaks to the human yearning to feel guiltless. God's profound response to Paul was "My grace is sufficient for you, for my power is made perfect in weakness."[16] [II Corinthians 12:9] Perhaps a more communicative way to say this would be: "My perfection is received in contrast to human imperfection. People do not need perfection, they only need my grace." In other words, within human frailty, God is best revealed. At this existential anxiety point in the life of faith, believers need to accept their limitations and be open to receive God's grace – the final and absolute forgiveness that God will, because of divine nature, unquestionably provide but in God's way and in God's time.

People are not going to be perfect; they are never going to do enough or believe enough to be guilt free – although humans will attempt to do so. Thus, God is not going to automatically absolve all hints of guilt until the time is right; to do so would mean that Christians would not need God. Absolutely, God can and will dissolve Christian's guilt – but only when God is ready. Surrendering to the fact that Christians cannot actually get rid of existential guilt is the first step – it is not fixable. Second, Christians are to trust that God will take them as they are and in God's time and God's way, will transform them completely. Third, Christians need to mantra that belief, in the face of feeling non-accepted. "Therefore, there is now no condemnation for those who are in Christ Jesus."[17] [Romans 8:1]

Ever listen to elderly people who are reflecting on their life? In my experience, they typically insert the regrets they feel with the desire to have lived differently. For long-term Christians, this guiltiness is not about not being saved or having Jesus as their savior; it is the human undertow current that powerfully flows to assert, "I am not good enough." This existential anxiety is not resolvable except in the free floating trust to be carried to God. With the rise and fall of each wave of guilt, Christians might continuously repeat "Surely God is my salvation; I will trust and not be afraid."[18] [Isaiah 12:2a] or "God please bring me into your Goodness."

MICRO-MANAGING MEANING

People want to have purpose. People feel empty without something to live for. **People have existential anxiety when their life in review questions the meaning and purpose for which they have been living**.

Viktor Emil Frankl,[19] Holocaust survivor and founder of Logotherapy, was famous for his books on finding meaning in life in spite of awful circumstances.[20] Frankl's experience in Nazi concentration camps increased his spiritual depth and formed his thought that people can live through physical and mental depravation when they have a higher purpose to live for – in love of others, a life project or in God. Having this meaning is absolutely necessary. Frankl's therapeutic approach profoundly assists people in living better in an age of meaninglessness. On the other hand, Frankl was aware that his basis of asserting life's meaning – the people loved, the projects aspired and even a person's own dignity – ends. When people realize that the end will come and with it life's meaning, they experience existential anxiety. Accordingly, Frankl also asserted that this "lonely" leads to the ultimate meaning of life which he called supra-meaning, transcendence or God. People are intimately connected with God; yet the recognition of such ultimate meaning cannot be completely affirmed except in the face of losing everything. This happened in the Holocaust when Frankl deepened his faith in God. This same dynamic occurs when Christians surrender to the fact that their life's meaning does not reside in the people they love or in the "life-changing" projects they adopt – but ultimate meaning comes only in their relationship with Jesus; this happens after people have released their hold on Micro-managing Meaning.

Indeed, life needs to have meaning so people can have something to live for. Accordingly, people strive to find their soul mate, an organization, family relationships or projects to invest in (even trying to know God can be a human attempt to make meaning). While such meaning manifests in that which is "beyond themselves," **all human-made meaning leaves, dies, seems incomplete or becomes unobtainable.** When loss of meaning commences, depression (or fear) can accompany, even hide, the sense of the "lonely." For example, some parents react to the end of child-rearing with an "empty nest syndrome" that manifests in bouts of crying and the inability to sleep or function well in the world. Psychological help is recommended. However, the therapy and medication can keep such parents from recognizing the "lonely" and the new attitudes that God is inviting. Jesus' radical proclamation begins to make some sense, "Anyone who loves his father or mother more than me is not worthy of me; anyone who loves his son or daughter more than me is not worthy of me."[21] [Matthew 10:37] The value placed in being a good parent that has been removed brings an emptiness that cannot be fixed. However, this "lonely" can bring parents closer to God as the only one who is ultimate meaning.

For a second example, people who are professional helpers, especially pastors, can succumb to compassion fatigue. Since they are convinced that helping others spiritually is important, they come to build their life's meaning in the successful accomplishment of doing so. They cannot actually help everyone, although they may try. Thus, they may begin making promises they cannot keep, lying when they don't do what they had hoped. They are likely to "work themselves to death" or at least into a state of physical and emotional exhaustion. Consequently, the professional helpers' world of meaning comes crashing down. Psychological help is recommended. Again, the therapy and the medication may hide the sense of the "lonely." Professional helpers have to admit in real-life practical ways that the world already has a savior (and it is not them), and that they actually need to receive (not give) that help for themselves. In the midst of their own life's loss of meaning, Jesus' apostles were told to "Trust in God; trust also in me."[22] [John 14:1] They had to let the unseen power of God in the guise of the Holy Spirit take charge and provide the meaningful direction for their lives. In the midst of the "lonely," Christian helpers must also make such transition, either with or without the need of therapy.

Having meaning in life is essential to healthy living. On the other hand, human-made meaning always has limits that lead to its loss. Releasing what held meaning is difficult; hopefully spiritual helpers can assist people in letting go of humanly-created values and meaning in order to allow them to rely on God's fulfillment. Nevertheless, people are tempted to fill the angst of meaning with other finite forms. In fact, when people believe they have lost the purpose for which they have been living, they are in crisis and liable to do any "crazy" thing to reclaim that sense of purpose. Consider the unhappy story of George.

For a few sessions, I met with George who was a very intelligent and competent ordained minister having served some large congregations. George, about fifty years old with a wife and family, expressed some discomfort with his life in general and about being a minister in particular. George had an award-winning, stellar career. While he talked about some difficulties in his personal life and in his new congregation, they did not seem to be out of the ordinary or insurmountable. He decided that a personal retreat might help him to process what was going on in his life and discern what God wanted for him. Afterward, he described a sunrise that he experienced on retreat. While anticipating the appearance of the sun, it got "trapped" behind some morning clouds and trees. He was visibly despondent until he suddenly exclaimed, "Then the clouds broke open and the sun shined through. I thought I had lost it but I got a second chance." While this experience appeared to be filled with surprise and beauty, it didn't seem to contain anything extraordinary – at least until the following month. When George didn't arrive for his spiritual direction session, I telephoned to see if he was all right or had an emergency. I was told that he was nowhere to be found. He and his personal assistant had suddenly left town, leaving his wife of twenty-five years and family behind.

Indeed, God orchestrates second chances. However, God was not the author of George's wake of destruction. George was exhausted from building a life of faith for himself and others that no longer made his life meaningful. His life that seemed empty and insincere caused significant ambiguity. He was experiencing existential anxiety because he had "played by the rules" all of his life and he was "supposed" to be happy. Instead of paying attention to the truth that only God makes ultimate meaning, George choose to run away. Indeed, bad things happen when people run when they are in the Dark. Certainly, "Once the angel in us is repressed, (s)he turns into a demon."[23] **Every Christian comes to this existential "choice-point" which, with sensitivity to God's leading, can result in exhilaration and an ease of living that goes beyond anything that has been previously experienced – a form of Christian contentment**.

One of my directees finally surrendered to the immoveable forces of existential anxiety and it made a huge difference in his life. The picture of this fifty-five-year-old person is crucial to appreciate the transition. Phillip was a successful business man, highly education, extremely capable in interpersonal relationships, a leader of others as well as a long-term active Christian who practiced faithfulness. Life and God had blessed his living in numerous ways. In the last few years, however, major parts of his life seemed to be disintegrating: uncertain and disturbing events removed contact with his daughter and grandchildren and his thriving business nose-dived under the weight of an economic down turn. Concurrently, Phillip had begun to respond to God's call to move toward ministry, both unofficially and as a second "career." This movement had increasingly grown over a decade and a half as his inherent life fears had been dissolved and his spiritual gifts had been revealed and exercised. He was also motivated to boldly move into new arenas – behaviors that would have previously petrified him.

As all of the difficulties invaded, Phillip increased his prayer life only to discover he "could not pray" like he had always done. Changing his prayer routine and moving into a much simpler, less expectant way of connecting with God helped as God choose to engage with him. The "lonely" was in him as evidenced in the lack of feeling fulfilled, a depressive attitude with accompanying tears and most certainly the inability, although he tried mightily, to change his life situations.

His spiritual crucible occurred after working through an intensely emotional and spiritual dream that basically reflected new understandings and nakedness before God in the midst of surrendering before the altar of God. Quite spontaneously while worshiping at a Sunday service, this man who was a model of goodness and faith responded to an "altar call." In reflection, Phillip compared his action to his original response to accept Jesus as his savior, which he described as pale in comparison to what he had just done. Of course, with more life experience, with greater understanding of faith and with an accumulated devotion of following Jesus, his action was more intentional, deliberate and costly – it meant more personally without discounting any of what God did at his original conversion.

Phillip exhibited an overwhelming joy, excitement and motivation which was such a contrast to what had previously been his demeanor. While God most certainly can cause such a radical change, I cautiously affirmed this euphoria, until I could celebrate its validity as it continued in subsequent months. Re-prioritizing had taken place. As Phillip reflected, "I always said (my priorities were) God, family, business but my actions said family, business, God. Now I feel much more in alignment with what I said in my heart and in my actions." While the hurts and worries from the demise of family and business were still present, neither held the power over him that they had previously had. Phillip no longer micro-managed meaning either by what he accumulated in his business or by what he valued via his family. In the face of existential anxiety, he had released determining meaning, value and worth through human means.

People, even Christians, live by means of temporary meaning. Only God provides ultimate meaning. This supra-meaning comes via an act of trusting faith in the midst of non-meaning. "Now we see but a poor reflection as in a mirror; then we shall see face to face. Now I know in part; then I shall know fully, even as I am fully known."[24] [I Corinthians 13:12] This biblically-expressed clarity comes from surrender, not in resignation to meaninglessness, but to the One who has the words of eternal life. It comes with the prayer, "God, I am yours. If you will, please bring me into your Oneness – where all will be meaningfully integrated and reconciled."

DEALING WITH DEATH

People do not want to die. People are driven to be young, be productive and independent. **People have existential anxiety when they realize that they are not going to get out of this world alive**.

In a sense, everything people do in regard to chasing certainty, reliving guilt and micro-managing meaning is in essence attempting to avoid the end of life. My tongue in cheek comment to enable people face this truth is, "Nobody gets out of this world alive." Presumably, Christians' goal is to go to God after this life is done which means that they will be Dealing with Death. <u>Yet, people attempt to fill the angst of death with building legacies, including any combination of the above approaches, which will last the test of time</u>. No one has returned from the "other side" and if some had, what they would have said with finite words could not describe what eternity is. People have always sought to interpret "life after death" experiences and the biblical imagery of Revelation in order to be assured from their angst of death and dying. <u>However, it is ultimately an act of trusting faith in the midst of non-being</u>.

Dealing with Death is as uneasy as it is final. However, spiritual helpers may assist with some very simple, almost rhetorical questions. "Do you believe that God knows what is best for you?" (This can release Chasing Certainty to God) "Do you believe that God loves and takes care of what God creates?" (This can release Relieving Guilt to God) "Do you believe that God will give you what is best for you?" (This can release Micro-managing Meaning to God) "Are you willing to trust God in the face of dying?" The ultimate question is not "How will you live your life?" Instead, it is "How will you live your death?" Hopefully, with a prayer like, "God, I trust you to bring me into the beauty of your Life." or "Into your hands I commit my spirit."[25] [Luke 23:46]

SUMMARY

The "lonely" can happen all through spiritual life, especially in transitional moments, but culminates in the experience of Dark Night quandaries. The "lonely" manifests itself in the existential anxiety conditions of uncertainty, guilt, meaningless and death. "Does God exist and how can people know for sure?" This is the angst of uncertainty. "Can sin and its guilt really be removed even though people still feel the weight of their sins?" This is the angst of guilt. "How does all that has been lived result in anything truly meaningful in the big picture?" This is the angst of meaning. "How can that which is limited and finite and flesh ever merge into that which is eternal and God?" This is the angst of death. <u>Each dimension of existential anxiety is only ultimately resolved "in God." No human answer will suffice. The only adequate response is to hope in the promise and qualities of God</u>.

That's what the lonely is for – to bring people to God.

CHAPTER 21

"Monsters from the Id"

When I was a teen, I was captivated by a televised science-fiction film "The Forbidden Planet."[1] The great impact of the movie came not because it featured Robby the Robot, a human-sized fully-functional android with a conscience. Although really cool, neither did the precursive "Star Trekish" teleporting mode of transportation nor the sophisticated special effects provide lasting influence on me. It was a phrase – "Monsters from the Id."

In the film's storyline, a brilliant scientist-father, Dr. Edward Morbius, and his beautiful daughter, Alta, in her twenties had been marooned on a distant planet, Altair-4. The planet had been the home of an extremely advanced species called the Krel. Morbius had learned some of their secrets from their left behind data. The Krel knowledge had been collected in a seemingly endless storage facility that only the father had been able to successfully access. When he gained some of their knowledge, he was able to light up only one power panel of the thousands that were present. When other people tried to do so, they had all died.

After decades a rescue spaceship arrived which was seen by the father as an intrusion. When the ship's commander, John J. Adams, and Alta became romantically involved, Dr. Morbius was even more incensed. As the story developed, a huge unstoppable invisible monster attacked the spaceship and some of its crew. To escape the destruction, the ship planned to depart taking everyone. The scientist-father furiously objected. He simply wanted the rescuers to go away, but his daughter insisted on leaving with her newly found love. At this point, the monster began savagely attacking. Everyone fled to the underground storage facility of Krel knowledge and sealed the ten foot thick doorway made from specially constructed, impenetrable Krel metal. Nevertheless, the monster's image could be seen burning its way through the door. Simultaneously, the Krel knowledge panels sequentially alighted accessing a seemingly limitless supply of power. During the confusion, the crew member with the highest IQ successfully accessed the Krel knowledge system. As he lay dying, he shared that the danger could not be stopped because it was a "Monster from the Id."

As a teen, I had never heard the term "Id" but opened a dictionary to discover that it was a word used to describe the unknown, subconscious part of the human mind. In "The Forbidden Planet" the vast power of the Krel had become available for the scientist-father to use and unconsciously was providing all the ability he needed to destroy the unacknowledged object of his anger. When he became conscious of what he was doing with his subconscious, the father repented and relented. Immediately, the monster's attack stopped.

While people's brains record every moment of their lives, individuals cannot be aware of everything that has happened all at one time. Thus, what is not in people's present awareness is relegated to what has been called the unconscious or the subconscious – a vast storage facilitate of life events and the emotions that accompany them. **Events housed in the subconscious that are perceived as negative have been called the Shadow,[2] which can be unconsciously released into real-life situations. Then, they become "Monsters from the Id."** This seemingly unlimited power of the subconscious was highlighted in the 1956 film, "The Forbidden Planet."

Consider a commonplace example of how this process is true. People often use the same phrases that their parents said to them without even being aware of what they have said. After becoming aware, people may exclaim, "I can't believe that I am turning into my father!" **The more negative a past event, the greater possibility it has to inflict, unconsciously, harm in the current situation. More importantly, such involuntary damage has the ability to slow or stop spiritual growth.**

The apostle Paul knew about the monsters from the Id; he just didn't know exactly what to do with them or how to clearly name them. He noted, "I have the desire to do what is good, but I cannot carry it out. For what I do is not the good I want to do; no, the evil I do not want to do – this I keep on doing."[3] [Romans 7:18b-19] Even a limited reading of the New Testament reveals that Paul was a disciplined, strong-willed man. So how is it possible that he does what he says he does not want to do? His struggling rationalization is that it is the sin that is in him which causes him to do the bad things. Indeed, the Christian faith labels whatever attitudes or behaviors that are not in accord with God as "sins." However, Paul wrestles with this issue because it sneaks up on him and propels him into actions that he would not choose to do. In other words, if Paul would have been fully conscious of what he was about to do, he would have behaved differently. He would have defeated his sin with the power of Christ. This understanding of what was happening in **Paul postulates that something other than his fully awake consciousness prompted and propelled what he did.** While the Devil could be cited to explain that force, **an unresolved and unforgiven unconscious part of him** could equally be the cause. Of course, the apostle Paul did not have the terminology of the "unconscious" which was not officially labeled until the late nineteenth century.

This chapter deals with the last of the ways that Christians get stalled on the side of the Spiritual Road: the negative influences of the subconscious. What is externally observable are **Christians who do not actually do what they say they want to do or who sabotage themselves from doing it.** Their external actions are initiated internally from memories of past negative events that inflict pain or negativity into their lives and upon others. This chapter primarily focuses on how the subconscious causes negativity. However, people also have past experiences that keep themselves from accepting positive direction in their lives.

For example, when I was in spiritual direction training, I had a totally humbling and extremely embarrassing experience. While most of my cohorts were dealing with hellish monsters, I kept having positive dreams with bright colors, laughter, balloons and people providing affirmations; similar things were happening in my guided faith meditations. I strongly reacted that something must be really wrong with me for "manufacturing" such inappropriate experiences. Upon further work, leaders of the program helped me to realize that for a long time I had been consistently denying my value and my gifts – a process which "thankfully" was caused by a "critical judge" monster within me. However, what was most important at the time was for me to accept the positive; later I would have the opportunity to forgive the monsters and even surrender the ego-gifts that God had given. I find this same scenario in people who have been abused – their monsters keep them from accepting the positive truth of who they are and the intrinsic values they have. Validating this genuineness helps them access the strength to confront the monsters who caused such unfounded belittling.

RECOGNIZING THE MONSTER

Dealing with the unconscious realm is typically the realm of psychotherapy. However, **a very simple and basic way exists to recognize the presence of monsters from the Id – when people have a much stronger emotional reaction to a current event than the situation would normally elicit**. For example, when a parent yells and throws a temper tantrum because her two-year-old accidently spilled her milk, be sure that this parent is not "really" mad at the toddler, but at the parent who did the same to her when she was two. Many parents will be sorry for their explosive reactions. However, typically people, especially children, remember the first things that were said and always the emotions expressed rather than the apologies received. Consequently, children are damaged and spiritual growth is halted due to such repetitive unconscious eruptions. While most spiritual helpers who I know are not equipped to do therapy, they most certainly can recognize when disproportional emotion is expressed. <u>The more often spiritual helpers detect such behavior, the more they might suspect that something in the subconscious is triggering or trapping people into their reactions</u>.

Another way to identify the influence of the subconscious occurs when people repeatedly say they want to do something but never complete the task. Sometimes, people may only need to evoke their personal will (instead of their desires) to follow through with their intention. Thus, discovering whether people <u>really</u> want to do what they say they want to do may be all that is necessary. Spiritual helpers can do so by asking people what they really choose to do – not what they say they want to do or should do. This "Evoking the Will" technique, inviting people to consciously choose, is simple, powerful and often all that is needed. Nevertheless, if the inconsistency between desire and its completion continues, spiritual helpers might consider that such folks have, at least, a mini-monster in their Id that is causing the problem.

For example, Ted who kept saying that he wanted to establish a pattern of regular prayer always found excuses not to do so. Suspecting an unconscious influence to this repeated behavior, I began some discussion about the praying people in his memory. Ted reported that his saintly grandmother had taught him to pray, yet she was always correcting the way he did so and insisted that he needed to pray more. I summarized, "So, it would seem that you could never pray as well as your grandmother. If you could never measure up to her standards, why would you even want to start?" Ted's mental light bulb turned on. He became aware of how this subconscious memory controlled his real-life actions. "What do I need to do?" was his immediate question. To which I responded, "First, you need to consciously and intentionally forgive your grandmother for her sin (intentional or unintentional) of critically holding you to a higher standard than you were able. And I recommend that we do that right now."

As I anticipated, Ted vocalized **a typical objection, "But how can I say something like that to my grandmother? She died long time ago."** "Yes, of course," I agreed. "I know your grandmother passed, but I guarantee that she is very much alive inside of you and her re-animated criticism is destroying your efforts. As such, you would be primarily saying these things to the memory of her that you have imposed on yourself and allowed to control your good intentions. Besides, prayer goes through the Divine, who is not restrained by time and space. That means that your grandmother receives your forgiveness as you speak it."

Moving to **another typical objection, Ted replied, "But how can I say something so mean to my grandmother, even to her memory?"** With assurance I replied, "Well, first of all I certainly do not want you to be mean, only correctly truthful and with the corresponding emotion. Do you think that Jesus would suggest that you pray regularly? Of course, you do. Do you think that Jesus would want whatever is in the way of that recommendation to be removed? Remember, when Jesus said, "Anyone who loves his father or mother more than me is not worthy of me; anyone who loves his son or daughter more than me is not worthy of me."[4] [Matthew 10:37] That applies to even saintly grandmothers. Also, I don't see why you and Jesus together can't confront your grandmother and offer forgiveness as well. I don't believe he will let you be mean, do you?" The prayer that Ted prayed was as passionate in his confrontation as it was gracious in its forgiveness. Afterward, Ted was visible exhausted and peaceful. Over the next few sessions, he reported how much more regular and easier his prayers had become ... to the joy of his forgiven grandmother.

People will typically object, "You can't change the past." Of course, not. However, this protest confuses what actually happened in the past with the part of it which is remembered. Social science experiments consistently confirm that people do not accurately remember past events. While the actual past cannot be change, what people recall and use to run their lives can most certainly be changed. Sometimes a simple conscious decision can do that. On the other hand, the power of God is often necessary to heal the more intense and deep-seated hurts held in the subconscious.

WHY ENGAGE THE MONSTERS

But why should spiritual helpers be concerned with dealing with these unconscious monsters?

First, people's relationships with others and with God can be scuttled more by what is unseen than by what is obvious. What kind of role model was the above parent to her two-year-old? And because children receive their first image of God from the attitudes of their parents, what impression of God would they likely receive? Like an iceberg, what floats above the water is not what wretches the ship, it is the seven-eighths of the iceberg unseen under the water that destroys lives. Spiritual helpers can be effective lookouts, "Ahoy. That looks like an iceberg. What do you think?"

Second, spiritual helpers need to work with the subconscious because primarily forgiveness of those subconscious events, not therapy, is necessary to move forward when traveling the later part the Spiritual Road, especially from the middle of the Illuminative Way onward. While God can truly work through therapy and bring about forgiveness, it is the job of spiritual helpers. Some demons can only be tamed and transformed by the raw power of God. In rare cases, exorcisms have been indispensable. Reportedly, the late Dr. Gerald May resigned from his lucrative psychiatric practice to become a spiritual director partly because he had come to believe that therapy could not heal and spiritual direction could facilitate it.

Third, spiritual helpers need to assist in removing or transforming the unconscious monsters because they are part and parcel to the sins that need to be eliminated so that the perfect abiding with God can occur. In the history of the church, Christians have been taught to confess and pray for forgiveness both for their sins of commission and also their sins of omission. Sins of commission are clearly the willing violations, via an external deed or an inner attitude, of a spiritual precept or law. An example is where Adam and Eve violated God's directive to not eat of the Tree of Good and Evil (external deed).[5] [Genesis 2:16-17] An inner attitude sin of commission is: "But I tell you that anyone who looks at a woman lustfully has already committed adultery with her in his heart."[6] [Matthew 5:28] Christians, especially during the Purgative Way, primarily deal with purging these sins of commission.

The official definition in the history of Christianity is that <u>sins of omission</u> are failures of do something that people "can and ought to do."[7] The scripture also teaches, "Whoever knows the right thing to do and fails to do it, for him (or her) it is sin."[8] [James 4:17] Accordingly, sins must be intellectually known and willfully omitted (or committed) to be considered "real sins" – with "full knowledge and free consent." However,

Q. 285. What are sins committed without reflection or consent called?

A. Sins, committed without reflection or consent, are called material sins; that is, they would be formal or real sins if we knew their sinfulness at the time we committed them.[9]

In other words, until the time that wrong actions and attitudes (omitted or committed) are realized, they are labeled "material sins." Likewise, in the history of Christian doctrine, people are not responsible for either sins of commission or omission, if they are unaware of them as sinful.[10] Nevertheless, as soon as people become aware, they are responsible. So, in orthodox Christian teaching ignorance truly is bliss.

While knowledge and willpower can be effective with eliminating sins of commission and omission, when it comes to Monsters from the Id, a problem exists. The above doctrinal position regarding sin is based on early nineteenth century assessment of human beings such as, "Man differs from all irrational creatures in this precisely that he is master of his actions by virtue of his reason and free will."[11] However, people are not controllers of their actions as evidenced by modern psychological understanding of the subconscious and if the plight of Paul of Tarsus is taken seriously. Paul not only does not do the good he wants to do; but he also "keeps on doing it" – compulsively. **People can be unable to control and actually don't freely choose the "evil" they do or omit. They are trapped or triggered into action (or non-action) and they are unaware of their sin until after it has occurred because its source originated in the subconscious. I call this "unconscious sin."** Ecclesiastically, while people are not held responsible for sins of which they are unaware (although Jesus seems to disagree),[12] they still are sinful nonetheless. <u>**Truly, any sin, whether material (unrealized or unconscious), committed (action), or omitted (non-action), hinders spiritual growth and keeps people from getting closer to God**</u>. That which causes or tends to cause separation from God is sin.

Seriously, this discussion is not justification to allow people do keep on doing the sins they can't seemingly control. However, I have personally struggled with the issue of unconscious sins because I did not want to be held accountable for the sins of which I was not aware. Officially, according to historical Christian doctrine, people are not. On the other hand, unconscious sins still affect people's relationship with God. Thus, **reframing the picture of "unconscious sin" can be helpful**. Sin is often seen as morally pungent and devastatingly awful – the result is that it renders people "bad." In the beginning half of the Christian life, conceiving of sin as very, very "bad" is actually helpful for the process of spiritual growth. At this place on the Spiritual Road, sin is predominant and unchecked; and it needs to be purged as soon as possible. Also, people are usually emotionally young and so respond to a "pre-conventional" ethic that is personal and punishment-oriented. "Repent because you are bad." Repent so you won't go to Hell."

However, by the latter half of the spiritual growth process (assuming that Christians have been faithful and true) observable sins have mostly been confessed and countered via living for God. Thus, labeling mature Christians with sins will often elicit an adverse reaction. They know that they are not "bad" people and don't want the label of "sin" to imply that. Long-term Christians can easily and unfortunately become defensive, compare themselves to beginning Christians as did the religious man who sought to inherit eternal life did with Jesus, "'Teacher' he declared. 'All these (commandments) I have kept since I was a boy.'"[13] [Mark 10:20] Implied in his declaration is this man's reaction to the possibility that he might not have been doing the right things. This seeker of eternal life did not want any insinuation that he had sinned against God.

By definition, sin is anything that moves people in the opposite direction from God, regardless of whether people are aware of their sin or not. Yet, **while Christians who have traveled far along the Spiritual Road are still "responsible" for even the sins they are unaware of, framing them as very "bad" is neither helpful nor necessary.** These Illuminative Way and Unitive Way Christians, once they become aware of sin, almost immediately want to repent and change their ways, which is all that God wants. Thus, spiritual helpers would be advised to assert, "Sin is what keeps us from unity with God. While your obvious behavioral sins have been mostly eliminated, whatever keeps us from God still needs to be addressed. These are mostly unconscious. They don't render you 'awful,' they just hinder your further spiritual growth." It is not that God holds these sins against Christians (like at the beginning of their life of faith); it is that these unconscious sins hold God away. Thus, Christians who deeply desire to draw closer to God will spend time expelling these "monsters from the Id." Spiritual helpers can assist in this work especially if they distinguish between sin that makes people "bad" and the effect of "unconscious sin" that encumbers spiritual growth.

THERE'S A MONSTER IN THE HOUSE

I have often used the analogy of a house to explain how the subconscious functions inside people as well as a visual approach for seeing what to do.

Cross-culturally, the "house" has been identified as an archetypal symbol of the individual person – the Self. Jesus referred to himself and his forthcoming resurrection, not the Jewish Temple in Jerusalem, when he told the religious leaders, "Jesus answered them,

'Destroy this temple, and I will raise it again in three days.'"[14] [John 2:19] While Jesus' house was a glorious Temple, William Paul Young envisioned a dilapidated shack. As he spoke in one of his interviews: "The Shack is the house of the soul of a human being that has become all broken up."[15] Both structures represented the condition of the individual. In addition, the apostle Paul talked about the human body being the "Temple of the Holy Spirit."[16] [I Corinthians 6:19-20] He also described it as a tent which would be torn down when people died only to receive a glorious new edifice for them, their soul-self, to live in.[17] [II Corinthians 5:1]

Intervarsity Christian Fellowship has used the booklet, "My Heart Christ's Home"[18] as a tool to invited people to accept Jesus emotionally into the center of their lives as Savior and Lord. The pamphlet pictures Jesus entering into the human heart and the author saying, "Let me show you around and introduce you to the various features of the home that you may be more comfortable and that we may have fuller fellowship together." This begins the process of having Jesus live personally inside the house of the Self. Subsequently, Jesus is personally invited into various parts of the house – the library, the dining and living rooms, the workroom and so forth. After living together for quite a while, Jesus indicated the existence of a secret room that contained "dead and rotting things left over from the old life." This needed the cleansing touch of Jesus. While this place is described as being a second floor locked closet, I will depict it below as the basement. Both ways, there was a monster in the house and it was stinking up the place.

In his famous work, Mere Christianity, C. S. Lewis picks up this same theme of Jesus being invited to come and live inside the individual Christian's house. But he furthers the analogy and notes what happens when the Divine resides within the human.

Imagine yourself as a living house. God comes in to fix that house at your request. At first, perhaps, you can understand what he is doing. He is getting the drains right and stopping the leaks in the roof and so on; you knew that those jobs needed doing and so you are not surprised. But presently he starts knocking the house about in a way that hurts abominably and does not seem to make sense. What on earth is he up to? The explanation is that he is building quite a different house from the one you thought of... You thought you were going to be made into a decent little cottage. But (instead) God is building a palace. (You see) He intends to come and live in it (with you).[19]

If houses of individual Christians are to be transformed into the structures in which God is willing to live, then at least two things need to happen: Jesus has to be invited to move into every part of those houses, and be given permission to totally remodel even the deepest recesses of the Self – including the subconscious where the monsters live.

THE THREE LEVEL HOUSE

I met Rev. Cliff Custer in the early 1980s and consider him my first teacher in regard to the process of spiritual growth. He was leading a workshop in the local congregation where I was serving as an associate minister. Over the years, I have sketched his "Three Level House" for many of the people with whom I have worked. Recently, I re-connected with Cliff and he graciously provided me with an official copy of his Three Level House (Graphic 17), which has been expanded and detailed over the years as a teaching tool in his Ministry of Inner Healing, a way of dealing with the Monsters from the Id. **I have included the Three Level House to illustrate the place of the subconscious in people, why it yields so much power and how to employ the process of "inner healing" for personal spiritual growth.**[20]

The individual person can be described using <u>the divisions of heart, mind and soul</u> which correspond to the Great Commandment to love God with heart, mind and soul. The heart is at the basement level; the mind level is on the ground floor; and the soul correlates to the attic. In addition, **the heart-basement is the subconscious; the mind-ground floor is the conscious world; and the soul-attic is the superconscious/spiritual dimension of the person.**

The subconscious-heart level gets lots of detail. It includes a computer room, an art room and a mind projection room. This is to communicate that <u>people store all their memories in the subconscious; and they perceive these memories in particular created ways which they project into the conscious realm.</u> In the Art Room of the subconscious, people paint, Photoshop and film-edit how they remember and interpret the life data from the Memory Storage Room. These selected and interpreted slices of life are projected into consciousness when elicited by parallel current events. While Cliff's house particularly focuses on the projection of male and female images, it is equally true that events, values and principles are also imposed onto life. **People create these Art Room renditions; and people, with God's help, can re-canvas, re-record and re-film what will be projected into their lives.**

People live their lives on the conscious-mind level, using all five senses to experience life. Each new experience is retired to the basement level for storage and artful integration with all other memories. <u>On this conscious level, people respond to and value most with whatever is projected from the subconscious.</u>

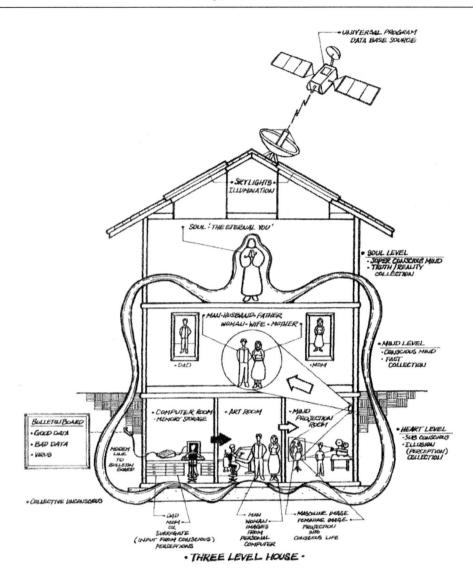

Graphic 17: The "Three Level House" is used here to represent how people unconsciously hold, revision and project their memories onto life events. Negative subconscious memories sabotage good spiritual intentions. (Created by Rev. Cliff Custer, used by permission)

At some point, the soul, the eternal Self, comes to awareness, is born from above, or beamed in. By whatever terminology, the soul becomes alive and active. In Christian terms, this occurs when people accept Jesus as Lord and Savior. This does not make them perfect only that the Holy Spirit become present and available for them.

Using the "Three Level House," note that God's messages are received via the "universal program data base source" satellite. After being communicate to the soul, the message is received in the heart and lived in the world. In other words, the satellite receives and transmits the information down to the heart where it is stored, processed and finally projected into "real" life. **So, what people receive in the soul (from God) is filtered through the lenses of subconscious perceptions before it is brought into conscious living**. As an example, people may receive the message that God is their Heavenly Father. However for some people, this truth might have to be processed through the memories of a father who beat the stuffing out of them or sexually abused them for the first fifteen years of their life. Such negative life experiences distort the intension of God. Obviously, inner healing needs to take place in the subconscious so that message of God can be authentically lived in the conscious world. Therapy will help; but this is ultimately a spiritual issue. In less dramatic examples, people who have low self-esteem have a difficult time living like (and believing that) they are valued children of God. People who live in childhood homes or churches that manifested a critical spirit will look at the world with criticism, focus more on law than grace, and often become like Christians baptized in dill pickle juice. These are all lurking unconscious monsters in the Id that need to be transformed.

TRANSFORMING THE MONSTERS

Healing in the subconscious always requires the power of God, which can be accessed in various ways. If a specific spiritual atmosphere is present, it can occur through therapy. However, more intentional forms of intervention are best. I have included three below.

Prior to healing, since the subconscious is unconscious, the monsters of the Id must be clearly and consciously identified. This is not always an easy task. Much of what is hidden in the subconscious is done so to protect the ego – the image and actions which people want to show to the world. Thus, many rationalizations, emotional reactions, blaming projections, sublimations and just pure denial conceal and bury the true soul-self, which is what is freed when the monsters are dissipated. Therapy can reveal these hidden elements which take time and trust as well as skilled insightful intervention. In my experience, people who have gone through extensive therapy actually identify their monsters and usually receive some good coping skills to relieve the stress and difficulties they cause. However, rarely are the monsters transformed. Thus, when Christians struggle with excessive emotional eruptions or the repeated inability to follow through with intentions, I suspect a monster from their Id. Accordingly, I often ask whether they have done therapy and ask if they would be willing to revisit those events and their revelations from therapy. My intention is not to re-do the therapy but to build upon it.

The first tool I use to heal the subconscious is the least intrusive and most helpful for mini-monsters. I call the process "Raising the Unconscious" because <u>it simply involves bringing the negative to consciousness, changing it to be positive with God's blessing and then letting it resurface changed</u>. This process must be repeated over a long time but actually works. It is a re-painted art project in process. A cute little example may help. Soon after Pat and I married, I noticed that just as she was going to sleep, and even during the night, she would utter the sound "un-uh" which was form of "no." When I asked her about it, she didn't realize what she had said. Since she claimed that nothing was wrong and since it was such a happy time in our lives, I suggested that she replace the negative sound with the more positive "uh-hu." In playful reinforcement, whenever she would semi-consciously say "uh-uh," I would immediately counter with the positive replacement and smile with a toothy grin. Over the years, Pat would unintentionally still say "un-uh" but would immediately substitute the positive phrase. And today she always utters the positive phrase "uh-hu" – even while she is asleep, really! **The negative unconscious had been raised to consciousness, altered often enough so that it actually lives in the unconscious as positive!**

As a spiritual director, I have assisted many people using this tool. Chapter nineteen, "Words Can Sometimes," employs this technique as the basis of changing the words people repeat to themselves. Many directees have broken free from the negative rules or obligations that were inflicted upon them which they held and projected into their world and their spiritual lives. Implementation was however, always preceded by conversation about what God really wanted for them, which included the contrast between freely choosing and being begrudgingly obligated. In conclusion, I would always offer prayer that God would increase the awareness of these people and keep them moving in the direction of God's discerned will for their lives. After a time, no longer were they controlled by what they thought the "should" do or believe but had broken free to be their true self – becoming the child that God created them to be. **"Raising the Unconscious" takes repetition, an act of the personal will and often the consistent assistance of another person**. But it works, is non-invasive and allows people to be in charge of their own healing.

After the completion of "Raising the Unconscious" as well as after the following two techniques, I have found it helpful to invite the people I accompany to prayerfully consider: "What is the lie that Satan whispered into your soul when that happened?" They may have an immediate intuitive response or they may need to take a moment of passive contemplative prayer to listen for that truth. When the lie is exposed to the Light of God's Truth, people can more easily become the authentic and transparent people that God is creating them to be. In addition, a particular word, phrase or visual reminder can help anchor this newness into people.[21]

The second technique is to specifically pray for the Holy Spirit to work within. This method is particularly suited for times of great stress, when the Id monsters become more active and have the tendency to take over. As such, this is prayer both for protection and healing. In a way, this has most often been the approach of traditional spiritual direction – "just take it to prayer." <u>People must intentionality "give God permission" to do whatever is necessary; and they must totally trust the results</u>.

It is as if people say, "God, I am not able to manage my own life and do not want to be at the mercy of nameless demons, please intercede with your Holy Spirit in those unknown parts of me according to your perfect will." If people cannot pray as often happens during times of great difficulty, I invited them to write down, carry with them and read the following scripture with the byline "This I choose."

In the same way, the Spirit helps us in our weakness. We do not know what we ought to pray for, but the Spirit himself intercedes for us with groans that words cannot express. And he who searches our hearts knows the mind of the Spirit, because the Spirit intercedes for the saints in accordance with God's will.[22] [Romans 8:26-27]

If people are musical, I invite them to hum or sing "Sweet Hour of Prayer"[23] with special emphasis on "in seasons of distress and grief my soul has often found relief" so "I'll cast on Him my every care and wait for Thee." This is an intentional action of surrendering all to God for protection and healing. In addition, people in this condition often need others to pray this prayer along side of them and even for them. Thus, I always move them to the very top of my prayer list and engage God very seriously on their behalf.

Third, the work of "inner healing" can use the power of God to provide saving redemption to what is in the subconscious. This method, which I learned from Cliff Custer and is specifically detailed in his book, is often needed for the meanest monsters from the Id because it is powerful and invasive enough to be effective. Accordingly, I have used in judiciously over the years. Nevertheless, this method personally assisted me when nothing else helped because it totally transformed my life when my monster was cut down to size and my Soul-self became fully alive. Cliff Custer's specified steps are 1) Face your Shadows, 2) Forgive your perceived Shadow-makers and 3) Form a new model to replace old shadowed mental images.[24]

I approach "inner healing" in this way. <u>First</u>, whatever "monster" is unconsciously causing the problem or compulsion needs to be identified – remembered in as much detail as necessary so that people can re-enter the experience as if they were living it (a very Gestalt therapy technique). <u>Second</u>, invite people to re-immerse themselves in a very sensory way it that past event. They are to morph into their Art Room story so as to re-experience that moment, not unlike entering into a biblical story in the Ignatian Exercises. <u>Third</u>, have the Divine (in whatever audio-visual-tactile form the faith imagination will allow) to come between the person and the adversary or the incongruence. <u>Fourth</u>, have the person ask the Divine for whatever is necessary to remove, stop or destroy the perceived "monster" that has caused harm to them and is preventing them from being what God wants for them. <u>Fifth</u>, when the adversary is eradicated (sometimes quite dramatically and graphically depending on the level of the pain behind the image), ask people to have the Light of God shine on whatever is left (even on the "nothing.") If the adversary returns in a more humble or positive form, invite the image of the Divine to merge into it. If the antagonist re-appears basically unchanged, then the healing is incomplete and needs to be repeated, perhaps at a later time. <u>Finally</u>, I conclude with a short prayer of gratitude for what God has done.[25]

The process of Inner Healing is particularly necessary for significant life-altering events. The destroying of the monsters from the Id is akin to the crucifixion of the "sins of the world" to the cross; upon resurrection both Jesus and the world become transformed. However, the process is powerful, enveloping and can feel invasive. I use it only after I have engaged in serious prayer confident that it seems appropriate; and I also ask for permission. The process is not unlike surgery with a scalpel – cutting and removing the offending part with time after for recovery. People who are assisted through this process will be totally spent physically and emotionally because it is both purging and cleansing. After an encounter with a particular demon, I remember having sore muscles for three days.

This chapter has focused on unconsciously harbored events that become sin and affect the personal spiritual growth of individuals. Spiritual helpers need to be aware that "Monsters from the Id" often have a profound effect on the process of spiritual growth. When Christians, particularly those who seriously desire to keep moving along the Spiritual Road, seem to be going nowhere fast, consider whether something in the subconscious is causing the delay, the compulsion or the inability to do what is consciously chosen. Spiritual helpers may definitely need to refer people to psychotherapy. On the other hand, the people that have successfully been released from therapy may still need the healing-forgiveness of the past which only God can do. Both injuries and injurers as well as the unconsciously held memories that slip into sin need healing and forgiveness. May spiritual helpers be graced by the power of God to assist in this process.

Praxis for Spiritual Helpers

When examining a map the particular legend that guides the understanding of the map is important. Some map readers may prefer miles and others kilometers – with each map available in a variety of languages. Some people may need great details because they intend to "take it slow, enjoy the ride and see everything along the way." On the other hand, some travelers may simply want a basic overview because they desire the spontaneous approach of what to do, how far to go and when to sleep.

Spiritual helpers are to be … well, helpful spiritually. Thus, they need to adjust their map legends according to the travelers they advise. In other words, **spiritual helpers need to understand who they are talking to, have a helpful and measured way to be an accompanying guide but also be clear about what they are doing and why they are doing it**. This section is about those practical details. Since the Spiritual Road is long with different surfaces and difficulties along the way, being especially sensitive to "Who Are You Talking To?" is essential. Spiritual helpers need to acquire this intuitive sense, aided by the Holy Spirit, because different people require different approaches. In addition, there is a "Spiritual Helper Mode of Operation" that goes along with how similar helping professions approach their clients. I have described some of the principles that I have found useful for having effective spiritual conversations, which include details and techniques of being a spiritual helper. Finally, I conclude with an emphasis on the ultimate purpose of spiritual helpers – assisting people with their relationship with God – which is truly the last word I want to leave with the reader.

CHAPTER 22

Who Are You Talking To?

I have noticed through the years of practicing spiritual conversations how important it is to understand with whom I am talking. At first, I had to concentrate on the
details of the individuals – how old they were and what were their life situations as well
as their place along the Spiritual Road. I added to this assessment what they said they
needed combined with as much personal history as I could glean. Over time, I adapted to
a more intuitive approach but always gathering the information that would personalize the
individuals so as to be the most help to them. And of course, I have learned to listen to and
trust the still small voice of the Holy Spirit who still whispers seemingly foolish insights.

This kind of appraisal needs to strongly determine the specific questions that are
asked and the suggestions that are given. It is always about "Who Are You Talking To?"
As a way to communicate this spiritual helpers' praxis, I have included in this chapter
four examples: how Jesus' parable communicates different spiritual truths to two groups
of individuals at the same time (with a contemporary illustration of how to do the same),
how a particular biblical teaching is helpful to some people but not to others because they
are at different spiritual places in their respective lives, how people's move from one congregation to another can be needed for spiritual growth and finally how a mother provided
practical spiritual guidance at different times in her daughter's life.

JESUS' PARABLE

In Jesus' parable which has been named the Parable of the Prodigal Son,[1] [Luke 15:11-
32] Jesus was actually speaking to two different groups of people with two non-inter-
changeable messages. The context clearly indicates that "tax collectors and sinners were
gathering around to hear him" (verse 1) but the "Pharisees and the teachers of the law"
(verse 2) were also listening. When Jesus began the parable in verse eleven about a
certain man who had two sons, he had two audiences who were in two very different
places in their spiritual lives. The "sinners" may have had an on-again off-again relationship with God and probably didn't practice religion; whereas the official teachers of
Judaism were in daily contact with the divine and "practiced the faith." (I want to assume

319

the best case scenario for these religious leaders. Although some may have been hypocritical, I believe in the sincerity of many.)

I presuppose that readers have read and gleaned the basic narrative from this parable; if not, I highly recommend doing that. According to the traditional interpretation, the younger son corresponds to the "sinners" group and the "leaders" group is a match with the older son. Jesus was simultaneously teaching each group. The elementary principles regarding the younger son storyline are: God desires loving relationships with people. When they make poor choices that harm that relationship, God waits for them to "come to their senses" and offers total and complete forgiveness to re-establish the relationships. While it is possible to apply this same teaching to the older son (if you imagine that he is basically a fraud and out of relationship with the father), that conclusion is not what Jesus teaches nor is it the implied tenor of his voice. When the father near the end of the story goes out to the older son for a personal conversation, his words begin with an affectionate tone "my son." The most important points that Jesus wants to communicate to this older son are "You are always with me!" and secondarily, "Everything I have is yours!"

In regard to their spiritual conditions, at the very least, the younger son is out of relationship with God and the older son is included within a relationship with his father. In addition, at the climactic moment the younger son has nothing and the older son has everything.

When working with "younger son/daughter" types of people, the primary hope is to help move those people into a committed relationship with God. These people are roughly in the classical stage of faith called the Purgative Way[2] or even the Pre-Christian Way stage. **When working with "older son/daughter" types of people, an important intention is to affirm that these people are in a very valued committed relationship**. These people are typically on the Illuminative Way or at least near the end of the Purgative Way.[3] The spiritual tools to use for these diverse purposes are very different. What is needed from the younger son is a particular kind of confession, feeling welcomed and afterward to begin to learn the "rules" of the household. The older son, on the other hand, needs to affirm that all of the hard work and all of the thoughtful learning are worth the relationship; such assertion actually grows a person at this spiritual stage into the more mature mind of the father.

WORKING WITH THE "YOUNGER"

Younger sons and daughters are "coming to their senses" which means they have come to understand that God is important and they are starting to desire a committed relationship with God. Now, this "coming to their senses" spiritual moment can happened as an original realization or in the case of the Prodigal Son parable, it can be about returning home and back to a previous relationship with the divine (although it will be a different one.) Those people who help others grow spiritual will want to focus on the turning point of the "coming to their senses" spiritual moment and help younger sons/daughters move toward establishing a relationship with God.

Recently, I heard the disturbing story of an older gentleman who after fifty plus years lost his wife. Ray was sad and lonely. A local church leader listened to his story and invited him to come to church. Ray said, "Oh, I haven't been in church for twenty or thirty years. I don't know if I could do that." By this, of course, he meant that he had been in the far country and out of relationship with God; so this would be a major change in his life – something very difficult to do. After some encouragement, Ray finally came to "his senses" and attended the small rural church. His immediate need: community, love and companionship. After worship, he asked a widowed lady to go for some coffee with him. Word of this "romantic" rendezvous spread rapidly, but not in any positive way. The gossip was that the person who had originally invited Ray was trying to be a matchmaker to a woman who had no interest in being in a partnered relationship. Consequently, on the next Sunday the group of gossipers surrounded the widow who had been invited for coffee, shunned the visitor and all whisked away out an alternative exit in order to avoid the returning "younger" son.

Besides being a commentary of the state of the church, the visiting gentleman was not welcomed. The church people did not see Ray "while he was still a long way off" nor were they "filled with compassion for him." And they certainly did not run to him and "throw their arms around him."[4] [Luke 15:20] As a result, one more "sinner" went back into the far country away from the arms of faith.

If the congregational members had responded to the visitor's spiritual need, they would have rallied around the new visitor who clearly needed community. They all would have gone for coffee together and talked about the importance of being surrounded by the love of God incarnated in the people of the church. If the widow in question had no desire to pursue a personal relationship, she needed to say so with or without the support of others. But it was the responsibility of the church people to communicate and model the Love of God that this man really needed.

When a "younger son" gets shunned, he will run. When the church fathers and mothers do not have compassion for the one who has been lost plus understanding of how hard it is to come back home, the younger son will roam. A person on the Purgative Way needs to feel the unearned and undeserved acceptance of God which is called grace. How do modern day "Pharisees and teachers of the law" go out of their way, with over the top expression, so that contemporary "younger sons/daughters" feel wanted? Unless "sinners" feel undeniably graced, they will not stay. If they do not stay, they do not offer confession which is necessary for a committed relationship with the divine.

Dr. Kenneth E. Bailey[5], formerly the New Testament professor at the Near East School of Theology in Beirut, Lebanon, has truly amazing teachings of the parables of Jesus which are laced with the cultural understandings he gained by living for decades in that part of the world. Dr. Bailey tutors that **Jesus was using this parable to show a particular kind of forgiveness**. While Bailey refers to these as a Jewish form of forgiveness versus a Christian form of forgiveness, I prefer to label them as true confession versus works righteousness.

When the younger son decided to return home, he really felt his unworthiness to do so. Accordingly, he "rehearsed" what he would say when he would encounter that terribly tense moment that he would see his father. (Dr. Bailey claims that the request of the younger son for inheritance was the same thing as saying to his father, "Drop dead.") So, the son practiced: "Father, I have sinned against heaven and against you. I am no longer worthy to be called your son; make me like one of your hired servants."[6] [Luke 15:18-19] In other words, I will work for and earn whatever I'm allowed. This self-judgment was justifiable and to be expected. However, a careful reading of the parable shows that the father of the sinner allowed him to begin his earnestly-felt confession but stopped him in mid-sentence and does not allow him to say, "Make me one of your hired servants." Dr. Bailey rightly observes that confession for which one works does not contain grace; it is "works righteousness." It is trying to obtain a relationship with God via earning it, which can never be accomplished.

Coaching such authentic confessions from younger sons/daughters is of paramount importance for entrance into relationship with God and the community of the church. <u>What is necessary for this to happen</u>? First, without a loving welcome and excessive acceptance, such confessions will likely never occur. Second, younger daughters/sons need to feel unworthy to be accepted and that nothing they can do will change that. When they verbalize this, they need to hear, "God (and we) loves you anyway." This affirmation bonds them into God and into the church. However, people (and ministers) of the church are prone to give a new person a job as a way of helping them feel good about the church and to stay connected to the community. Unfortunately the typical effect of this "work-giving" is to allow younger sons/daughters to believe they can "earn" their way. What younger son/daughter people truly need is to feel that God as well as the Church loves and forgives them even though they do not deserve nor can they earn such a gift! That is the Truth that sets them free. Accordingly, the church should responsibly assert, "Your new life is God's gift to you; what you do with it is your gift back to God." Subsequently, younger sons/daughters need to be encouraged to readjust their lives morally and ethically according to the way that God wants them to live. Certain Bible studies, catechisms and basic Christianity classes are excellent to encourage this behavior. Henceforth, the younger sons/daughters will live in relationship with God and God's church being eternally grateful for the best gift anyone could ever receive – a positive relationship with God now and an Eternal Life one later.

Applying this above information would have helped Father Carl's spiritual direction approach to a younger son type who was actually a young man.

Father Carl was very responsible spiritual director who worked with many young men who were assigned for his assistance. Typically, spiritual directors, especially from the classical Roman Catholic tradition, understand their craft from the model of contemplative spirituality which deals with Christians who are not at the beginning of the spiritual growth process. In practical terms, this style includes helping a directee to discern, "Where have you sensed God's presence in your life?" or "How have you felt God prompting you?" The importance of this approach is to help others figure out or clarify what God is doing and how they may or may not wish to cooperate with God. This would be accomplished, as Father Carl knew, by asking lots of open-ended, reflective questions which are designed to allow directees to claim for themselves what God was doing in them and with them. It is kind of like the questions implied by the father in Jesus' parable, "Don't you sense that God is with you always... and especially in this moment?" "Don't you understand that all that God has is yours if you stay the course of working in the fields?" "What would it mean if you choose to celebrate with a lost younger brother who has just now found God?" These are older sons/daughters' types of questions.

On more than one occasion, I heard <u>Father Carl express concern about not being of much help to some particular young men</u>. It bothered him. In fact, he articulated that he didn't know why they kept returning for his counsel. Carl described how he had asked appropriate spiritual direction questions about where God was sensed. To such questions, the directees responded that they felt good at a candlelight Christmas Eve mass, sensed God even when they visited the church alone and also noted that they lives were full of chaos. One young man noted that he really wanted to get married; but the details about how he was going about that were not only inappropriate but also potentially harmful. Father Carl also asked if this younger son prayed and was told, "Not as much as I should but I do say the 'Our Father' (i.e., The Lord's Prayer) sometimes."

In reflection, <u>Father Carl's perceived problem could be resolved by simply shifting his spiritual direction approach</u>. Typically, the young men in question were still growing toward the contemplative form of Christian reflection and prayer. However, since they were still on the Purgative Way part of the Christian journey, they would be better facilitated by a different approach and alternative questions. For example, consider that one young man kept returning for help when Father Carl was sure that no help had been given. When budding Christians are in trouble, over-stressed or don't know what to do, they go to church, read their Bibles or offer a "fox-hole" prayers. As many modern films have depicted, younger sons/daughters wandered into sanctuaries because they were seeking what to do in their lives; there in film land, they sometimes met a priest or minister who offered words of consolation and counsel that proved insightful. When the above young man returned to the "sanctuary that was Father Carl," he was doing the same. Actually, the very act of returning to Father Carl was his attempt to communicate with God – it was his form of prayer.

While beginning or pre-Christians don't have an established time for formal prayer, they do talk to others (and God). In addition, their praying is not very contemplative – done in silence awareness as they actively listen for God's communication. Instead, they would more likely "say their prayers" – pre-authorized or route prayers. The conversation between Father Carl and his directee was had the potential to be extremely prayerful. However, Purgative Way Christians cannot be counted on to offer prayer on their own or even for what is needed. (Thus pre-authorized prayers, like Jesus did for his apostles when they asked for his guidance, are needed). More than anything, younger son directees need regular contact with God (and to establish other regular spiritual habits), to initiate godly moral and ethical practices and to have simple sentence prayers to use daily.

With this recognition, Father Carl would have easily changed his technique. First, Carl would have affirmed that "Yes, you need to come see me regularly and more often" which would be the spiritual discipline of coming close to God. Second, he would focus more on this young man's moral/ethical behaviors and ask whether he thought his behaviors were according to God's rules. In addition, using biblical passages could be helpful because younger sons/daughters respond to "following the rules" which will assure that they would be good and receive rewards for their actions. Father Carl could still use his open-ended questions like, "Do you think that God is happy when you manipulate young women?" or "Is it important to be in love with a woman before deciding to marry her?" and "What does God think? Is getting married about loving someone else or about satisfying your own needs?" These and similar questions would help connect the directee's concerns with God. It would even be appropriate for Father Carl to say gently, "If you want God to do for you what you want, then you probably ought to do what God wants. Don't you think?" Third, when this directee came to the moment of realizing that what he were doing was not what God wanted, then Father Carl needed to suggest that confession was necessary, and this confession needed to be done in the moment not as an assignment for this directee to do later. Since such young men are not equipped to create a prayer of this type, Carl might have offered to pray short phrases out loud and have his directee repeat them. Such a prayer might be: "Dear Heavenly Father, I am thankful that you hear me when I talk in this place. I am sorry that I am so selfish when it comes to wanting to get married. Help me to think about what _____ (the woman) wants and needs. I know you will help me when I do what is right so help me to do your Will. In your holy name, I pray. Amen." Following the verbal prayer, a sigh of relief or even tears would confirm the accuracy of this method. Finally, Father Carl could have his directee write a "love others" Bible verse to take with him to read daily and remind him of his confession and new life.

WORKING WITH THE "OLDER"

Older sons/daughters are in a much different place along the spiritual pathway. They are not beginners nor are they extremely skilled. They are aware of God and God's importance; they have a set of morals and ethics; and they have basically committed their lives to following/trusting God. These are the primary lessons of the Purgative Way. As the older sons/daughters have entered the Illuminative Way, they are in a long process of learning which includes increased and clarified beliefs as well as consistent application of those beliefs – all for the purpose of becoming a mature Christian.

The older son in the Parable of the Prodigal Son stayed at home and committed himself to be in the relationship with his father. Certainly, this older son had previously realized how deeply his father loved him and accepted him just as he was. He also must have known that he was not perfect nor did he deserve the vast fortune or inheritance that was to be his. So, he invested in this established relationship and in his future, actually increasing its value with his work. He worked hard and faithfully. He probably wanted his father to be proud of him; perhaps he forgot that his father had always been proud of him even when the older son talked angrily and disrespectfully to him.

What do the older sons/daughters need spiritually? As part of their development, such people have previously made confessions, struggled with temptations and adopted more helpful patterns of behavior including some spiritual disciplines. As a result, they have come to have a basic trust of God with their lives. Now, they are in the long process of learning, growing and applying divine truths/principles into real life. They need to remember that they have come a long way. But more than that, **they need to recall why they decided to live the spiritual life – because having God's Love is worth all the trouble!**

When working with older sons/daughters, first remind them of Christian Basics –

✟ how much God loves them
✟ they are forgiven but don't deserve it
✟ they have God's promise of eternal life
✟ they have lived their new lives as a gift back to God

In the parable, the father reminded the older son, I am with you always and all I have is yours. First of all, remembering enables Illuminative Way Christians to re-up their commitment and keeps them living a positive life. Worship, especially in the Protestant tradition that strongly emphasizes re-telling the Gospel message, has this effect.

Secondly, older sons/daughters are not to be demoted, but encouraged and challenged to follow their convictions. Let it be said that persons at the beginning of the Illuminative Way can still slip back into former sins. However, once they understand their mistake, do not shame them! They know what is right and feel badly when they have been angry, dishonest, disrespectful and so forth. Many older sons/daughters are adaptive children (those who try to please those in authority) and will hide or pretend to be good when internally they don't feel positive. If they withdraw or become defensive, they will not transform or mature as Christian people. Instead, they need to come to the realization that in order to become good they need to be transparent when they don't behave correctly, especially when they feel negative inside.

So, affirm for them that "Therefore, there is now no condemnation for those who are in Christ Jesus."[7] [Romans 5:1] Provide a lot of grace for them. Say to older sons/daughters, "You are not bad because you are already redeemed. When you act poorly or make inappropriate/unhealthy choices, you can change direction or re-decide without disapproval. You just need to confess and decide what you want to do." Contemplative spiritual direction works well for older sons/daughters because it helps them process what is going on inside with a divine perspective and then gives them time to think and re-decide between sessions. Personal "silent retreats" are even better because in such a setting they are assigned something to think about followed by spiritual conversation about that subject.

Third, be sure to follow up with "What did you learn/decide/experience?" kinds of questions. **Above all, the task of Christians on the Illuminative Way is to learn spiritually (about themselves and about God) and APPLY that in real life**. What have they learned? What do they choose to do about it? What exactly is the plan or practical action they will begin? As this process unfolds, spiritual helpers could make summaries of how those they assist have become better, using whatever particular words or phrases communicate best. Often in my time of praying with the Christians near the end of a session, I will thank God for bringing such growth.

Finally, put the spiritual growth of older daughters/sons into the larger perspective. They are in a long, often slow learning process. Accordingly, affirming the way they used to be and how far they have grown can be very supportive. What they are doing is allowing the Spirit to rule in their hearts. Identifying when they actually were doing God's Will and acting with the mind of Christ can be extremely helpful to further growth. Furthermore, encourage them to put on the mantel of spiritual leadership/mentoring for those who have not traveled as far down the spiritual road as they have, saying: "When you choose to celebrate with younger brothers/sisters who seems to be getting all the attention that they don't deserve (and that you are not getting), then you are affirming the transformative love which the Father-God gives. The only way you can authentically behave this way is if you are getting better, maturing and growing spiritually."

In summary, spiritual helpers are strongly encouraged to understand who they are talking to. The method of working with younger sons/daughters people on the Pre-Christian/Purgative Ways is different than working with older daughters/sons who are on or near the Illuminative path of Christian spiritual growth. Making such distinctions is absolutely essential for effective spiritual growth to continue.

CAREFUL SCRIPTURAL APPLICATION

Jesus' command to his disciples, "If anyone would come after me, he must deny himself and take up his cross and follow me"[8] is, without question, one description of the ultimate goal of the Christian spiritual life. [Matthew 16:24] However, this directive can be either helpful or destructive depending on the particular spiritual condition of the individuals who receive it.[9]

Jesus is the literal application of this statement. In other words, he exemplified self-denial, carrying his cross to and dying on Golgotha in order to communicate God's love and grace. Obviously, Jesus did not follow God in this way until the end of his life and even asked that he "not have to drink this cup." He could have resisted his arrest with a "legion of angels" coming to his rescue; but instead he stopped the violence of Peter and healed the ear of the high priest's servant. He could have clearly and forcefully proclaimed the truth as he did numerous times in the Temple court and countryside; but he surrendered to silence before his accusers. Actually during most of his life and ministry, Jesus did not deny himself or surrender to carry a cross; instead he proactively made choices and took action. Indeed, Jesus followed his own teaching "to deny, carry and follow" when it was spiritually appropriate to do so. Undoubtedly, Jesus would not assert that others follow his teachings in ways that he did not. Spiritual helpers would be most effective to apply this teaching (and others like it) as judiciously.

This instructional axiom "Deny yourself, take up your cross and follow me" is often applied to self-surrender – that is, "Give up living life on your own terms with your own will in your own way." Consequently, Christians are told to become "nothing" in order that Jesus might live for them, in them or with them.

For those in the Pre-Christian and Purgative Ways, this rendering of Jesus' command can be very helpful, especially if they need "external control" when they do not seem to have any self-control. In order to proceed successfully, they need to have clear rules and structure which they are not able to provide or follow. They need power from above, outside of and greater than themselves, in order to succeed. Thus, to deny themselves – that is their ability to establish and follow a helpful way of living – is absolutely necessary! HOWEVER, this kind of self-denial is not the ultimate goal – a lovingly optional self-denial is.

Effectively, people at this point in their lives are making themselves into a marionette inviting God to pull the strings because when they attempt to do it themselves, they become spasmodic and even destructive to themselves and others. Most certainly, God is willing to provide this control for people who need and ask for this intervention. It is the most loving thing for God to do – for spiritual helpers as well. However, if God wanted to have puppets for followers, God could have easily made that happen. The ideal situation is to have fully skilled individuals voluntarily surrender those talents to the service of God's purposes and whose personal wills are naturally in accord with God's Will. In order for this to happen, Christians must be restrained from going their own destructive way and at the same time develop positive spiritual habits and attitudes that become who they grow into. With such strength, they will be able to voluntarily deny themselves.

Accordingly, Illuminative Way Christians may begin to view Jesus' teaching with deeper discernment. They may say, "If I deny myself including my abilities, then how can I have any strength to 'take up my cross and follow Jesus?" Those who help others grow spiritually can respond, "I understand what you are saying. Jesus never asked us to deny our loving self, our compassionate self or our honest self. However, our 'negative self' most certainly needs to be eliminated." In this "Clarifications," Illuminative Way Christians are not reading what the scripture says but what it means. Truly, Jesus never did or ever would require people to deny their compassionate self, their honest self or their loving self. These and other God-qualities, which are to become aspects of mature Christian individuals, are not to be denied but fully enhanced and embraced.

As a result, this transformation builds a strong, independent and confident sense of Self. When such people deny themselves in order to take up a cross and follow Jesus, it comes with love and voluntary surrender. **Accordingly, God has received willing and capable servants who can manage the vineyard as a stand-in for the Master**. Such followers voluntarily build the Holy Community of God and also love God in the process, which can only be accomplished when Christians release and relinquish control they could keep.

Just like the developmental growth process, children will exhibit out of control behaviors that need to be controlled by an outside force. Then they need to obtain their God-given gifts, skill, talents and abilities; and, as a result, they become strong-willed, self-confidence and independent. Subsequently, these adults come to realize that they are not the center of the universe and that no one is essentially better than anyone else. They understand that everyone is connected to the same eternal source and are designed to return to God and live eternally in God's Holy Community. This new life perspective provides the opportunity for free self-denial with full knowledge but without the necessity to do so. **Their response to God's love is now truly an optional choice which greatly deepens their spiritual relationship as they take up their "cross" and follow in a much different manner – one which begins to allow Jesus to unite and live through them**. Jesus modelled such spiritual maturity: "No one takes it (my life) from me, but I lay it down of my own accord. I have authority to lay it down and authority to take it up again. This command I received from my Father."[10] [John 10:18]

When spiritual helpers succinctly apply biblical teachings such as "Deny yourself, take up you cross and follow me" according to "whom they are talking to," Christians grow and develop spiritually wherever they are along the Spiritual Road.

MARY'S SPIRITUAL MOVE

Sometimes people cannot grow spiritually because of the circumstances and experiences in their lives. They need to be in a different situation. While it is possible that people run away from what they do not like, the story of Mary describes such a situation in which moving was the best thing for her to do. Spiritual helpers need to make such discernment by considering "who they are talking to."

I remember Mary who came to the congregation where I was the senior minister. When we sat down to talk about her religious experience,[11] I discovered that she had recently moved from a different city where she had been a practicing Christian for eight years. Her former church had strongly insisted on a lot of rules, the do's and do not's of faith. Mary reluctantly expressed some discomfort with that approach, probably expecting some degree of correction from me. However, the atmosphere of the congregation was much more unstructured and would allow Mary the freedom to take the faith she already had and make conscious decisions about what she really believed.

Understanding where Mary was in the process of her growing Christian faith, I encouraged her to become part of the congregation saying, "You will find support and encouragement to strengthen your faith without others making you feel guilty." Mary joined the church and experienced rapid spiritual growth because she needed a different expression of faith at this point in her faith life, which in no way made her former congregation a bad place. In fact, Mary's former congregation was perfect for her first eight years as a Christian. (One of the reasons I do not want to identify with particular doctrinal teachings of faith is because most every approach for transmitting Christianity has purpose and value at different phases in a Christian's life; and people need the freedom to move where God leads them to grow best.)

If Mary had associated with Christians and/or a congregation that preached that there is only one way (even if that is true), she would have continued to be reserved, guiltier and growth-stunted. Parents who recognize and accept that adolescents somewhere between eight and eighteen have the tendency to "try on all kinds of roles and attitudes and relationships" understand what was happening to Mary. Those parents also know that "this phase they are going through" will change to some other phase and they rarely stay with anything too long.

Think about it this way. Parents tell children, "Try your spinach; how will you know you don't like it if you don't try it." Then, when children want to taste all of the different flavors of ice cream, parents balk at the idea. The good parenting principle, of course, is to let children have as much freedom as needed for them to experience and choose for themselves – but without harming themselves or others in the process – an art form, certainly. Spiritual adolescents also need this same kind of balanced mentoring that is devoid of negative, "critical parent" overtones. Obviously, Mary had been a spiritual baby and was now growing into spiritual adolescence and needed a different situation in order to do so. Spiritual helpers can provide such assistance if they remember "who they are talking to."

A PARENT'S GUIDANCE

Consider the example of the following two stories from the life of Samantha Anne and how her mother, Beverly, provided spiritual guidance for the different eras of her life. This real-life illustration provides an analogy for how spiritual helpers might modify their approach depending on the particular people and different situations.

Little Sam was five years old and was already in love with soccer. She was always running and kicking her soccer ball with reckless abandon everywhere around her home in the suburbs that bordered a busy street. Her mother instructed her not to play close to the street and if her ball went across the road that she was not to go get it.

One morning after one of her power kicks bounced off a tree and sailed toward the street, Sam instinctively bolted to retrieve it. The blaring of an automobile horn and the screeching of tires halted her, wide-eyed, looking right into the head light of a dark blue sedan. The woman driving jumped from her vehicle and the commotion caused Sam's mother, Beverly, to come screaming from the house to swoop up her little girl. Mom thanked the cautious driver and took little Sam into the living room and sat her on the couch. They were both shaking and crying and hugging. Finally, mom took a deep breath and scolded, "Samantha Anne, what have I told you about playing soccer near the street; and what did I say about chasing the ball into the street?" Sad-faced Sam slurred, "Don't do it; but I needed to go get it." Mom knew what she had to do. "Well, young lady, you will not need to go get the ball for the next two weeks because it will be on top of the refrigerator. And you are not allowed to go into the front yard by yourself or the ball will be put away for another two weeks. Do you understand?" "Yes … but mom …" "No buts, Samantha Anne; that's the way it's going to be!" And the discipline was enforced strictly. …

… Years later, Samantha was stunning with her auburn hair flowing across tanned shoulders in her strapless, scarlet, form-fitting senior prom gown. Beverly was so proud that her baby girl had grown into such a beautiful, young woman – smart, confident and capable. Soon Jerome, her boy friend of two years plus, would be arriving to sweep her away into the night of dress up and maturity and freedom – beauty and dinner and dancing and friends and after-prom activities. "Samantha, you are so beautiful and I'm so proud of you," exclaimed her mom with tears starting to form in her eyes. "Can we sit down a minute?" "Sure, Mom." They positioned themselves on the same couch, thirteen years more worn, where they had sat after mom had rescued little Sam from the soccer ball near-tragedy.

"I remember when I was getting ready for my senior prom," mom started. "I was so alive and excited … I felt so pretty. I hope you feel the same way. I really hope you have fun and will remember this day for a long, long time." Samantha assured her mother that she kind of felt the same way and was planning to have a good time. "I also wanted to let you know that I accidently overheard you and Jerome talking last night. You were speaking about the prom and about having sex; and you told him that you had condoms in your purse just in case." Sam started to speak but mom softly interrupted, "Let me finish, honey." "I know that you and Jerome are very close and have been together for a couple of years. I know that you love each other. That is all wonderful and I would never take that away from either of you. We have talked about how having sex is much more than physical pleasure. God made it as an ultimate confirmation and affirmation of our togetherness. It is a bonding of a relationship – both psychologically and physically and spiritually too. In order words, when you make love, when you share love in this way, you are saying, 'I am committed to this relationship long-term, knowing that we will both change and need to adapt to make the relationship grow.' If you and Jerome think you are ready to have sex, then you need to decide if you are ready to be committed like that to each other. After you have talked, you will know what you choose to do or not do. Sex is too beautiful and powerful to leave to chance – to just be caught up in the glitz of a senior prom night."

"Now, I am just about done saying what I wanted to say, except for one more thing. Do you remember when you were five years old and ran out into the street to retrieve your soccer ball?" "Yes," came Sam's wondering why response. "Well, we sat right here on this couch and I told you that I was putting your soccer ball on top of the frig. I had to limit you and your activities because even if you promised not to run into the street, you would have followed the ball wherever it went. You didn't understand why I set a rule that seemed so mean. I'm sure that you know now I did that to keep you safe because you didn't have the ability you have now to make a decision and stick to it. You are not a five-year-old little girl; you are a lovely eighteen-year-old young woman – and I am not going to try to put your condoms on top of the refrigerator. I love you as much as I ever have and I will love you the same tomorrow. Since you are thinking about sex, I hope you will talk with Jerome first about your relationship. If you are not totally sure that your relationship commitment is long-term, don't do it. … All I want now is a hug."

Beverly not only knew what was best for five-year-old Sam but also knew how to be God's angel whispering into the ear of developing Samantha. Practically and realistically speaking, parents cannot control the lives of their eighteen-year-old children. In fact, attempting to control or manipulate whatever is being taught to a teenage will pretty sure backfire with the opposite result. In addition like everyone, Samantha needed and had God's spirit within her in order to make this decision instead of going with the default "whatever feels right" selfish nature. She was on the verge of spiritual growth or spiritual decline – confirming or rejecting her "belief" with the "deeds" of real life application. At age five, Sam needed clear-cut, strict rules to grow in the difference between right and wrong – a very spiritual basic. To grow spiritually at age eighteen, Samantha needed knowledge, encouragement and the freedom to decide.

In some ways, spiritual helpers are parents to those they guide. What type of parent they are best depends on who they accompany. The younger sons/daughters need clear-cut basics with strongly stated limits. They may not understand why at the time, but good parents do what is needed. Spiritual helpers need to do the same for younger Christians. On the other hand, at the appropriate age and moment in time, parents and spiritual helpers do what is most helpful when they assert their love and simultaneously allow greater freedom for the blossoming adolescents. Oh yes, it is certainly scary to do so; but nonetheless what is necessary.

SUMMARY

As part of the praxis for spiritual helpers, even before they think about how they are to function, they need to be sensitive to the individuals they are serving. Being receptive of the type of people, the circumstances of their lives and the status of their current relationship with God are essential. <u>Awareness of "who you are talking to" is the first step in spiritual guidance</u>.

Thus, in this chapter, I have used various real-life vignettes to sensitize spiritual helpers to this practical way to be with others. The stories and examples are intentionally different. I began with a biblical example of how Jesus was a master of communicating to the spiritual needs of people – even when they were at developmentally dissimilar spiritual places in their lives. Younger sons and daughters as well as older sons and daughters are typically on different parts of the Spiritual Road. Using scripture in itself takes appropriate discernment for spiritual helpers as illustrated in the basic Christian teaching to "deny yourself, take up your cross, and follow me." Father Carl for some young men, I for Mary and Beverly for Samantha Anne each had unique opportunities to apply "Who Are You Talking To" with the assistance they provided. Each situation was different; all required careful discernment certainly prior to any guidance given. <u>Because individuals are complicated complex composites, spiritual helpers are advised to proceed cautiously and within the presence of God's Holy Spirit – who must always be the ultimate spiritual helper.</u>

CHAPTER 23

The Spiritual Helper Mode of Operation

The ways that spiritual helpers employ their craft, their mode of operation, can be summarized with some very basic principles which I have included in this chapter. In the above chapters, I have supplemented such fundamental spiritual guidance with the theory and process of spiritual growth, some additional maps to overlay as well as some specific tools to assist spiritual helpers when the people they accompany get stuck alongside the Spiritual Road. However, **do spiritual helpers need to understand the process of spiritual growth in order to assist others toward a deeper and closer relationship with God? Absolutely not!** God will lure people into such a relationship without any outside help – God has been doing that for centuries and will continue to work in that way. **So, why bother? I believe that God has given accumulated knowledge and spiritual tools so that spiritual helpers can be co-builders with God.**

I remember fondly the endless hours of putting together Lego sets with our son who always wanted to construct the coolest and the most complex space ships. He was only four years old at the time we started Lego building. So who do you think did ninety-eight per cent of the work? Dear ol' dad, of course. I did not need our son's help but it was so much fun doing it together. In fact, I have an incredible wide smile on my face right now just thinking about those days. It was a real joy! I suspect that our son felt that as well; since, while in high school, he voiced his displeasure that we had passed all of the Lego sets on to someone one else. Do you think it might have something to do with the being together and working together? In addition, it was also skills training for bigger and better life tasks that were ahead. Space ships to Mars begin with play in family romp rooms.

God can build the most complex human being without any help from people – but why would God want to miss the fun-filling, relational love-work? I am convinced that God desires the camaraderie. God is all about loving. God is all about relating. God is all about creating. Doing that together with other people just multiplies God's Joy to its fullest. After explaining how Jesus shared in God's spiritual connectedness with people, he noted, "I have told you this so that my joy may be in you and that your joy may be complete."[1] [John 15:11] Helping others grow spiritually is about loving and relating and creating – all which God desires. Truly, God does not need people to help others but yearns to be part of that joyful experience whenever God's children work and play together.

Now in regard to Lego building, I could have let our four-year-old son sit in a sea of red, yellow and blue plastic blocks and he probably would have learned to push some of them together. However, he could not have read the instructions and would have never been able to finish what he wanted. As a result, he would have become frustrated and would not have loved playing with Lego sets nor would he have relished the time we had together. Certainly, I did not need him in order to finish a Lego project; and consequently I could have unintentionally not allowed him to participate as much as he could. As every teaching parent knows, there is a balance between doing too much and not doing enough – and of course the proper balance is necessary for the good of all God's children.

The same is true for the way that spiritual helpers assist others. **People, by themselves, can grow spiritually as they respond to God. However, they can do so more easily in the presence and with the help of others**. The scripture clearly states: "For where two or three come together in my name, there am I with them."[2] [Matthew 18:20] This "spiritual law" seems to indicate that <u>the divine wants to be part of personal spiritual faith and growth. Surely, God could have designed it otherwise, but where would be the fun in that?</u>

YOU CAN DO IT

In order to grow spiritually in the beginning, most people simply need the listening and encouraging skills that mature Christian people normally develop over the years. These established Christians actually do a wonderful job of helping others grow spiritually. This happens around the kitchen table, in Bible studies, via parental conversation with their children, through Sunday school classes and small groups as well as between folks on the phone, with Skype, at lunch or doing the work of the church. **Long-term Christians who have seriously engaged in prayer over many years need to be spiritual helpers** … especially for new Christians or those on the Pre-Christian Way!!! Christianity does not have enough of these folks helping others who are just getting started on the Spiritual Road. I have had numerous conversations attempting to convince Illuminative Way Christians that they <u>by far</u> know enough to accompany others, who are not asking the same kinds of difficult questions that these potential helpers are. In addition by doing so, they would also enhance their own spiritual journey and not be so bored with the same old churchy stuff. In my experience teachers always learn more than their students. Furthermore, <u>the fastest growing congregations understand and implement the concept that committed Christians need to be ministers of others, with individuals and for groups</u>. Average Christians need to love others by listening and encouraging beginners in the faith. However, they also need to realize when they have reached the limit of their ability.

As spiritual growth gets more complex, more skill is necessary so everyone "in charge of" guiding others spiritually (pastors and parents included) need to refer the people to whom they are listening to someone with more skill and experience in the spiritual life. While making referrals is necessary, knowing the quality of the people to whom spiritual helpers refer is even more important. So many people go into the helping fields because they needed help; but unless they have recovered and experienced healing, they will not do a good job of assisting others. Thus, **personal recommendations are usually the best way to assess the value of professional helpers.** Spiritual helpers who need to refer should take the initiative to find suitable people to suggest because they are likely to ask the better questions. Talk with these optional persons (physicians, therapists, social workers, other spiritual guides and others.) but also ask for references and talk to them with some particular and pointed questions. These "advanced" helpers may be a professionally trained person or simply someone older, a more experienced pastor, priest, religious or spiritual director; and they need to have a good combination of life experience, more learning about the spiritual life as well as personal sensitivity to what God hopes for others. Then provide a couple of names from which people can select – knowing that any choice will be acceptable and truly helpful.

At the later stages of the spiritual life journey, having a seasoned spiritual guide who often is blessed with the accompanying presence of the Holy Spirit is absolutely essential. These folks have a special ability to help others from God's own heart, in God's own way, because God has actually blessed them in such a manner. Such spiritual guides are rare indeed and to be highly valued.

MO DETAILS

After deciding that "you can do it" with God's help of course, **some initial details need to be considered.** Conversation about the <u>meeting time and place</u>, practice of <u>confidentiality</u>, <u>payment</u> expectations (if any) and <u>how to end meeting together</u> with an exit interview requested are all best to be concluded upfront and as soon as possible. The frequencies of meetings can be negotiated and varied according to the needs of people. Spiritual helpers must be able to <u>stay current with their people's lives</u> and so need to suggest how often they need to meet in order to do so. I typically have monthly meetings and suggest communicating more often when people are in crisis or have a lot happening. I have also found that <u>the fifty-minute therapeutic hour is extremely unhelpful</u>. When people know that they have fifty minutes, they often (unconsciously) wait until five minutes prior to time to end before they speak the most important topic. Obviously, not much can be done in such a short span of time. Since my intent is to be helpful, I tell the people with whom I work that I start with a beginning time, but have no firm end time. (In order to put aside concerns, I also have a maximum fee no matter how long it takes; and I am in charge of how much time I provide.)

This procedure has proved to be effective for having enough time to deal with any subject and often people introduce what they know as most important soon after beginning so long sessions have not been typically an issue. Some of those I assist bring a written list of what they would like to discuss and share that at the beginning of each session.

As indicated in the previous chapter, spiritual helpers need an intuitive sense of who they are assisting. Some people call this having the "gift" from God of knowing how to say what is needed to whom. Having this "spiritual" gift is awesome, but it can also be developed in some people; and while the best spiritual helpers have been blessed by God, they can actually learn copious things even to be intuitive and sensitive. Spiritual helpers begin with these sensitive perceptions and estimations. However, proceeding with a structure designed to enhance the Holy Spirit's involvement is essential. I have learned that **spiritual guidance is all about being P-L-A-S-T-I-C**, by which I mean flexible and Spirit-led, not artificial and human-made.

PRAY

First of all, I pray for all of the people I help spiritually – both prior to meeting and in between sessions. Immediately before I meet with a person, I pray between five and twenty minutes. This is not generic prayer, but is specifically tailored to the people I will be seeing. I pray for God's assistance for the people I will be helping and God's intervention if needed. I most consistently and fervently pray for a "professional" distance to occur: "Keep me out of their stuff and don't let me inflict my stuff on them!" I also seek to be sensitive to when the Holy Spirit speaks and to have the courage to repeat what I have heard. In addition, I ask for guidance about when to offer instruction and when to just listen. I explicitly seek the best questions to ask that will assist the person to where God wants them to go – and I consistently receive those directives during this prayer time. Accordingly, I limit my talk to God; and default to listening and relaxing.

I also have some involvement in the lives of the people I assist, through praying for them, providing summaries of sessions, reading the journal entries they provide and with in-between session emails that answer questions they have. I do this selectively; considering the people, where they are on the Spiritual Road and whether transference (and counter-transference) is likely. In therapy supervision, professionals would claim that this is over-involvement. I am cautious with some people, but mostly my attempt is to establish a deep level of caring, compassion and trust with these spiritually maturing people. Trust and involvement are essential for building the Community of God. A strong level of trust is also indispensable when it comes to times that I suggest something with which people disagree, times when they are scared to try or believe something different and times when they need to accept that the darkness is where they need to be. People can sometimes only push through such difficulties solely based on the trusting relationship.

LISTEN

In recent decades, many have labeled the ministry of spiritual direction as a "listening" ministry – listening to others and listening for the Holy Spirit. In the broader historical perspective, originally spiritual direction was definitely instructive, dogmatic and even authoritative – people were told what to believe and what to do. Spiritual guidance as re-defined in this past century has often been contrasted with psychotherapy which is to solve problems, answer questions and give advice – which spiritual direction is not to be. However, honestly spiritual directors do sometimes participate in giving advice, answering questions and solving problems. Certainly, telling people what to do never fixes their problems because they have to realize the solutions on their own. On the other hand, if they have no idea how to do that, they will only become frustrated and stop. **I am convinced that the proper balance between letting others figure out how God wants them to grow spiritually and suggesting what they might try is essential for effectively helping others grow spiritually**.

How do spiritual helpers keep that balance? The adage, "God gave people two ears and one mouth so that they will listen twice as much as they talk" is a good rule for spiritual helpers. However, while talking, even advice-giving, is important, be sure to keep the PLASTIC order of first praying, listening and asking before even thinking about talking.

In regard to listening, active listening skills are indispensable. The ability, innate or learned, to retain spoken information and be able to repeat it may be the best skill a spiritual helper can have. If need be, take a class or study the techniques via the internet or other media. People, after hearing what they have said, will be altered. They may feel grateful to be heard, validated for what they believe, challenged by the inconsistency, surprised that they were not understood or even gain additional insight from their own words. Spiritual helpers are responsible for stopping conversations when they have reached their own ability to retain what has been said. Unless this is done, spiritual helpers do injustice to the people talking. They need to summarize what has been said before moving forward. For those people I help who talk a lot or tend to flit randomly from topic to topic, I interrupt quite often. However, this is not the "Talk or Teaching" that takes place later because at this point spiritual helpers are simply parroting what they have heard not saying what they think about it.

Furthermore, always pay attention to the first subject people talk about. The gestalt therapy class I took in seminary taught me to listen to the very first words and the topics included in them. Literally! Very truly I say I have been astounded how the seemingly casual, chit-chat conversation at the beginning of a session has bearing on the spiritual conclusion for that day. For example, how people react to the rainy weather can be precursive to the tragedy accident they choose to talk about. Or how their child was such a handful may have direct reference to the resistance they have about doing what they know God requires of them.

Getting people to talk and listening to them, of course, is only part of the task. **Spiritual helpers need to remember the words and important phrases spoken by those they accompany**. I write down what I hear; people always wonder what I record so I tell them and show them what I have written. I keep notes which almost exclusively include the important words and phrases that people say. First of all, I want to have a good summary for them, which they sometimes record for themselves. In addition, people can even answer their own questions but do not recognize them until they hear them or read them. Spiritual helpers, who can offer back what they have heard from "some wise adviser" or "famous philosopher," not only assist well but also instill both greater awareness and confidence in the people to whom they listen.

I believe what is most instructive about listening and recording well is the ability to recall the important words spoken from previous months by those I accompany. Reminding people of what they have concluded or what they said they wanted to do can have great value. However, such reminding best takes place after the steps of listening and asking have taken place.

ASK

People always ask questions. When they do, I smile and probably chuckle before I say, "I'm sorry. You have got it wrong (again). I ask the questions; you give the answers." None of the people I assist actually like that comment; but they have come to expect it. **Asking questions puts the responsibility for spiritual growth where it belongs – with the one doing the growing**. Spiritual helpers who provide lots of direction and dogma are actually taking responsibility for the lives of other people. It is no wonder that they get upset when those people don't accept that advice. Even the talk or teaching (discussed below) needs to be framed with the questions, "Would you like me to say what I think?" followed by "But it is totally your choice whether you believe or do that or not."

Questions have different purposes. **Mostly, spiritual helpers need to ask open-ended questions**, which means that they can never be answered with "yes" or "no" and the answers are not expected or included in the questions. Instead of asking "Do you believe in God?" say, "Tell me about believing in God." In other words, people are free to respond however they choose. Rhetorical questions that expect particular answers are acceptable if used to follow a logical progression or bring people to a specific open-ended question. Also, avoiding the word "why" whenever possible is advisable since people often feel defensive when asked "why" questions.

Especially when commencing to work with people, questions help in the process of getting to know them. At a first session, I might say, "Tell me about yourself." I expect the response, "What do you want to know?" Immediately I rejoin, "Whatever you want to tell me." If people share about an event that seems important or about which I don't completely understand, I will probably ask, "Could you tell me more about that?" This same approach works even with people who I know well, "Tell me what happened this past month?" As people describe events without personally relating to it, I wonder "why" they shared about this particular topic. So, I will ask, "Could you explain how (Why) this holds such meaning for you?"

Asking questions also has the advantage of actually discovering what people understand. People can only retain so much information; and spiritual helpers never know what part of what has been discussed people garner. Thus, I may invite people to summarize a particular session saying, "What are you going to take with you as you leave today?" Or when beginning the next session, I will ask, "What do you remember from our last conversation?" **What was remembered is what is important, not what actually transpired**. In addition, people often misinterpret what has been said or apply it in ways that were not intended.

Questions are also well-suited for identifying and encouraging spiritual growth. If, for example, spiritual helpers have appraised that Pre-Christian Way people need to identify God, they may simply, ask, "Where have you noticed the presence of God lately?" Or if they need to focus on grace, spiritual helpers may inquire, "When have you ever received what you did not really deserve?" For Purgative Way Christians, spiritual helpers may want to center on rules or ethical concerns. Thus, asking about what people have seen as fair or unfair can lead to whether that incident is in accord with God's ways. Asking beginning Christians to describe how a particular spiritual habit might be practiced can lead to the suggestion that they might try that for thirty days and report back. Also asking "What have you learned during this past month?" is an open-ended question that can be helpful. This could be about God, life, spiritual principles, the Bible, scripture verses, prayers, the church and so forth. Especially if Christians are near the beginning of the spiritual journey, this question can be used to affirm and solidify the rules, the moral and ethical principles and the spiritual habits that are being established. It also determines what most interests these Christians.

Questions are perfect ways to enable people to apply faith to life or to discern how they have done so. Thus, the question, "How have you applied your faith to life?" is especially useful for those Illuminative Way Christians who need to connect and confirm the application of spirituality. On the other hand, people may only be able to talk about what life happenings have been most important. After which, spiritual helpers can assist them to adjoin faith to the event with a comment-question, "It seems that God had a lot to do with that; how do you think that is true?" Or after people have finished talking, spiritual helpers may query, "Where in particular was God working in what you just described?" This question can have a variety of uses. For individuals who are on the Pre-Christian Way or Purgative Way, naming God can specifically help to enrich their understanding of God. However, the question is also effective when dealing with "Dark Night" moments as people either see God's light in the darkness or clearly claim the absence of the divine in their lives.

When I have asked people, "When did you feel closest to God or when did you grow spiritually?" they most often described a difficult time in their lives from which they have recovered. Helping people grow spiritually often means helping them in the midst of these situations or to make sense of the difficulties after they have ended. Indeed, sensing what people need and asking appropriate questions is a semi-gentle method that can enable them to grow spiritually.

SPIRIT-EYES

To have Spirit-eyes is to spiritualize, by which I mean to see God in the midst of life. In essence, this is the spiritual helper's primary task. Asking the above kinds of questions coupled with intuitive individuals often allows the spiritual light bulb to ignite. Spiritual helpers, of course, need to immediately affirm the insight.

On the other hand, other people may not notice these "God-sightings." After people describe what they are doing in their life and the comment has been offered "Maybe God is at work here," they still may not make the connection. Spiritual helpers might offer a different perspective. For example, the loving action of taking care on someone else may not be seen as God acting in the midst of life. Spiritual helpers may wish to probe whether the people they accompany believe that God can actually work in the world and in particular through other people. They may wish to inquire whether it is possible that the loving event just described might be God doing exactly that. Even if people cannot confirm God's activity, spiritual helpers can provide spirit-eyes by matter-of-factly commenting, "I see God working there." They may wish to add, especially for rule-requiring Purgative Way Christians, Jesus' statement, "Anyone who has seen me has seen the Father."[3] [John 14:9] or "I will show you my faith by what I do."[4] [James 2:18]

Another way that spiritual helpers can have Spirit-eyes for those they accompany is by connecting the dots between life events. However, doing so is more appropriately shared later and belongs to the "Connect" section below. When people repeat the past, they may be in a pattern of behavior or thinking the same things. God can use or be involved in such recurrences to either teach a lesson, call attention to sin or even affirm a talent or ability. Noticing the correlation between past and present happenings can be an extremely valuable in-sight for spiritual helpers to make. Because spiritual helpers are not emotionally involved, they are well-suited to reveal such perceptions. However, those being assisted still must take responsibility for the insights; so helping them to notice a good place to fish does not mean spiritual helpers catch the fish. Guides on the huge lake of life who have spiritual sonar are especially helpful, saying, "Cast your nets on the other side of the boat; I see Spirit there."

Having Spirit-eyes may also involve the simple act of accountability. Occasionally, people will conclude where God is leading them and that they choose to follow. Recalling those times months hence can be particularly helpful when people don't follow through on what they intended. Doing what someone else tells them to do can be dismissed. However, when people's own words provide the instruction, it is much harder to ignore. Thus, quoting their own words that spiritual helpers recorded in previous sessions has a special kind of authority. In addition, reminding people of what they have said can reveal inconsistencies which may be keys to unlock the lack of spiritual progress. For example, indicating that forgiveness has already occurred can be countered by the anger just expressed. Or a promise to never "be like my father" may be enlightened by reading words the father used to say that were written in notes from months before (which had just been spoken.)

Spirit-eyes draw attention to God in the midst of living. Spirit-eyes provide a new perspective that may be the next steps along the Spiritual Road.

TALK – AND TEACH

The spiritual insights of Spirit-eyes can lead to talking or teaching. In fact, **the purpose of "Talk" is to confirm and expand how God has already been identified as working within people's lives**. In terms of a Bible study example, after the exegesis (understanding the situation and recognizing God in it) is done, then the commentary (applications to individual lives) can begin. <u>Accordingly, "Talk" can involve further explanations or additional examples; it can also be about understanding how others (including biblical characters) have had similar experiences.</u>

Commentary and explanations are helpful. This is certainly true about the spiritual journey. Yet, **spiritual helpers who are eager to talk or teach before people have gone through the experience are not being helpful**. Because I am a teacher at heart, I tend to want people to learn quickly and fully understand. However, unless people learn to build the Lego set and read instructions mostly on their own, they will not retain what they received. Butterflies struggle mightily to work themselves out of their cocoons. Spiritual helpers might like to help by using a knife to open the cocoons. However, when that is done, the result is that the butterfly dies because the effort to get out of the cocoon is absolutely necessary to develop the strength to fly and produce the vivant colors they display. The same is true for those on the spiritual path – the struggle has purpose for strong living. <u>Do not talk or teach in order to spare people the pain of the struggle</u>. Struggle has purpose like Jacob's wrestling with the angel was essential for his life adjustment and the resultant limp reminded him of how God intervened to make it so.[5] [Genesis 32:22-30]

Accordingly, **after people have understood a particular life event or personal experience as coming from God, then "Talk" is supportive**. Help people interpret what they have experienced, after they have felt it. This may take the form of asking, "Do you know what God has done?" This enlarges the meaning of the experience which is not the same as telling people what to believe or how to feel. For a simple example, after people have come to the conclusion that their tendency to criticize is really anger held inward and inflicted outward, teaching what God wants people to do with such realization is important. However, telling people that they must not be so critical to everyone oversteps the boundaries of spiritual helpers and is not good teaching. In addition, talking about how these same people have successfully reduced criticism in the past is effective instruction and encouragement.

Another simple approach to "Talk," is to seek what people understand from their life's incidents, asking "What do you think that God is teaching you through all of this?" This type of open-ended talk initiative is especially crucial because people will often express unexpected thoughts. Sometimes, their account includes putting themselves down, to which spiritual helpers may need to express, "God is more interested that you learn and change than if you are belittled." Sometimes, people will make some erroneous conclusion, which needs to be countered with, "That makes no sense to me; and I don't believe that God would like that either." On the other hand, people may express exceptionally precise and helpful responses. Nevertheless, inviting people to talk allows them to articulate what they have actually received. After which, spiritual helpers can join the conversation.

Once a new perspective and has been gleaned, those being helped can better value the experiences of others, especially if those experiences confirm their own. Besides, stories are always an excellent way to communicate truth. At this point in the process, spiritual helpers can feel free to talk and share appropriately related parts of their own lives. If there is any doubt about whether to do so or not, simply interject something like, "Something similar to what you have gone through has occurred in my life. I would be willing to share if you would find that valuable." However, spiritual helpers should absolutely NEVER share any part of their lives that they are still working through! In addition, referencing biblical characters that have gone through similar experiences can be helpful for growing Christians. Talking about contemporary people and what they have done or reading autobiographies can also be ways to expand or maximize spiritual growth.

"Talk" is also important when nothing much seems wrong in people's lives. When people are in a good place say, "Tell me about what is good." or "What is it like to have so much goodness in your life?" Often a sense of humility or unworthiness can be expressed, which can give rise to a relationship that more deeply appreciates the greatness and compassion of God. Then, offer thanksgiving and understanding of the ways in which God has been blessing. Remind people to stay in the "goodness" because God has given it. I often note my personal belief that "We will be held accountable in heaven for each blessing that we were not thankful for as well as each sin we failed to repent." If spiritual helpers intuit that people are really not in as good a place as they say they are, then they might explore whether the attitude hides boredom, lethargy, indifference or the "lonely." Spiritual helpers might ask people to talk about what is not happening in their prayers or their spiritual life. Occasionally, people will "say all the right things" but internally they are not "feeling it." Having people expound and illustrate about all the good may reveal what is really not right. As their talking reveals the inconsistency, note it and stay in the contradiction because God will be attempting to work there.

When it comes to "Talk," I have a rule for myself. The farther along the spiritual road that people have traveled the less direct help, advice or instruction they need. On the other hand, those on the Pre-Christian Way or the Purgative Way need clearly stated unambiguous words. They have not developed the regular habit of deeply listening for God and often have conflicting attitudes and behaviors that limit what they assimilate. In a sense, spiritual guides have the heavy burden of being a vehicle for God's voice. What would God say to such folks? Does God knock them off of their high horse and ask, "Why do you persecute me?"[6] [Acts 9:4] or get them to say what is obvious, "What do you want me to do for you?"[7] [Mark 10:51] or if you want eternal life, then "obey the commandments."[8] [Matthew 19:17] For those on the Illuminative Way or farther, encouraging broad-perspective thinking and being sensitive for revelation is best. Thus, telling them is not as good as discovering with them. However, teaching or commenting on what has happened is extremely valuable.

Remember, the words which spiritual helpers speak are exceptionally important. God spoke a word and the world was created. Spiritual helpers use words that in reality change the world of others. Thus, carefully weigh the words about to be spoken. Giving comfort and hope in the midst of crisis is especially important. During such times, criticism or conservative realism is not helpful nearly one-hundred per cent of the time. Be harsh, or even just not encouraging, and people die. Goethe's famous words apply doubly to the spiritual life, "Treat a man (or woman) as he is, he will remain so. Treat a man (or woman) the way he can be and ought to be, and he will become as he can be and should be."[9]

INITIATIVE

Initiative is about action, having an application plan and accountability.

American inventor Thomas Edison said, "Genius is one percent inspiration, ninety-nine percent perspiration."[10] The truth of this hyperbole is that work is required in order to complete a task – including spiritual growth. All of the insights and revelations will make little difference until they are applied. If spiritual helpers understand their job as to assist in spiritual growth, then they must focus on the actions and applications in the lives of those they accompany. On the other hand, the spiritual helping job is to offer assistance; it is not to make sure that people get it right. This means that what people actually do is up to them, but assisting with the plan is a necessary part of the process of spiritual conversation.

For those people not too far along the Spiritual Road, I assign homework, gently. Doing homework is a rule that needs to be followed. The part of the important work of Purgative Way Christians is to establish new habits – both in ethics and spiritual disciplines. Thus, they need to practice. Whether or not they have a task is not optional if they are going to grow spiritually. On the other hand, for Christians who are farther along the Spiritual Road, I make homework more optional. Actually, a primary task for Illuminative Way Christians is to apply faith to experience and most of them will do that automatically. However, they can use some assistance in designing their initiative and of course with accountability.

Accordingly, after people have talked and come to conclusions about their spiritual life, spiritual helpers need to ask, "What would you like to do about that insight or new understanding?" Or "How would you be willing to apply that in your life?" **In initiating this call to action spiritual helpers need to make sure that what is decided is practical, specific and measurable**. In the moment of realization, people will tend to generalize with broad sweeping intentions, which will set them up for failure. Spiritual helpers can best serve by helping people avoid this self-imposed trap.

One of my personal spiritual insights was that I needed to love the strong-willed women in my life; this insight proved to be absolutely true and what God wanted for me. However, the task was too big to actually complete … all at once. Instead, I first needed to refrain from speaking criticism about one particular woman for a specific length of time. This was practical because I was in charge of my speech (to stop what others said about women would have been impractical). This was specific because the attempt had a beginning and an ending (to do so forever would guarantee failure). This plan was measurable because I could record when I did and when I did not withhold criticism (having others do the measuring is of course better).

After the agreed upon length of time, **spiritual helpers need to ask for a report about the application. This is accountability**. Accountability is NOT for the spiritual helper; but it is for the people being helped. Spiritual helpers are responsible to ask for a report because they were given that responsibility by the people who are being helped. In other words, at the time that the action-plan is initiated, spiritual helpers need to specifically ask, "At our next meeting, would you like me to ask how you did with this assignment?" In addition, if the report is given that nothing was actually done or that it was a total and complete disaster, spiritual helpers must not shame, guilt or harshly criticize people. Spiritual helpers are not responsible for the successful accomplishment of the initiatives only for helping to establish them.

As noted in the first section of the book, "Overview of Spiritual Growth", belief without action is useless. On the other hand, application leads to a faith that becomes concentric and moves toward the maturity of Christ. Providing "Initiative" is actually not easy but an essential part of being an effective spiritual helper.

CONNECT

Connecting is a summary of the themes of the current session with the overall spiritual progress in the spiritual process. "Connect" may join previous information, tendencies, words said and actions promised. In a sense, "Connect" is about identifying life patterns and claiming how God is working through and with them.

Accordingly, this "Connect" portion of a spiritual conversation may not occur every time that people meet because it involves uniting various parts of people's lives. Spiritual helpers, of course, need to understand multiple parts of people's lives in order to be able to help put them together. In addition, people need to have come to conclusions and closures before spiritual helpers can actually suggest that what they have gone through connects with what they have previously experienced. Thus, spiritual helpers must remember and intuit whether the current stories, words, lessons and events are actually appropriate to be linked. Reliance upon the promptings of the Holy Spirit is absolutely necessary. When God's still small voice speaks within, spiritual helpers prayerfully need to suggest what they have heard.

Indeed, life understood gains passion and purpose that enables people to approach the future with a great difference. Thus, after people have successfully gone through the wilderness wandering and arrived at the Promised Land, I will spend time helping them to review that process. This summary includes how they were, what changes were made and how they got to where they are; it concludes by offering God the praise and the glory for guiding all the way. Explaining the process of spiritual growth not only enables them to appreciate and be grateful for what has happened but it also provides them with tools to help others in the future. The greatest joy that I have felt is when people have decided to officially pass on what they have received in some form of spiritual ministry. When people deal with their own life issues and claim their related God-given gifts, they naturally evolve toward using their lives for the glory of God. Whether in official or unofficial ways, they are the absolutely perfect people to pass on what they have experienced to the people who have similar experiences. It is real life action of the spiritual mandate, "Love one another. As I have loved you, so you must love one another."[11] [John 13:34]

"Connect" is about dovetailing the current conversation with what has previously happened. Connect with previous lessons learned. Connect with the use of spiritual gifts. Connect with similar personalities and types of individuals. Connect with signature sin tendencies. Connect with personal past experiences. Connect with life patterns. **When people can see consistent tendencies and patterns unfolding and running through their life actions, they understand that these repetitions are not accidental. God intentionally**

works in people's lives. In my experience, most people have only a few themes that flow through their lives. God wants people to heal from these hurts and to make full use of the particular spiritual gifts given in order to grow into the maturity of Christ. Spiritual helpers, by summarizing with "Connect," can significantly assist in assembling the pieces of people's lives into a consistent whole that God has brought together. Then, they can affirm together, "'For I know the plans I have for you,' declares the LORD, 'plans to prosper you and not to harm you, plans to give you hope and a future.'"[12] [Jeremiah 29:11]

PRAY

Prayer is the most basic privilege that Christians have in common. Practice the privilege. **I conclude all of my spiritual helping sessions with vocal prayer with the people I assist**. Occasionally, I will invite people to pray for themselves, but always I pray for them. I absolutely praise God for the work accomplished, which so often is beyond my personal expectations and with greater insights than could come from me. I also affirm what has been decided and what still needs further development – using as many of the exact words spoken by those I accompany that I can remember. When people hear their own words coming back to them and being offered to God, they are encouraged and validated, but mostly they realize their lives have been connected with God.

AD-ONS

The above discussion centered on what the spiritual helper's mode of operation is when guiding others. However, spiritual helper's MO also extends beyond the one-to-one relationships. Spiritual helpers can be better at their craft in three additional ways: carefully assessing those they help, not being a lone wolf and understanding discernment.

ASSESSMENT

At some point in the helping relationship, spiritual helpers need to do an overview assessment of those they are assisting. This appraisal does not need to be shared with those helped; and I recommend that spiritual helpers do so as an annual review. The purpose of the "Assessment" is to make sure that all aspects of people are being included and considered. Furthermore, it provides opportunity for the Holy Spirit to enter into the process as the review is offered in prayer. I use a list of questions, which of course can be modified according to the need and situation of different people.

Personal Review:
1) How old is the client?
2) What is their status in life? (Married, work, education, family etc.)
3) What are the basic relationships? Names?
4) What are the primary, life-changing historical events/activities?
5) What are the current life events/activities?
6) Where do they put their energy?
7) What is their physical condition and illnesses?
8) What medications are they taking? (Some medications limit abilities.)
9) How well do the take care of their body?

Developmental Review:
1) What stressors do they have in their life?
2) What major life trials have happened in their life? How have they responded?
3) What are their emotional strengths?
4) What are their typical negative emotional reactions?
5) Do they have a default emotional response to life?
6) What are their night-time dreams, especially repeated themes?
7) Where are they on the Psycho-Social Map?
8) Do they have "arrested development" in the basic emotions along Erickson's developmental progression?
9) Does this "unfinished business" limited or inhibited their spirituality (faith and/or growth)? Does it affect their belief or application? Does it affect their relationship with God or others?
10) Where are they on the Moral/Ethical Map?
11) Is the way they make justice decisions coincide with their psycho-social and spiritual development?

Spiritual Review:
1) What part of the Spiritual Road are they on?
2) If Pre-Christian, what tasks are they dealing with?
3) Have they formally started on the Purgative Way (are they a Christian)?
4) Does their personal/moral/ethical developmental correspond with their spiritual progress?
5) What kind of consistent spiritual habits do they practice?
6) Do they have or know their signature sin?
7) If on the Illuminative Way, how is their level of anxiety compared to basic trust?
8) Are there any particular "Learnings" or "Clarifications" they are working on?
9) How is their "Devotion" expressed?

10) What particular spiritual gifts, talents or abilities do they exhibit?
11) Where do they need to apply faith to life or work toward mission/generativity?
12) Do they have symptoms of a "Dark Night?"
13) Are non-spiritual factors included in this pain? Are they being addressed?
14) Which "Dark Night" are they likely experiencing? How are they responding? What would be the most helpful manner to respond?

Spiritual Tool Assessment:
1) Where are they in regards to faith values and knowledge perspective along Fowler's stages of faith?
2) Are they stuck in a roundabout? Does this relate to an emotional issue?
3) Has emotional "unfinished business" limited or inhibited their spirituality (faith and/or growth)? Does it affect their belief or application? Does it affect their relationship with God or others?
4) What type of prayer is typical in their life? Does their prayer form correspond with their place on Spiritual Road?
5) Do they have persistent unforgiveness in their life? Do they need CPR?
6) What is the source of their pain? Are they ready to consider what God is teaching or encouraging?
7) What words do they use that limit or inhibit spiritual growth?
8) Are they dealing with the unanswerable questions of existential anxiety?
9) Do they have deep-seeded emotional monsters that need inner healing? Is referral to a competent psychotherapist needed?

After making personal, developmental and spiritual assessments, spiritual helpers need to reflect on where are the places they are corresponding and conflicting? Of paramount importance, spiritual helpers need to deal with whatever will increase the personal relationship between God and the people they accompany.

SUPERVISION

All spiritual helpers need to have a designated spiritual helper and/or a peer supervision group. Everyone needs others in order to see what they do not see and also to help them to continue to grow personally. Supervision groups are great for staying focused on what is most important and also dealing with issues beyond spiritual helpers' expertise and experience. All who guide others spiritually need to find a group, a like-minded friend or clergy-person to meet with regularly, or even create a supervision group. Keep the conversation confidential, both regarding those in the group as well as about those being accompanied. Trained spiritual directors can meet with other spiritual directors. In congregations, pastors (with spiritual helping skills) can regularly meet with lay people who function as spiritual helpers. Clergy can do the same for each other as long as the task for the discussion is limited to the topic of the spiritual helping process.

Spiritual supervision groups are designed to deal with self-questions that spiritual helpers have about those they guide, they are NOT to focus on talking about the people being helped. The best supervision groups are immersed in a prayerful attitude and structure. Built in time needs to be given to listening for the guidance the Holy Spirit. Borrowing from my small group training, supervision groups could be structured using a VHS composition – Vision, Huddle and Skills.[13]

Vision is to specifically focus on the purpose of the spiritual helping relationship. Spiritual helpers need to be reminded that their one to one time with others is for growing a personal faith relationship between those they assist and God. Vision can be implemented in various ways: each person in the group could monologue or provide a meditation on the importance of the spiritual relationship; poems, literature, media or speakers could be used; or various parts of spiritual relationship development could be highlighted. Whatever lifts up God's attempt to connect with people is appropriate for the Vision part of the supervision group.

Huddle is the segment that is personal and interactive, via the Holy Spirit's direction, with special emphasis on processing concerns. Everyone could have some time to express how they are feeling about their spiritual helping ministry; and then, after a time for silent prayer, receive feedback. More profitable option would be to have one person per meeting present a matter that needs oversight, reflection or suggestions from the group. These concerns, questions and issues brought to a supervision group need to be about what has happened to the spiritual helper before, during and after they have assisted others. What did spiritual helpers experience during a session that distracted them from helping? Did they identify too much with the issues of those they accompany? What emotions surfaced? Do they have a sense of helplessness or uncertainty about what to do or not do? Do they have a lingering angst about the people they help long after those people have left? Is the Holy Spirit prompting them in regard to these folks and how are they responding to such divine directives? Always after prayerful consideration, the group would provide comments designed to reflect God's way of speaking.

The final part of each supervision group could be spent in Skill Development. Practical topics from how to start a first session to how to make a referral could be addressed. An expert could be invited to teach on a particular subject or a regional workshop/speaker could be reviewed. A book, read by all participants, could be used to gain skills on spiritual guidance. The group as a whole could research a specific topic and collect their knowledge in conversation. Learning must not stop if spiritual helpers want to effectively assist whose they serve – God and others. For example a typical concern when practicing spiritual guidance revolves around: "How do spiritual mentors guide without doing too much...

or too little?" "Am I being too directive or too passive?" "Do I need to say something or be silent?" Researching the topic or bringing in a facilitator for a presentation would be an excellent way to spend skill development time.

A group of quality, like-minded colleagues because they care about the people they are trying to help not only can guard against unconscious mistakes of transference (and counter-transference) but also can sustain and increase their effectiveness as spiritual helpers.

ABOUT DISCERNMENT

Entire books have been written on spiritual discernment. So I want to make only a couple of observations regarding discernment. Nevertheless, a clear understanding of the role and importance of discernment in providing spiritual help is essential. **Discernment is the figuring out what is what. When it comes to spiritual information, discernment is about determining if what has been received is what God wills or if what has been understood is from God**.

First, discernment is NOT something that people can do alone – human beings are way too good at fooling themselves!!! Talking with a trusted, mature spiritual Christian about the content and interpretation of one's prayers and spiritual faith is the only way to discern well – because it allows the divine to be actively engaged in their relationship. Scripture, tradition, reason and revelation are all important for getting to the truth; but people on their own can easily distort any of them. Make sure to regularly practice the art of discernment – both personally and in supervision.

Second, when receiving spiritual information (via prayer, scripture, other people, media, interpreted life events, dreams and so forth), there are three potential sources – from God, from the person or from the demonic. There is good reason why the scripture strongly warns, "Dear friends, do not believe every spirit, but test the spirits to see whether they are from God..."[14] [I John 4:1]

Near the beginning of the Spiritual Road, the solidity and maturity of people's faith are not strong. Accordingly, they can be easily persuaded, led astray or make ill-advised decisions. Identifying the source of their influence is an especially important task for spiritual helpers. If the source is God, that is good. If from the demonic, strong and immediate action is required. If the source comes from self-interest, it may result in a harmless choice to learn from or cause serious damage. After discernment, spiritual helpers may need to assert, "I seriously doubt if this comes from God and may be just your psyche acting on its own." Nevertheless, those being helped need the freedom to make their own choices.

Christians who are farther along the Spiritual Road also need discernment. Since these Christians are more mature in their faith and practice, the discernment they need has less to do with their external behavior and more to do with interior spirituality. Especially as Christians enter into Contemplative Prayers, they need greater discernment in regard to their prayer conversations. Contemplative Prayers includes praying from the heart; and those emotions do not always correspond with accurate discernment. In addition, evil is real and it can take any form. The demonic uses the same "Spirit World" to communicate as does God. Be aware that the further along the Spiritual Road that Christians travel the greater motivation the demonic has to interfere – especially during the difficult Dark Nights. Having Christians share from their often very personal journals is not easy but a valuable help for such discernment. Personal retreats, monitored and processed alongside a spiritual guide, is another excellent way to enter into the interior for the purpose of discernment.

When **dealing with discernment**, I always ask myself and invite others to ask, "Does it come from God? And does it lead to God?" In other words, is the motivation or the initiative divine? Does the conclusion bring honor and glory to God? It is the old philosophical axiom: Does the means justify the ends? Does the end justify the means? When it comes to spiritual discernment, the means and the ends must coincide – they both must be clearly from God, of God and for God. These questions only touch the surface of a very complex subject. Consideration needs to be given to the thoughts, emotions, desires, fears and anxieties as well as the patterns and tendencies of the person affected. All of which are often subtle and sometimes hidden; however they influence the tendencies of Christians to be attracted or repulsed by a particular choice. In other words, if discernment was easy, everyone would be able to do it pretty well. Nevertheless, discerning well, especially in regard to prayer, is essential.

While there are a variety of discernment methods and techniques, Ignatius of Loyola summarized what he knew regarding discernment into twenty-two rules which are readily available. Spiritual helpers would strengthen their ability by employing them.[15]

CONCLUSION

What is the mode of operation of a spiritual helper?

- ✟ Praying receptively.
- ✟ Listening well.
- ✟ Assessing clearly.
- ✟ Speaking where the presence of God is seen.
- ✟ Teaching Tactfully
- ✟ Initiating effective plans for change with accountability.
- ✟ Connecting moments to help people see how God in sovereignty and love is directing the course of their lives.

✞ Prayerfully affirming God's Work.
✞ Regularly doing an overall assessment.
✞ Consulting with and being supported by other spiritual helpers.
✞ Discerning God always.

The mode of operation is all about the purpose of assisting people to grow in their personal spiritual faith with God so as to build God's reign of salvation and truth, justice and love in the world.

Jesus announced the focus of his spiritual ministry. "The kingdom of God is near (at hand). Repent and believe the good news!"[16] [Mark 1:15] Following this edict and helping others to do the same puts spiritual helpers in good company. Jesus believed that God, and that which is from God, is close enough to touch. Thus first and foremost, the mode of operation for spiritual helpers is to make God real! Second, the task is to help people turn from what is not God and head in the direction of God – in a personal spiritual relationship and in life applications.

The Spiritual Road is a developmental journey of growing into unity with God. It is modeled by Jesus; and empowered via the Holy Spirit. It includes personal spiritual transformation that allows the will of God to be done on earth as it is in Heaven. God is able to accomplish this extreme makeover. However, I am convinced that God desires mature Christians to help others grow spiritually – those who know the limits of their abilities, who continue to grow personally and spiritually as well as those who always keep close to God's purposes. **So, I pray that Christians keep in mind the ultimate purpose of spiritual helpers – assisting people traveling The Spiritual Road to mature in their relationship with God and in the process allow and assist God in transforming the world to be the Holy Community that God desires for the transformation of all creation. Amen.**

Endnotes

Chapter 1 – Defining Spiritual Growth

[1] In his "high priestly prayer" of John 17:1-26, Jesus asked that God would help his disciples, as well as his followers in future generations, to become "one as we are one." In Jesus' Garden of Gethsemane prayer (Matthew 26:39), he sought that he would act according to God's Will which would make his personal will coincide with God's Will. In the history of Christianity, allowing God's Will and the human will to be the same has often been concluded as the goal of the Christian life. Further in John 17:3, when Jesus defined "eternal life" which is the goal of "being saved" he said, "Now this is eternal life: that they may know you, the only true God, and Jesus Christ, whom you have sent." Thus, the purpose of Christian faith and spiritual growth is becoming one with God – described in a variety of ways.

[2] Paul Tillich, Dynamics of Faith (New York, New York: Harper Publishing Company, 1958).

[3] II Corinthians 5:19 and John 3:16 are from The Holy Bible, New International Version (Grand Rapids, Michigan: Zondervan Publishing House, 1973). I will regularly reference biblical sections, using translations not paraphrases, because I believe it is important for Christians to grow in biblical literacy. However, I want to avoid any particular doctrinal approach of describing spiritual faith/growth because as the reader shall see Christians actually grow by using a variety of different techniques/tools, methods of thinking and forms of behavior.

Chapter 2 – Making It Real

None

Chapter 3 – Uniting Belief and Deeds

[1] James 2:14-26
[2] Matthew 18:20
[3] Romans 1:16a
[4] Luke 18:35-42

Chapter 4 – Concentric Faith

[1] Clara H. Scott, The Royal Anthem Book, "Open My Eyes That I May See," (Lyons, Iowa: The Ladies' Seminary, 1882). The words and music were written by Clara H. Scott (1841-1897), who was a native of

Illinois and taught music at the Ladies' Seminary in Lyons, Iowa. In 1882, she published the <u>Royal Anthem Book</u>, the first volume of anthems published by a woman.

Open my eyes, that I may see glimpses of truth thou hast for me;

Place in my hands the wonderful key that shall unclasp and set me free.

Silently now I wait for thee, ready, my God, thy will to see.

Open my eyes, illumine me, Spirit divine!

[2] Philippians 4:12-13; (New International Version is used unless otherwise noted.)

[3] Take a moment to relax with some deep breaths. Then do it again. You are invited to stand in a place where you are not surrounded by stuff. With your faith imagination, picture Jesus Christ standing directly in front of you. See a radiant, glowing aura or halo around him. Take your time until this image is clear. Then, invite Jesus to turn around so that you are now in the position to follow him. See the circle of light in front of you. Now step forward into that radiance and sense what happens.

[4] Matthew 5:48

[5] Gerhard Kittel and Gerhard Friedrich, eds. <u>Kittel's Theological Dictionary of the New Testament</u>, Geoffrey W. Bromiley, trans. (Grand Rapids, Michigan: Eerdmans Publishing Company, 1976). From http://www. biblestudytools.net/Lexicons/Greek. The New Testament Greek Lexicon based on Thayer's and Smith's Bible Dictionary plus others; this is keyed to the large Kittel and the "Theological Dictionary of the New Testament." These files are public domain.

[6] Likewise, when spiritual authorities in the history of Christianity write about "The Way of Perfection," they are talking about the path of spiritual growth, not a moral and ethical perfectionism.

Chapter 5 – The Roads We Travel

[1] Acts 9:1-2; "Meanwhile, Saul was still breathing out murderous threats against the Lord's disciples. He went to the high priest and asked him for letters to the synagogues in Damascus, so that if he found any there who belonged to the **Way**, whether men or women, he might take them as prisoners to Jerusalem." Bold added by the author.

[2] R. Garrigou-Lagrange, <u>The Three Ages of the Interior Life</u>, trans. M. T. Doyle, vol. 2, (Charlotte, North Carolina: The Catholic Company, 1947-48).

[3] In order to become a Christian, most Christian traditions require both personal acceptance of Jesus as Savior and Lord plus baptism. Some parts of Christianity believe that confession must come prior to baptism while others allow baptism that is later confirmed. Nevertheless, The Three Ways begins at the point when both baptism and acceptance, in whatever order, have occurred.

Chapter 6 – The Pre-Christian Way

[1] Ernest Cassirer, <u>Philosophy of Symbolic Forms</u>, trans. Ralph Manheim, (New Haven, Connecticut: Yale University Press, 1955).

[2] Ana-Marie Rizzuto, <u>The Birth of the Living God: A Psychoanalytic Study</u> (Chicago, Illinois: University of Chicago, 1979).

[3] Romans 1:20

[4] Philippians 4:13; "I can do everything through him who gives me strength."

[5] II Corinthians 4:8-9; "We are hard pressed on every side, but not crushed; perplexed, but not in despair; persecuted, but not abandoned; struck down, but not destroyed."

[6] II Corinthians 12:9; "But he said to me, 'My grace is sufficient for you, for my power is made perfect in weakness.' Therefore I will boast all the more gladly about my weaknesses, so that Christ's power may rest on me."

[7] An "awakening" is a moment of clarity in which a new insight or understanding is gained. With this new awareness the experience of life is seen differently, and new possibilities are opened. Changes in patterns of thought, emotions, and behavior occur. An awakening allows the possibility of growth to new levels of psychological and spiritual maturity. From Awakenings: Simple Solutions for Life's Problems' web site from http://www.lessons4living.com.

[8] Proverbs 1:7; "The fear of the Lord is the beginning of knowledge, but fools despise wisdom and discipline."

[9] Matthew 10:28; "Do not be afraid of those who kill the body but cannot kill the soul. Rather, be afraid of the One who can destroy both soul and body in hell."

[10] James W. Fowler, Stages of Faith: The Psychology of Human Development and the Quest for Meaning (New York, New York: Harper Collins Publishing Company, 1981). These stages will be more fully explored and overlaid onto the spiritual road in chapter fifteen, "Overlaying the Faith Development Map."

[11] Paul Tillich, The Courage To Be (New Haven, Connecticut: Yale University Press, 1952).

[12] Isaiah 55:8-9

[13] Paul Tillich, The Shaking of the Foundations, "You Are Accepted," (New York, New York: Charles Scribner and Sons, 1948).

[14] Romans 3:23

[15] Romans 6:23; "For the wages of sin is death, but the gift of God is eternal life in Christ Jesus our Lord."

[16] John Newton, "Amazing Grace," Olney Hymns in Three Books, John Newton and William Cowper, eds. (London, England: W. Oliver, 1779) 53-54. Newton's work was originally written as a poem entitled 'Faith's Review and Expectation.' While various tunes were used with Newton's poem, the current one used was assigned by composer William Walker. William Walker, The Southern Harmony, and Musical Companion tune: "New Britain" (New Haven, Connecticut: E. W. Miller Publisher, 1835).

Amazing grace! (how sweet the sound),

That sav'd a wretch like me!

I once was lost, but now am found,

Was blind, but now I see.

'Twas grace that taught my heart to fear,

And grace my fears reliev'd;

How precious did that grace appear

The hour I first believ'd!

Thro' many dangers, toils, and snares,

I have already come;

'Tis grace hath brought me safe thus far,

And grace will lead me home.

The Lord has promis'd good to me,

His word my hope secures;

He will my shield and portion be

As long as life endures.

Yes, when this flesh and heart shall fail,

And mortal life shall cease;

I shall possess, within the veil,

A life of joy and peace.

The earth shall soon dissolve like snow,

The sun forbear to shine;

But God, who call'd me here below,

Will be forever mine.

The following verse was added by Harriet Beecher Stowe:

When we've been there ten thousand years,

Bright shining as the sun,

We've no less days to sing God's praise,

Than when we first begun.

[17] Dietrich Bonhoeffer, The Cost of Discipleship (New York, New York: Macmillan Publishing Co., Inc., 1963).

[18] Charlotte Elliott, "Just As I Am" Christian Remembrancer in 1836, (London, England: Religious Tract Society, 1873). William B. Bradbury, "Woodworth," Third Book of Psalmody (New York, New York: Thomas Hastings and William Batchelder Bradbury Publishers, 1849) 60.

Just as I am - without one plea,

But that Thy blood was shed for me,

And that Thou bidst me come to Thee,

-O Lamb of God, I come!

Just as I am - and waiting not

To rid my soul of one dark blot,

To Thee, whose blood can cleanse each spot,

-O Lamb of God, I come!

Just as I am - though toss'd about

With many a conflict, many a doubt,

Fightings and fears within, without,

-O Lamb of God, I come!

Just as I am - poor, wretched, blind;

Sight, riches, healing of the mind,

Yea, all I need, in Thee to find,

-O Lamb of God, I come!

Just as I am - Thou wilt receive,

Wilt welcome, pardon, cleanse, relieve;

Because Thy promise I believe,

-O Lamb of God, I come!

Just as I am - Thy love unknown

Has broken every barrier down;

Now to be Thine, yea, Thine alone,

-O Lamb of God, I come!

Just as I am - of that free love

The breadth, length, depth, and height to prove,

Here for a season, then above,

-O Lamb of God, I come!

[19] Romans 5:1, 5; "Therefore, since we have been justified through faith, we have peace with God through our Lord Jesus Christ, … And hope does not disappoint us, because God has poured out his love into our hearts by the Holy Spirit, whom he has given us."

[20] St. John of the Cross coined the phrase the "Dark Night" which he divided into two parts – the "Dark Night of the Senses" and the "Dark Night of the Spirit." For further explanation see the section entitled "Dark Night of the Senses" in chapter seven, "The Purgative Way," as well as chapter ten "The Illuminative Way – the Dark Night of the Spirit."

[21] Matthew 3:17

[22] Matthew 4:1; the gospel of Mark uses the phrase "at once" to indicate that the temptation took place immediately after the baptism. The underlining for emphasis is supplied by the author.

Chapter 7 – The Purgative Way

[1] "God's Holy Community" is a term that I have gleaned from somewhere (or coined) which replicates the meaning in the biblical phrase "Kingdom of God" which some have re-phrased the "Reign of God" in order to de-genderize it. "Holy Community" emphasizes the important and necessary relational aspect of life with God and God's people while still maintaining the theological and biblical teaching inherit to its meaning.

[2] I Thessalonians 4:3-7; II Timothy 2:19-21; Hebrews 5:11-14. Sometimes "sanctification" is confused with "justification." "Justification" is God's action based on simple acceptance of Jesus as Lord and Savior, whereas "sanctification" is God's action in co-operation with our efforts. Justification is OKness with God; sanctification is growing spiritually toward God.

[3] Philippians 2:12b-13

[4] Synesius of Cyrene, "Lord Jesus Think on Me," Allen W. Chatfield, ed. Songs and Hymns of Earliest Greek Christian Poets (London, England: Oxford Press, 1876). William Daman Psalms of David in English Meter, Tune: "Southwell" (London, England: 1579).

Lord Jesus, think on me

And purge away my sin;

From earthborn passions set me free
And make me pure within.
Lord Jesus, think on me,
With many a care oppressed;
Let me Thy loving servant be
And taste Thy promised rest.
Lord Jesus, think on me
Amid the battle's strife;
In all my pain and misery
Be Thou my Health and Life.
Lord Jesus, think on me
Nor let me go astray;
Through darkness and perplexity
Point Thou the heavenly way.
Lord Jesus, think on me
When floods the tempest high;
When on doth rush the enemy,
O Savior, be Thou nigh!
Lord Jesus, think on me
That, when the flood is past,
I may th'eternal brightness see
And share Thy joy at last.
Lord Jesus, think on me
That I may sing above
To Father, Spirit, and to Thee
The strains of praise and love.

[5] This is discussed in detail in chapter seventeen, "C-P-R for New Life."

[6] How God uses "pain" as a motivating method to keep Christians growing spiritually is discussed in chapter eighteen, "Dealing with Pain."

[7] Galatians 5:19-21 list seventeen "sins of the flesh" which include, but are not limited to, adultery, emulation, fornication, wrath, uncleanness, strife, lasciviousness, sedition, idolatry, heresies, witchcraft, envying, hatred, murder, variance, drunkenness and reveling. While this list from the Kings James Version of the Bible needs interpretation and explanation, there is no shortage of people who will delineate exactly what is meant.

[8] Galatians 5:16-18, 24-26

[9] Matthew 25:31-46

[10] Matthew 13:41-42, 49-50; "The Son of Man will send out his angels, and they will weed out of his kingdom everything that causes sin and all who do evil. They will throw them into the fiery furnace, where there will be weeping and gnashing of teeth." Also, "This is how it will be at the end of the age. The angels will come and

separate the wicked from the righteous and throw them into the fiery furnace, where there will be weeping and gnashing of teeth."

[11] John 8:32; "Then you will know the truth, and the truth will set you free."

[12] Matthew 7:12; "So in everything, do to others what you would have them do to you, for this sums up the Law and the Prophets."

[13] Matthew 22:38-39; "This is the first and greatest commandment. And the second is like it: 'Love your neighbor as yourself.'"

[14] The Sermon on the Mount is the collection of teaching found in chapters 5-7 of the gospel of Matthew.

[15] The seven deadly sins were originally used in early Christian teachings to educate and instruct followers. The early church also recognized that each sin had a corresponding virtue that would be obtained as the sin was removed. The vice of lust lead to the virtue of chastity, gluttony to temperance, greed to charity, sloth becomes diligence, wrath transforms into kindness, envy into patience and pride to humility.

[16] Philippians 1:6 (Revised Standard Version)

[17] Psalm 25:7

[18] Lyman Coleman, "Growing the Church Through Small Groups," First Baptist Church, Wheaton, Illinois, 6 March 1993. Lyman Coleman, one of the pioneers of the small group movement, trained over 500,000 people in seminars held throughout North America. This reference comes from information supplied at the seminar.

[19] Luke 11:24-26; "When an evil spirit comes out of a man, it goes through arid places seeking rest and does not find it. Then it says, 'I will return to the house I left.' When it arrives, it finds the house swept clean and put in order. Then it goes and takes seven other spirits more wicked than itself, and they go in and live there. And the final condition of that man is worse than the first."

[20] Matthew 23:25-26; "Woe to you, teachers of the law and Pharisees, you hypocrites! You clean the outside of the cup and dish, but inside they are full of greed and self-indulgence. Blind Pharisee! First clean the inside of the cup and dish, and then the outside also will be clean."

[21] Bruce Wilkinson, Secrets of the Vine: Breaking Through to Abundance (Sisters, Oregon: Multnomah Publishers, Inc., 2001) 29ff.

[22] Richard Foster, Celebration of Discipline: The Path to Spiritual Growth (New York, New York: Harper Collins Publishers, 1988).

[23] The increase of pain can be, and was in this case, an indicator that God is attempting to get people's attention so that they will make constructive changes. See the chapters eighteen and twenty, "Dealing with Pain" and "That's What the Lonely is For" for additional information.

[24] Hebrews 5:11-14

[25] The "Dark Night of the Senses" is the first part of the spiritual process called the "Dark Night" by St. John of the Cross. The second part is called "The Dark Night of the Spirit." In addition, I have included a third "Dark Night" called "Confessional Temptation." For further explanation see the section entitled "The Dark Night of the Soul" in chapter ten, "The Illuminative Way – Dark Night of the Spirit."

[26] Mark 10:17-30

[27] Luke 23:39-43, "Jesus answered him, "I tell you the truth, today, you will be with me in paradise." And Matthew 21:31, Jesus said to them, "I tell you the truth, the tax collectors and the prostitutes are entering the kingdom of God ahead of you."

[28] Friedrich von Hugel, The Mystical Element in Religion, 4th ed. (London, England: James Clark Publishers, 1961).

[29] Benedict J. Groeschel, Spiritual Passages: The Psychology of Spiritual Development (New York, New York: Crossroads Publishing Company, 1983) 120-121.

[30] Matthew 16:23

[31] John 13:8

[32] John of the Cross (1542-1591) was a Spanish Christian priest, theologian, poet, mystic and intellectual who is well-known for his deeply insightful and profound writings on the spiritual journey. He introduced the phrase the "Dark Night of the Senses" and the "Dark Night of the Spirit." "The Dark Night of the Soul" is a popularized phrase that amalgamates both of St. John's "Dark Nights."

[33] John of the Cross, The Ascent of Mount Carmel, book II, chapter 3, K. Kavanaugh and O. Rodriquez, eds. and trans. The Collected Words of St. John of the Cross, (Washington, D. C.: ICS Publications, 1973) 110-111.

[34] Matt and Beth Redman, "Blessed Be Your Name," Blessed Be Your Name: The Songs of Matt Redman, Vol. 1, Brentwood, Tennessee: EMI Christian Music Group, 1999.

Blessed Be Your Name
In the land that is plentiful
Where Your streams of abundance flow
Blessed be Your name
Blessed Be Your name
When I'm found in the desert place
Though I walk through the wilderness
Blessed Be Your name
Every blessing You pour out
I'll turn back to praise
When the darkness closes in, Lord
Still I will say
Blessed be the name of the Lord
Blessed be Your name
Blessed be the name of the Lord
Blessed be Your glorious name
Blessed be Your name
When the sun's shining down on me
When the world's 'all as it should be'
Blessed be Your name
Blessed be Your name

On the road marked with suffering
Though there's pain in the offering
Blessed be Your name
Every blessing You pour out
I'll turn back to praise
When the darkness closes in, Lord
Still I will say
Blessed be the name of the Lord
Blessed be Your name
Blessed be the name of the Lord
Blessed be Your glorious name
Blessed be the name of the Lord
Blessed be Your name
Blessed be the name of the Lord
Blessed be Your glorious name
You give and take away
You give and take away
My heart will choose to say
Lord, blessed be Your name

[35] John 9:25

[36] I Corinthians 7:9

[37] The concepts of marriage, divorce, remarriage and adultery in the Bible have been discussed and debated for centuries. Various conclusions have been drawn that are reflected in the dogma or theological teaching of different Christian traditions. Check with individual denominations to discern the official position. Nevertheless, the issues center on the interpretation of the "original" Greek (and Hebrew) texts. Of particular note is whether the Greek phrase μὴ ἐπὶ πορνείᾳ in Matthew 19:9 is to be applied to one or both verbs. ("I tell you that anyone who divorces his wife, except for marital unfaithfulness, and marries another woman commits adultery.")Translators can make a case for both choices which, of course, makes it impossible for non-translation skilled lay persons to make definitive conclusions. In the actual terms of the text the question is: does this exceptive clause apply to the words γαμήσῃ/ἄλλην and therefore to μοιχᾶται as well as to the verb ἀπολύσῃ? The subject is extremely complex; be cautious of those who offer simple authoritative conclusions.

[38] Matthew 20:1-16

[39] Matthew 20:13-15

[40] I Timothy 5:14; "So I counsel younger widows to marry, to have children, to manage their homes and to give the enemy no opportunity for slander."

[41] Matthew 19:9; "I tell you that anyone who divorces his wife, except for marital unfaithfulness, and marries another woman commits adultery." See also note nineteen.

42 While some strict-constructionist, biblically-oriented Christians might want to raise the objection that no one can be above the Law of God. God is above the scripture. God corrected the scripture with some of Jesus' teachings. Even after Jesus had ascended, God, through Peter and Cornelius' dreams, re-oriented the total Christian focus (Acts 10). If what had previously been recorded strictly followed, then only Jews would be offered the salvation that came through Jesus. While the revelation of God in the Bible must be revered, the scripture can become bibliolatry when its status is raised above the sovereignty of God. Using the Bible's teachings, as in Timothy's story, to control one's life – to make sure that God will do exactly what it says in the book – will lead to a "Dark Night of the Senses." Why? Because: Christians, to be in a genuine relationship with God, must trust God above all things.

43 Benedict J. Groeschel, <u>Spiritual Passages: The Psychology of Spiritual Development</u> (New York, New York: Crossroads Publishing Company, 1983) 118.

Chapter 8 – The Illuminative Way
An Introduction

1 Donald S. Browning, <u>Atonement and Psychotherapy</u> (Philadelphia, Pennsylvania: Westminster Press, 1966).

2 Dallán Forgaill, "Be Thou My Vision," trans. Mary E. Byrne, comp. David Evans, <u>Church Hymnary</u>, 2nd ed. (Church of Scotland, 1927). "Be Thou My Vision" is an early Irish poem/hymn used by Irish monks and attributed to saint Dallán Forgaill in the 6th century AD.; translated from Old Irish by Mary E. Byrne in 1905 and put into verses by Eleanor Henrietta Hull in 1912; the music tune is "Slane" which was combined with the words by David Evans in the Church of Scotland's <u>Church Hymnary</u>, 2nd edition, in 1927.

Be Thou my Vision, O Lord of my heart;

Naught be all else to me, save that Thou art.

Thou my best Thought, by day or by night,

Waking or sleeping, Thy presence my light.

Be Thou my Wisdom, and Thou my true Word;

I ever with Thee and Thou with me, Lord;

Thou my great Father, I Thy true son;

Thou in me dwelling, and I with Thee one.

Be Thou my battle Shield, Sword for the fight;

Be Thou my Dignity, Thou my Delight;

Thou my soul's Shelter, Thou my high Tower:

Raise Thou me heavenward, O Power of my power.

Riches I heed not, nor man's empty praise,

Thou mine Inheritance, now and always:

Thou and Thou only, first in my heart,

High King of Heaven, my Treasure Thou art.

High King of Heaven, my victory won,

May I reach Heaven's joys, O bright Heaven's Sun!

Heart of my own heart, whatever befall,

Still be my Vision, O Ruler of all.

Chapter 9 – The Illuminative Way
The Process

[1] In order to become a Christian a certain about of information is necessary to understand; this is outlined in the chapter six, "The Pre-Christian Way."

[2] II Timothy 2:15; "Do your best to present yourself to God as one approved, a workman who does not need to be ashamed and who correctly handles the word of truth." ὀρθοτομοῦντα (correctly handles) comes from the two words compounded together ὀρθός meaning "straight" and τέμνειν "to cut."

[3] Chapter twenty-two, "Who Are You Talking To?" specifically addresses how and why to spiritual conversation based on where people are along the spiritual road.

[4] I Corinthians 3:1-2; "Brothers, I could not address you as spiritual but as worldly—mere infants in Christ. I gave you milk, not solid food, for you were not yet ready for it. Indeed, you are still not ready."

[5] Some of these passages include Matthew 5:21, 27, 33, and 43.

[6] These types of questions often occur when the age and life situation encourages believers to "think for themselves." Going to college or moving out of one's parents' house to live on one's own is times that require such assessments. Contrary to Purgative Way oriented spiritual leaders, it is not the world or the college that is "bad" for kids' "losing their faith." It is what normally happens. During this time of developmental transition, having a spiritual mentor who understands the process of spiritual growth is invaluable not only for keeping people's Christian faith but expanding it, and handling it rightly, as God desires.

[7] James 1:6-8; "But when he asks, he must believe and not doubt, because he who doubts is like a wave of the sea, blown and tossed by the wind. That man should not think he will receive anything from the Lord; he is a double-minded man, unstable in all he does." The Greek word for double-minded, δίψυχος (dipsuchos), literally means that a person has two "souls." The passage indicates that asking is good if people want knowledge for the purpose of increasing faithfulness. As one example of genuine doubt, James 1:5 indicates that people should ask God, who gives and doesn't find fault with the asker, when they do not understand or lack wisdom.

[8] Ephesians 3:14-19

[9] Philip H. Pfatteicher, New Book of Festivals and Commemorations: A Proposed Common Calendar of Saints (Minneapolis, Minnesota: Fortress Press, 2008) 159.

[10] Godspell, dir. John Michael Tebelak, comp., Stephen Schwartz (Broadway Musical, 17 May 1971). Godspell, based primarily on the Gospel According to St. Matthew, was conceived and originally directed by John Michael Tebelak, and offers music and new lyrics by Stephen Schwartz including "Day By Day." The show opened May 17, 1971 Off-Broadway and transferred to Broadway in 1976.

[11] Rick Warren, The Purpose Driven Life (Grand Rapids, Michigan: Zondervan Publishing, 2002) and The Purpose Driven Church (Grand Rapids, Michigan: Zondervan Publishing, 1995).

[12] Workplace Spirituality or Spirituality in the Workplace is a movement that began in the early 1990s. It emerged as a grassroots movement with individuals seeking to live their faith and/or spiritual values in the workplace. It has been formalized in organizations such as International Center for Spirit at Work.

[13] Matthew 7:9-11

[14] Matthew 25:40

[15] The parable of the Good Samaritan in Luke 10:25-37 is especially suited for this purpose.

[16] Benedict J. Goeschel, Spiritual Passages: The Psychology of Spiritual Development (New York, New York: Crossroads Publishing Company, 1983) 145.

[17] Galatians 5:22-23; "But the fruit of the Spirit is love, joy, peace, patience, kindness, goodness, faithfulness, gentleness and self-control. Against such things there is no law."

[18] Janet K. Ruffing, Spiritual Direction: Beyond the Beginnings (New York, New York: Paulist Press, 2000) 90.

[19] Philippians 1:10-11

[20] Philippians 1:27-29, "Whatever happens, conduct yourselves in a manner worthy of the gospel of Christ. Then, whether I come and see you or only hear about you in my absence, I will know that you stand firm in one spirit, contending as one man for the faith of the gospel without being frightened in any way by those who oppose you. This is a sign to them that they will be destroyed, but that you will be saved—and that by God. For it has been granted to you on behalf of Christ not only to believe on him, but also to suffer for him."

[21] Philippians 2:5; "Your attitude should be the same as that of Christ Jesus:" The Greek phrase, τοῦτο φρονείσθω ἐν ὑμιν, which is literally "let this be thought in you" and translated "let this mind be in you" (King James Version) or with the NIV "Your attitude should be the same as Jesus Christ."

[22] Philippians 4:8-9; "Finally, brothers, whatever is true, whatever is noble, whatever is right, whatever is pure, whatever is lovely, whatever is admirable—if anything is excellent or praiseworthy—think about such things. Whatever you have learned or received or heard from me, or seen in me—put it into practice. And the God of peace will be with you."

[23] John 8:32b; "and the truth will set you free."

[24] I Corinthians 2:6-11; the author has added the notes and the italics.

[25] "Among the mature" literally is translated as "among they that are perfect" - (ἐν τοῖς τελείοις en tois teleios). This word teleios meaning "perfect" is here applied to Christians, as it is in Philippians 3:15a, "All of us who **are mature** should take such a view of things." (Bold added; NIV) or "Let us therefore as many as **be perfect**, be thus minded." (bold added; KJV) And it is clearly used to denote those who were advanced in Christian knowledge. The Greek word "teleios" is discussed more fully in chapter four, "Concentric Faith."

[26] Although not a direct quotation, this reference is from Isaiah 64:4, especially as read through the view of the Septuagint which is the Greek translation of the Old Testament Hebrew. The Septuagint reads: "From of old we have not heard, nor have our eyes seen a God beside you, and your works which you will do for those who wait for mercy." The Hebrew translates: "From of old men have not heard, not perceived with the ear, eye has not seen a God beside you who does (gloriously) for him who waits on Him."

[27] This word ἐρευνᾷ (ereuna) means to accurately, diligently and completely research so as to have thorough knowledge. Since the Holy Spirit is part and parcel of God, such profound knowledge could be assumed. However, its primary purpose is to point to the kind of information that is available to Christians who have the Spirit within – the Mind of Christ is imported.

[28] Here, I have inserted in italics the alternate translation *"interpreting spiritual truths to spiritual men"* for πνευματικοῖς πνευματικὰ συγκρίνοντες (pneumatikois pneumatika sugkrinontes) included in the NIV footnote from other manuscripts for "expressing spiritual truths in spiritual words" because it illuminates the process of spiritual growth and the step of "Clarifications" better. While many commentators make the point that the Spirit is revealing the meaning of Old Testament passages to refer to God's salvation in Jesus, the Spirit can also teach the current "thoughts of God." This is how Christians grow spiritually toward intimacy and oneness with the Divine.

[29] The word ἀνακρίνεται (anakrinetai) translated as "discerned" is used only in this place by the Apostle Paul. In classical Greek language and society it has a distinctive application: it was used technically 1) to examine magistrates with a view to proving their qualifications 2) and to examine persons concerned in a law suit, so as to prepare the matter for a grand jury. This is not superficial "discernment" but done for the purpose of a complete and proper understanding. In other words, there is clear evidence for the matter at hand – i.e., going forward with a trial is recommended or that the "spiritual truth" is from God. This includes precise intellectual consideration, not just a "sense of hearing God speak" but a confirmation of the words that were heard.

[30] Paul alludes to Isaiah 40:13 which is translated: "Who has understood the mind of the Lord, or instructed him as his counselor?"

[31] I Corinthians 2:16

[32] I Corinthians 2:11b

[33] Romans 8:9; "You, however, are controlled not by the sinful nature but by the Spirit, if the Spirit of God lives in you. And if anyone does not have the Spirit of Christ, he does not belong to Christ."

[34] I Corinthians 2:10; "but God has revealed it to us by his Spirit. The Spirit searches all things, even the deep things of God."

[35] John 14:9; "Jesus answered: "Don't you know me, Philip, even after I have been among you such a long time? Anyone who has seen me has seen the Father. How can you say, 'Show us the Father'?"

[36] John 14:26

[37] This inclination often occurs earlier in women who focus more on the traditional "have and take care of children" societal path than it takes place in men who by necessity think of their own agendas in order to "climb the corporate ladder." Later in life, women want to do more for themselves, like using and developing their own skills in a job, while men would rather stop that kind of activity and focus more on helping others. This makes for an interesting, and sometimes stressful, dynamic in couples' relationships, which also accounts for why men and woman do not go through this part of the Spiritual Road at the same time or in the same way. However, the working out of these differences can be instrumental in another "learning" – to appreciate and value differences that enable movement toward the divine attitude of "universal" harmony.

[38] Matthew 22:39; "And the second is like it: 'Love your neighbor as yourself.'"

[39] The section on "Reading the Maps," chapters twelve through fifteen, illustrates how spiritual growth and psychological development intersect.

[40] Pierre Teilhard de Chardin (1881–1955) was a French philosopher and Jesuit priest who trained as a paleontologist and geologist and took part in the discovery of both the Piltdown Man and Peking Man.

[41] This concept of the Noosphere is an extension of Teilhard's Law of Complexity/Consciousness, the law describing the nature of evolution in the universe. Teilhard argued the Noosphere is growing towards an even greater integration and unification, culminating in the Omega Point, which he saw as the goal of history and by which the Cosmic Christ is actively pulling all of creation.

[42] Pierre Teilhard de Chardin, The Phenomenon of Man, trans. Bernard Wall, (London, England: Wm. Collins Sons & Company, 1959) 53. Chardin's "common ground" between religion and science is specifically identified in this section.

[43] Pius XII, Encyclical. Humani Generis, 36. The 1950 encyclical Humani Generis condemned several of Teilhard's conclusions.

[44] Mark 10:7-9; "'For this reason a man will leave his father and mother and be united to his wife, and the two will become one flesh.' So they are no longer two, but one. Therefore what God has joined together, let man not separate."

[45] Matthew 26:39; "Going a little farther, he (Jesus) fell with his face to the ground and prayed, 'My Father, if it is possible, may this cup be taken from me. Yet not as I will, but as you will.'"

[46] Luke 8:40-56

[47] John 6:68-69

[48] Frances Ridley Havergal, "Take My Life and Let It Be" Songs of Grace and Glory ed. Charles B. Snepp (London, England: W. Hunt and Company, 1874) was first published in 1874. Current hymn tune: "Hedon" was composed by Henri A. Cesar Malan and included in The Psalter Hymnal, (Grand Rapids, Michigan: Christian Reformed Church Publications, 1927).

Take my life, and let it be consecrated, Lord, to Thee.

Take my moments and my days; let them flow in ceaseless praise.

Take my hands, and let them move at the impulse of Thy love.

Take my feet, and let them be swift and beautiful for Thee.

Take my voice, and let me sing always, only, for my King.

Take my lips, and let them be filled with messages from Thee.

Take my silver and my gold; not a mite would I withhold.

Take my intellect, and use every power as Thou shalt choose.

Take my will, and make it Thine; it shall be no longer mine.

Take my heart, it is Thine own; it shall be Thy royal throne.

Take my love, my Lord, I pour at Thy feet its treasure store.

Take myself, and I will be ever, only, all for Thee.

[49] Jeremiah 29:11

[50] John 17:20-21; "My prayer is not for them alone. I pray also for those who will believe in me through their message, that all of them may be one, Father, just as you are in me and I am in you. May they also be in us so that the world may believe that you have sent me."

[51] James 1:5

[52] I Corinthians 13:12

[53] John 14:9; "Jesus answered: "Don't you know me, Philip, even after I have been among you such a long time? Anyone who has seen me has seen the Father. How can you say, 'Show us the Father'?"

[54] Arthur Devine, "State or Way (Purgative, Illuminative, Unitive)," The Catholic Encyclopedia, Vol. 14, (New York, New York: Robert Appleton Company, 1912).

[55] Romans 8:28; "And we know that in all things God works for the good of those who love him, who have been called according to his purpose."

[56] John 15:15

[57] John 15:14

[58] Illuminative Way Christians may also make such a statement. This happens as a result of arrested emotional development. People, who have been "forced" in their lives and have not had the freedom to take their own initiative and make their own choices, will resist strongly obeying anyone, even the Divine. Until they have permission and ability to freely choose, they will typically not surrender themselves to "blind" obedience even for God. Consequently, the step of "Devotion" will also be latent, if it happens at all. Most often forgiveness needs to be offered and healing experienced most likely regarding issues of being controlled or forced beginning between ages three to twelve and perpetuated by successive life events.

[59] Romans 5:6; The Greek word for time is "καιρος" which means the "right time or appropriate time, in this case as chosen via God. "Χρονος" is an alternative word for "time;" but "chronos" like the word "chronological" refers to clock time, predictable time.

[60] Romans 12:7-8

[61] Carl Jung, Modern Man in Search of a Soul (New York, New York: Routledge & Kegan Paul, 1933) 244.

[62] Eric Erikson saw this opportunity in his "Generativity versus Stagnation" stage and James Fowler understood this challenge as part of his "Conjunctive Faith" stage.

[63] Galatians 2:20; Italics added by the author.

[64] Mark 8:34-35

[65] Genesis 12:1-3; "The Lord had said to Abram, 'Leave your country, your people and your father's household and go to the land I will show you. I will make you into a great nation and **I will bless you**; I will make your name great, and **you will be a blessing**. I will bless those who bless you, and whoever curses you I will curse; **and all peoples on earth will be blessed through you.**'" Bold added by the author.

[66] Matthew 28:19-20; "Therefore go and make disciples of all nations, baptizing them in the name of the Father and of the Son and of the Holy Spirit, and teaching them to obey everything I have commanded you. And surely I am with you always, to the very end of the age."

[67] John 15:8; "This is to my Father's glory, that you bear much fruit, showing yourselves to be my disciples."

[68] John 13:34

[69] John 17:1-26

[70] Revelation 21:1; "Then I saw a new heaven and a new earth, for the first heaven and the first earth had passed away, and there was no longer any sea."

[71] Matthew 6:10; Part of the Lord's Prayer: "your kingdom come, your will be done on earth as it is in heaven."

[72] Romans 12:1; "Therefore, I urge you, brothers, in view of God's mercy, to offer your bodies as living sacrifices, holy and pleasing to God—this is your spiritual act of worship."

Chapter 10 – The Illuminative Way
The Dark Night of the Senses

[1] Saint John of the Cross (1542-1591) was a Spanish mystic, priest, and reformer of the Carmelite Order and is considered, along with Saint Teresa of Ávila, as a founder of the Discalced Carmelites. He is also known for both his poetry and his studies on the growth of the soul which include Ascent of Mount Carmel, The Dark Night and A Spiritual Canticle of the Soul and the Bridegroom Christ.

[2] Scholastic Theology, an intellectual way of approaching spirituality, began with Anselm and was fully developed in Thomas Aquinas. It was based in the philosophical understandings of human nature via Plato and Aristotle. Scholastic Theology presupposed this philosophical approach and attempted to use and harmony its concepts. This is especially noticed in St. John of the Cross' use of "intellect, memory, and will" to summarize the rational human function. These were to be purified by the corresponding Christian virtues of faith, hope and love.

[3] Some of these scholars include: John O. Welch, When Gods Die: An Introduction to St. John of the Cross (Mahwah, New Jersey: Paulist Press, 1990); Susan Muto, John of the Cross for Today: The Ascent (Notre Dame, Indiana: Ave Maria Press, 1991); Thomas H. Green, Sr., Drinking from a Dry Well (Notre Dame, Indiana: Ave Maria Press, 1991); Gerald G. May, The Dark Night of the Soul: A Psychiatrist Explores the Connection between Darkness and Spiritual Growth (New York, New York: Harper Collins Publishers, 2004); Benedict J. Goeschel, Spiritual Passages: The Psychology of Spiritual Development (New York, New York: Crossroads Publishing Company, 1983).

[4] John Michael Talbot, "Holy Darkness," Table of Plenty (Eureka Springs, Arkansas: Troubadour for the Lord Records, 1997).

Holy darkness, blessed night,

Heaven's answer hidden from our sight,

As we await you, O God of silence,

We embrace your Holy Light.

I have tried you in the fires of affliction

I have taught your soul to grieve

In the barren soil of your loneliness

There I will plant my seed.

In the deepest hour of your darkness

I will give you wealth untold

When the silence stills your spirit,

Then my riches fill your soul.

Holy darkness, blessed night

Heaven's answer hidden from our sight,

As we await you, O God of silence,

We embrace your Holy Light.

[5] <u>Diagnostic and Statistical Manual of Mental Disorders DSM-IV-TR</u> Fourth Ed., (Washington, D. C.: American Psychiatric Association, 2000). Using of the <u>Diagnostic and Statistical Manual of Mental Disorders</u> is advised (or having a therapist available for consultation). The DSM-IV provides information to assist diagnosis, e. g., depression, that includes which symptoms need to persist for how long in order to determine if "clinical" referral is needed. Spiritual helpers do not need to be a therapist to use the book, just a therapist to do therapy.

[6] Gerald G. May, <u>The Dark Night of the Soul: A Psychiatrist Explores the Connection between Darkness and Spiritual Growth</u> (New York, New York: Harper Collins Publishers, 2004) 81. While St. John of the Cross describes the "Dark Night of the Senses" and the "Dark Night of the Spirit" as occurring in a linear process, Gerald May claims that "there is no hard-and-fast sequence; they overlap and often happen simultaneously."

[7] While, I will use this Scholastic model of human interiority because it has such spiritual history, more contemporary representations, including the Psychosynthesis approach, may be more adequate. However, it is far beyond the scope of this book to explore these alternatives.

[8] Spiritual masters explaining how to verify the authenticity of this "Dark Night" advise that these conditions must exist.

[9] This prayer process is described more fully in chapter sixteen "Prayer Forms."

[10] Hebrews 13:8; "Jesus Christ is the same yesterday and today and forever."

[11] Susan Muto, <u>John of the Cross for Today: The Ascent</u> (Notre Dame, Indiana: Ave Maria Press, 1991) 54.

[12] Ephesians 3:16-21; the underlining added by the author for emphasis.

[13] The <u>Summa Theologiae</u>, the best-known work of Thomas Aquinas (1225–1274), was one of the most influential works of Western Christianity.

[14] Brian Davies, <u>The Thought of Thomas Aquinas</u> (New York, New York: Oxford University Press, 1993) 9.

[15] Susan Muto, <u>John of the Cross for Today: The Ascent</u> (Notre Dame, Indiana: Ave Maria Press, 1991) 125.

[16] By "supernatural," St. John of the Cross means "coming from imagination or from beyond the individual." See Susan Muto, page 54.

[17] John of the Cross, <u>Ascent of Mount Carmel</u>, <u>The Collected Works of St. John of the Cross</u>, eds. and trans. Kieran Kavanaugh and Otillio Rodriguez (Washington, D. C.: ICS Publications, 1991) Book III, Chapter 7, #2.

[18] See chapter seventeen "C-P-R for New Life" for details about forgiveness.

[19] Romans 8:28; "And we know that in all things God works for the good of those who love him, who have been called according to his purpose."

[20] John of the Cross, <u>Ascent of Mount Carmel</u>, <u>The Collected Works of St. John of the Cross</u>, eds. and trans. Kieran Kavanaugh and Otillio Rodriguez (Washington, D. C.: ICS Publications, 1991) Book II, Chapter 6, #4.

[21] Gerald G. May, <u>The Dark Night of the Soul: A Psychiatrist Explores the Connection between Darkness and Spiritual Growth</u> (New York, New York: Harper Collins Publishers, 2004) 54. While Protestant psychiatrist and spiritual director Gerald May claimed that the "will" had a "familiar meaning" for St. John as it has for us today, clearly that is not true. More accurately reflecting the Roman Catholic tradition, both Susan Muto

and Thomas Green reveal that St. John of the Cross' description of the will consists of four "emotions" or "feelings" – joy, hope, sorrow and fear. The details of these parts of the "human will" clearly identify them as feelings: joy is a form of gratification related to bodily needs; hope refers to egocentric expectations; sorrow is a depreciative attitude; and fear refers to useless, rambling anxieties, in particular of not taking risks. (Susan Muto, John of the Cross for Today: The Ascent (Notre Dame, Indiana: Ave Maria Press, 1991) 144.) In addition, there is confusion between this human hope within St. John's description of the will and God's Hope that purifies human memory.

Unfortunately, John's writing of the Ascent ends abruptly and prematurely so as not to fully describe what he meant by the will. (Susan Muto, John of the Cross for Today: The Ascent (Notre Dame, Indiana: Ave Maria Press, 1991) 144; and Thomas H. Green, Sr., Drinking from a Dry Well (Notre Dame, Indiana: Ave Maria Press, 1991) 59. In Book III of the Ascent, St. John of the Cross discusses purification of the memory in chapters 1 through 15 and the various "feelings" of the will, but he suddenly stops in chapter 45 without finishing.) If the will consists of "joy, hope, sorrow and fear" as John suggests then it contains emotions (that need to be purged) and perhaps the mental-attitudes that drive those feelings. While Muto aptly explains some connections of these emotions to the human will, she concludes, "Once the intellect is purified by faith and the memory by hope, then the will in response to love chooses rightly." (Susan Muto, John of the Cross for Today: The Ascent (Notre Dame, Indiana: Ave Maria Press, 1991) 147.) In other words, when the cleansing of the intellect and memory is completed, the will is "automatically" done.

[22] Gerald G. May, The Dark Night of the Soul: A Psychiatrist Explores the Connection between Darkness and Spiritual Growth (New York, New York: Harper Collins Publishers, 2004) 54.

[23] Psychosynthesis was first formulated in 1910 by the Italian psychiatrist, Roberto Assagioli (1888-1974). Roberto Assagioli, Psychosynthesis: A Collection of Basic Writings (New York, New York: The Viking Press, 1965) and Roberto Assagioli, The Act of Will (New York, New York: Penguin Books, 1973). Psychosynthesis, the "fourth" school of psychology, claims that if the religious dimension of individuals is not considered then people cannot be properly understood. Accordingly, my spiritual direction training, which understood that some psychological system is always implicit when working with people, suggested that Psychosynthesis is a better model.

[24] Luke 24:36

[25] Matthew 6:22-23

[26] Janet K. Ruffing, Spiritual Direction: Beyond the Beginnings (New York, New York: Paulist Press, 2000) 66-70. Ruffing was referencing Karl Rahner, The Practice of the Faith: A Handbook of Contemporary Spirituality, eds. Karl Lehmann and Albert Raffelt, trans. John Griffiths (New York, New York: Crossroads Publishing Co., 1986) 80-84.

[27] Gerald G. May, The Dark Night of the Soul: A Psychiatrist Explores the Connection between Darkness and Spiritual Growth (New York, New York: Harper Collins Publishers, 2004) 88.

[28] Brian Kolodiejchuk, Mother Teresa: Come Be My Light: The Private Writings of the 'Saint of Calcutta' (New York, New York: Doubleday Publishing Co., 2007) 335.

[29] John 15:9; "As the Father has loved me, so have I loved you. Now remain in my love."

[30] Charles Wesley, "Love Divine, all Loves Excelling," <u>Hymns for those that Seek, and those that Have Redemption</u> (Bristol, England: Felix Farley, 1747).

Love divine, all loves excelling,
Joy of heaven to earth come down;
Fix in us thy humble dwelling;
All thy faithful mercies crown!
Jesus, Thou art all compassion,
Pure unbounded love Thou art;
Visit us with Thy salvation;
Enter every trembling heart.
Breathe, O breathe Thy loving Spirit,
Into every troubled breast!
Let us all in Thee inherit;
Let us find that second rest.
Take away our bent to sinning;
Alpha and Omega be;
End of faith, as its Beginning,
Set our hearts at liberty.
Come, Almighty to deliver,
Let us all Thy life receive;
Suddenly return and never,
Never more Thy temples leave.
Thee we would be always blessing,
Serve Thee as Thy hosts above,
Pray and praise Thee without ceasing,
Glory in Thy perfect love.
Finish, then, Thy new creation;
Pure and spotless let us be.
Let us see Thy great salvation
Perfectly restored in Thee;
Changed from glory into glory,
Till in heaven we take our place,
Till we cast our crowns before Thee,
Lost in wonder, love, and praise.

[31] Luke 22:42; "Father, if you are willing, take this cup from me; yet not my will, but yours be done."

[32] John 17:22; "I have given them the glory that you gave me, that they may be one as we are one."

[33] Philippians 3:10-11

[34] Galatians 2:20

[35] Edward Edinger, <u>Ego And Archetype</u> (Baltimore, Maryland: Penguin Books, 1972).

Chapter 11 – The Unitive Way

[1] Arthur Devine, "State or Way (Purgative, Illuminative, Unitive)," The Catholic Encyclopedia, vol. 14 (New York, New York: Robert Appleton Company, 1912).

[2] Teresa of Avila, Interior Castle trans. E. Allison Peers (New York, New York: Doubleday Publishing Company, 1961).

[3] Galatians 2:20

[4] John 17:3

[5] John of the Cross, The Collected Works of St. John of the Cross, eds. Kieran Kavanaugh and Otillio Rodriguez (Washington, D. C.: ICS Publications, 1991) Book I, Chapter 9.

[6] Gerald G. May, The Dark Night of the Soul: A Psychiatrist Explores the Connection between Darkness and Spiritual Growth (New York, New York: Harper Collins Publishers, 2004) 138-142.

[7] Casting Crowns, "Who Am I?" Casting Crowns, Reunion Label, Franklin, Tennessee, 10 October 2003.

[8] II Corinthians 12:1-4

[9] II Peter 1:4-7

[10] Philippians 4:12; the underlining added by author for emphasis.

[11] II Corinthians 11:23-28

[12] Romans 8:17; the underlining added by author for emphasis.

[13] Romans 5:3; "Not only so, but we also rejoice in our sufferings, because we know that suffering produces perseverance."

[14] II Corinthians 4:17; "For our light and momentary troubles are achieving for us an eternal glory that far outweighs them all."

[15] The Dis-identification Exercise, a guided meditation, was created by Roberto Assagioli, the developer of Psychosynthesis. Its purpose is to separate the things about a person from the true individual. Thus, the meditation suggests the internalization of phrases: "I have a body; but I am not my body." The same is done for emotions as well as intellect. When Christians use this psychological model, they identify the person as a Soul-Self or Conscious-I that God has created. When the sensations, feelings and thoughts are released from being who individuals are, then they can recognize that they are separate and distinct from the body, emotions and mind – they are a Soul-Self.

[16] The prayer "Take and Receive," also called The Suscipe, is included by Ignatius of Loyola (1491-1556 AD) as additional material in regards to the "contemplation for attaining love" at the end of his Spiritual Exercises, #234. While forms of it existed during the early monastic era, "Take and Receive" is attributed to Ignatius.

[17] Luke 18:18-25; verse 18 is "Indeed, it is easier for a camel to go through the eye of a needle than for a rich man to enter the kingdom of God."

[18] John of the Cross, Dark Night, eds. Kieran Kavanaugh and Otillio Rodriguez The Collected Works of St. John of the Cross (Washington, D. C.: ICS Publications, 1991) Book II, Chapter 10.

[19] Malachi 3:3

[20] Thomas H. Green, When the Well Runs Dry: Prayer Beyond the Beginnings (Notre Dame, Indiana: Ave Maria Press, 1979) 142-150.

[21] Jeremiah 18:4 and Isaiah 64:8; "But the pot he was shaping from the clay was marred in his hands; so the potter formed it into another pot, shaping it as seemed best to him." And "Yet, O Lord, you are our Father. We are the clay, you are the potter; we are all the work of your hand."

[22] Romans 8:26

[23] Constance FitzGerald, "Transformation in Wisdom," eds. K. Culligan and R. Jordan, <u>Carmelite Studies VIII: Carmel and Contemplation</u> (Washington, D.C.: Institute of Carmelite Studies, 2000) 309-310.

[24] Psalm 46:10

[25] Psalm 37:7

[26] John H. Sammis, "Trust and Obey," comp. Daniel B. Towner, (Public Domain, 1887).

[27] Eddie Espinosa, <u>Change My Heart, O God</u>, Mercy/ Vineyard, Stafford, Texas, Music Services, Inc., 1982. About the song Eddie Espinosa wrote: "Change My Heart O God is a heart cry song that came to me after a time of being in the presence of God during a private time of worship. The experience that I had was very similar to that of Isaiah, chapter 6. During my time of being in God's presence, sin and attitudes of the heart were suddenly glaring me in the face. I realized that in order for me to walk uprightly before the Lord, I needed a heart transplant. I desperately needed for God to change my heart in order to love the things that He loves and to hate the things that He hates. I also was aware that only He could change my heart. I began to sing without paying attention to the melody, it just flowed from the depths of my being." (http://www.worship.co.za/series/cmh-0101.asp)

[28] Philippians 1:21-24.

Chapter 12 – Understanding the Process … Developmentally

[1] Matthew 6:14-15; "For if you forgive men when they sin against you, your heavenly Father will also forgive you. But if you do not forgive men their sins, your Father will not forgive your sins."

[2] Psalm 22:9-10; "Yet you brought me out of the womb; you made me trust in you even at my mother's breast. From birth I was cast upon you; from my mother's womb you have been my God."

[3] Chapter twenty-two, "Who Are You Talking To?" expands on this assertion.

[4] Carl G. Jung, <u>Modern Man in Search of His Soul</u> (New York, New York: Harcourt, Brace and World, Inc., 1933), 264. "I have treated many hundreds of patients. Among those in the second half of life - that is to say, over 35 - there has not been one whose problem in the last resort was not that of finding a religious outlook on life."

[5] Ephesians 4: 7, 11-13

[6] I Corinthians 13:9-12

[7] I Corinthians 2:10-16; "but God has revealed it (what God has prepared for those who love him) to us by his Spirit. The Spirit searches all things, even the deep things of God. For who among men knows the thoughts of a man except the man's spirit within him? In the same way no one knows the thoughts of God except the Spirit of God. We have not received the spirit of the world but the Spirit who is from God, that we may understand what God has freely given us. This is what we speak, not in words taught us by human wisdom but in words taught by the Spirit, expressing spiritual truths in spiritual words. The man without the Spirit does not accept the things that come from the Spirit of God, for they are foolishness to him, and he cannot

understand them, because they are spiritually discerned. The spiritual man makes judgments about all things, but he himself is not subject to any man's judgment: 'For who has known the mind of the Lord that he may instruct him?' But we have the mind of Christ."

[8] Ontology is the part of metaphysical philosophy that describes what qualities we have when we come into existence. Genesis 1:26 is the beginning of biblical ontology.

[9] I Corinthians 2:12-14, 16b

[10] Romans 7:14-20

[11] My spiritual direction training introduced me to the psychological system called Psychosynthesis which is extremely compatible with the Christian faith and emphasizes that unless the religious dimension of a person is considered the whole person is not considered. Of course, this psychology is not handled in a doctrinal way but in a purely social scientific manner. See Roberto Assagioli, Psychosynthesis (New York, New York: The Viking Press, 1965).

[12] I Corinthians 3: 1-2; "Brothers, I could not address you as spiritual but as worldly--mere infants in Christ. I gave you milk, not solid food, for you were not yet ready for it. Indeed, you are still not ready." And Hebrews 5:11-14; "We have much to say about this, but it is hard to explain because you are slow to learn. In fact, though by this time you ought to be teachers, you need someone to teach you the elementary truths of God's word all over again. You need milk, not solid food! Anyone who lives on milk, being still an infant, is not acquainted with the teaching about righteousness. But solid food is for the mature, who by constant use have trained themselves to distinguish good from evil."

[13] These systems build upon the theory of Jean Piaget. Because Piaget's theory primarily deals with the development of children, I have elected to omit his work although it has important implications for spiritual growth. In fact, Christian educators have made good use of his research especially for writing Sunday school materials.

[14] For those spiritual helpers who are not familiar with these psycho-social models that have been officially titled the "psychology of religious development," these theories are totally unconcerned with all forms of doctrine, catechism or biblical interpretation. So, the content of any particular expression of Christianity is neither affected nor criticized. What is considered are the capacities of individuals in regard to emotional and cognitive ability, moral reasoning, locus of authority and the way they make sense of and relate to the divine.

Chapter 13 – Overlaying the Maps

[1] Pierre Teilhard de Chardin, The Phenomenon of Man, trans. Bernard Wall (London, England: Wm. Collins Sons & Company, 1959). Originally published in French as Le Phenomene Humain, copyright 1955 by Editions du Seuil, Paris, France. This quotation is regularly attributed to Chardin in The Phenomenon of Man. While consistent with his thought within the book, a computer word search in English of the text could not locate it.

[2] The summary of Erikson's Psycho-Social Developmental Growth comes from the following sources:
Erik H. Erikson, Childhood and Society (New York, New York: W. W. Norton and Company, 1950).
Erik H. Erikson, Identity and the Life Cycle (New York, New York: International Universities Press, 1959).
Gail Sheehy, Passages: Predictable Crises of Adult Life (New York, New York: E. P. Dutton, 1976).

[3] Thomas A. Droege, <u>Faith Passages and Patterns</u> (Philadelphia, Pennsylvania: Fortress Press, 1983) 39.

[4] Proverbs 22:6; scripture modified for emphasis to be gender inclusive by the author.

[5] Carl Friedrich Keil and Franz Delitzsch, <u>Commentary on the Old Testament</u>, 10 vol., trans. James Martin (Edinburg, England: T & T Clark Company, 1866), Revised Edition (Peabody, Massachusetts: Hendrickson Publishers, Inc., 1996) Proverbs 22:6.

[6] I John 4:20b; "If anyone says, 'I love God,' yet hates his brother, he is a liar. For anyone who does not love his brother, whom he has seen, cannot love God, whom he has not seen."

[7] Rudolf Otto, <u>The Idea of the Holy</u> (London, England: Oxford University Press, 1923). Rudolf Otto (1869–1937) was an eminent German Lutheran theologian and scholar of comparative religion.

[8] Mircea Eliade <u>The Sacred and the Profane: The Nature of Religion</u> trans. Willard R. Trask (New York, New York: Harper Torchbooks, 1961). Mircea Eliade (1907–1986) was a Romanian historian of religion and philosopher of religious experience.

[9] John Bradshaw, <u>Healing the Shame that Binds You</u>, Revised Edition (Deerfield Beach, Florida: Health Communications, Inc., 2005). I have found this book especially helpful in understanding the difference between shame and toxic shame, which hinders spiritual growth especially of those who have been abused and are recovering addicts.

Chapter 14 – Overlaying the Moral/Ethical Map

[1] Jean Piaget <u>The Origins of Intelligence in Children</u> (New York, New York: International University Press, 1952). Jean Piaget (1896–1980) was a Swiss developmental psychologist known for research with children and the development of his cognitive development theory regarding how they learn.

[2] Lawrence Kohlberg, "The Development of Modes of Thinking and Choices in Years 10 to 16," Ph. D. dissertation, Chicago, Illinois: University of Chicago, 1958.

[3] The legal system adopts this reasoning when it has different regulations and penalties for juveniles than adults. Case in point, some adults should not be even tried as adults.

[4] Clark Power, "Moral Development, Religious Thinking and the Question of a Seventh Stage" <u>Essays on Moral Development: Philosophy of Moral Development</u>, Vol. 1. ed., Lawrence Kohlberg (San Francisco, California: Harper and Row, 1981).

[5] Genesis 4:1-16

[6] Exodus 21:23-24; "But if there is serious injury, you are to take life for life, eye for eye, tooth for tooth, hand for hand, foot for foot, burn for burn, wound for wound, bruise for bruise."

[7] Matthew 7:12; "So in everything, do to others what you would have them do to you, for this sums up the Law and the Prophets."

[8] Romans 13:1-4

[9] Luke 10:25-37

[10] Acts 15:1-35

[11] Acts 5:29; "Peter and the other apostles replied: "We must obey God rather than men!"

[12] Romans 12:17-21

[13] Mitch Albom, <u>The Five People You Will Meet in Heaven</u> (New York, New York: Hyperion Press, 2003).

[14] Donald B. Kraybill, Steven M. Nolt and David L. Weaver-Zercher, <u>Amish Grace: How Forgiveness Transcended Tragedy</u> (Somerset, New Jersey: Jossey-Bass, 2007).

[15] Matthew 5:39; "But I tell you, Do not resist an evil person. If someone strikes you on the right cheek, turn to him the other also."

[16] Matthew 5:41; "If someone forces you to go one mile, go with him two miles."

[17] Luke 6:27-28; "'But I tell you who hear me: Love your enemies, do good to those who hate you, bless those who curse you, pray for those who mistreat you.'"

[18] Philippians 2:4-8

[19] This is evidenced from Abram's discussion with God about saving Sodom (Genesis 18:16-33); Jesus' original assertion that he came only for the Israelites (Matthew 15:24); and the early church's inclusion of gentiles (Acts 15:1-35).

[20] Isaiah 55:8-9; "'For my thoughts are not your thoughts, neither are your ways my ways,' declares the Lord. 'As the heavens are higher than the earth, so are my ways higher than your ways and my thoughts than your thoughts.'"

Chapter 15 – Overlaying the Faith Development Map

[1] James W. Fowler, <u>Stages of Faith: The Psychology of Human Development and the Quest for Meaning</u> (San Francisco, California: Harper Collins, 1981). Additional works by James Fowler expanded and corrected his original theory. These include: James W. Fowler, <u>Becoming Adult, Becoming Christian: Adult Development and Christian Faith</u> (San Francisco, California: Harper and Row, 1984). (Revised edition published by Jossey-Bass, 2000) and James W. Fowler, <u>Faith Development and Pastoral Care</u> (Philadelphia, Pennsylvania: Fortress Press, 1987). The purpose of this chapter is to overview Fowler's stages of faith in a simple enough way so that spiritual helpers will be able to use it in assisting other's spiritual growth. No consideration is given to the debate in the academic and the psycho-social communities. Those who wish to consider this discussion could review the five major books on the subject: Christiane Brusselmans, ed. <u>Toward Moral and Religious Maturity</u> (Morristown, NJ: Silver Burdett. 1980); Craig Dykstra and Sharon Daloz Parks, eds. <u>Faith Development and Fowler</u> (Birmingham, Alabama: Religious Education Press, 1986); Jeff Astley, and Leslie J. Francis, eds. <u>Christian Perspectives on Faith Development</u> (Grand Rapids, Michigan: Eerdmans Publishing Company, 1992); James W. Fowler, Karl Ernest Nipkow, and Friedrich Schweitzer, eds. <u>Stages of Faith and Religious Development</u> (New York, New York: Crossroad Publishing Company, 1991); and Richard R. Osmer and Friedrich L. Schweitzer, eds. <u>Developing a Public Faith: New directions in Practical Theology</u> (St. Louis, Missouri: Chalice Press, 2003).

[2] James W. Fowler and Mary Lynn Dell, "Stages of Faith from Infancy through Adolescence: Reflections on Three Decades of Faith Development Theory" <u>The Handbook of Spiritual Development in Childhood and Adolescence</u>, eds. Eugene C. Roehlkepartain, Pamela Ebstyne King, Linda M. Wagener, and Peter L. Benson (Thousand Oaks, California: Sage Publications, Inc., 2006), 36.

[3] James W. Fowler and Mary Lynn Dell, "Stages of Faith from Infancy through Adolescence: Reflections on Three Decades of Faith Development Theory" <u>The Handbook of Spiritual Development in Childhood and</u>

Adolescence, eds. Eugene C. Roehlkepartain, Pamela Ebstyne King, Linda M. Wagener, and Peter L. Benson (Thousand Oaks, California: Sage Publications, Inc., 2006), 40.

[4] James W. Fowler and Mary Lynn Dell, "Stages of Faith from Infancy through Adolescence: Reflections on Three Decades of Faith Development Theory" The Handbook of Spiritual Development in Childhood and Adolescence, eds. Eugene C. Roehlkepartain, Pamela Ebstyne King, Linda M. Wagener, and Peter L. Benson (Thousand Oaks, California: Sage Publications, Inc., 2006), 39

[5] Carol Gilligan, In a different voice (Cambridge, Massachusetts: Harvard University Press, 1982).

[6] James W. Fowler and Mary Lynn Dell, "Stages of Faith from Infancy through Adolescence: Reflections on Three Decades of Faith Development Theory" The Handbook of Spiritual Development in Childhood and Adolescence, eds. Eugene C. Roehlkepartain, Pamela Ebstyne King, Linda M. Wagener, and Peter L. Benson (Thousand Oaks, California: Sage Publications, Inc., 2006), 38.

[7] Robert L. Selman, The Developmental Conceptions of Interpersonal Relations (Boston, Massachusetts: Harvard-Judge Baker Social Reasoning Project, 1974).

[8] Nicholas of Cusa (1401–1464 AD), was a cardinal of the Catholic Church as well as a theologian, philosopher and mathematician. In his concern for a divided world, he re-invented the phrase the "coincidence of opposites" in order to approximate and to move toward unity both in real life and in Christian faith. His concept is significantly used in the writings of Mircea Eliade, Paul Tillich, Pierre Teilhard de Chardin and Meister Eckhart.

[9] Paul Tillich, The Eternal Now (New York, New York: Charles Scribner's Sons, 1963), 46.

Chapter 16 – Prayer Forms

[1] Gerald G. May, The Dark Night of the Soul: A Psychiatrist Explores the Connection between Darkness and Spiritual Growth (New York, New York: Harper Collins Publishers, 2004) 130.

[2] "Now I Lay Me Down to Sleep," The New England Primer, Benjamin Harris, ed. (Boston, Massachusetts: Benjamin Harris, 1687-1690). "Now I Lay Me Down to Sleep" is a classic children's prayer from the eighteenth century. The version printed in The New England Primer goes:

Now I lay me down to sleep,

I pray thee, Lord, my soul to keep;

If I should die before I wake,

I pray thee, Lord, my soul to take.

[3] Luke 11:1ff

[4] Philippians 4:13

[5] Genesis 31:49; "It was also called Mizpah, because he said, "May the Lord keep watch between you and me when we are away from each other."

[6] Psalm 143:5-6

[7] F. Antonisamy, An introduction to Christian Spirituality (Bangalore Publishing Company: St. Paul, Minnesota, 2000) 76-77.

[8] Fiddler on the Roof, Jerry Bock, writ., Sheldon Harnick, lyrics (New York, New York: Broadway Musical, September 24, 1964). "Fiddler on the Roof" is a musical with music by Jerry Bock, lyrics by Sheldon Harnick, and book by Joseph Stein Opened on Broadway September 24, 1964.

[9] Genesis 18:22-26; "The men turned away and went toward Sodom, but Abraham remained standing before the Lord. Then Abraham approached him and said: 'Will you sweep away the righteous with the wicked? What if there are fifty righteous people in the city? Will you really sweep it away and not spare the place for the sake of the fifty righteous people in it? Far be it from you to do such a thing--to kill the righteous with the wicked, treating the righteous and the wicked alike. Far be it from you! Will not the Judge of all the earth do right?' The Lord said, 'If I find fifty righteous people in the city of Sodom, I will spare the whole place for their sake.'"

[10] John 17:15; "My prayer is not that you take them out of the world but that you protect them from the evil one."

[11] Ignatius of Loyola (1491-1556 AD) created the Spiritual Exercises to enable Christians to deepen their relationship with God. The Exercises are divided into four sections (weeks) that focus on one's life, sin and God's love; following the life and ministry of Jesus; the last week in Christ's earthly life; and the resurrection and its implications for service in the world.

[12] Charles Austin Miles, "In the Garden" (Public Domain, 1912).

I come to the garden alone

While the dew is still on the roses

And the voice I hear falling on my ear

The Son of God discloses.

(Refrain)

And He walks with me, and He talks with me,

And He tells me I am His own;

And the joy we share as we tarry there,

None other has ever known.

He speaks, and the sound of His voice,

Is so sweet the birds hush their singing,

And the melody that He gave to me

Within my heart is ringing.

Refrain

I'd stay in the garden with Him

Though the night around me be falling,

But He bids me go; through the voice of woe

His voice to me is calling.

Refrain

[13] Cleavant Derricks, "Just a Little Talk with Jesus," Harbor Bells No. 6 (Chattanooga, Tennessee: Stamps-Baxter Music Company, 1937). Cleavant Derricks (1910-1977) was an African-American Baptist minister and songwriter of over 300 Gospel songs.

[14] John 4:5-42 and Mark 10:46-52.

[15] Morton T. Kelsey, God, Dreams, and Revelation: A Christian Interpretation of Dreams (Minneapolis, Minnesota: Augsburg Fortress Press, 1991) 159; and Louis M. Savary, Patricia H. Berne and Strephon K. Williams, Dreams and Spiritual Growth: A Judeo-Christian Way of Dreamwork (Mahwah, New Jersey: Paulist Press, 1984) 42-52.

In preparing the Latin Vulgate translation of the Bible, Jerome deliberately mistranslated a Hebrew word at least three times in order to include prohibitions against dreams and people attempting to understand them. Christianity is indebted to Morton Kelsey for uncovering this mistake. This error has been unfortunately extended to "guided imagery" and the use of any form of the imagination, part of the brain that God has given and uses to communication with humans.

The Hebrew word in question is *anan*, which means witchcraft, soothsaying and those who practiced magic. The word *anan* and various forms of it occur ten times in the Old Testament. In preparing the Latin translations of the Old Testament, Jerome gave *anan* two very different meanings. Seven times Jerome translated it correctly as "witchcraft" or one of its synonyms (Deuteronomy 18:14, II Kings 21:6, Isaiah 2:6, Isaiah 57:3, Jeremiah 27:9, Matthew 5:11 and Judges 9:37). However, the other three times (in Deuteronomy 18:10, Leviticus 19:26 and II Chronicles 33:6), where the Hebrew texts are condemning witchcraft (*anan*), Jerome translated it as "observing dreams."

Leviticus 19:26 and Deuteronomy 18:10 says, "You shall not practice sorcery and *anan*." Jerome's translation clearly noted that the Bible teaches not to practice "observing dreams" instead of "witchcraft." Jerome's mistranslation directly linked dream work with witchcraft in the sacred biblical text. We cannot absolve Jerome of the mistranslation by claiming that he did not know the meaning of *anan* because seven out of ten times he translated in correctly.

As a result, the emphasis of the Old Testament, the New Testament and Christians during the first 500 years of the early Christian Church on the understanding of God's message through the interpretation of dreams came to a screeching halt. Almost all translations of the Bible in use until the mid-twentieth century were made from Jerome's Latin Vulgate and perpetuated the false condemnation of dream work in the doctrine of the Roman Catholic Church and among the churches of the Protestant movement, but did not affect the Eastern Orthodox branch of Christianity as drastically. Not until the advent of new biblical scholarship initiated new translations in the 20th century from the original Hebrew and Greek manuscripts was Jerome's error discovery and is now slowly being corrected.

[16] Job 33:14-18, 26; the author has inserted the bracketed portions and has added the third person plural to the translation.

[17] Acts 10:1-48 is the story of God's connecting a centurion named Cornelius with the "head" of the Apostles' Simon Peter. God through a dream/trance instructed Peter to do what was against the traditional Jewish law with the implication for him (and all) to accept Gentiles (non-Jews) who received Jesus as Savior; these were the first "gentile Christians" and established the policy to receive "Christ believers" from the ranks of the Gentiles. This decision would be confirmed at the gathering of church leaders in Jerusalem as recorded in Acts 15:1-35.

[18] Using dreams as an indicator of what God is communicating can be extremely effective, especially since during sleep the resistance of Christians is basically non-existent and God can break through. Particularly helpful Christian dream resources for spiritual helpers to use include: Morton Kelsey, <u>Dreams, A Way to Listen to God</u> (New York, New York: Paulist Press, 1978) [classic]; Paul Meier and Robert Wise, <u>Windows of the Soul: A Look at Dreams and Their Meanings</u> (Nashville, Tennessee: Thomas Nelson Publishers, 1995) [evangelical]; and Louis M. Savary, Patricia H. Berne and Strephon K. Williams, <u>Dreams and Spiritual Growth: A Judeo-Christian Way of Dreamwork</u> (Mahwah, New Jersey: Paulist Press, 1984) [practical].

[19] Thomas Sugrue, <u>The Story of Edgar Cayce: There is a River</u> (New York, New York: Holt, Rinehart, and Winston, 1943). This book is a better summary of Edgar Cayce's life and his devout Christian spirituality than later works because it is written by a personal friend. While controversy surrounds some of what Cayce said, the simple sincerity of his Christian faith and his dedication to prayer cannot be denied. He is an example of passive "Contemplative Prayers."

[20] James 5:16. The Greek phrase [πολὺ (much) ἰσχύει (strong, is powerful) δέησις (prayer) δικαίου (of righteous man) ἐνεργουμένη (effective, energy)] has been translated with various emphases – some focus on the passion and even the continuousness of the prayer while others highlight the righteousness of the pray-er. However, it is not the prayer itself that is effective but the relationship of the pray-er with God. In other words, people cannot structure a prayer or emotionalize a prayer so that it will work; people can only live a life so that God comes into contact with it in such a way that power is received. The prayer itself has power and effect because of the interactive and affective nature of Christians. Righteousness refers to not to what a person can do, like being moral, but what God does in that person or in the case of "Contemplative Prayers" when God determines to engage.

[21] Benedict J. Goeschel, <u>Spiritual Passages: The Psychology of Spiritual Development</u> (New York, New York: Crossroads Publishing Company, 1983) 6-11.

[22] Thomas H. Green, <u>When the Well Runs Dry: Prayer Beyond the Beginnings</u> (Notre Dame, Indiana: Ave Maria Press, 1979) 32.

[23] Fredrick Brook, "My goal is God Himself, Not Joy, Nor Peace" (England: Public Domain, after 1870); Frederick Cook Atkinson (1841-1896), composer of Classic tune "Morecambe" (Norwich, England: 1870). The contemporary tune can be found at http://www.hymnal.net/hymn.php/nt/350.

My goal is God Himself, not joy, nor peace,
Nor even blessing, but Himself, my God;
'Tis His to lead me there—not mine, but His—
At any cost, dear Lord, by any road.
So faith bounds forward to its goal in God,
And love can trust her Lord to lead her there;
Upheld by Him, my soul is following hard
Till God hath full fulfilled my deepest prayer.
No matter if the way be sometimes dark,
No matter though the cost be oft-times great,
He knoweth how I best shall reach the mark,

The way that leads to Him must needs be strait.

One thing I know, I cannot say Him nay;

One thing I do, I press towards my Lord;

My God my glory here, from day to day,

And in the glory there my great Reward.

[24] Psalm 51:11-12

[25] Brian Kolodiejchuk, <u>Mother Teresa: Come Be My Light – The Private Writings of the "Saint of Calcutta"</u> (New York, New York: Doubleday Publishing Company, 2007). An example of the "media frenzy" is the 23 August 2007 <u>Time</u> magazine cover which read, "Mother Teresa's Crisis of Faith." Fr. Larry Voelker, a fellow spiritual director, recommended <u>Come Be My Light</u> to a parishioner who "hated" it – presumably because it painted a picture of a real Christian during the "Dark Night" experience instead of the idyllic one Christians want to aspire to be.

[26] Mark 8:35; parentheses added by the author.

[27] On the other hand, God can, of course, make "Unitive Prayers" happen at any time, even early in life. But they most often contain anxiety as well as a distinctive lack of freedom that makes them "unusual" and without the ability of transform the soul. People typically value them too highly or are petrified by them.

[28] Two basic categories of prayer are delineated by the words kataphatic and apophatic. Kataphatic means "with images;" apophatic means "without images."

[29] John 17:18 and John 17:15; "As you sent me into the world, I have sent them into the world. … My prayer is not that you take them out of the world but that you protect them from the evil one." together with John 17:16; "They are not of the world, even as I am not of it."

[30] Tim Dowley, ed., <u>Eerdman's Handbook to the History of Christianity</u>, (Berkhamsted, Herts, England: Lion Publishing, 1977).

[31] Teresa of Avila, "Autobiography," <u>The Collected Works of St. Teresa of Avila</u>, vol. 1, trans. Kieran Kavanaugh and Otilio Rodriguez (Washington D.C.: ICS Publishing Company, 1976) Chapters 11-22.

[32] Gerald G. May, <u>The Dark Night of the Soul: A Psychiatrist Explores the Connection between Darkness and Spiritual Growth</u> (New York, New York: Harper Collins Publishers, 2004) 114.

[33] Devine, Arthur, "Recollection," <u>The Catholic Encyclopedia</u>, vol. 12 (New York, New York: Robert Appleton Company, 1912). The term "recollection" in the classical spiritual literature often confuses "thinking about God," "interior solitude," "contemplation" and "infused contemplation;" and so does Teresa as she attempts to fits the experiences of praying into the structure of Classical Theology. That language and descriptions are not helpful. It does not differential between rational and intuitive functions of the brain and focuses on the relinquishing of intellect, memory and will – the way used to describe human psychology and brain functioning in that day which is sustained in orthodox forms of mystical Roman Catholic theology. This chapter "Prayer Forms" is an attempt to provide more helpful descriptions while still including the insights of the mystical and classical Christians.

[34] Psalm 46:10

[35] Thomas H. Green, <u>When the Well Runs Dry</u> (Notre Dame, Indiana: Ave Maria Press, 1979) 29-32. His summary excludes "Formal Prayers."

[36] Basil Pennington, <u>Lectio Divina: Renewing the Ancient Practice of Praying the Scriptures</u> (New York, New York: The Crosswords Press, 1998). Lectio Divina may be translated as "Sacred Reading." It is a prayer form that came from the spirituality of the fourth century desert fathers and mothers. As Abba Isaac taught him, John Cassian introduced Lectio Divina into Western Christianity; and St. Benedict employed it in his monastic movement. Lectio still remains a much used form of prayer.

Chapter 17 - CPR for New Life

[1] In 2009, I put together a paper for the people that I helped spiritually, which I called "CPR for New Life," which makes up the bulk of this chapter. I wrote that paper mostly because I was always sharing the information about how to deal with the issue of forgiveness with just about everyone; so I figured that it would be better to have it written. I knew what I wanted to convey but also did lots of research in order to make sure that I had the details correct. At that time, I did not footnote the sources I used, so I apology ahead of time for inadvertently using another's words, if in fact I did. However, the following sources are included in this chapter; I just don't know which words, if any, should have quotation marks around them and which words come from which source. They include:

Gary Thomas, "The Forgiveness Factor," <u>Christianity Today</u>, vol. 44 no. 1, 10 January 2000.

Robert D. Enright and Joanna North, eds., <u>Exploring Forgiveness</u> (Madison, Wisconsin: University of Wisconsin Press, 1998). This book contains an extensive bibliography on forgiveness literature and research, including works on forgiveness from a Christian, theological perspective.

Beverly Flanigan, <u>Forgiving the Unforgivable: Overcoming the Bitter Legacy of Intimate Wounds</u> (New York, New York: Macmillan Publishing, 1992).

L. Gregory Jones, <u>Embodying Forgiveness: A Theological Analysis</u> (Grand Rapids, Michigan: Eerdmans Publishing Company, 1995).

Lewis Smedes, <u>Forgive and Forget: Healing the Hurts We Don't Deserve</u> (New York, New York: Harper Collins Publishers, 1984).

Donald S. Browning, <u>Atonement and Psychotherapy</u> (Philadelphia, Pennsylvania: Westminister Press, 1966).

[2] Micah 6:8: "He has showed you, O man, what is good. And what does the Lord require of you? To act justly and to love mercy and to walk humbly with your God."

[3] This requirement is initiated in Leviticus 19:2, but echoed in the words of Jesus to be perfect/merciful as God is (Matthew 5:48 and Luke 6:36); and the original law is reaffirmed in I Peter 1:16 as necessary for Christians.

[4] Matthew 6:12; and also in Luke 11:4a as "Forgive us our sins, for we also forgive everyone who sins against us."

[5] Revelation 7:9-15; Revelation 4:6-11; Revelation 22:1-4 all depict this image of Heaven.

[6] Matthew 6:14-15; the author has added the inclusive language for emphasis.

[7] I John 4:20; the author has added the inclusive language for emphasis.

[8] Romans 10:10; underlining added by author.

[9] James Strong, <u>The New Strong's Exhaustive Concordance of the Bible</u> (Nashville, Tennessee: Thomas Nelson Press, 1991) #4982. The Greek word σῴζω (sozo) is the root word used for salvation. It is also the

same root word used for "to heal, to be made whole, and to save." The interconnectedness of physical, emotional and spiritual restoration is implicit in the use of the same Greek word σῴζω. Accordingly, the same power of God is employed for whatever kind of σῴζω is needed.

[10] John 4:4-42

[11] Mark 1:40-45

[12] Luke 8:40-48

[13] James Strong, The New Strong's Exhaustive Concordance of the Bible (Nashville, Tennessee: Thomas Nelson Press, 1991) #3339-3340.

[14] I John 1:9

[15] Psalm 8:3-6; "When I consider your heavens, the work of your fingers, the moon and the stars, which you have set in place, what is man that you are mindful of him, the son of man that you care for him? You made him a little lower than the heavenly beings and crowned him with glory and honor. You made him ruler over the works of your hands; you put everything under his feet."

[16] Jeremiah 29:11; "For I know the plans I have for you," declares the Lord, "plans to prosper you and not to harm you, plans to give you hope and a future."

[17] Psalm 103:10-13; "He (God) does not treat us as our sins deserve or repay us according to our iniquities. For as high as the heavens are above the earth, so great is his love for those who fear ("respect" conveys the meaning better); as far as the east is from the west, so far has he removed our transgressions from us. As a father has compassion on his children, so the Lord has compassion on those who fear him;"

[18] Ephesians 4:26 (Revised Standard Version)

[19] Matthew 5:39; "But I tell you, Do not resist an evil person. If someone strikes you on the right cheek, turn to him the other also."

[20] Romans 8:1

[21] Matthew 5:44

[22] Agape (ἀγάπη) means unconditional love that is associated with God's ability to love perfectly. Eros (ἔρως) is passionate love, with sensual desire and longing. Eros is not used in the New Testament but implied in sections referring to "worldly" passions. Philia (φιλία) means friendship or brotherly love. Storge (στοργή) means "affection" and mostly refers to relationships within the family.

[23] Romans 12:21

[24] Francis of Assisi (1181–1226 A.D.) was an Italian Roman Catholic friar and iterant preacher. The religious orders of Franciscans and St. Claire were formed by him.

[25] Lisa Vischer "The Forgiveness Song" (Brentwood, Tennessee: EMI Christian Music Group, 1994.)

Chapter 18 - Dealing with Pain

[1] Dietrich Bonhoeffer, Letters and Papers From Prison, Eberhard Bethge, ed., Reginald H. Fuller, trans. (New York New York: Macmillan Publishing Company, 1953).

[2] However, individual sickness and disease, if necessary, can be used by God as a pain that lures people in particular directions and influences their choices. I find this first true about my personal life as a recipient of

polio; and cautiously consider the possibility that God may use similar sickness in others – always giving them the option of whether they consider that true for themselves.

[3] Some Christians consider that some forms of human-wide pain is caused by human-wide error/sin through which God communicates i.e., the Sodom and Gomorrah Syndrome) – although discussion of this possibility is beyond the scope of this chapter. I discount this option at least because it is not the norm and discussion about it typically sidetracks the healing.

[4] Further discussion of this and similar phrases as road blocks along the Spiritual Road will be considered in chapter nineteen "Words Can Sometimes."

[5] Matthew 26:11, "The poor you will always have with you, but you will not always have me." John 16:20; "I tell you the truth, you will weep and mourn while the world rejoices. You will grieve, but your grief will turn to joy."

[6] Hebrews 12:10

[7] Acts 5:1-10

[8] II Corinthians 12:7-9; "To keep me from becoming conceited because of these surpassingly great revelations, there was given me a thorn in my flesh, a messenger of Satan, to torment me. Three times I pleaded with the Lord to take it away from me. But he said to me, 'My grace is sufficient for you, for my power is made perfect in weakness.' Therefore I will boast all the more gladly about my weaknesses, so that Christ's power may rest on me."

[9] John 4:39; "Many of the Samaritans from that town believed in him because of the woman's testimony, "He told me everything I ever did.""

[10] Sarah Hart and Brian White, "Awakening" (New York, New York, BMG Music Publishing, Inc. BMI/BMG Songs, Inc., 2001).

Is this love or madness

Is this cruelty or grace

You have given this dry season

I'm thirsting for the reason

You have brought me to this place.

This is death and living

I am empty and fulfilled

And all that's left for me

Is the abundance that I see when I

Open my eyes to Your will.

(Chorus)

Awakening to You

Awakening to You

To love, to mercy

To the beauty of truth

Awakening to You.

In the fire I flourish
In the testing of my faith
And the evidence is clear
It's Your hand that moved me here
To be born into this new day. (Chorus)

And through all my unbelieving
Even then, oh You were teaching
For me to see
This glorious dawn. (Chorus)

[11] Genesis 50:20

[12] A Jo-Hari window is a psychological tool created by Joseph Luft and Harry Ingham; its purpose is to help people better understand their interpersonal communication and relationships. The "window" is segmented into four quadrants that describe types and levels of awareness. Quadrant two indicates what people are "blind" but others like a spiritual director can see.

1. "The Arena" – what is known by the person about him/herself and is also known by others.

2. "The Blind Spot" – what is unknown by the person about him/herself but which others know.

3. "The Facade" – what the person knows about him/herself that others do not know.

4. "The Unknown" – what is unknown by the person about him/herself and is also unknown by others.

[13] Bruce Wilkinson, Secrets of the Vine: Breaking Through to Abundance (Sisters, Oregon, Multnomah Publishers, Inc., 2001). I highly recommend the reading of this book.

[14] Hebrews 12:4-6 which references Proverbs 3:11-12.

[15] Romans 8:1

[16] Bruce Wilkinson, Secrets of the Vine: Breaking Through to Abundance (Sisters, Oregon, Multnomah Publishers, Inc., 2001) 34-36.

[17] Bruce Wilkinson, Secrets of the Vine: Breaking Through to Abundance (Sisters, Oregon, Multnomah Publishers, Inc., 2001) 33. Evidencing the translation error: of the 102 times that "airo" is used in the Kings James Version, it is translated as take up 32 times, take away 25, take 25, away with 5, lift up 4, bear 3, miscellaneous 8. The primary definitions are listed as "to raise up, elevate, lift up, to raise from the ground, take up: stones to raise upwards, elevate, lift up: the hand to draw up: a fish to take upon one's self and carry what has been raised up, and to bear to bear away what has been raised, carry off." The Greek lexicon used is based on Thayer's and Smith's Bible Dictionaries as well as the Kittel "Theological Dictionary of the New Testament." These references are public domain.

[18] Bruce Wilkinson, Secrets of the Vine: Breaking Through to Abundance (Sisters, Oregon, Multnomah Publishers, Inc., 2001) 56-57.

[19] John 15:1a, 2b.

[20] Bruce Wilkinson, Secrets of the Vine: Breaking Through to Abundance (Sisters, Oregon, Multnomah Publishers, Inc., 2001) 58.

[21] John Hartley and Gary Sadler, "Love By Degree" (Brentwood, Tennessee: EMI Christian Music Group, 2002).

When You try my heart like silver

And test my soul with fire

When You cut away the beauty

Of the treasures I desire

One by one I lay them down

Through the working of Your hand.

(Chorus)

And if it takes my whole life through

And if it breaks my heart in two

But if it makes me more like You

Lord, let it be in me

Love by degree

Will You flood in like the waters

Melt my castles made of sand

Until You're my deepest longing

In the depths of who I am

Every dream I will lay down

To the working of Your hand

(Chorus 2X)

[22] John 15:4

[23] "Hands," De Beers Jewelers Television Commercial, JWT (New York Advertising Agency, July 2000). Video Location: http://www.advertolog.com/de-beers/adverts/hands-2333005/.

[24] John 16:22; "So with you: Now is your time of grief, but I will see you again and you will rejoice, and no one will take away your joy."

[25] Jamie Rickert, "New Wine," New Wine (Suffern, New York: Parish Mission Team, 1989).

Lord, do I believe

That you are building me a house full of pain

Father, I do.

Lord, do I believe

That when I'm drowning you'll be sending me rain

Father, I do.

Lord, do I believe

That you're pushing me harder than I've ever been pushed before

And that you're going to be pushing me harder, and harder

'Till there is nothing to push anymore

Father, I do

(Chorus)

And the fresh new wine is so raw when it's young

Brings tears to the eyes and it burns on the tongue

And it carries the cries of the grapes that they are ripped from the vine.

And the flesh has been torn from my back and my bone

My hide has been cut; my hide has been sown

For my father has need of a new skin

Because he's making new wine

Lord, do I believe

That you're carving out the heart of my heart

Father, I do

Lord, do I believe

That you're ever going to break me apart

Father, I do

Lord, do I believe

That you're tearing from my hands the things I am dying to hold

And you're pouring me out 'till I'm empty, 'till I'm empty

And there is nothing inside anymore, Father but you

Father, I do.

(Chorus)

And the flesh has been torn from my back and my bone

My hide has been cut; my hide has been sown

For my father has need of a new skin

Because he's making new wine

New Wine!

Chapter 19 – Words Can Sometimes …

[1] Elie Wiesel, <u>Night</u>, trans. Stella Rodway (New York, New York: Bantam Books, 1982). Elie Wiesel (born in 1928) is a contemporary Jewish writer, professor, political activist and Holocaust survivor. He is the author of over forty books, the best known of which is <u>Night</u>, a memoir describing his experiences during his imprisonment in several concentration camps. Wiesel was awarded the Nobel Peace Prize in 1986.

[2] Numbers 13:1-33

[3] John 8:32; "Then you will know the truth, and the truth will set you free."

[4] Romans 3:20b; "through the law we become conscious of sin."

[5] Ephesians 4:26a (Revised Standard Version)

Chapter 20 – "That's What the Lonely Is For"

[1] David Wilcox, "That's What the Lonely Is For" (Irving Music, Inc. Midnight Ocean Bonfire Music, 1993.)

The depth of your dreams

The height of your wishes

The length of your vision to see

Your hope of your heart is much bigger than this

For it's made out of what it might be

Now picture your hope

Your heart's desire

As a castle that you must keep

In all of its splendor

It's drafty with lonely

This heart is too hard to heat.

CHORUS:

When I get lonely

That's only a sign some room is empty

And that room is there by design

If I feel hollow

That's just my proof

That there's more for me to follow

That's what the lonely is for.

Is it a blessing or a curse

This palace of promise

When the empty chill makes you weep

With only the thin fire of romance to warm you

These halls are too tall and deep

(CHORUS)

But you can seal up the pain

Build walls in the hallways

Close off a small room to live in

But those walls will remain

And keep you there always

And you'll never know

Why you were given

Why you were given the lonely.

(CHORUS)

[2] GLAD is a contemporary Christian pop/rock group formed in 1972 and specializing in a cappella music. They are known for their tight harmonies as well as their free-flowing, intricate arrangements which often include some classical and jazz overtones.

[3] Martin Heidegger, Sein und Zeit (1927), Being and Time trans. John Macquarrie and Edward Robinson (Oxford: Basil Blackwell, 1978).

[4] See endnote #5 in chapter ten, The Illuminative Way – The Dark Night of the Spirit, for a suggested resource for distinguishing between depression and spiritual Dark Nights.

[5] Paul Tillich, The Courage To Be (New Haven: Connecticut: Yale University Press, 1952) 155. Tillich listed three categories for the nonbeing and its resulting anxiety: ontic (fate and death), moral (guilt and condemnation), and spiritual (emptiness and meaninglessness).

[6] Teresa of Avila, Interior Castle, trans. E. Allison Peers (New York, New York: Doubleday Publishing Company, 1961). An excellent treatment of Teresa's journey of faith with accompanying insights from developmental psychological growth is written by Fr. John O. Welsh in his book Spiritual Pilgrims: Carl Jung and Teresa of Avila, (Mahwah, New Jersey: Paulist Press, 1982).

[7] Robert Detweiler and David Jasper, "The Interpretative Tradition of Literature and Religion," Religion and Literature: a Reader (Louisville, Kentucky: Westminster John Knox Press, 2000) 48.

[8] Francis Thompson, "Hound of Heaven," The Oxford Book of English Mystical Verse, eds. D. H. S. Nicholson and A. H. E. Lee (Oxford, England: Clarendon Press, 1917). The "Hound of Heaven" is a 182 line poem written by English poet Francis Thompson (1859-1907 A. D.) which depicts how God relentlessly pursues people until they turn and surrender.

[9] Ecclesiastes 1:17

[10] Romans 5:3-5; "Not only so, but we also rejoice in our sufferings, because we know that suffering produces perseverance; perseverance, character; and character, hope. And hope does not disappoint us, because God has poured out his love into our hearts by the Holy Spirit, whom he has given us."

[11] Isaiah 11:6-9; "The wolf will live with the lamb, the leopard will lie down with the goat, the calf and the lion and the yearling together; and a little child will lead them. The cow will feed with the bear, their young will lie down together, and the lion will eat straw like the ox. The infant will play near the hole of the cobra, and the young child put his hand into the viper's nest. They will neither harm nor destroy on all my holy mountain, for the earth will be full of the knowledge of the Lord as the waters cover the sea."

[12] II Peter 3:13; "But in keeping with his promise we are looking forward to a new heaven and a new earth, the home of righteousness." And Revelation 21:1ff; "Then I saw a new heaven and a new earth, for the first heaven and the first earth had passed away, and there was no longer any sea."

[13] Proverbs 29:18; KJV

[14] I John 3:2-3

[15] II Corinthians 12:7-9; "To keep me from becoming conceited because of these surpassingly great revelations, there was given me a thorn in my flesh, a messenger of Satan, to torment me. Three times I pleaded with the Lord to take it away from me. But he said to me, "My grace is sufficient for you, for my power is made perfect in weakness." Therefore I will boast all the more gladly about my weaknesses, so that Christ's power may rest on me."

[16] II Corinthians 12:9

[17] Romans 8:1

[18] Isaiah 12:2a

[19] Viktor Emil Frankl (1905-1997) was an Austrian neurologist, psychiatrist and Holocaust survivor. Frankl was the founder of Logotherapy, which focused on the necessity of meaning making in order to deal with the difficulties in life. The ultimate meaning is found in God.

[20] Viktor Emil Frankl, Man's Search for Meaning: An Introduction to Logotherapy, trans. I. Lasch (New York, New York: Washington Square Press, 1963). Viktor Emil Frankl, The Doctor and the Soul: From Psychotherapy to Logotherapy. trans. R. and C. Winston (New York, New York: Vintage Books, 1973).

[21] Matthew 10:37

[22] John 14:1

[23] Viktor Emil Frankl, The Unconscious God: Psychotherapy and Theology (New York, New York: Simon and Schuster, 1975) 70.

[24] I Corinthians 13:12

[25] Luke 23:46

Chapter 21 – "Monsters from the Id"

[1] The Forbidden Planet, dir. Fred Wilcox, writ. Cyril Hume (MGM Productions, Turner Entertainment Company, 1956). Actors: Walter Pidgeon, Leslie Nielsen, Anne Francis.

[2] In Jungian psychology, the Shadow is a part of the unconscious mind consisting of repressed weaknesses, shortcomings, and instincts. Jung claims that these qualities are often projected on others. Cliff Custer defines the term Shadow as "any negative perception we have buried, composed of ugly feelings we have swept under the rug of our consciousness." (The Gift of Peace, page 55.)

[3] Romans 7:18b-19

[4] Matthew 10:37

[5] Genesis 2:16-17; "And the LORD God commanded the man, 'You are free to eat from any tree in the garden; but you must not eat from the tree of the knowledge of good and evil, for when you eat of it you will surely die.'"

[6] Matthew 5:28; "But I tell you that anyone who looks at a woman lustfully has already committed adultery with her in his heart."

[7] Joseph Delany, "Omission," The Catholic Encyclopedia, vol. 11 (New York, New York: Robert Appleton Company, 1912). "It may be asked at what time one incurs the guilt of a sin of omission in case he fails to do something which he is unable to do, by reason of a cause for which he is entirely responsible. For instance, if a person fails to perform a duty in the morning as a result of becoming inebriated the previous night, the guilt is not incurred at the time the duty should be performed because while intoxicated he is incapable of moral guilt. The answer seems to be that he becomes responsible for the omission when having sufficiently foreseen that his neglect will follow upon his intoxication he does nevertheless surrender himself to his craving for liquor."

[8] James 4:17; parenthesis added by author for inclusion.

[9] Baltimore Catechism #3, LESSON SIXTH: "On Sin and Its Kinds" (Baltimore, Maryland: Public Domain, 1891). A Catechism of Christian Doctrine of the Roman Catholic Church prepared and enjoined by Order of the Third Council of Baltimore (Maryland) in 1884.

[10] Arthur Charles O'Neil, "Sin," The Catholic Encyclopedia, vol. 14 (New York, New York: Robert Appleton Company, 1912).

[11] Arthur Charles O'Neil, "Sin," The Catholic Encyclopedia, vol. 14 (New York, New York: Robert Appleton Company, 1912).

[12] Matthew 25:44-46; "They also will answer, 'Lord, when did we see you hungry or thirsty or a stranger or needing clothes or sick or in prison, and did not help you?' He will reply, 'I tell you the truth, whatever you did not do for one of the least of these, you did not do for me.' Then they will go away to eternal punishment, but the righteous to eternal life."

[13] Mark 10:20

[14] John 2:19

[15] William Paul Young, "Atlanta Live," Interview (Atlanta, Georgia: WATC Television Station Channel 57, June 27, 2008).

[16] I Corinthians 6:19-20; "Do you not know that your body is a temple of the Holy Spirit, who is in you, whom you have received from God? You are not your own; you were bought at a price. Therefore honor God with your body."

[17] II Corinthians 5:1; "Now we know that if the earthly tent we live in is destroyed, we have a building from God, an eternal house in heaven, not built by human hands."

[18] Robert Boyd Munger, My Heart Christ's Home (Downers Grove, Illinois: Intervarsity Press, 1986).

[19] C. S. Lewis, Mere Christianity (New York, New York: MacMillan Co., 1960), 160. (My words are inserted in parentheses.)

[20] Cliff Custer, The Gift of Peace: Three Essential Steps to Healing and Happiness (Grants Pass, Oregon: Cyber Publishing Company, 2004) 82. For a full description of inner healing, I highly recommend Cliff Custer's book. People may purchase this book through www.cliffcuster.com. Cliff Custer's approach to Inner Healing is very Christ-centered; nevertheless, he has realized the value of reaching people who reject Christianity by referring to Jesus as the Inner Advisor, similar to how Bill Wilson in Alcoholics Anonymous called God the Higher Power. He also has an explicitly Jungian approach using terms like the Shadow, anima, animus, the collective unconscious and others.

[21] This question comes from the work of Dr. Edward M. Smith's, a Baptist minister and licensed pastoral counselor, Theophostic Prayer Ministry (www.theophostic.com). This is an acknowledgement of the source and not an endorsement of the ministry. "Theophostic is a ministry of helping emotionally wounded people to acknowledge and to identify the true source of their inner emotional pain and find lasting peace through receiving personalized truth directly from the Lord." [Smith, Ed M. "Freedom from Performance-based Spirituality," DVD, Theophostic Prayer Ministry (2004)]. Controversy surrounds this and similar approaches as to whether it is to be considered a religious intervention or a counseling procedure. Smith strongly asserts that Theophostic "is not counseling" although psychological language and techniques are used to allow "healing of the memories" through God's intervention. Smith encourages people to seek "professional mental health care" as needed. These objections are typically initiated by those of the scientific community and their legitimate questions require consideration and response.

[22] Romans 8:26-27

[23] William W. Walford, "Sweet Hour of Prayer," recorder, Thomas Salmon, comp. William Batchelder Bradford (Coleshill, Warwickshire, England, 1845). "Sweet Hour of Prayer" was a poem recited by the

blind preacher William W. Walford to Thomas Salmon in Coleshill, Warwickshire, England during 1845; it appeared in *The New York Observer* on September 13, 1845. In 1861, William Batchelder Bradford composed the music "Sweet Hour" traditionally associated with the poem.

Sweet hour of prayer! Sweet hour of prayer!

That calls me from a world of care,

And bids me at my Father's throne

Make all my wants and wishes known.

In seasons of distress and grief,

My soul has often found relief

And oft escaped the tempter's snare

By thy return, sweet hour of prayer!

Sweet hour of prayer! Sweet hour of prayer!

The joys I feel, the bliss I share,

Of those whose anxious spirits burn

With strong desires for thy return!

With such I hasten to the place

Where God my Savior shows His face,

And gladly take my station there,

And wait for thee, sweet hour of prayer!

Sweet hour of prayer! Sweet hour of prayer!

Thy wings shall my petition bear

To Him whose truth and faithfulness

Engage the waiting soul to bless.

And since He bids me seek His face,

Believe His Word and trust His grace,

I'll cast on Him my every care,

And wait for thee, sweet hour of prayer!

Sweet hour of prayer! Sweet hour of prayer!

May I thy consolation share,

Till, from Mount Pisgah's lofty height,

I view my home and take my flight:

This robe of flesh I'll drop and rise

To seize the everlasting prize;

And shout, while passing through the air,

"Farewell, farewell, sweet hour of prayer!"

[24] Cliff Custer, The Gift of Peace: Three Essential Steps to Healing and Happiness (Grants Pass, Oregon: Cyber Publishing Company, 2004) 21.

[25] This procedure can also be very effectively used by re-entering disturbing dreams, which of course come from the subconscious. This procedure is not to be considered professional therapy; but employs "inner healing" techniques to allow God's healing, just like prayer could be understood as a "technique."

Chapter 22 – Who Are You Talking To?

[1] Luke 15:11-32

[2] See references to the Three Ways of spiritual development especially the Pre-Christian and Purgative Ways in chapters six and seven.

[3] See reference to the Three Ways of spiritual development especially the Illuminative Way in chapters eight through ten.

[4] Luke 15:20

[5] Kenneth E. Bailey, Through Peasant Eyes: More Lucan Parables, Their Culture and Style (Grand Rapids, Michigan: Eerdmans Publishing Company, 1980).

[6] Luke 15:18-19

[7] Romans 5:1

[8] Matthew 16:24

[9] This is especially true when using some of the cross referenced passages such as the Luke 9:23 passage that indicates that denial, carrying and following must be done "daily." The Matthew 10:38 adds guilt saying, "and anyone who does not take his cross and follow me is not worthy of me." Luke 14:27 disallows people from Christianity with the phrase "And anyone who does not carry his cross and follow me cannot be my disciple." I Peter 2:21 can even be interpreted that Christians need to suffer, "To this you were called, because Christ suffered for you, leaving you an example that you should follow in his steps." This classic phrase needs to be judiciously applied according to spiritual development – unless everyone is considered to be the same emotionally, psychologically, spiritually and in their life experiences.

[10] John 10:18

[11] My traditional "get acquainted with the new parishioner" opening question is, "Tell me about your religious background?" People will normally respond, "What do you want to know?" and I say, "Whatever you want to tell me." Pay attention to the first words. Most often, people will say what they really need at the very beginning and then talk about lots of other things. Mary said, "My other church was ok, but some things I didn't like."

Chapter 23 – The Spiritual Helper Mode of Operation

[1] John 15:11

[2] Matthew 18:20

[3] John 14:9; "Jesus answered: 'Don't you know me, Philip, even after I have been among you such a long time? Anyone who has seen me has seen the Father. How can you say, "Show us the Father"?'"

[4] James 2:18; "But someone will say, 'You have faith; I have deeds.' Show me your faith without deeds, and I will show you my faith by what I do."

[5] Genesis 32:22-30; verse 28 reads, "Then the man said, "Your name will no longer be Jacob, but Israel because you have struggled with God and with men and have overcome."

[6] Acts 9:4; "He fell to the ground and heard a voice say to him, 'Saul, Saul, why do you persecute me?'"

[7] Mark 10:51; "'What do you want me to do for you?' Jesus asked him. The blind man said, 'Rabbi, I want to see.'"

[8] Matthew 19:17' "'Why do you ask me about what is good?' Jesus replied. 'There is only One who is good. If you want to enter life, obey the commandments.'"

[9] Johann Wolfgang von Goethe (1749 - 1832) was a German dramatist, novelist, poet, and scientist.

[10] Thomas Alva Edison, Harper's Monthly Magazine (September 1932).

[11] John 13:34

[12] Jeremiah 29:11

[13] Richard A. Haynes, "Designing Small Groups for Church Renewal," Doctoral Thesis available at the Northern Baptist Theological Seminary Library, 660 E. Butterfield Road., Lombard, Illinois, 60148; http://www.seminary.edu/current-students/library/ or 630-620-2104, 2 June 1995, 94-99.

[14] I John 4:1; "Dear friends, do not believe every spirit, but test the spirits to see whether they are from God, because many false prophets have gone out into the world."

[15] William A. Barry, Paying Attention to God: Discernment in Prayer (Notre Dame, Indiana: Ave Maria Press, 1990). It contains Barry's insights about discernment based on the Spiritual Exercises of St. Ignatius of Loyola.

[16] Mark 1:15; alternative translation in parentheses.

Bibliography

_____. Baltimore Catechism #3, LESSON SIXTH: "On Sin and Its Kinds." Public Domain, 1891.

_____. Fiddler on the Roof. Jerry Bock, writ., Sheldon Harnick, lyrics. Broadway Musical, September 24, 1964.

_____. Godspell, dir. John Michael Tebelak, comp. Stephen Schwartz. Broadway Musical, 17 May 1971.

_____. "Hands," De Beers Jewelers Television Commercial, JWT New York Advertising Agency, July 2000. Video Location: http://www.advertolog.com/de-beers/adverts/hands-2333005/.

_____. "Now I Lay Me Down to Sleep," The New England Primer, Benjamin Harris, ed. Boston, Massachusetts: Benjamin Harris, 1687-1690.

_____. The Forbidden Planet, dir. Fred Wilcox, writ. Cyril Hume. MGM Productions, Turner Entertainment Company, 1956.

_____. "The New Testament Greek Lexicon," Bible Study Tools: Growing Deeper in the Word. Salem Communications Corporation, 9 Feb 2012 <http://www.biblestudytools.net/Lexicons/Greek.

Albom, Mitch. The Five People You Will Meet in Heaven. New York, New York: Hyperion Press, 2003.

Antonisamy, F. An introduction to Christian Spirituality. St. Paul, Minnesota: Bangalore Publishing Company, 2000.

Astley, Jeff and Leslie J. Francis, eds. <u>Christian Perspectives on Faith Development</u>. Grand Rapids, Michigan: Eerdmans Publishing Company, 1992.

Assagioli, Roberto. <u>The Act of Will</u>. New York, New York: Penguin Books, 1973.

Assagioli, Roberto. <u>Psychosynthesis: A Collection of Basic Writings</u>. New York, New York: The Viking Press, 1965.

Atkinson, Frederick Cook. "Morecambe," comp. Norwich, England: Public Domain, 1870.

Bailey, Kenneth E. <u>Through Peasant Eyes: More Lucan Parables, Their Culture and Style</u>. Grand Rapids, Michigan: Eerdmans Publishing Company, 1980.

Barry, William A. <u>Paying Attention to God: Discernment in Prayer</u>. Notre Dame, Indiana: Ave Maria Press, 1990.

Bonhoeffer, Dietrich. <u>Letters and Papers from Prison</u>, ed. Eberhard Bethge, trans. Reginald H. Fuller. New York New York: Macmillan Publishing Company, 1953.

Bonhoeffer, Dietrich. <u>The Cost of Discipleship</u>. New York, New York: Macmillan Publishing Co., Inc., 1963.

Bradbury, William B. "Woodworth," <u>Third Book of Psalmody</u>. New York, New York: Thomas Hastings and William Batchelder Bradbury Publishers, 1849.

Bradshaw, John. <u>Healing the Shame that Binds You</u>, Revised Edition. Deerfield Beach, Florida: Health Communications, Inc., 2005.

Brook, Fredrick. "My Goal is God Himself, Not Joy, Nor Peace." England: Public Domain, appx. 1870.

Browning, Donald S. <u>Atonement and Psychotherapy</u>. Philadelphia, Pennsylvania: Westminster Press, 1966.

Brusselmans, Christiane, ed. <u>Toward Moral and Religious Maturity</u>. Morristown, NJ: Silver Burdett. 1980.

Cassirer, Ernest. <u>Philosophy of Symbolic Forms</u>, trans. Ralph Manheim. New Haven, Connecticut: Yale University Press, 1955.

Casting Crowns. "Who am I?" <u>Casting Crowns</u>. Reunion Label, Franklin, Tennessee, 10 October 2003.

Coleman, Lyman. "Growing the Church Through Small Groups." First Baptist Church, Wheaton, Illinois, 6 March 1993.

Custer, Cliff. <u>The Gift of Peace: Three Essential Steps to Healing and Happiness</u>. Grants Pass, Oregon: Cyber Publishing Company, 2004.

Daman, William. "Southwell," <u>Psalmes of David in English Meter</u>. London, England: 1579.

Davies, Brian. <u>The Thought of Thomas Aquinas</u>. New York, New York: Oxford University Press, 1993.

de Chardin, Pierre Teilhard. <u>The Phenomenon of Man</u>, trans. Bernard Wall. London, England: Wm. Collins Sons & Company, 1959.

Delany, Joseph. "Omission," <u>The Catholic Encyclopedia</u>, vol. 11. New York, New York: Robert Appleton Company, 1912.

Derricks, Cleavant. "Just a Little Talk with Jesus," <u>Harbor Bells No. 6</u>. Chattanooga, Tennessee: Stamps-Baxter Music Company, 1937.

Detweiler, Robert and David Jasper. "The Interpretative Tradition of Literature and Religion," <u>Religion and Literature: a Reader</u>. Louisville, Kentucky: Westminster John Knox Press, 2000.

Devine, Arthur. "Recollection," <u>The Catholic Encyclopedia</u>, vol. 12. New York, New York: Robert Appleton Company, 1912.

Devine, Arthur. "State or Way (Purgative, Illuminative, Unitive)," <u>The Catholic Encyclopedia</u>, vol. 14. New York, New York: Robert Appleton Company, 1912.

Dowley, Tim ed. <u>Eerdman's Handbook to the History of Christianity</u>. Berkhamsted, Herts, England: Lion Publishing, 1977.

Droege, Thomas A. <u>Faith Passages and Patterns</u>. Philadelphia, Pennsylvania: Fortress Press, 1983.

Dykstra, Craig and Sharon Daloz Parks, eds. Faith Development and Fowler. Birmingham, Alabama: Religious Education Press, 1986.

Edinger, Edward. Ego and Archetype. Baltimore, Maryland: Penguin Books, 1972.

Edison, Thomas Alva. Harper's Monthly Magazine. September 1932.

Eliade, Mircea. The Sacred and the Profane: The Nature of Religion, trans. Willard R. Trask. New York, New York: Harper Torchbooks, 1961.

Elliott, Charlotte. "Just As I Am," Christian Remembrancer in 1836. London, England: Religious Tract Society, 1873.

Enright, Robert D. and Joanna North, eds. Exploring Forgiveness. Madison, Wisconsin: University of Wisconsin Press, 1998.

Erikson, Erik H. Childhood and Society. New York, New York: W. W. Norton and Company, 1950.

Erikson, Erik H. Identity and the Life Cycle. New York, New York: International Universities Press, 1959.

Espinosa, Eddie. "Change My Heart, O God." Mercy/Vineyard, Stafford, Texas, 1982.

FitzGerald, Constance. "Transformation in Wisdom," Carmelite Studies VIII: Carmel and Contemplation, eds. K. Culligan and R. Jordan. Washington, D.C.: Institute of Carmelite Studies, 2000.

Flanigan, Beverly. Forgiving the Unforgivable: Overcoming the Bitter Legacy of Intimate Wounds. New York, New York: Macmillan Publishing, 1992.

Forgaill, Dallán. "Be Thou My Vision," trans. Mary E. Byrne, comp. David Evans. Church Hymnary, 2nd ed. Church of Scotland, 1927.

Foster, Richard. Celebration of Discipline: The Path to Spiritual Growth. New York, New York: Harper Collins Publishers, 1988.

Fowler, James W., Karl Ernest Nipkow, and Friedrich Schweitzer, eds. Stages of Faith and Religious Development. New York, New York: Crossroad Publishing Company, 1991.

Fowler, James W. and Mary Lynn Dell. "Stages of Faith from Infancy through Adolescence: Reflections on Three Decades of Faith Development Theory," <u>The Handbook of Spiritual Development in Childhood and Adolescence</u>, Eugene C. Roehlkepartain, Pamela Ebstyne King, Linda M. Wagener, and Peter L. Benson, Eds. Thousand Oaks, California: Sage Publications, Inc., 2006.

Fowler, James W. <u>Becoming Adult, Becoming Christian: Adult Development and Christian Faith</u>. San Francisco, California: Harper and Row, 1984.

Fowler, James W. <u>Faith Development and Pastoral Care</u>. Philadelphia, Pennsylvania: Fortress Press, 1987.

Fowler, James W. <u>Stages of Faith: The Psychology of Human Development and the Quest for Meaning</u>. New York, New York: Harper Collins Publishing Company, 1981.

Frankl, Viktor Emil. <u>Man's Search for Meaning: An Introduction to Logotherapy</u>, trans. I. Lasch. New York, New York: Washington Square Press, 1963.

Frankl, Viktor Emil. <u>The Doctor and the Soul: From Psychotherapy to Logotherapy</u>, trans. R. and C. Winston. New York, New York: Vintage Books, 1973.

Frankl, Viktor Emil. <u>The Unconscious God: Psychotherapy and Theology</u>. New York, New York: Simon and Schuster, 1975.

Garrigou-Lagrange, R. <u>The Three Ages of the Interior Life</u>, vol. 2, trans. M. T. Doyle. Charlotte, North Carolina: The Catholic Company, 1947-48.

Gilligan, Carol. <u>In a Different Voice</u>. Cambridge, Massachusetts: Harvard University Press, 1982.

Green, Sr., Thomas H. <u>Drinking from a Dry Well</u>. Notre Dame, Indiana: Ave Maria Press, 1991.

Green, Sr., Thomas H. <u>When the Well Runs Dry: Prayer Beyond the Beginnings</u>. Notre Dame, Indiana: Ave Maria Press, 1979.

Groeschel, Benedict J. <u>Spiritual Passages: The Psychology of Spiritual Development</u>. New York, New York: Crossroads Publishing Company, 1983.

Hart, Sarah and Brian White. "Awakening." New York, New York, BMG Music Publishing, Inc. BMI/BMG Songs, Inc., 2001.

Hartley, John and Gary Sadler. "Love By Degree." Brentwood, Tennessee: EMI Christian Music Group, 2002.

Havergal, Frances Ridley. "Take My Life and Let It Be," Songs of Grace and Glory, ed. Charles B. Snepp. London, England: W. Hunt and Company, 1874.

Haynes, Richard A. "Designing Small Groups for Church Renewal," D. Min. dissertation. Lombard, Illinois: Northern Baptist Theological Seminary Library, June 1995.

Heidegger, Martin. Sein und Zeit (1927), Being and Time, trans. John Macquarrie and Edward Robinson. Oxford: Basil Blackwell, 1978.

John of the Cross. Ascent of Mount Carmel, eds. and trans. Kieran Kavanaugh and Otillio Rodriguez, The Collected Works of St. John of the Cross. Washington, D. C.: ICS Publications, 1991.

Johnson, Dan. "Awakenings: Simple Solutions for Life's Problems," Lessons4living. 2 Feb 2012 <http://www.lessons4living.com.

Jones, L. Gregory. Embodying Forgiveness: A Theological Analysis. Grand Rapids, Michigan: Eerdmans Publishing Company, 1995.

Jung, Carl G. Modern Man in Search of His Soul. New York, New York: Harcourt, Brace and World, Inc., 1933.

Keil, Carl Friedrich and Franz Delitzsch. Commentary on the Old Testament, 10 vol., trans. James Martin. Edinburg, England: T & T Clark Company, 1866; Revised Edition. Peabody, Massachusetts: Hendrickson Publishers, Inc., 1996.

Kelsey, Morton T. Dreams, A Way to Listen to God. New York, New York: Paulist Press, 1978.

Kelsey, Morton T. God, Dreams, and Revelation: A Christian Interpretation of Dreams. Minneapolis, Minnesota: Augsburg Fortress Press, 1991.

Kittel, Gerhard and Gerhard Friedrich, eds. <u>Kittel's Theological Dictionary of the New Testament</u>, trans. Geoffrey W. Bromiley. Grand Rapids, Michigan: Eerdmans Publishing Company, 1976.

Kohlberg, Lawrence. <u>The Development of Modes of Thinking and Choices in Years 10 to 16</u>, Ph. D. dissertation. Chicago, Illinois: University of Chicago, 1958.

Kolodiejchuk, Brian. <u>Mother Teresa: Come Be My Light: The Private Writings of the 'Saint of Calcutta'</u>. New York, New York: Doubleday Publishing Co., 2007.

Kraybill, Donald B., Steven M. Nolt and David L. Weaver-Zercher. <u>Amish Grace: How Forgiveness Transcended Tragedy</u>. Somerset, New Jersey: Jossey-Bass, 2007.

Lewis, C. S. <u>Mere Christianity</u>. New York, New York: MacMillan Co., 1960.

Malan, Henri A. Cesar. "Hedon," <u>The Psalter Hymnal</u>. Grand Rapids, Michigan: Christian Reformed Church Publications, 1927.

May, Gerald G. <u>The Dark Night of the Soul: A Psychiatrist Explores the Connection between Darkness and Spiritual Growth</u>. New York, New York: Harper Collins Publishers, 2004.

Meier, Paul and Robert Wise. <u>Windows of the Soul: A Look at Dreams and Their Meanings</u>. Nashville, Tennessee: Thomas Nelson Publishers, 1995.

Miles, Charles Austin. "In the Garden." Public Domain, 1912.

Munger, Robert Boyd. <u>My Heart Christ's Home</u>. Downers Grove, Illinois: Intervarsity Press, 1986.

Muto, Susan. <u>John of the Cross for Today: The Ascent</u>. Notre Dame, Indiana: Ave Maria Press, 1991.

Newton, John. "Amazing Grace," <u>Olney Hymns in Three Books</u>, eds. John Newton and William Cowper. London, England: W. Oliver, 1779.

O'Neil, Arthur Charles. "Sin," <u>The Catholic Encyclopedia</u>, vol. 14. New York, New York: Robert Appleton Company, 1912.

Osmer, Richard R. and Friedrich L. Schweitzer, eds. <u>Developing a Public Faith: New Directions in Practical Theology</u>. St. Louis, Missouri: Chalice Press, 2003.

Otto, Rudolf. <u>The Idea of the Holy</u>. London, England: Oxford University Press, 1923.

Pennington, Basil. <u>Lectio Divina: Renewing the Ancient Practice of Praying the Scriptures</u>. New York, New York: The Crosswords Press, 1998.

Pfatteicher, Philip H. <u>New Book of Festivals and Commemorations: A Proposed Common Calendar of Saints</u>. Minneapolis, Minnesota: Fortress Press, 2008.

Piaget, Jean. <u>The Origins of Intelligence in Children</u>. New York, New York: International University Press, 1952.

Power, Clark. "Moral Development, Religious Thinking and the Question of a Seventh Stage," <u>Essays on Moral Development: Philosophy of Moral Development</u>, vol. 1, ed., Lawrence Kohlberg. San Francisco, California: Harper and Row, 1981.

Rahner, Karl. <u>The Practice of the Faith: A Handbook of Contemporary Spirituality</u>, eds. Karl Lehmann and Albert Raffelt, trans. John Griffiths. New York, New York: Crossroads Publishing Co., 1986.

Redman, Matt and Beth Redman, "Blessed Be Your Name," <u>Blessed Be Your Name: The Songs of Matt Redman</u>, vol. 1. Brentwood, Tennessee: EMI Christian Music Group, 1999.

Rickert, Jamie. "New Wine," <u>New Wine</u>. Suffern, New York: Parish Mission Team, 1989.

Rizzuto, Ana-Marie. <u>The Birth of the Living God: A Psychoanalytic Study</u>. Chicago, Illinois: University of Chicago, 1979.

Ruffing, Janet K. <u>Spiritual Direction: Beyond the Beginnings</u>. New York, New York: Paulist Press, 2000.

Sammis, John H. "Trust and Obey," Daniel B. Towner, comp. Public Domain, 1887.

Savary, Louis M., Patricia H. Berne and Strephon K. Williams. <u>Dreams and Spiritual Growth: A Judeo-Christian Way of Dreamwork</u>. Mahwah, New Jersey: Paulist Press, 1984.

Scott, Clara H. "Open My Eyes That I May See," Royal Anthem Book. Lyons, Iowa: The Ladies' Seminary, 1882.

Selman, Robert L. The Developmental Conceptions of Interpersonal Relations. Boston, Massachusetts: Harvard-Judge Baker Social Reasoning Project, 1974.

Sheehy, Gail. Passages: Predictable Crises of Adult Life. New York, New York: E. P. Dutton, 1976.

Smedes, Lewis. Forgive and Forget: Healing the Hurts We Don't Deserve. New York, New York: Harper Collins Publishers, 1984.

Strong, James. The New Strong's Exhaustive Concordance of the Bible. Nashville, Tennessee: Thomas Nelson Press, 1991.

Sugrue, Thomas. The Story of Edgar Cayce: There is a River. New York, New York: Holt, Rinehart, and Winston, 1943.

Synesius of Cyrene. "Lord Jesus Think on Me," Songs and Hymns of Earliest Greek Christian Poets, Allen W. Chatfield, ed. London, England: Oxford Press, 1876.

Talbot, John Michael. "Holy Darkness," Table of Plenty. Troubadour for the Lord Records, Eureka Springs, Arkansas, 1997.

Teresa of Avila. "Autobiography," The Collected Works of St. Teresa of Avila, vol. 1, trans. Kieran Kavanaugh and Otilio Rodriguez. Washington D.C.: ICS Publishing Company, 1976.

Teresa of Avila. Interior Castle, trans. E. Allison Peers. New York, New York: Doubleday Publishing Company, 1961.

Thomas, Gary. "The Forgiveness Factor." Christianity Today, vol. 44 no. 1, 10 January 2000.

Thompson, Francis. "Hound of Heaven," The Oxford Book of English Mystical Verse, eds. D. H. S. Nicholson and A. H. E. Lee. Oxford, England: Clarendon Press, 1917.

Tillich, Paul. "You Are Accepted," The Shaking of the Foundations. New York, New York: Charles Scribner and Sons, 1948.

Tillich, Paul. <u>Dynamics of Faith</u>. New York, New York: Harper Publishing Company, 1958.

Tillich, Paul. <u>The Courage To Be</u>. New Haven, Connecticut: Yale University Press, 1952.

Tillich, Paul. <u>The Eternal Now</u>. New York, New York: Charles Scribner's Sons, 1963.

Vischer, Lisa. "The Forgiveness Song." Brentwood, Tennessee: EMI Christian Music Group, 1994.

von Hugel, Friedrich. <u>The Mystical Element in Religion</u>, 4th ed. London, England: James Clark Publishers, 1961.

Walford, William W. "Sweet Hour of Prayer," Thomas Salmon, recorder. Coleshill, Warwickshire, England, 1845, William Batchelder Bradford composer, 1861.

Walker, William. "New Britain," <u>The Southern Harmony, and Musical Companion</u>. New Haven, Connecticut: E. W. Miller Publisher, 1835.

Warren, Rick. <u>The Purpose Driven Church</u>. Grand Rapids, Michigan: Zondervan Publishing, 1995.

Warren, Rick. <u>The Purpose Driven Life</u>. Grand Rapids, Michigan: Zondervan Publishing, 2002.

Welch, John O. <u>When Gods Die: An Introduction to St. John of the Cross</u>. Mahwah, New Jersey: Paulist Press, 1990.

Wesley, Charles. "Love Divine, all Loves Excelling," <u>Hymns for those that Seek, and those that Have Redemption</u>. Bristol, England: Felix Farley, 1747.

Wiesel, Elie. <u>Night</u>, trans. Stella Rodway. New York, New York: Bantam Books, 1982.

Wilcox, David. "That's What the Lonely Is For." Irving Music, Inc. Midnight Ocean Bonfire Music, 1993.

Wilkinson, Bruce. <u>Secrets of the Vine: Breaking Through to Abundance</u>. Sisters, Oregon: Multnomah Publishers, Inc., 2001.

Young, William Paul. "Atlanta Live," interview. Atlanta, Georgia: WATC Television Station Channel 57, June 27, 2008.

Index of Scripture Passages

General Index

CPSIA information can be obtained at www.ICGtesting.com
Printed in the USA
LVOW120938110612

285520LV00001B/7/P